GEARS OF WAR
JUDGMENT

THE CHARGES AGAINST YOU

You and your squad might have killed a lot of Locust today, Lieutenant. But this war has only just begun. Our survival depends on one thing: Gears follow orders.

But I look at you and I don't see a Gear—I see something more dangerous. I see a hero. Well, congratulations, hero. Millions of citizens you've sworn to protect might die because of what you did today.

I hereby charge Kilo Squad with desertion, cowardice, trespassing, the theft of experimental military technology, and treason. Does that sound about right to you, Lieutenant Baird?

ABOUT THIS GUIDE

Gears of War: Judgment represents a major shift for the franchise in campaign structure, characters, and the rules of multiplayer combat. Our team of writers spent nearly a month on-site at Epic Games ensuring that our guide evolved alongside it. We've packed this book with proven strategies for all game modes, various difficulty settings, and multiplayer modes to ensure that players of all skills and preferences find what they're looking for.

Here are just a few of the features you'll find inside this guide:

> Proven campaign coverage that includes tactics for both standard and Declassified mission objectives, with advanced scoring tips for maximizing your Star count.

> Complete walkthrough coverage of the unlockable Aftermath campaign. Now you can learn how Baird and Cole made it to Azura in *Gears of War 3*.

> Four dozen maps complement the campaign walkthrough and reveal the location of every COG Tag, weapon pickup, and ammo crate.

> Comprehensive descriptions of enemy and weapon behavior, with a full listing of all applicable stats and ratings.

> Extensive coverage of the all-new OverRun mode includes detailed tactics for every character class for each map.

> Proven strategies for lasting all 10 waves in the new Survivor mode, including detailed maps showing elevations, fortifications, and more.

> Complete listing of all unlockable Ribbons and Medals, Weapon Skins, Character Skins, Achievements, and more.

BASIC TRAINING

Gears of War: Judgment takes a step back in time, to the early days of the war against the Locust. Set three short weeks after Emergence Day, the members of Kilo Squad are only now starting to appreciate the severity of their situation, and the strength of their adversary. Fresh off the battlefields of the Pendulum Wars, the COG soldiers must adapt to a new enemy. So too must you adapt to a completely new Gears of War experience. This installment in the franchise represents a significant shift in structure, controls, and gameplay. For this reason, we strongly recommend all players—rookies and veterans alike—consult both the Basic Training and Multiplayer Basics portions of this book in preparation for the fight to come.

It's the purpose of this chapter to supplement—not replace—the in-game tutorials and user's manual that accompany the game. Our goal is to expand on the information those sources already provide and help you understand some of the game's finer elements before you charge headlong into battle. The following pages touch upon the fundamental aspects of the game while devoting extra attention to the changes made since the previous *Gears of War* games. Some of the topics we cover include:

> Controls

> Difficulty and Co-Op Damage Multipliers

> Utilizing Cover and Movement

> Declassified Mission Objectives and Star System

> Active Reloads, Executions, and Meatshields

CONTROLS

The basic controls in *Gears of War: Judgment* are simple to learn and very intuitive. Veterans of the series will note that some of the controls have been streamlined and certain actions have shifted to other buttons as a result of the switch to a two-weapon system. Nevertheless, *Gears of War: Judgment* is a third-person shooter that utilizes many of the same controls you're likely familiar with from other games. Use the Left and Right Trigger buttons and Thumbsticks to control movement, aim, and fire your weapon. The A button controls the game's trademark cover and movement system while the X button serves as your all-purpose interaction button.

GENERAL CONTROLS

COMMAND	ACTION
LEFT THUMBSTICK	MOVEMENT; CLICK WHILE AIMING TO SPOT
RIGHT THUMBSTICK	LOOK; CLICK TO ZOOM
A BUTTON	ROADIE RUN (HOLD); ROLL (PRESS WHILE POINTING WITH THE LEFT THUMBSTICK); ENTER COVER (PRESS NEAR COVER)
X BUTTON	INTERACT; USE; PICK UP MEATSHIELD
B BUTTON	MELEE, GRENADE TAG; CURB STOMP (TAP); SPECIAL EXECUTION (HOLD)
Y BUTTON	SWAP WEAPONS
L TRIGGER	AIM WEAPON
R TRIGGER	FIRE WEAPON
L BUMPER	THROW GRENADE
R BUMPER	RELOAD/ACTIVE RELOAD
D-PAD	TAC-COM DISPLAY (DOWN)

COVER & MOVEMENT COMMANDS

COMMAND	ACTION
ROADIE RUN	HOLD [A]
RIGHT-ANGLE TURN	WHILE ROADIE RUNNING, TAP AND HOLD [A] WHILE POINTING LEFT THUMBSTICK LEFT OR RIGHT
180-DEGREE TURN	WHILE ROADIE RUNNING, TAP AND HOLD [A] WHILE POINTING LEFT THUMBSTICK DOWN.
ENTER COVER	APPROACH COVER AND PRESS [A]
EXIT COVER	POINT LEFT THUMBSTICK AWAY FROM COVER
COVER SLIP	PRESS FORWARD WITH LEFT THUMBSTICK WHILE AT THE EDGE OF COVER AND HOLD [A]
COVER SWAP	WHILE IN COVER, POINT LEFT THUMBSTICK TOWARD ANOTHER NEARBY PIECE OF COVER AND PRESS [A]
MANTLE	POINT LEFT THUMBSTICK TOWARD LOW COVER AND PRESS [A]
MANTLE KICK	POINT LEFT THUMBSTICK TOWARD LOW COVER WITH AN ENEMY ON THE OTHER SIDE, AND PRESS [A] TO MANTLE AND KICK ENEMY

The way the characters move and utilize the surrounding terrain and architecture for cover has long been a hallmark of the Gears of War experience. This sophisticated system of maneuvering across the battlefield is all done with the A button and Left Thumbstick. Use these controls to quickly enter and exit cover, sprint, and mantle over obstacles to maintain movement. It's even possible to turn 90-degrees or instantly reverse direction during a Roadie Run without breaking stride. Mastering this system of movement allows for very quick, precise motions that make it possible to avoid enemy fire and close on your prey in an instant. Though not as important during Campaign play, this art of "wall bouncing" is virtually essential in competitive multiplayer matches.

GAMEPLAY MODES & DIFFICULTIES

Gears of War: Judgment is divided into two main components: Campaign and Multiplayer. The Campaign portion, including both Judgment and Aftermath, can be played solo or with up to three friends co-operatively. The Multiplayer portion of the game contains many of the familiar Versus modes that fans have come to love, as well as several new modes such as OverRun and Survival. This chapter deals exclusively with the Campaign portion of the game. The Multiplayer Basics chapter later in this guide covers everything you need to know about playing the game's numerous multiplayer offerings.

SOLO PLAY: You control each chapter's primary protagonist, as defined by the testimony being given, while the in-game AI controls the rest of Kilo Squad. They help revive you, offer covering fire, and alert you to threats and points of interest.

CO-OP PLAY: Play with up to three of your friends. Players aren't required to have played through prior on their own, and each player is free to choose the difficulty setting that suits their skill. Players are split across the four characters that star in any given scene, with the party host taking the lead role. Note that the game spawns additional enemies into some encounters when playing with three or four players.

CO-OP MULTIPLIERS

CO-OP PLAYERS	ENEMY DAMAGE MULTIPLIER	PLAYER DAMAGE MULTIPLIER
+1 PLAYER	1.2X	0.9X
+2 PLAYERS	1.4X	0.9X
+3 PLAYERS	1.6X	0.85X

JUDGMENT CAMPAIGN

The Judgment Campaign represents the bulk of the Campaign experience and consists of six chapters, comprising a total of 42 sections. Unlike previous installments in the *Gears of War* series, the Judgment Campaign consists of short, scenario-based missions that reward your skill and efficiency through a brand new scoring system. It's not enough to simply survive a section, but to do so with style!

Stars are awarded based on how well you perform in a number of categories ranging from the number of enemies you kill, the quantity of ribbons you earn, to the amount of time you spend down but not out (DBNO). The goal is to earn three Stars in each section, with the color of Stars corresponding to the difficulty mode you selected.

STAR COLORS AND DIFFICULTIES

DIFFICULTY MODE	STARS
CASUAL	⭐
NORMAL	⭐
HARDCORE	⭐
INSANE	⭐

For every 50 points you earn, a new Star is awarded up to a maximum of three. Getting downed drains the Star Meter, but you cannot lose a Star once it has been earned. Points are tracked behind the scenes and run through a series of multipliers customized for each individual section in order to account for those battles with fewer enemies or greater difficulty.

STAR POINTS

ACTION	STAR POINTS
KILL (GIB)	1
KILL (HEADSHOT)	2
KILL (EXECUTION)	3
EARNING A RIBBON	5
DBNO PENALTY	-2 (PER SECOND)

In addition to the points listed in the table, each individual enemy is also worth a certain number of points, as shown in the Hostile Forces chapter and throughout the Campaign Walkthrough.

Not all Stars are equal, however. There is also a multiplier that progressively makes it more difficult to earn subsequent Stars. Kills and ribbons are worth twice as many points toward earning your first Star as they are toward earning your second. They're worth even less toward a third Star. The difficulty in earning a third Star can be offset by accepting the Declassified conditions present near the start of each section. This additional mission-based objective adds a layer of challenging conditions that Kilo Squad must overcome. Declassified conditions are unique to each section and range from decreased visibility, additional Locust units, limited ammo, or even an inability to regenerate health. We've included a Declassified Star Multiplier for every section of the walkthrough that reveals how much faster Stars accumulate once the Declassified option is accepted.

EARNING THREE STARS

Is it possible to earn three Stars without accepting the Declassified option? That depends. Though it is possible on some sections if you avoid being downed and maximize your headshots, executions, and ribbons, there is very little margin for error. Consult the Declassified Star Multiplier listed in each section to get an idea how likely earning three Stars is without the Declassified challenge. The closer that number is to 1.0x, the greater your chances of earning three Stars without the additional challenge. On the other hand, if the multiplier is 2.0x or greater, you'll almost certainly need to accept the Declassified option to get three Stars. The Ribbons and Scoring sections throughout the walkthrough detail how to earn the most points in each mission and increase your chances of earning the maximum Stars.

AFTERMATH CAMPAIGN

Unlocked after earning 40 Stars in Judgment Campaign.

The Aftermath Campaign serves as a "Missing Act" from *Gears of War 3*. These six chapters reveal what Baird, Cole, and Carmine were up to while Marcus and the others were securing the submarine needed to reach Azura. Those who played *Gears of War 3* will certainly remember Baird and Cole arriving at Azura aboard a decrepit looking ship, out in front of a fleet of reinforcements. This is your chance to learn how they got that ship, who those reinforcements were, and why Cole was so excited when radioing with Anya.

There are no Stars or Declassified mission challenges in the Aftermath Campaign. This is just an extra dose of the good old-fashioned *Gears of War* Campaign. The only thing that matters is surviving to the next checkpoint and continuing the story. Of course, that doesn't mean it's easy. You'll need every tip we've packed into the walkthrough portion of this guide if you're going to survive this trip into the future.

CAMPAIGN DIFFICULTY MODES

Gears of War: Judgment contains four different difficulty settings: Casual, Normal, Hardcore, and Insane. We recommend newcomers to the series give the game's Normal difficulty setting a try, especially if they have previous action game experience. Those who are brand new to modern video games should probably go ahead and start on Casual mode, then adjust upwards if it feels too easy. Veterans of the series, depending on their skill, should feel at home on Normal or Hardcore mode during their first playthrough. Hardcore offers just enough challenge without getting too frustrating. Insane difficulty is best left to very experienced players, and only after they've completed Hardcore mode.

MULTI-FACETED WALKTHROUGH

Our coverage for the Judgment Campaign offers two levels of guidance. For those who only want a general overview of each mission and are declining the Declassified option, we have a "Classified Intel" section that offers tips for the major encounters only. We also include a "Declassified: Three-Star Tactics" section for each mission that provides step-by-step strategy and tips for earning three Stars on the Hardcore difficulty. These tactics apply to Insane mode as well, although players attempting the game's ultimate difficulty must take care to spend more time in cover and be more judicious in their weapon usage.

CAMPAIGN DIFFICULTY DIFFERENCES

ATTRIBUTE	CASUAL	NORMAL	HARDCORE	INSANE
PLAYER HEALTH	1200	840	510	300
PLAYER HEALTH RECHARGE DELAY	0.80	0.80	1.00	1.20
PLAYER HEALTH RECHARGE SPEED	1.20	1.20	1.00	1.00
CAN BE DOWNED (DBNO)?	YES	YES	YES	NO
CAN SELF REVIVE?	YES	NO	NO	N/A
BLEEDOUT TIME WHILE DBNO (SECS)	45	20	15	N/A
PLAYER REVIVE PROTECTION (SECS)	4.0	2.0	2.0	N/A
PLAYER WEAPON DAMAGE MODIFIER	2.00X	1.50X	1.25X	1.00X
FRIENDLY AI HEALTH MODIFIER	3.50X	3.00X	3.00X	2.50X
FRIENDLY AI DAMAGE MODIFIER	1.80X	1.60X	1.45X	1.30X

As a rule of thumb, there are no global behavioral differences throughout the Campaign from one difficulty to the next. The differences are almost entirely statistical. In short, the player does less damage and has less health on the harder difficulty settings. This not only reinforces the need to stay in cover and keep your enemies at a distance, but it also places a premium on ammunition. Pick your shots carefully and practice those headshots!

NAVIGATING THE BATTLEFIELD

UTILIZING COVER

The gameplay in the *Gears of War* franchise is based around the use of cover. Though you can achieve a fair amount of success on the lower difficulty modes (and in Multiplayer) by running-and-gunning, this simply will not work on the harder difficulties. It's imperative that you present your enemies with as small a target as possible. This is achieved by crouching or standing behind solid objects such as walls, cars, sandbags, and other bulletproof barriers. There are essentially two types of cover: low and high.

LOW COVER

Most cover falls into this category. Low cover, as its name implies, is any solid object behind which the player can take refuge, but that is low enough to be mantled over (i.e. hurdle). Low cover is generally waist-high and forces the character to crouch behind it for maximum protection. A small amount of the player is often exposed to standard enemies, but he or she can blind-fire over the top of the object and even manually lean over the cover and aim, still concealing most of his or her body. It's also possible to move left and right along low cover and attack from different positions. Grenades can be blind-tossed over the top of low cover.

Low cover is the most flexible cover to use, but it does leave the player vulnerable. For starters, enemies can perform a mantle-kick by running toward the other side of the barrier and mantling over directly into the player's position. The mantle-kick knocks the unit in cover backwards into a stagger, while giving the mantling player a perfect opportunity for a point-blank shotgun blast!

Low cover is also ineffective against elevated or flying Locust or larger beasts such as the Reaver. Enemies in elevated positions can angle their shots downwards at the player and inflict damage even while the player is behind low cover.

HIGH COVER

High cover refers to any solid object that's tall enough to provide complete coverage to a player standing behind it. As a rule, high cover offers more protection than low cover, but at the risk of maneuverability. High cover tends to be a solid wall or column. The player's only choice is to lean out and fire around the structure's end, such as at a doorway or on the left and right sides of a column. Though the player can click the Left Thumbstick to manually crouch and keep his opponents guessing in that regard, he cannot blind-fire over the top of tall cover.

Players can blind-fire from the sides of high cover and even cover swap between two adjacent pieces of tall cover. That said, high cover does somewhat limit the player's field of view and can make it difficult to spot an enemy moving along your flank. Nevertheless, high cover does provide near-absolute protection from taller enemies such as a Reaver or an arcing Boomshot projectile.

ENEMIES IN COVER

The Gears aren't the only ones who know how to utilize cover. The Locust are more than capable of employing many of the same techniques described above. Grenadiers and Theron Guard are particularly savvy when it comes to using cover. The Campaign Walkthrough includes case-by-case tips for flushing enemies from cover wherever appropriate, but there are a few general purpose strategies that can be used throughout the game.

> Depending on the weapons in your possession, it sometimes makes sense to keep your distance and target the enemy while it's in cover. Wait for it to expose itself during an attack and quickly counterattack. This is best done with a precise weapon such as the Markza or OneShot. Enemies often reveal a small portion of themselves while crouched behind low cover—take the shot!

> Explosives provide another excellent way of forcing an enemy out of cover. Lobbing a Frag Grenade or firing the Booshka at the enemy's area will certainly send it fleeing, if not kill it outright. Take care when doing this so you don't waste the grenade. Try to bounce the grenade off cover behind the enemy or to its side. Pay attention to the trajectory indicator to know exactly where the grenade or Booshka shell will go.

> An ideal way to expel an enemy from behind cover is by Spotting and flanking. Spot the enemy to focus your squad's fire on the foe. This will likely keep the enemy pinned down and may even soften it up. This gives you time to flank the enemy safely. Use cover to move up alongside the enemy to get a clean shot at it from a lateral position. You can do this without Spotting the enemy, provided the area is large and the enemy is distracted. Otherwise, the enemy might see you coming.

> Another way to flush enemies out of cover, albeit one exclusive to the Aftermath Campaign, is to use the Digger Launcher. The Digger Launcher's projectile burrows through the ground, beneath cover, and rises up to explode alongside the hiding enemy.

GEARS ON THE RUN

Movement is another aspect of the gameplay that sets the *Gears of War* franchise apart from others. Players can make their character sprint, otherwise known as Roadie Run, but they can also use the cover system to wall-bounce, cover slip, and slam into cover faster than the character can run. These techniques are actually far more important in multiplayer than they are in the campaign. While you may have to occasionally run for your life during the campaign, these moments are few and far between. In general, it's often much safer to take a slower, methodical approach to combat. Keep your enemies at a distance and sweep across the field of battle to play the angles before advancing. While staying in cover for too long in multiplayer will likely get you killed, leaving cover too soon in campaign play often yields a similar result.

Mastering the art of steering your character while Roadie Running serves you well during the campaign. Practice 90-degree and 180-degree Roadie Run turns, and always tap the A button when nearing cover to slide into it from several steps away. Though you are best served by staying in cover and picking off enemies from the safety it affords, it's important to move with urgency when out of cover.

COMBAT: THE FINER POINTS

The Campaign Arsenal and Hostile Forces chapters provide a wealth of information, tactics, and data concerning all of the game's numerous weapons and enemies. While those are critical aspects of combat, the remainder of this chapter is devoted to some of the advanced concepts that make *Gears of War: Judgment* so unique. Newcomers to the series are encouraged to continue reading before jumping ahead to the walkthrough.

The Active Reload meter appears on the screen's upper-right corner. As soon as you press the Reload button (or once the weapon runs out of ammo), the needle begins to move across the meter from left to right. Pressing the Reload button a second time while the needle is in the black area results in a failed Active Reload which actually *prolongs* the reload process. You'll undoubtedly grumble alongside the character on the screen when this happens.

ACTIVE RELOADS

There are two ways to reload your weapons in the game: you can press the Reload button and wait for the process to conclude; or you can tap the Reload button to start the process, and then tap it a second time as the needle moves into the gray area to perform an Active Reload. The second method results in a much faster reload process.

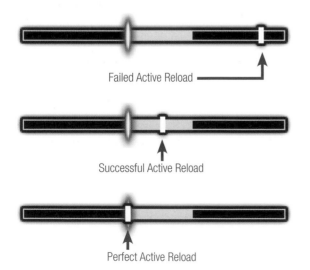

Failed Active Reload

Successful Active Reload

Perfect Active Reload

Stopping the needle inside the meter's gray area counts as a successful Active Reload, speeding the reload process. There's a third option: the Perfect Active Reload. Stop the needle in the sliver of white within the success zone to complete this feat. Performing a Perfect Active Reload not only speeds up your reload time, but also earns a weapon-specific bonus. Perfect Active Reloads often yield a 20% damage bonus for the reloaded rounds, but some weapons benefit in other ways such as increased range or a faster firing rate.

Performing the Active Reload isn't hard once you get the hang of it. The meter on each weapon varies along with the width of the Perfect Active Reload zone. Monitor the needle's progress when first getting used to this system. It won't be long before muscle memory takes over and you can Active Reload any weapon without looking.

PRELOADING THE ACTIVE RELOAD

Make room for the Perfect Active Reload's more potent rounds by firing off some of the bullets already in your magazine. This is a great way to give yourself an edge when heading into battle against a tough foe. Expend some bullets at nothing in particular, and then perform the Perfect Active Reload to gain plenty of high-damage rounds. Use them fast, as the effect wears off after several seconds.

EXECUTIONS

Not every enemy dies immediately after being drained of health. As long as they aren't killed with a headshot or explosion, humanoid Locust (Drones, Grenadiers, Theron Guards, and so forth) drop to their knees in a state often referred to as DBNO (Down But Not Out). As with the Gears, Locust that are DBNO try to crawl toward their teammates with the hope of being revived. In the absence of nearby Locust, they try to crawl behind cover, hoping to be revived or to eventually bleed out.

You can finish off a downed opponent from distance, but it's much more fun—although a bit risky—to rush in for an execution. You can perform multiple types of executions. For instance, you can simply melee a downed enemy to kill it. You can also switch to a pistol and line up a true execution-style shot to the head from pointblank range. Another option is the old-fashioned curb stomp, an icon of the franchise. Approach the downed enemy and lightly tap the Melee button to perform the curb stomp. Lastly, and exclusive to the Campaign portion of the game, are the weapon-specific executions.

Each and every primary and power weapon in the game can be used to perform a special one-of-a-kind execution. Down an enemy, switch to the weapon you wish to use for the execution, and then hold the Melee button while standing next to the downed enemy. These animations tend to take several seconds and leave you extremely vulnerable as they play out. It's best to refrain from performing any lengthy weapon-specific executions (aside from the chainsaw) until you're sure no other enemies are nearby. Stick to the faster executions to claim your point bonus while playing the Judgment Campaign.

MEATSHIELDS

As fun as it may be to perform an execution, it's a terrible waste of a perfectly good bullet sponge. Why kill a downed enemy when you can use it as a meatshield? Press the X button while standing next to a downed enemy to take it hostage as a meatshield. Using a meatshield is a lot like wielding the Boomshield. New to *Gears of War: Judgment* is the ability to wield any weapon you have equipped (even a two-handed one) while in possession of a meatshield.

Meatshields have been known to save the lives of the hostage taker. They can soak up the blast from a Torque Bow and even absorb a close-range blast from the Gnasher. The meatshield eventually disintegrates as it continues to take damage. You can drop the meatshield intentionally by switching weapons or by pressing the X button to snap its neck. Don't worry about freeing a meatshield, as the enemy is considered to be executed as soon as you grab it.

BAG AND TAG

If taking a meatshield is a good idea, using it to blow up other Locust is a great one! Take a Locust hostage as a meatshield while in possession of a grenade and tap the Grenade button while facing a group of other Locust. Your character plants the grenade in the back of your meatshield and kicks it toward the group of enemies. This is best performed while standing no more than five to ten yards from the other Locust. This maneuver is particularly useful in Judgment missions in which you're finding it hard to earn three Stars.

CAMPAIGN ARSENAL

The *Gears of War* franchise has always been known for its unique and powerful weaponry. From the chainsaw-equipped Lancer assault rifle to the explosive-tipped arrows of the Torque Bow, the COG and Locust have been wielding imaginative tools of war since Emergence Day. And now, in *Gears of War: Judgment*, four new weapons join the arsenal. As longtime fans of the series know all too well, each weapon's stats and usefulness differs substantially between Campaign and Multiplayer modes. This portion of the book deals exclusively with the weapons used in the Judgment and Aftermath Campaigns. Please consult the Multiplayer Arsenal portion of the guide to see how each weapon's performance has been tweaked for each of the multiplayer modes.

PRIMARY WEAPONS

> Players beginning from the New or Select section begin each Judgment mission equipped with the Lancer and Gnasher. Continuing or Loading a game gives players the weapons they had at the last saved checkpoint. Those playing the Aftermath Campaign begin with the Lancer and Sawed-Off Shotgun.

> Unlike in previous *Gears of War* games, only two weapons can be equipped at once. Press the Y button to swap between them.

> Players can equip any two primary weapons they choose, regardless of type. This includes power weapons, assault rifles, and shotguns.

> Depending on the situation, it's usually a good idea to always carry at least one assault rifle or shotgun.

ASSAULT RIFLES

LANCER

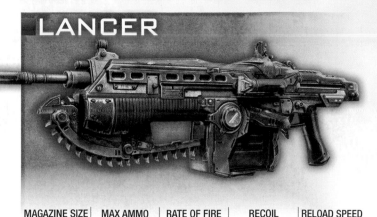

Damage Statistics

BASE	HEADSHOT	MELEE	STOPPING POWER
50	1.0X	305	MODERATE

This jack-of-all-trades weapon has received a boost to its rate of fire this time out, making it even deadlier than ever before! The Lancer offers a near-perfect blend of power, range, and accuracy and is at home in any situation. Though capable of inflicting damage at long range, the Lancer is best suited for close- to medium-range combat. The Lancer's impressive rate of fire and expansive magazine make it capable of downing almost any enemy in record time. Its under-barrel chainsaw attachment provides a way to instantly execute an enemy at close range without firing a bullet.

MAGAZINE SIZE	MAX AMMO	RATE OF FIRE	RECOIL	RELOAD SPEED
60	420	850/M	VERY LOW	FAST

Range Finder

0M	10M	20M	30M	40M	50M	60M	70M	80M	90M	100M

RETRO LANCER

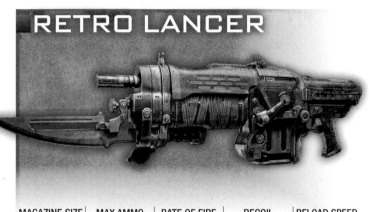

Damage Statistics

BASE	HEADSHOT	MELEE	STOPPING POWER
93	1.0X	400	MODERATE

The Retro Lancer is outfitted with an under-barrel bayonet attachment. What the Retro Lancer lacks in magazine size and capacity, it makes up for in base damage. The Retro Lancer deals nearly twice the damage of the traditional Lancer, albeit with greater recoil and a slightly slower rate of fire. In the right hands, the Retro Lancer is one of the deadliest weapons on Sera. Due to its moderate recoil and smaller magazine size, the Retro Lancer is most effective when fired in short bursts. It is an ideal close- to medium-range weapon that rapidly loses effectiveness at range. Lastly, the Retro Lancer's bayonet allows the user to perform a Retro Charge execution attack—just watch the charge meter on the screen to make sure momentum isn't lost before the execution is performed.

MAGAZINE SIZE	MAX AMMO	RATE OF FIRE	RECOIL	RELOAD SPEED
30	240	650/M	MODERATE	FAST

Range Finder

0M	10M	20M	30M	40M	50M	60M	70M	80M	90M	100M

HAMMERBURST

Damage Statistics

BASE	HEADSHOT	MELEE	STOPPING POWER
105	2.0X	305	MODERATE

The Hammerburst isn't encountered very often during the Judgment Campaign, but it's widely available during the Aftermath Campaign. This standard-issue Locust assault rifle has received a larger max ammo capacity this time out and continues to be a semi-automatic rifle that can be fired as fast as you can pull the trigger. Despite inflicting more than twice the damage of the Lancer, the lack of an automatic firing mode makes the Hammerburst less effective at close range, particularly going against a foe with a shotgun in hand. In contrast, the greater headshot capabilities and increased accuracy afforded by the semi-automatic nature of the weapon make it more suitable for medium- to longer-range combat.

MAGAZINE SIZE	MAX AMMO	RATE OF FIRE	RECOIL	RELOAD SPEED
20	200	250/M	VERY LOW*	FAST

The Hammerburst suffers additional recoil per successive shot fired.

Range Finder

0M	10M	20M	30M	40M	50M	60M	70M	80M	90M	100M

MARKZA

Damage Statistics

BASE	HEADSHOT	MELEE	STOPPING POWER
230	2.5X	305	N/A

The Markza is one of the new additions to the COG arsenal, thanks to the UIR's surrender to end the Pendulum Wars. The Gorasni-made Markza is a high-capacity, semi-automatic assault rifle outfitted with a scope. The Markza straddles the line between assault rifle and sniper rifle and is best thought of as a precision rifle. It excels at medium- to long-range combat and inflicts heavy damage to the head. The Markza's scope doesn't have the magnification of the Longshot, but it is much faster to reload and fire. The Markza is ill-suited for close-range combat, but its larger magazine and ease of use enable it to be useful in defending yourself if suddenly attacked while sniping.

MAGAZINE SIZE	MAX AMMO	RATE OF FIRE	RECOIL	RELOAD SPEED
10	120	300/M	LOW	FAST

Range Finder

0M	10M	20M	30M	40M	50M	60M	70M	80M	90M	100M

SHOTGUNS

GNASHER

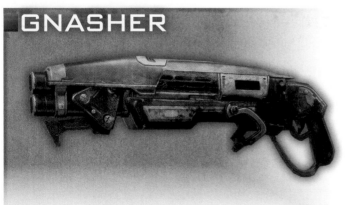

Damage Statistics

BASE	HEADSHOT	MELEE	STOPPING POWER
500	1.0X	305	HIGH

The Gnasher is to shotguns what the Lancer is to assault rifles. This powerful shotgun has enjoyed a long and storied existence as the go-to weapon in the COG arsenal, regardless the arena. The Gnasher inflicts bone-breaking damage at close to medium range and is capable of delivering headshot kills if aimed properly. The Gnasher can be found throughout the battlefield and is ideally suited for battle against Locust of all types. The Gnasher is best used in open terrain, outside of cover, where its short range and lack of precision don't hinder it. That said, the Gnasher is the perfect weapon to equip when charging an enemy behind cover. Mantle-kick the foe to stun it, then open fire with the Gnasher for a one-shot kill at point-blank range! The Gnasher is capable of inflicting one-shot kills to all but the largest of Locust units.

MAGAZINE SIZE	MAX AMMO	RATE OF FIRE	RECOIL	RELOAD SPEED
8	39	60/M	VERY HIGH	SLOW

Range Finder

0M	10M	20M	30M	40M	50M	60M	70M	80M	90M	100M

SAWED-OFF SHOTGUN

Damage Statistics

BASE	HEADSHOT	MELEE	STOPPING POWER
2500	1.0X	305	HIGH

The Sawed-Off Shotgun is a double-barrel shotgun capable of delivering five times the damage as the Gnasher. Capable of killing multiple foes with a single blast thanks to its wide spread, the Sawed-Off Shotgun is now more potent than ever before! The Sawed-Off Shotgun can now be loaded with two shells that can be fired in quick succession. This makes it possible to kill multiple enemies even if the first squeeze of the trigger only hits one. The Sawed-Off Shotgun is still very slow to reload and is only useful in close-range combat. Use a more versatile weapon to close in on enemies armed with long-range power weapons (or a group of unsuspecting Locust), and then switch to the Sawed-Off Shotgun for the kill. A single shot at close range is capable of killing a Boomer or Mauler, and there aren't many weapons that can boast that claim!

MAGAZINE SIZE	MAX AMMO	RATE OF FIRE	RECOIL	RELOAD SPEED
2	12	45/M	VERY HIGH	SLOW

Range Finder

0M	10M	20M	30M	40M	50M	60M	70M	80M	90M	100M

PISTOLS

SNUB PISTOL

Damage Statistics

BASE	HEADSHOT	MELEE	STOPPING POWER
90	2.0X	225	LOW

The Snub Pistol was once part of every COG soldier's standard issue, but the move to lighten the load of the Gears has left the Snub Pistol by the wayside. Occasionally found on the battlefield, the Snub Pistol is a fast-firing semi-automatic pistol capable of inflicting nearly as much damage as the Retro Lancer per bullet fired. The Snub Pistol has a much lower magazine size than a rifle, but deals double the damage when shot at an enemy's head. Nevertheless, the Snub Pistol should be considered little more than a weapon of last resort.

MAGAZINE SIZE	MAX AMMO	RATE OF FIRE	RECOIL	RELOAD SPEED
12	84	625/M	VERY LOW	VERY FAST

Range Finder

0M	10M	20M	30M	40M	50M	60M	70M	80M	90M	100M

BOLTOK PISTOL

Damage Statistics

BASE	HEADSHOT	MELEE	STOPPING POWER
300	3.5X	225	VERY HIGH

The Boltok Pistol enjoys a loyal following by those who have come to master its classic style. This revolver pistol is second only to the Longshot in headshot capability and packs enough punch to halt the progress of most any Locust charging the COG's position. Despite having a small magazine size and sluggish rate of fire, the Boltok Pistol is still a fine option, particularly against the tougher Locust units. The Boltok Pistol's iron sight offers a slight zoom that can help bring distant enemies into range for a well-placed headshot.

MAGAZINE SIZE	MAX AMMO	RATE OF FIRE	RECOIL	RELOAD SPEED
6	42	60/M	LOW	VERY FAST

Range Finder

0M	10M	20M	30M	40M	50M	60M	70M	80M	90M	100M

GORGON PISTOL

Damage Statistics

BASE	HEADSHOT	MELEE	STOPPING POWER
70	1.0X	225	MODERATE

The Gorgon Pistol is, in all practical terms, a sub-machine gun in a pistol form factor. The gun is fully automatic and boasts the third fastest firing rate of any known weapon on Sera. The Gorgon inflicts greater damage on a per-bullet basis than the Lancer, but unfortunately doesn't have the accuracy or range of the Lancer. The Gorgon is rarely found as a pickup unless dropped by a Kantus or Armored Kantus. It is most effective when aiming at a close- to medium-range target, preferably a larger one where accuracy is less important.

MAGAZINE SIZE	MAX AMMO	RATE OF FIRE	RECOIL	RELOAD SPEED
32	224	700/M	VERY LOW	VERY FAST

Range Finder

0M	10M	20M	30M	40M	50M	60M	70M	80M	90M	100M

POWER WEAPONS
LONGSHOT

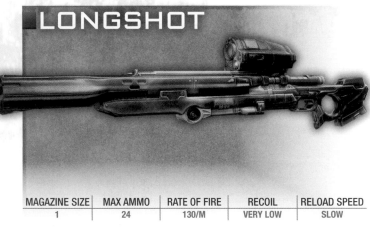

Damage Statistics

BASE	HEADSHOT	MELEE	STOPPING POWER
500	5.0X	305	N/A

The Longshot is the marquee sniper rifle in the COG arsenal. Its powerful optics makes it possible to headshot a Locust from across the battlefield for a one-shot kill. The Longshot is far more powerful than the Markza, deals five times the standard damage when striking an enemy's head, and suffers from no gun sway. The Longshot's only drawbacks are its single-bullet magazine and relatively slow reload speed. Those capable of consistent active reloads gain the most out of the Longshot.

MAGAZINE SIZE	MAX AMMO	RATE OF FIRE	RECOIL	RELOAD SPEED
1	24	130/M	VERY LOW	SLOW

Range Finder

0M	10M	20M	30M	40M	50M	60M	70M	80M	90M	100M

BREECHSHOT

Damage Statistics

BASE	HEADSHOT	MELEE	STOPPING POWER
330	2.2X	405	LOW

The Breechshot is what happens when the Locust get their hands on a Markza and decide to eliminate its scope and add a blade attachment. The Breechshot is an iron-sighted semi-automatic rifle that excels in medium-range combat. The weapon inflicts considerably more damage than a Markza and is every bit as accurate at medium range. Best of all, its four bullets can be fired in quick succession with virtually no recoil. The Breechshot inflicts above-average melee damage and can be hip-fired in times of emergency. Line the targeting reticle up with an enemy's head and watch for it to turn red before firing—the Breechshot inflicts the third most headshot damage, behind only the Longshot and Boltok.

MAGAZINE SIZE	MAX AMMO	RATE OF FIRE	RECOIL	RELOAD SPEED
4	36	66.6/M	VERY LOW	VERY FAST

Range Finder

0M	10M	20M	30M	40M	50M	60M	70M	80M	90M	100M

TORQUE BOW

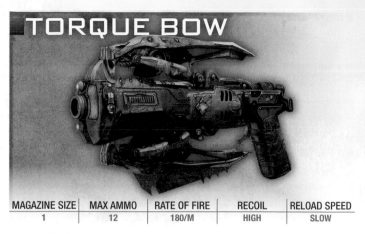

Damage Statistics

BASE	HEADSHOT	MELEE	STOPPING POWER
20/708*	1.1X	400	N/A

*The Torque Bow's arrow inflicts minimal damage compared to the resulting explosion.

The Torque Bow is the weapon of choice for the Locust's elite Theron Guard. This precision bow fires an explosive-tipped arrow that can stick into an enemy or wall when fully drawn. The arrow explodes after a brief delay and is large enough to kill multiple enemies, particularly if they have already been weakened. When using the Torque Bow, it's imperative that you draw the bow back long enough to make sure the arrow sticks into its target—the targeting reticule will tighten into a straight line when the bow is ready to be fired. This weapon inflicts heavy melee damage, but is otherwise best left for medium- to long-range combat only. This is a weapon to be used from behind cover, when you have the time to fire it accurately. The Torque Bow can be used to headshot an enemy, and it's not unheard of for the arrow to continue through one enemy's head and stick into another.

MAGAZINE SIZE	MAX AMMO	RATE OF FIRE	RECOIL	RELOAD SPEED
1	12	180/M	HIGH	SLOW

Range Finder

0M	10M	20M	30M	40M	50M	60M	70M	80M	90M	100M

SCORCHER

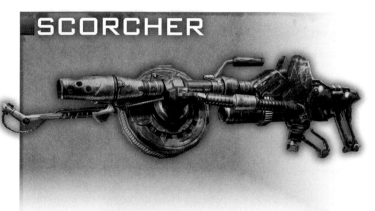

Damage Statistics

BASE	HEADSHOT	MELEE	STOPPING POWER
40	1.0X	305	LOW

The Scorcher is one of the best options for dealing with large numbers of enemies at close to medium range. This impressive flamethrower offers no threat of backdraft and can be fired continuously for nearly 10 seconds, engulfing enemies in a wall of flame. The Scorcher's flame not only delivers low amounts of stopping power, slowing an enemy's advance, but it can even cook enemies within their armor. The Scorcher is ideally suited for use against armored enemies. The only downside to using the Scorcher is that the flame can only reach so far and damage instantly falls to zero beyond the edge of the flame. Always try for an Active Reload to extend the reach of the flame.

MAGAZINE SIZE	MAX AMMO	RATE OF FIRE	RECOIL	RELOAD SPEED
34	334	850/M	NONE	FAST

Range Finder

0M	10M	20M	30M	40M	50M	60M	70M	80M	90M	100M

BOOMSHOT

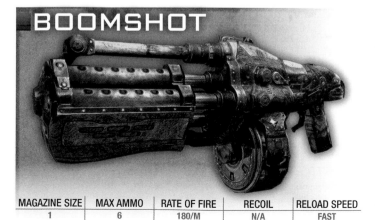

Damage Statistics

BASE	HEADSHOT	MELEE	STOPPING POWER
900X6	1.1X	305	N/A

The Boomshot is one of the most potent weapons on Sera, capable of launching a miniature barrage of bomblets in a tight cluster. The Boomshot is accurate—it can be used to earn a headshot kill—and immensely powerful. A well-aimed Boomshot attack can kill multiple enemies in an instant, and the splash damage can circumvent cover and even those enemies hiding behind Boomshields. A weapon of this magnitude does require practice to master, as the projectile's mass causes the trajectory to drop with distance. It's important to account for gravity and arc long-distance shots up and over cover to hit the desired target. Lastly, it's often good to aim slightly lower at the target in order to not risk shooting the projectile over the enemy's head. And never, ever, fire it at close range!

MAGAZINE SIZE	MAX AMMO	RATE OF FIRE	RECOIL	RELOAD SPEED
1	6	180/M	N/A	FAST

Range Finder

0M	10M	20M	30M	40M	50M	60M	70M	80M	90M	100M

DIGGER LAUNCHER

MAGAZINE SIZE	MAX AMMO	RATE OF FIRE	RECOIL	RELOAD SPEED
1	6	300/M	VERY HIGH	VERY SLOW

Damage Statistics

BASE	HEADSHOT	MELEE	STOPPING POWER
900	1.0X	305	N/A

Exclusive to the Aftermath Campaign, the Digger Launcher is once again wielded by the Savage Boomers forced to do without their trusty Boomshots. The Digger Launcher fires an explosively-charged creature that burrows through the ground, beneath cover and past allies, until it emerges next to its target for a point-blank explosion. The Digger Launcher packs as much damage as the Boomshot and is capable of inflicting heavy damage over a large blast area. The Digger Launcher makes it possible to attack enemies hiding behind cover, provided there are no interruptions in the ground surface between the weapon's wielder and the targeted foe. And because the weapon launches its live munitions in an arc, it can be fired directly at a nearby enemy—watch as the Digger burrows into the enemy's chest and erupts from within! Though effective, the Digger Launcher's slow rate of speed makes it easy to avoid, both for Locust and COG.

Range Finder

0M	10M	20M	30M	40M	50M	60M	70M	80M	90M	100M

BOOSHKA

MAGAZINE SIZE	MAX AMMO	RATE OF FIRE	RECOIL	RELOAD SPEED
3	12	60/M	LOW	SLOW

Damage Statistics

BASE	HEADSHOT	MELEE	STOPPING POWER
700	1.0X	305	N/A

The Booshka is another UIR weapon that made its way to the shores of Halvo Bay where the members of Kilo Squad could put it to good use. As Paduk would say, "Booshka is Gorasni for boom!" This grenade launcher is capable of firing its three projectiles in quick succession to blanket a small area with explosive firepower. The Booshka packs a tremendous amount of damage, but does take some getting used to. Its projectiles can be launched at enemies for a direct hit or bounced off of walls and other surfaces to reach enemies behind cover. The Booshka delivers concussive force that can even damage Maulers hiding behind their Boomshields.

Range Finder

0M	10M	20M	30M	40M	50M	60M	70M	80M	90M	100M

HEAVY WEAPONS

> Heavy weapons can be picked up in addition to your two equipped primary weapons.

> True to their name, heavy weapons encumber the player, slow movement speed, and limit the ability to utilize cover (the Tripwire Crossbow is an exception to this).

> Heavy weapons disappear from the battlefield once the last of their ammo has been used.

> These weapons are positioned throughout the battlefield strategically, often where a large influx of Locust is fast approaching.

> The only way to replenish their spent ammo is by picking up an Onyx Ammo Cache or another of the same heavy weapon.

MULCHER

Damage Statistics

BASE	HEADSHOT	MELEE	STOPPING POWER
77	N/A	N/A	N/A

The Mulcher is an unmounted chaingun that can be fired from the hip or placed on the ground or atop cover. This heavy machine gun fires a blistering 1200 rounds per minute and can rip apart any sized Locust in seconds. The Mulcher has a brief wind-up period as its barrels begin to rotate. It also has to be cooled off periodically, or it will overheat. Hold the Reload Button to manually cool the weapon before the temperature gauge fills and a forced three-second cooldown initiates. The Mulcher is best used from cover, while resting the weapon down atop a piece of wall or other object. Its accuracy diminishes when fired while walking.

MAGAZINE SIZE	MAX AMMO	RATE OF FIRE	RECOIL	RELOAD SPEED
N/A	200	1200/M	MODERATE	FAST

Range Finder

0M	10M	20M	30M	40M	50M	60M	70M	80M	90M	100M

MORTAR

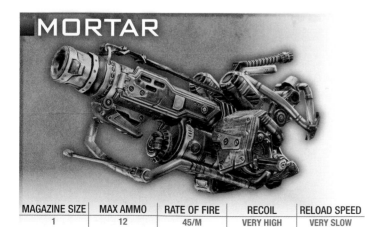

Damage Statistics

BASE	HEADSHOT	MELEE	STOPPING POWER
800X10	N/A	N/A	N/A

The Mortar is the go-to weapon for combating large groups of Locust, especially if they are at long range. The Mortar's shell splits into 10 separate bomblets while airborne and rains fiery destruction down across a wide area. The Mortar is perfect for taking out large numbers of enemies that are hiding behind obstacles, as long as they're not under a roof or other overhead cover. To use the Mortar, tilt its tube forward or backward with the movement controls to angle the trajectory, then hold the trigger to set the power of the shot—the longer you hold it, the further the shell will fly. The hash mark shows the previous shot's setting so you can adjust accordingly. Take care to make sure that you're not under an awning or other overhead obstruction when firing the Mortar, as the shell will be deflected right down at your position. An "X" will appear on the Mortar's rangefinder to indicate an unsafe firing position.

MAGAZINE SIZE	MAX AMMO	RATE OF FIRE	RECOIL	RELOAD SPEED
1	12	45/M	VERY HIGH	VERY SLOW

Range Finder

0M	10M	20M	30M	40M	50M	60M	70M	80M	90M	100M

TRIPWIRE CROSSBOW

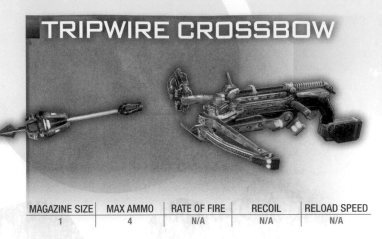

Damage Statistics

BASE	HEADSHOT	MELEE	STOPPING POWER
2000	1.1X	305	N/A

The Tripwire Crossbow is the new addition to the COG's heavy weapon arsenal. Unlike other heavy weapons, it does not encumber the user. This defensive weapon allows the Gears to set laser-tripwires throughout an area that can trigger heavy, directional explosives. To use the Tripwire Crossbow, hold the trigger down to draw the bow back just as with the Torque Bow. Fire the arrow at a flat surface, perpendicular to the direction you want the tripwire to extend. Make sure to set the tripwires low enough so that enemies don't walk underneath them. The lasers extend outward a long distance from the explosive charge, making it possible for an enemy to trip the explosion while being safely out of harm's way. Consider limiting the Tripwire Crossbow to narrow chokepoints such as halls and doorways where the enemies are sure to be close by the explosion. It's also possible to fire the Tripwire Crossbow directly at the ground to transform the traps into mines. This guarantees a direct-hit if the enemy steps anywhere near the mine. Another effective tactic is to place two mines in the same area, facing one another from opposing surfaces to emit a blast from each direction.

MAGAZINE SIZE	MAX AMMO	RATE OF FIRE	RECOIL	RELOAD SPEED
1	4	N/A	N/A	N/A

Range Finder

0M	10M	20M	30M	40M	50M	60M	70M	80M	90M	100M

ONESHOT

Damage Statistics

BASE	HEADSHOT	MELEE	STOPPING POWER
5500	5.0X	N/A	VERY HIGH

The single most powerful weapon that can be moved by hand, the OneShot is capable of instantly killing multiple Locust with a single shot. Once focused, the powerful projectile can shoot straight through Maulers, Bloodmounts, and even Reavers with a single pull of the trigger. This precision instrument of death isn't without its drawbacks, however. For starters, the OneShot is not the exclusive property of the COG; Locust have grown quite fond of it. Additionally, the OneShot can only be used while looking through its scope, thus significantly limiting your field of view. Never use the OneShot if there are enemies close by. The OneShot can only be used while resting atop cover or on the ground. Hold the Weapon Aim button to focus its targeting laser and squeeze the trigger to fire it. An Active Reloaded OneShot can fire straight through a Boomshield. Even a standard shot can obliterate multiple foes at once, regardless of where the projectile hits their body. The OneShot's targeting laser betrays your position while in use. But you'll only ever hear the whine of its targeting systems if it's being used by the enemy, a surefire cue to duck!

MAGAZINE SIZE	MAX AMMO	RATE OF FIRE	RECOIL	RELOAD SPEED
1	8	60/M	MODERATE	SLOW

Range Finder

0M	10M	20M	30M	40M	50M	60M	70M	80M	90M	100M

CLEAVER

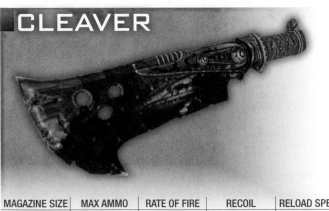

Damage Statistics

BASE	HEADSHOT	MELEE	STOPPING POWER
500	1.0X	500	N/A

The Cleaver is a dedicated melee weapon without a ranged capability. This heavy Locust blade is wielded by Theron Guard and Butchers and can be used in a pinch to fight your way through close encounters with other melee foes. Unlike the other heavy weapons, it's possible to roadie run while carrying the Cleaver, though it drags on the ground behind you, slowing your advance. The Cleaver can be used to guard against a chainsaw attack from an enemy Lancer, but it's best used against Wretches, Formers, and other unarmed enemies. The Cleaver can be fun to swing—and doesn't break until it hits 12 enemies—but it's not very practical in a world where nearly every enemy has a firearm.

MAGAZINE SIZE	MAX AMMO	RATE OF FIRE	RECOIL	RELOAD SPEED
N/A	12	66.6/M	N/A	N/A

Range Finder

0M	10M	20M	30M	40M	50M	60M	70M	80M	90M	100M

BOOMSHIELD

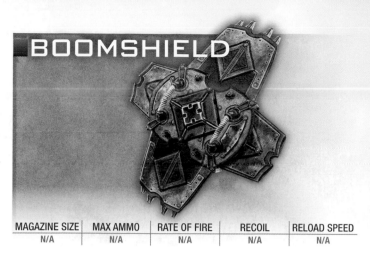

MAGAZINE SIZE	MAX AMMO	RATE OF FIRE	RECOIL	RELOAD SPEED
N/A	N/A	N/A	N/A	N/A

Damage Statistics

BASE	HEADSHOT	MELEE	STOPPING POWER
N/A	N/A	N/A	N/A

The Boomshield is a heavy piece of armor that can be carried into combat as a shield or planted in the ground as deployable cover. The Boomshield can deflect nearly all frontal attacks, with only an Active Reloaded OneShot able to pierce it. Kilo Squad is the first Gears unit to wield a two-handed weapon while carrying the Boomshield in front of them. This ability makes it possible to pair the Boomshield with a Lancer, Boomshot, Gnasher, etc. Throwing a grenade or swapping weapons causes the COG to drop the Boomshield momentarily, but it can be picked back up. Holding the Aim Weapon button slows character movement but keeps the Boomshield out in front, obscuring all but the slightest bit of the COG's body and vision. Though it's possible to roadie run while carrying the Boomshield, doing so negates the shield's purpose and leaves its user vulnerable to attack from all sides. Press the Roadie Run button while holding the Boomshield in front to plant it in the ground as cover, whether to hide behind or to block enemy advances. Melee attacks performed while holding the Boomshield result in a backhanded swipe with the shield.

Range Finder

0M	10M	20M	30M	40M	50M	60M	70M	80M	90M	100M

GRENADES

> Gears can carry up to four grenades of a single type in addition to their two weapons.

> Grenades can be thrown while wielding a gun, without the need to holster your firearm first.

> Grenades can be thrown, planted in the ground as a proximity mine, or blind-tossed from behind cover.

> Onyx Ammo Caches yield one grenade of the last type that you had equipped.

FRAG GRENADES

MAGAZINE SIZE	MAX AMMO	RATE OF FIRE	RECOIL	RELOAD SPEED
1	4	N/A	N/A	N/A

Range Finder

0M	10M	20M	30M	40M	50M	60M	70M	80M	90M	100M

Damage Statistics

BASE	HEADSHOT	MELEE	STOPPING POWER
1500	N/A	N/A	N/A

Frag Grenades are the most common and most lethal of all of the grenade types. Frag Grenades deliver intense damage across a 10-meter radius and are capable of killing multiple foes with a single explosion. Frag Grenades can be thrown with tremendous accuracy over considerable distances and offer a superb way of closing Emergence Holes from afar. Hold the Aim Weapon button to bring up the targeting reticle and maneuver the trajectory path to hit your mark. Try bouncing the grenade off of walls or the ceiling to hit enemies behind cover. Frag Grenades make excellent proximity mines—plant them inside chokepoints to lure enemies to their death. It's possible to "bag and tag" a meatshield by pressing the Throw Grenade button while in control of a downed enemy. The COG sticks the hostage with a grenade and kicks him forward, ideally toward a group of enemy reinforcements! Frag Grenades are extremely critical in "no health regen" scenarios and very useful for helping to take out Serapedes.

INK GRENADES

MAGAZINE SIZE	MAX AMMO	RATE OF FIRE	RECOIL	RELOAD SPEED
1	4	N/A	N/A	N/A

Range Finder

0M	10M	20M	30M	40M	50M	60M	70M	80M	90M	100M

Damage Statistics

BASE	HEADSHOT	MELEE	STOPPING POWER
100 (PER SECOND)	N/A	N/A	N/A

Rather than explode with instantaneous damage, Ink Grenades release a cloud of toxic gas that damages over time. Enemies caught in the cloud will most certainly be downed—or worse—if unable to extricate themselves from the situation in a speedy manner. These ink clouds don't just inflict damage, but they also blur enemy vision and stun those in the affected area as well. While not as lethal as a Frag Grenade, a well-thrown Ink Grenade can temporarily neutralize multiple Locust and buy the Gears time to scavenge for weapons and ammo, seek cover, or move in for the kill. Ink Grenades are relatively rare during both the Judgment and Aftermath Campaigns, and are seldom found away from the corpse of a Kantus. Ink Grenades can be planted as a proximity mine, but it will rarely result in a kill. Tagging an enemy with an Ink Grenade is far more effective.

INCENDIARY GRENADES

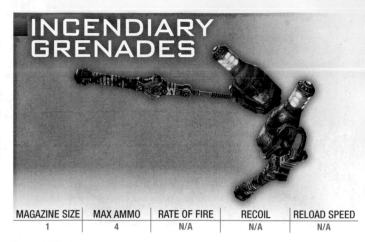

Damage Statistics

BASE	HEADSHOT	MELEE	STOPPING POWER
80 (PER SECOND)	N/A	N/A	N/A

Incendiary Grenades are extremely rare in the Campaign portion of the game and can only be found in the Aftermath Campaign, if dropped by a Locust. Incendiary Grenades are similar to Ink Grenades in that they inflict damage over time, but they neither stun nor blur enemy vision. That said, a direct hit is almost guaranteed to result in a kill. Incendiary Grenades are useful for softening up multiple kills, cutting off the enemy's advance, and for flushing enemies out of cover.

MAGAZINE SIZE	MAX AMMO	RATE OF FIRE	RECOIL	RELOAD SPEED
1	4	N/A	N/A	N/A

Range Finder

0M	10M	20M	30M	40M	50M	60M	70M	80M	90M	100M

SMOKE GRENADES

Damage Statistics

BASE	HEADSHOT	MELEE	STOPPING POWER
N/A	N/A	N/A	N/A

There are at least two instances of usable Smoke Grenades in the Judgment Campaign. Smoke Grenades can be used to stun or obscure enemy vision (or conceal COG movements) but are primarily the domain of multiplayer play. Please consult the Multiplayer Arsenal section of this book for more information concerning the tactical usage of Smoke Grenades in the online arena.

MAGAZINE SIZE	MAX AMMO	RATE OF FIRE	RECOIL	RELOAD SPEED
1	4	N/A	N/A	N/A

Range Finder

0M	10M	20M	30M	40M	50M	60M	70M	80M	90M	100M

STIM-GAS GRENADES

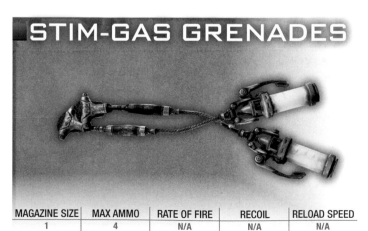

Damage Statistics

BASE	HEADSHOT	MELEE	STOPPING POWER
N/A	N/A	N/A	N/A

Kilo Squad comes into contact with Stim-Gas Grenades on several occasions during the Judgment Campaign. These unique grenades instantly heal anyone within the area of effect. They are particularly helpful during those few Declassified missions in which the squad's ability to recover health has been disrupted. To use a Stim-Gas Grenade, simply toss it at the ground and note the circular area of effect. A cloud of "+" icons surrounds the character, alerting you to the benefits they provide. Stim-Gas Grenades, like Smoke Grenades, are far more common in the multiplayer portion of the game and are described in greater detail in this book's Multiplayer Arsenal chapter.

MAGAZINE SIZE	MAX AMMO	RATE OF FIRE	RECOIL	RELOAD SPEED
1	4	N/A	N/A	N/A

Range Finder

0M	10M	20M	30M	40M	50M	60M	70M	80M	90M	100M

HOSTILE FORCES

Taking place just 30 days after Emergence Day, the Judgment Campaign primarily features those basic species of Locust initially encountered in the original *Gears of War*, albeit with some variations. Kilo Squad is also introduced to a breed of Locust known as the Rager, a species confined to the shores of Halvo Bay. The Aftermath Campaign, set many years later during the events of *Gears of War 3*, includes some of the savage varieties of Locust from that time period, including Lambent Formers.

SMALLER ENEMIES

TICKER

JUDGMENT AND AFTERMATH CAMPAIGNS

HP	SPEED	STAR SCORE	THREAT	COVER USAGE	ATTACKS
250	VERY FAST	2	MINOR	LOW	MELEE, EXPLOSIVE

One of the few enemies you can hear long before you see them, Tickers are pint-sized scavengers fitted with explosive canisters. Though capable of clawing and scratching at their prey, they prefer to detonate their bombs in suicidal fashion. The detonation takes roughly two seconds to commence, allowing ample time to either roll away or, better yet, kick the Ticker into the air and shoot it. A single Ticker explosion isn't likely to down a player unless playing on Insane difficulty, but Tickers rarely travel alone. Tickers are a pack species and often attack as a swarm. Listen for the clip-clop-clop of their scurrying approach and back away while switching to a weapon you can dispatch them with from afar. The Lancer will do, but a single round from the Boltok pistol can detonate them from afar. Their short height makes them difficult to spot beyond cover.

WRETCH

JUDGMENT AND AFTERMATH CAMPAIGNS

HP	SPEED	STAR SCORE	THREAT	COVER USAGE	ATTACKS
350	VERY FAST	3	MINOR	LOW	CLAWS, TEETH

Wretches are among the least intelligent Locust species, but their sharp teeth and lengthy claws combine with their single-track ferocity to make them a feared beast nonetheless. Wretches travel in large, hopping packs and are capable of clambering along most surfaces, even the ceiling. With no need for doors, they can launch an attack from anywhere. A lone Wretch can be kicked aside or shot and killed with little effort, but Wretches rarely travel alone. As with the Tickers, Wretches become dangerous in groups and can swarm their prey with little warning. Fortunately, Wretches lack a ranged attack and can be killed safely from afar, but this isn't always as easy as it sounds. Their short height and fast, hopping gait can make them hard to hit, especially in areas with ample cover or large obstacles. Wretches are prime targets for chainsaw kills, Sawed-Off Shotgun multi-kills, and setting aflame with the Scorcher.

LAMBENT WRETCH

JUDGMENT AND AFTERMATH CAMPAIGNS

HP	SPEED	STAR SCORE	THREAT	COVER USAGE	ATTACKS
300	VERY FAST	4	MINOR	LOW	CLAWS, IMULSION BLAST

This rare version of Locust was, for a long while, the only breed to be contaminated by Imulsion—and that continues through the events of the Aftermath Campaign set in Halvo Bay. Lambent Wretches behave much the same way as standard Wretches, but their slight decrease in health is more than offset by their toxic explosion upon death. Lambent Wretches don't simply bleed and die upon receiving fatal damage; they explode. Anyone standing too close is immediately doused in the hazardous Imulsion running through their veins. As with the Ticker's explosion, a lone Lambent Wretch's rupture isn't going to down anyone not playing on Insane difficulty (unless previously damaged), but Lambent Wretches travel in groups. Keeping your distance from the Lambent Wretch is vital. Be sure to kick any that get too close. Open fire on them with the assault rifle, Scorcher, or Gnasher before they get too close. And whatever you do, don't chainsaw them!

FORMER

AFTERMATH CAMPAIGN ONLY

HP	SPEED	STAR SCORE	THREAT	COVER USAGE	ATTACKS
300	FAST	N/A	MINOR	LOW	MELEE, IMULSION BLAST

The Former isn't Locust, but rather humans that have become so sickened by Imulsion that they've transformed into Lambent Humans. Formers are often lurking en masse, in areas quarantined by those humans who were still healthy. Thanks to the large populations on Sera that worked with Imulsion, there's no such thing as a solitary Former. If you encounter one, you can be sure that dozens are nearby. Formers possess superhuman athletic ability and strength. They can leap from rooftops, crash through doors, and even deliver a hefty mantle kick. Formers explode in a burst of toxic gas that is only the slightest bit harmful. Formers can be shot and killed with any weapon, but there is no more satisfying and efficient way to kill them than with the Retro Lancer. It's possible to Retro Charge through three or more Formers in a single attack, bursting right through them without firing a single bullet. Firing a Lancer or Gnasher from the hip is also a great way to keep them at bay.

SHRIEKER

JUDGMENT CAMPAIGN ONLY

HP	SPEED	STAR SCORE	THREAT	COVER USAGE	ATTACKS
500	MODERATE	7	MODERATE	N/A	CUSTOM GORGON SMG, EXPLOSION

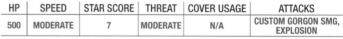

These floating, gas-filled sentries pose a far greater threat than their diminutive size might suggest. Armed with customized Gorgon sub-machine guns, Shriekers attack from the sky in large numbers. They boast considerable health and are capable of evading when shot to avoid additional damage. Shriekers can only evade once every two seconds so it's best to fire in a short burst, let them evade, then open fire on them once you regain the target. Though their weaponry is indeed powerful, what really makes Shriekers dangerous is their dive-bomb explosion. The flammable gas that keeps them aloft doesn't explode while airborne. Instead, Shriekers target the nearest living creature—human or Locust—and dive towards it for an explosive kamikaze collision. This explosion is far more dangerous than their gunfire and you must take care to not target a Shrieker directly overhead! Instead, use your Lancer, Retro Lancer, or Marzka to shoot Shriekers out of the air while they are near other Locust.

NEMACYST

HP	SPEED	STAR SCORE	THREAT	COVER USAGE	ATTACKS
25	FAST	0	MINOR	N/A	INK EXPLOSION

Nemacysts are airborne creatures, spewed into the air by distant Seeders. Nemacysts can be shot out of the air with relative ease (an assault rifle is best for this) and can also be evaded with a well-timed roll or by sprinting behind cover. Their impact inflicts very little damage, but they erupt in a cloud of poisonous gas, not unlike an Ink Grenade. Nemacysts are never a primary threat, but rather a complicating factor that can force you to stay in cover and split attention between ground-based threats and those in the sky. Fortunately, you're rarely going to encounter any Nemacysts without the presence of a Range Sentinel. These auto-targeting turrets are well-suited for shooting Nemacysts out of the air and can free you to focus on larger threats.

STANDARD LOCUST
DRONES

JUDGMENT AND AFTERMATH CAMPAIGNS

VARIETY	HP	SPEED	STAR SCORE	THREAT	COVER USAGE	WEAPONRY
DRONE	1000	NORMAL	3	MODERATE	MODERATE	ASSAULT RIFLES, SHOTGUNS, PISTOLS, TURRETS
DRONE GRAPPLER	600	NORMAL	3	MODERATE	MODERATE	ASSAULT RIFLES, SHOTGUNS, PISTOLS
DRONE W/ MORTAR	1000	NORMAL	9	HIGH	MODERATE	MORTAR, ASSAULT RIFLES, PISTOLS
SAVAGE DRONE	1000	NORMAL	N/A	MODERATE	MODERATE	RETRO LANCER, TURRET

Drones are the most common unit in the Locust army and can equip themselves with a variety of weapons, excluding power weapons. Drones are the closest thing the Locust have to a human in terms of size, speed, and appearance. Drones are brutish creatures that make up for their lack of intellect with a ferociousness that can be problematic in tight spaces. Drones typically eschew flanking maneuvers and rarely utilize available cover. Instead, the aggressive Drones charge across the battlefield and try to attack from close to medium range. Drones often attack in groups and commonly lead the way for heavier, more powerful units in the Locust army. Deal with them from afar, while taking advantage of their predictability. Drones can be dispatched with any number of weapons, including the Lancer's chainsaw. Avoid using power weapons against them unless you're certain you can kill multiple Drones with a single attack.

CYCLOPS

HP	SPEED	STAR SCORE	THREAT	COVER USAGE	WEAPONRY
550	NORMAL	5	MODERATE	MODERATE	ASSAULT RIFLES, PISTOLS

The Cyclops is a cousin of the Drone, outfitted with a special targeting system in its helmet. The Cyclops is more accurate than a Drone or Grenadier and takes pleasure in scavenging the battlefield for COG weaponry. It's not at all uncommon to encounter a Cyclops with a Lancer or Boltok, and some even attempt to use the Lancer's chainsaw. The Cyclops is far rarer than the Drone and has lower HP, but is a more valuable quarry to hunt. Always look for the lone targeting eye in the Cyclops' helmet and prioritize accordingly. These enemies should be dispatched quickly, and before they get too close. Spot them for assistance from other COGs to reduce the chance of them sneaking up for a chainsaw kill.

SNIPER

HP	SPEED	STAR SCORE	THREAT	COVER USAGE	WEAPONRY
450	NORMAL	6	HIGH	HIGH	LONGSHOT, ONESHOT

Snipers are among the most cunning enemies in the Locust army, thanks to their skilled use of cover, their reluctance to engage at close range, and their accurate aim. The other members of Kilo Squad seldom fail to alert you to the presence of Snipers. Immediately duck into cover and look for the glimmer reflecting off their rifle's scope or the laser of the OneShot's targeting system. You'll rarely be able to reach the position occupied by Snipers on the battlefield, so duck into cover, watch their movement, then counterattack with a long-range weapon of your own. The Longshot or Markza are the obvious choices, but the Breechshot and Boltok can be used successfully as well.

GRENADIER

JUDGMENT AND AFTERMATH CAMPAIGNS

VARIETY	HP	SPEED	STAR SCORE	THREAT	COVER USAGE	WEAPONRY
GRENADIER	1000	NORMAL	7	MODERATE	MODERATE	SHOTGUNS, PISTOLS, GRENADES
FLAME GRENADIER	1000	NORMAL	7	MODERATE	MODERATE	SCORCHER, GRENADES
SAVAGE GRENADIER	1000	NORMAL	N/A	MODERATE	MODERATE	SHOTGUNS, PISTOLS, GRENADES

Grenadiers outrank Drones in the Locust military and deserve your attention as soon as they're spotted. Unlike Drones, Grenadiers utilize cover to close in on your position and either blind-toss a Frag Grenade at your feet or put their Gnasher to use. Savage Grenadiers are more likely to utilize Incendiary Grenades instead of Frag Grenades, but otherwise differ in appearance only. In contrast, Flame Grenadiers attack with a Scorcher and can be difficult to distinguish from a Flame Boomer from afar. Fortunately, the Flame Grenadier has less than half as much HP as a Flame Boomer and can be killed with a single headshot, just like the other Drones. If no precision weapon is available, open fire on the fuel tanks on the Flame Grenadier's back for an explosive kill. Grenadiers are quite rare compared to Drones. Fortunately, they're far more vocal and often announce their arrival. Take them out from afar, as you don't want to risk getting into a close-range shotgun battle with them on higher difficulties.

THERON GUARD

JUDGMENT AND AFTERMATH CAMPAIGNS

VARIETY	HP	SPEED	STAR SCORE	THREAT	COVER USAGE	WEAPONRY
THERON	1075	NORMAL	8	HIGH	HIGH	ASSAULT RIFLES, TORQUE BOW
THERON W/ CLEAVER	1075	NORMAL	8	HIGH	LOW	CLEAVER

The Theron Guards are the elite members of the Locust military and surpass the Drones and Grenadiers in every measurable quality from health to intellect. The Theron Guard come in two varieties: standard and those armed with a Cleaver. Typical Theron Guard attack with either a Torque Bow or assault rifle, utilize cover exceptionally well, and can maintain their distance. By contrast, the Therons armed with a Cleaver charge into battle and attempt to cut the Gears to pieces without hesitation. They run right past cover and don't stop until they're on top of you swinging away with their heavy metal blades. Therons can be difficult to spot, but you'll either hear their hoarse whispers or spot the glow of their Torque Bows as they draw them back for firing. Beware the splash-damage from an exploding Torque Bow, as you needn't suffer a direct hit to take heavy damage.

HEAVY FORCES
RAGER

JUDGMENT AND AFTERMATH CAMPAIGNS

HP	SPEED	STAR SCORE	THREAT	COVER USAGE	WEAPONRY
1000	NORMAL	8	HIGH	MODERATE	BREECHSHOT, LANCER

The Rager is the newcomer to the *Gears of War* landscape. Beneath the wrinkled skin of this crazed beast lurks a boiling cauldron of hatred and anger. When left to its own devices, the Rager is content to lurk behind cover and use its Breechshot or Lancer to fire on enemy Gears. But any attack on the Rager had better be fatal, or the Rager will throw down its weapon and enter its enraged state. Once enraged, the hulking, red creature sprints across the battlefield and attacks with all the intensity of a Berserker. Not only is it safer to deliver fatal damage before they enrage, but your attacks only inflict 40% of their normal damage once the Rager has entered its enraged state. The Rager can be killed with a single headshot, explosives, or a chainsaw attack while in its standard state. Once enraged, however, you'll need to pile on the damage to account for its increased durability. Lastly, an enraged Rager can only be chainsawed from behind, by surprise.

KANTUS

HP	SPEED	STAR SCORE	THREAT	COVER USAGE	WEAPONRY
1350	SLOW	12	HIGH	LOW	GORGON PISTOL, SCREAM, INK GRENADE, TICKERS, RESURRECTION

The Kantus is a shaman-like unit within the Locust army. Relatively rare, this support unit is armed with Ink Grenades and one Gorgon Pistol. But its true power lies beyond its offensive capabilities. The Kantus is capable of reviving fallen Locust from across the battlefield. The Kantus raises its arms, turns white in prayer, and revives any Drone, Grenadier, or Theron knocked to its knees. Though it can't bring back the dead, the Kantus' ability to revive the fallen makes it a top priority target. And if its healing powers weren't reason enough to take it out first, the Kantus can also summon Tickers into battle! The Kantus rarely uses cover and moves only sparingly, though almost always with a somersault. Look for a Markza or Longshot to snipe the Kantus as soon as its presence is known. Otherwise, try to get in close and use the Sawed-Off Shotgun on it. Approach cautiously, as its piercing scream can stop you in your tracks and leave you vulnerable to its Ink Grenades and allies.

BOOMER

JUDGMENT AND AFTERMATH CAMPAIGNS

VARIETY	HP	SPEED	STAR SCORE	THREAT	COVER USAGE	WEAPONRY
BOOMER	2500	VERY SLOW	11	HIGH	LOW	BOOMSHOT
FLAME BOOMER	2500	VERY SLOW	9	MODERATE	LOW	SCORCHER
SAVAGE BOOMER	2500	VERY SLOW	N/A	HIGH	LOW	DIGGER LAUNCHER

Boomers are the quintessential heavy unit and one of the most feared Locust forces. The base Boomer stomps into battle armed with a Boomshot and a bellowing voice that announces each shot. Boomers are deadly accurate with their Boomshot, even if they eschew cover and often stand out in the open while firing. Boomers have a very high amount of HP and can withstand tremendous punishment before falling in battle. Flame Boomers are less common than their Boomshot-wielding brethren, but pose a large threat in tight spaces. Their Scorcher doesn't have the range of a Boomshot—and their fuel tanks can be detonated for an easy kill—but they are not to be ignored. Lastly, the Savage Boomer only appears during the Aftermath Campaign, but utilizes the Digger Launcher to circumvent your attempts at taking cover. The Digger Launcher can burrow through the ground, under cover, and automatically rises up to detonate when an enemy is detected. Savage Boomers are arguably the most dangerous Boomer of all.

GRINDER

HP	SPEED	STAR SCORE	THREAT	COVER USAGE	WEAPONRY
2750	VERY SLOW	15	HIGH	LOW	MULCHER

Similar to the Boomer, the Grinder is a Locust heavy unit armed with a single namesake weapon, with the tendency to announce its use. Grinders march headlong into battle armed with their trusty Mulcher and an impressive supply of ammo. The Mulcher's accuracy diminishes significantly with range, rending the Grinder's attack little more than a nuisance at long range. The Grinder often attacks when you least expect it, typically while occupied with other Locust. Take cover at once and switch to a power weapon if possible. Otherwise, wait for the Mulcher to overheat and launch your attack while the Grinder is forced to cool down its Mulcher. The Grinder is less dangerous at close range, provided you can circle-strafe around him, staying away from the business end of the Mulcher. The faster you kill the Grinder, the more ammo available for you to use with the Mulcher.

MAULER

JUDGMENT CAMPAIGN ONLY

VARIETY	HP	SPEED	STAR SCORE	THREAT	COVER USAGE	WEAPONRY
MAULER	2500	SLOW	15	HIGH	LOW	BOOMSHIELD, EXPLOSIVE FLAIL
ELITE MAULER	5000	SLOW	5	HIGH	LOW	BOOMSHIELD, EXPLOSIVE FLAIL

Maulers are perhaps the most intimidating of all the Locust bipeds. Immense in size, clad in armor, and capable of short gallops at a surprising speed, the Mauler demands your full attention as soon as it emerges from the shadows. Maulers (and Elite Maulers with double the HP) use their Boomshield for protection from gunfire, forcing you to target their feet, use a OneShot, or aim an explosive device at the ground nearby. Maulers possess surprising range with their explosive Flail and are not as quick to walk away from a downed Gear as the rest of the Locust. Their explosive Flail can down a Gear with one swing and another swing won't be far behind for those who can't quickly crawl to safety. OneShots and Mortars are extremely helpful when combating a Mauler, but distance is always your number one weapon. These lumbering beasts may be deadly, but they pose no threat from afar.

BUTCHER

HP	SPEED	STAR SCORE	THREAT	COVER USAGE	WEAPONRY
2750	VERY SLOW	9	MODERATE	LOW	CLEAVER

The massive Butcher is among the rarest Locust unit in this corner of Sera. Slow moving, but heavily armored, the Butcher strides into battle armed with nothing more than the same Cleaver that many of the Theron Guards use. Butchers are considerably slower than Theron Guards, but use their immense girth to bring the Cleaver down far harder than a Theron ever could. Depending on the difficulty setting, a Butcher can down a Gear with a single slash of the Cleaver, especially if taking damage from elsewhere. Unlike the Maulers, however, Butchers have no shield to protect them. Simply back away and open fire with an assault rifle or shotgun to kill them. They can soak up a lot of bullets, but they're harmless from a distance.

LOCUST BEASTS

SERAPEDE

JUDGMENT CAMPAIGN ONLY

HP	SPEED	STAR SCORE	THREAT	COVER USAGE	ATTACKS
800	SLOW	15	MODERATE	LOW	ELECTRIC BITE

The multi-segmented creature known as a Serapede is unlike any other on Sera. Essentially an armor-plated insect resembling a centipede, the Serapede is all but bulletproof except for the last segment of its body. Gunfire aimed at its armor-plated segments inflicts just 50% of normal damage, whereas shots to the final segment on its body rupture with ease. Serapedes pick a single enemy on which to focus their pursuit until another enemy ruptures three or more of its tail segments. Then the Serapede turns and focuses its aggression on the attacker. Serapedes pick up speed as they get shorter. The increased speed, paired with a tighter turning radius, makes the Serapede an ideal enemy to tackle with a friend. Have one player flee the Serapede in a straight line while the other targets its tail, then reverse the roles. The Serapede isn't a particularly dangerous enemy, but its bite renders its victim stunned, low on health, and vulnerable to follow-up attacks.

CORPSER

JUDGMENT CAMPAIGN ONLY

HP	SPEED	STAR SCORE	THREAT	COVER USAGE	WEAPONRY
3500	NORMAL	25	HIGH	LOW	CLAW, STAB

There is only one variety of Corpser present in Halvo Bay, an armored juvenile whose thick metal plating deflects all bullets that strike its legs. The Corpser crawls across the ground like a crab in an attempt to claw at its enemies. It can also rear back on its tail and bring its mighty, barbed legs down in a stabbing motion. Corpsers are also capable of burrowing underground to launch a surprise leg-stab attack from underfoot. Corpsers are particularly vulnerable to explosives, provided you can land a direct hit on their body. Gunfire, particularly from the Sawed-Off Shotgun, is also effective from a flanking position. Don't waste any ammo firing on the Corpser head-on when its legs are curled in front of it like a shield; your bullets will merely bounce off. Instead, try to shoot between the legs, Spot it for assistance, or roll to the side and attempt to flank it.

BLOODMOUNT

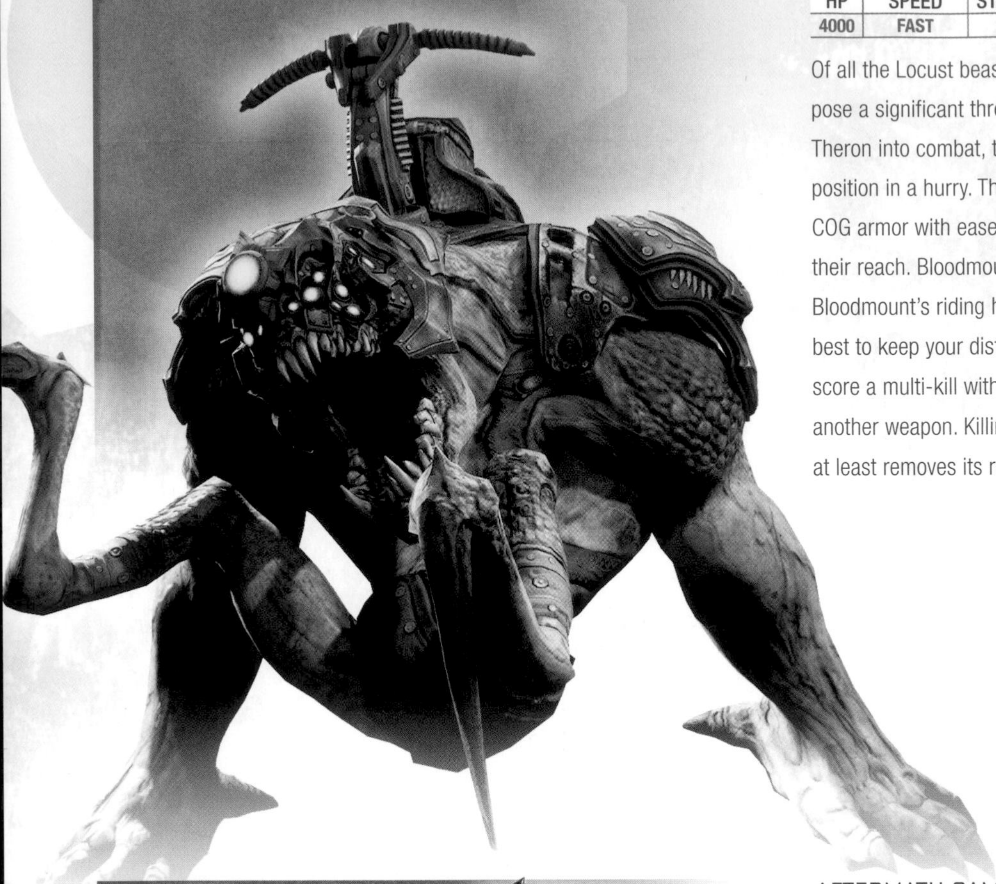

HP	SPEED	STAR SCORE	THREAT	COVER USAGE	ATTACKS
4000	FAST	12	HIGH	LOW	TEETH, LEG STAB

Of all the Locust beasts, the Bloodmount is among the smallest, but it can pose a significant threat nonetheless. Capable of quickly carrying a Drone or Theron into combat, the Bloodmount can mantle over cover and close on your position in a hurry. Their dagger-like front legs and spiny teeth can pierce COG armor with ease, making it essential to seek higher ground and avoid their reach. Bloodmounts are vulnerable to all weapon fire and a shot to the Bloodmount's riding helmet can stun both the beast and its rider. Though it's best to keep your distance, those with a Sawed-Off Shotgun can oftentimes score a multi-kill with a single shot if they first soften the Bloodmount with another weapon. Killing the Bloodmount's rider doesn't injure the beast, but it at least removes its ranged threat.

ARMORED KANTUS

HP	SPEED	STAR SCORE	THREAT	COVER USAGE	ATTACKS
4800	SLOW	N/A	HIGH	LOW	TWIN GORGON SMG, ROLL ATTACK, RESURRECTION

The Armored Kantus may resemble the standard Kantus in shape and armament, but it is significantly more deadly and far harder to kill. True to its name, the Armored Kantus is completely covered in armor that reduces all standard bullet damage to just 20% of its normal damage rating. Fire from Incendiary Grenades and the Scorcher is reduced to just 70% of its normal damage rating. Fortunately, there is another way to damage the Armored Kantus. Unless in the midst of one of its damaging roll attacks, the Armored Kantus can be stunned with an explosive attack—whether by a Torque Bow, Boomshot, or Frag Grenade—and lets out a blood-curdling scream while stunned. Its open mouth is extremely vulnerable to gunfire and almost any direct hit to its open mouth can prove fatal. The Armored Kantus is vulnerable to an attack on its mouth for roughly four seconds as it screams. It also periodically screams on its own as a way of reviving fallen Locust. Use this time to fire the Boltok, Torque Bow, or Hammerburst straight through its mouth.

REAVER

JUDGMENT AND AFTERMATH CAMPAIGNS

HP	SPEED	STAR SCORE	THREAT	COVER USAGE	ATTACKS
6500	FAST (FLY), SLOW (WALK)	25	HIGH	LOW	ROCKETS, TENTACLES

Reavers are the primary aerial unit of the Locust military and are capable of bombarding the battlefield with their Boomshot-like rockets from the skies. Reavers in the skies are best ignored, as your ammo is only wasted in trying to hit them. Instead, wait for the Reaver to land, then open fire. A grounded Reaver likely continues to use its rockets to attack, unless its prey happens to be directly beneath it. In that case, the Reaver uses its massive tentacle-like legs to trample and stab the enemy to death. Though Reavers are often ridden by a Drone or Theron that fires on the Gears once the Reaver lands, it's best to ignore the riders and focus entirely on the Reaver itself. Aim for its head or, if directly beneath it, the soft pink underbelly. Targeting the pink belly and the mouth yield a 50% damage boost to whatever weapon you use. Of course, the single best way to kill a Reaver is with the OneShot—line it up with the riders for a multi-kill!

BERSERKER

JUDGMENT CAMPAIGN ONLY

HP	SPEED	STAR SCORE	THREAT	COVER USAGE	ATTACKS
30000	SLOW (WALK), FAST (SPRINT)	20	HIGH	LOW	MELEE

Berserkers are the largest and most formidable Locust outside the leadership ranks. These blind, hulking beasts aren't armed, but pack considerable punch thanks to their immense size and strength. Berserkers stomp across the battlefield listening for the sounds of enemy movement and gunfire. Once detected, the Berserker sprints directly towards the sounds in an effort to trample its foe. It inflicts heavy damage with body slams and overhead strikes, but can be avoided with a well-timed roll to the side. The Berserker's thick skin is virtually bulletproof and reduces most standard gunfire to just 10% of its normal effectiveness. The only way to efficiently harm a Berserker is by setting it alight with a Scorcher or Flame Sentinel. Berserkers turn molten red for roughly 10 seconds after being doused in flame. Use this time to open fire with your Lancer or other weapon to inflict the normal amount of damage each weapon is capable of. Continue to alternate between the Scorcher and the Lancer and try to keep a piece of cover between you and the Berserker at all times. Even a fallen column or half-wall stops a Berserker in its tracks.

JUDGMENT CAMPAIGN

THE MUSEUM OF MILITARY GLORY

BAIRD'S TESTIMONY

SECTION 1: OLD TOWN

"OUR MISSION WAS TO RENDEZVOUS WITH A SUPPLY CONVOY. BUT THEN THINGS STARTED TO GO WRONG."

DAMON S. BAIRD, COG LIEUTENANT

Following the loss of Baird's commanding officer, Colonel Loomis promoted him to Lieutenant and gave him command of Kilo Squad. He intends to do well.

Baird is a skilled technician and mechanic with a biting, sarcastic sense of humor that can easily grate on the nerves of his fellow soldiers, especially his superiors. He joined the COG on Emergence Day and was soon promoted to lead Kilo Squad. Fourteen long years of battling the Locust would eventually bring Baird, along with his good friend Augustus Cole, to the Alpha and Delta Squads. And ultimately, adrift aboard the CNV Sovereign...

Baird is a constant throughout the *Gears of War* saga. His wit, intelligence, and technical know-how have helped lead his squadmates out of more jams than they care to remember. He's a diligent observer and knows more about the Locust—and their intent—than anyone else in the COG.

	START
X	FINISH
1	CLASSIFIED INTEL STEP
T	TURRET

MISSION OBJECTIVES

> Get to the convoy.

> Find a route to the museum.

HOSTILES ENCOUNTERED

③	③	⑥	⑪	⑮	④
DRONE	WRETCH	GRINDER	BOOMER	SNIPER	LAMBENT WRETCH*

☆ = Star Score

*Declassified Mission only.

RIBBONS AND SCORING

Use the Lancer's chainsaw to execute any Wretches or Drones that charge your position, both for the execution bonus and in an effort to earn a Lumberjack ribbon. Refrain from tossing a Frag Grenade during the initial enemy encounter. It can be difficult to earn a Clusterluck ribbon in this initial fray, so save Frag Grenades for where the enemies are more tightly bunched. During the second encounter, try to race across the street beyond the convoy site to lob a grenade at the E-Hole as soon as it appears (before your squadmates close it for you). This earns the Plug the Hole ribbon. Depending on what type of enemy emerges, the opportunity to earn a Boombardier ribbon might present itself if you claim a Boomshot and quickly fire it at a group of remaining foes.

CLUSTERLUCK: Kill multiple enemies with one grenade.

LUMBERJACK: Chainsaw 3 enemies in a row.

PLUG THAT HOLE: Close an E-Hole with explosives.

COG TAGS

FRAG GRENADE

LANCER

DECLASSIFY

LANCER

AMMO

CLASSIFIED INTEL

1 Drop into cover near the flaming tree and blind-fire at the Drones that approach. Move to the column to the left and ready the chainsaw to cut down any Wretches that approach.

2 Stick close to the stairs leading to the terrace on the right to avoid being cornered by the Wretches and Drones that attack here. Wretches attack en masse and it's not uncommon for a number of Drones to attack from the rear.

3 Advance from cover to cover, grab the Frags, and quickly toss one at the Emergence Hole that opens in the street ahead. This E-Hole has a tendency to spawn anything from Drones to Boomers to Snipers. Shut it down quickly!

DECLASSIFIED: THREE-STAR TACTICS

Kilo Squad enters Old Town via a quiet abandoned alley. There's no sign of life, human or otherwise, but the ground is alive with tremors. Make your way past the flaming building to the debris in the alley and kick it out of the way. Lift the bar off the gate on the left and continue to the second section of Old Town.

Press the X button to kick the couch out of the way after the tremor.

Wend your way through the alley to the courtyard ahead and descend the stairs to the fallen Onyx Guard. Take the additional Lancer ammo. Then duck into cover near the wall down the steps, near the ammo crate.

Stick close to the left pillar to shoot the Drones and be ready to step out and chainsaw the Wretches.

A small group of Drones and Wretches attacks. Stay in cover and blind-fire at the Drones. Don't waste Frag Grenades here; they come in handy later. Keep firing until the Wretches appear. Then move a few steps to the left and take cover near the pillar. Watch as the Wretches hop up the stairs and over the crates in front of you. Rev the chainsaw, step out, and execute them one by one as they round the corner. Gather the ammo from the crate on the lower landing and continue around the corner past the flaming tree.

DECLASSIFY

LAMBENT WRETCHES REPLACE NORMAL WRETCHES

Kilo Squad claimed to encounter unknown Locust variant.

Difficulty Increase: Low

Star Multiplier: 1.44x

Lambent Wretches behave similarly to normal Wretches, but their Lambent nature means that they will erupt in an explosion of Imulsion upon death. Imulsion is highly toxic and the blast can be lethal on Hardcore and Insane difficulties, even if you're previously uninjured. Accepting this Declassified information requires that you approach the right-hand walkway with caution. Keep your distance and do not, under any circumstance, chainsaw a Dark Wretch on Insane difficulty!

There are two paths to take here: one leads through the buildings on the far left side of the street and the other goes across the terrace on the right. Start high on the right to take out the initial wave of Lambent Wretches and use the upper walkway for cover against the numerous Drones in the street below. Avoid the corners of this terrace. The Lambent Wretches can easily overwhelm you and their Imulsion explosions can prove deadly if you can't roll out of the blast radius. Try to stick close to the near-side stairs to give yourself an exit. Lob a Frag Grenade across the terrace at the Drones and Lambent Wretches as they attack.

Hang back near the stairs to avoid being surrounded by Lambent Wretches when heading onto the terrace.

Use the walls on this terrace for cover and toss any remaining Frag Grenades down the steps to beat back the next wave of attackers. Use the cover of the trees and short walls in the street and quickly pick up the Frag Grenades in the yard. Toss one immediately at the E-Hole that opens on the street, slightly around the corner to the right.

Multiple Drones emerge from this E-Hole, along with a Boomer, Grinder, or Sniper. Grab the Frags in the street and lob one into the hole to close it as quickly as possible and to potentially earn a Clusterluck ribbon (in addition to a Plug That Hole ribbon). Additional enemies may attack from further down the street, possibly including a Sniper. Keep your head down and look for any fallen Boomshots or Longshots to pick up.

Toss Frags at the road around the corner to close the E-Hole as soon as it opens.

E. Kogan, Sgt, Jacinto

K.I.A. when a glowing Wretch that pounced on him was shot and exploded.

The first COG Tag is located near the mission's end, in the small courtyard to the right of the roadblock. The COG Tag is on the ground, to the right of the Crimson Omen. This is directly opposite where the rest of Kilo Squad will be waiting for you.

COG TAG

AMMO

COG TAGS

MORTAR

SAWED-OFF

FRAG GRENADE

3

T

4

2

1

X

MULCHER

FRAG GRENADE

AMMO

DECLASSIFY

MARKZA

AMMO

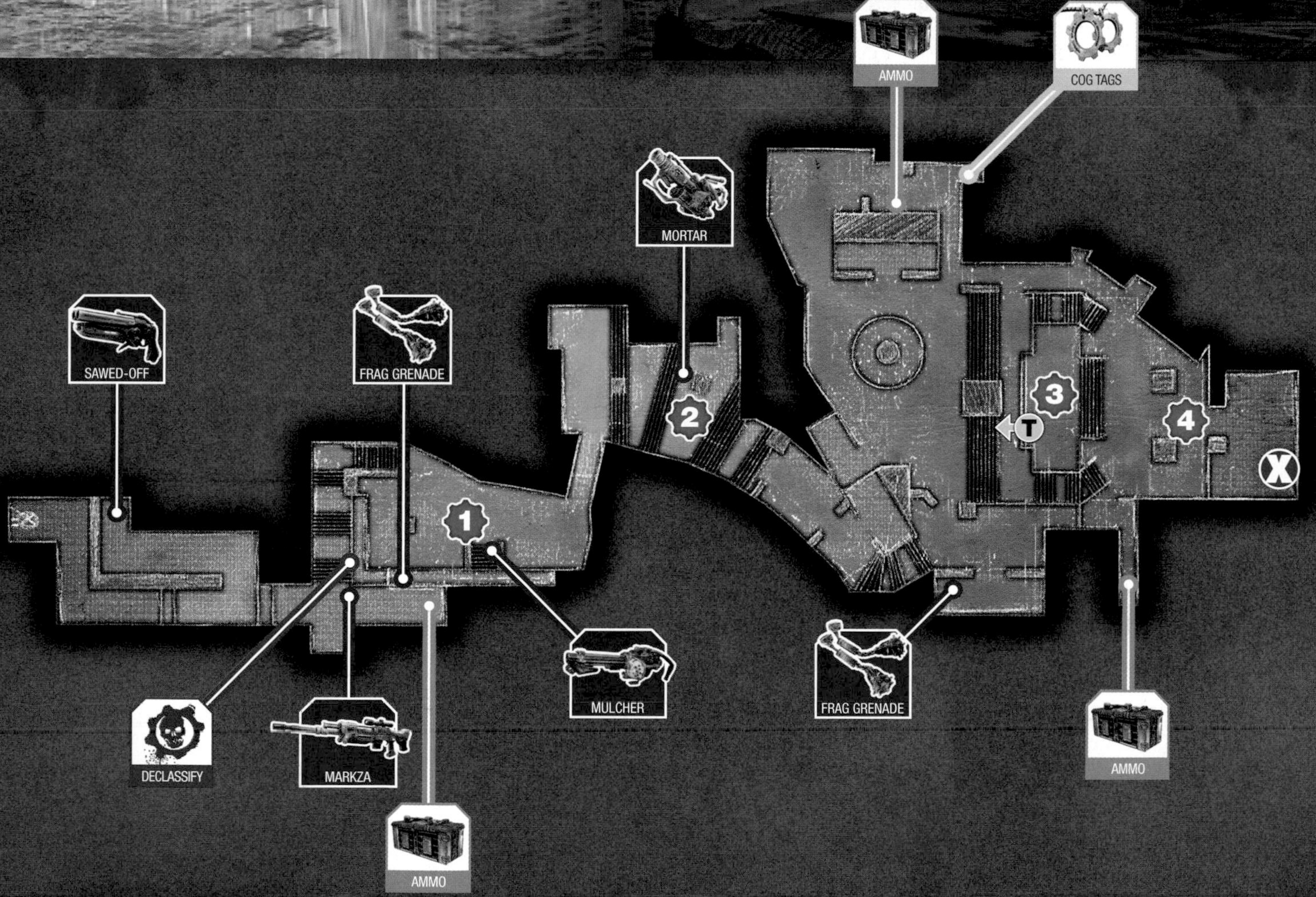

MISSION OBJECTIVES

> Find a route to the museum.

> Get to the museum.

> Deal with the Locust outpost.

HOSTILES ENCOUNTERED

②	③	③	⑥	⑪	⑮
TICKER	WRETCH	DRONE	SNIPER	BOOMER	GRINDER

☆ = Star Score

"THE MUSEUM WAS ON THE OTHER SIDE OF THE RIVER— THE SIDE THE COG NO LONGER CONTROLLED. I THOUGHT MAYBE WE COULD SLIP THROUGH UNNOTICED."

RIBBONS AND SCORING

Grab the Frags near the Mulcher and look up the hill to see what kind of enemy is coming first. If they are Wretches, then use the Lancer to chainsaw them as they make their way across the bridge. This should earn one or even two Lumberjack ribbons. If they are Snipers and Drones, use the Markza from the walkway near the Frags and snipe a few enemies for headshots. Use the Mortar to get up the stairs with at least 1:40 on the clock. Then clear the upper walkway to claim the Frags before the E-Holes open near the fountain. Use the Frags to earn one or two Plug That Hole ribbons to further boost your Star count. Keep your eyes peeled for a Boomshot left on the stairs early on in the mission; swap out the Markza or Gnasher for it and try using it to get a Boombardier ribbon after closing the E-Holes.

CLUSTERLUCK: Kill multiple enemies with one grenade.

LUMBERJACK: Chainsaw 3 enemies in a row.

HAT TRICK: Score 3 headshots in a row without dying.

PLUG THAT HOLE: Close an E-Hole with explosives.

CLASSIFIED INTEL

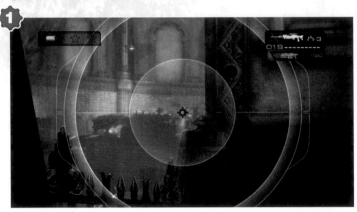

1 Grab the Frag Grenades near the Mulcher and start sniping with the Markza, or rev your chainsaw and cut a path through the Wretches streaming across the bridge. Either way, be sure to watch out for the Grinders and Boomers.

2 Secure the Mortar and fire one of its three shells up the stairs to bombard the heavy units moving to your position. Ascend the stairs to the sandbags and fire the second shell to draw out any stragglers. Fire the third shot from the top of the stairs towards the turret.

3 Use Frag Grenades to clear out the upper platform near the turret. Then grab the Frags behind the sandbag on the right. Toss them to close the two E-Holes that open below. Then use the Lancer, turret, and your Markza to finish off the remaining Locust. Take your time and stay in cover.

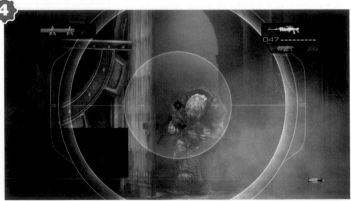

4 A final heavy unit will burst through the doors behind you with a couple of Tickers or Wretches in tow. Let your squadmates deal with the peons while you target the heavy's head with the Markza. Expect either a Grinder or Boomer.

DECLASSIFIED: THREE-STAR TACTICS

Kilo Squad has found themselves alone in a wine cellar, but this no time for a sip of the grape. Unless you're playing on Insane difficulty, swap out the Gnasher for the Markza. Then grab the ammo crate at the end of the hall *before* accepting the Declassify option—this will help save some time. A Sawed-Off Shotgun is also in the wine cellar, but wc don't recommend picking it up if you're trying to three-Star the mission.

DECLASSIFY

FINISH BEFORE HAMMER OF DAWN STRIKES

Lt. Baird claimed unauthorized Hammer of Dawn strikes took place in Old Town.

Difficulty Increase: High

Star Multiplier: 2.54x

Countdown to Hammer of Dawn Strikes

CASUAL	NORMAL	HARDCORE	INSANE
5:00	4:00	3:30	4:00

This isn't an easy goal to meet, particularly on the harder difficulties, as it really forces you to charge into the action a bit more than you may like. Get across the bridge without much hesitation and use the Mortar to clear the stairs. Try and save one shell, if possible, and carry the Mortar up the stairs. Use it to clear the area near the turret up top. Quickly close the E-Holes that open near the fountain. Then, if out of grenades, turn back to the corner and pick up the Frag Grenades behind the sandbag. Use them against the heavies that approach from the alleys down the stairs on the right. You'll have to get past one final heavy unit at the building before rushing in to safety.

Head up the stairs and sprint across to the steps on the right, near the Mulcher. Collect the Frag Grenades on this narrow walkway. Scan the upper path to see which type of enemy is coming first. There will either be a stream of Wretches hopping down the steps or a number of Drones and Snipers out in front of a Grinder or two. If the latter, post up on the walkway near the Frag Grenades and use the Markza to quickly bag a few headshots. Then rush across the bridge to the Mortar. If you see the Wretches instead, stay in cover and wait for the Wretches to reach the bridge. Chainsaw at least three of them to earn a Lumberjack ribbon. Lob a grenade at the others for a Clusterluck ribbon.

It's not necessary to earn several ribbons at the start of the battle to earn three Stars if you're going to Declassify the Hammer of Dawn Strikes. It's more important to not waste time. Fight your way across the bridge to the left soon after getting the Frag Grenades (ignore the Mulcher on the right) and lay claim to the Mortar. Use two of its three shells to clear out the stairs. Carry it up the stairs and then onto the dirt to the right of the path running alongside the turret. Fire the third Mortar shell at the terrace where the turret is.

From the dirt beside the tree, fire the third Mortar shell at the enemies near the turret.

Earning a Lumberjack ribbon against the Wretches before grabbing the Mortar is a good start to earning three Stars.

Mantle the wall at the top of the hill and fling a Frag Grenade at the other Locust. Then grab the Frags in the center and rush into cover near the wall by the turret. Two Emergence Holes are about to open near the fountain below. Use the two grenades to close them immediately. The first opens directly in front of the turret, to the left of the fountain. The second opens far to the right, beyond the fountain. Close them right away with the Frags. Then brace for multiple Boomers coming from the alley on the far right.

Close the E-Hole on the left first, since failure to do so will enable more enemies to attack at closer range.

Scan the area below (and behind you) for enemies and see if there are any Boomshots that can be put to use. Use the turret if you have a chance to gun down any heavy units. Otherwise stick with the Lancer and focus on the enemies coming up the stairs. A number of Locust will make their way up the stairs to the right (as viewed facing the fountain). Hold the higher ground and use the brick wall for cover.

Kill off the Boomers and any remaining Drones. Then turn and brace for one final attack from within the building behind your position. The doors burst open and a Boomer or Grinder emerges, accompanied by a pair of Tickers or Wretches. Kick the Tickers aside and then Spot the heavy unit to have your squad focus their fire on it. This is particularly important if there are only a few seconds remaining before the Hammer of Dawn strikes. Sprint into the building and tap Up on the D-pad as soon as possible to end the mission before time runs out.

Use the Spot command so your squad knows which enemy to focus their firepower on.

J. Los, CPL, Kinnerlake

K.I.A. from friendly fire when he accidentally ran in front of his fire team.

This COG Tag is down the alley at the base of the stairs beneath the turret. Clear the area of all Locust. Then, if there's time remaining before the Hammer of Dawn strikes (if applicable), descend the right-hand stairs, as viewed from the area near the turret, and head down the alley on the right. The small Crimson Omen is on the wall at the end of the alley. The COG Tag is on the ground to the right of it. It's best to get this COG Tag while playing without the Declassified option, as time is usually of the essence.

COG TAG

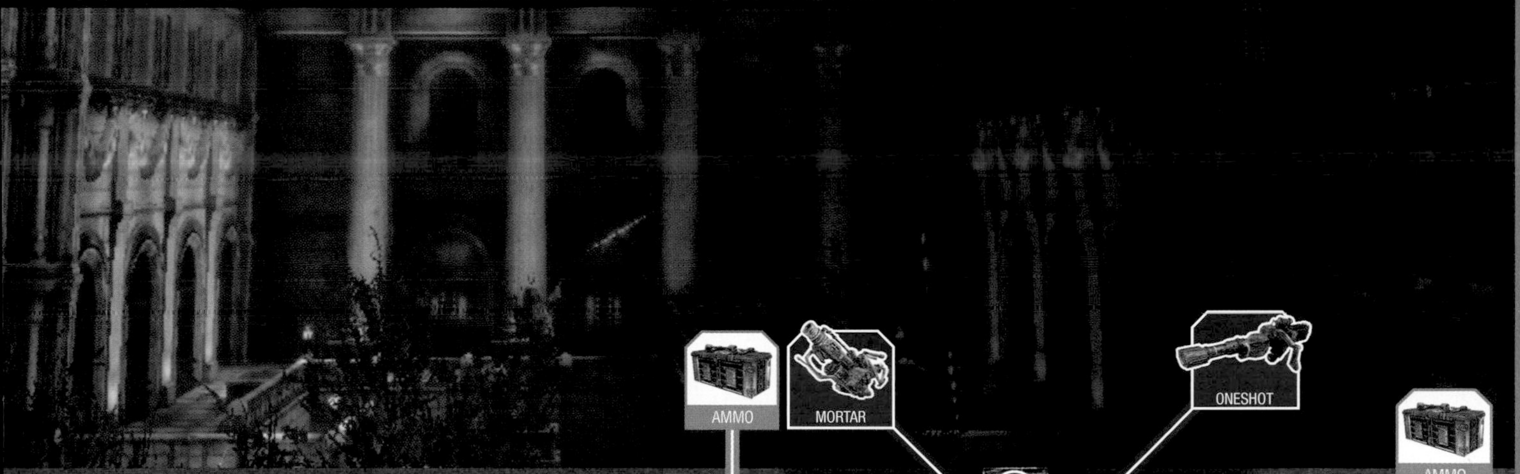

MISSION OBJECTIVES

> Get to the museum.
> Stop the Locust assault on the museum (optional).

HOSTILES ENCOUNTERED

TICKER

DRONE

BOOMER

KANTUS

 = Star Score

AMMO

MORTAR

ONESHOT

AMMO

ⓧ

③

②

ONYX AMMO

LONGSHOT

LANCER

DECLASSIFY

BOOMSHIELD

①

HAMMERBURST

FRAG GRENADE

COG TAGS

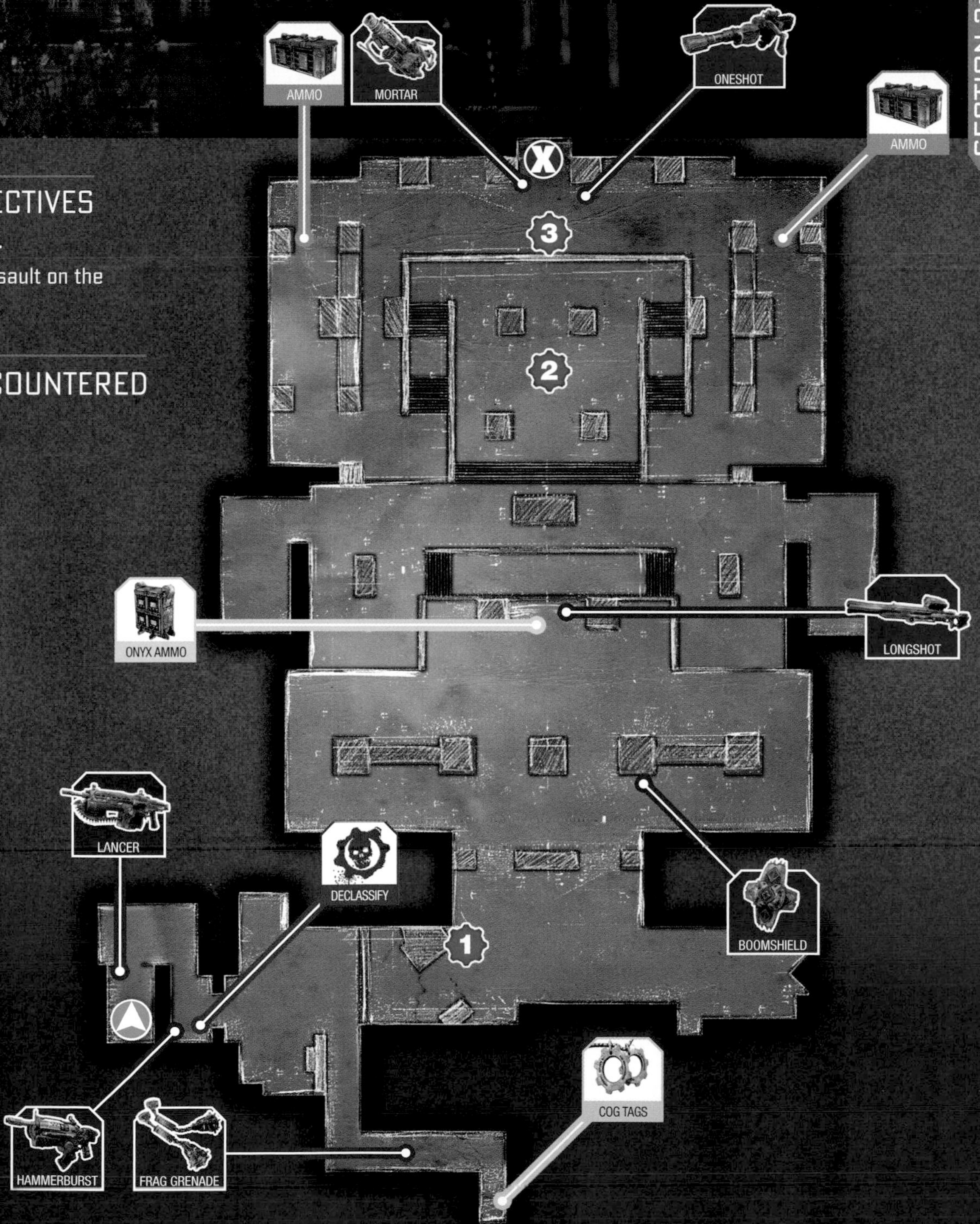

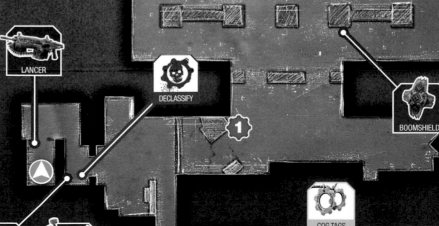

"IT WAS FASTER TO GO THROUGH THE EMPTY BUILDINGS THAN AROUND THEM. THEY WERE ALL SO...ABANDONED. IF NO ONE HERE HAD BEEN EVAC'D, WHERE WAS EVERYONE?"

RIBBONS AND SCORING

Accept the Declassify option and put the Hammerburst to use against the first Kantus that appears. Then switch to the Sawed-Off Shotgun and move through the gardens in search of an opportunity to kill two or more enemies at once for a Nothin' But Bits ribbon. Should no such opportunities arise, aim low on the Drones to down them. Then rush in and grab one for a meatshield and snap its neck for an execution bonus. Clear the upper walkway and then grab the OneShot leaning against the column and take cover near the rail. Other than the occasional Clusterluck ribbon possibly earned if the Declassified option isn't accepted (or a Hat Trick earned with the Longshot), your big scoring chance comes from the Shish-Kashot ribbon. The key to earning three Stars on this mission is to rack up as many Shish-Kashot ribbons as possible, and that means using the OneShot to kill two or more enemies at once. Keep your head down and watch for a Boomer and Kantus to approach single file, then open fire with the OneShot. Try to get three Shish-Kashot ribbons before killing the last Locust. Listen for your squad's alerts to incoming Tickers and quickly switch to a rifle or shotgun. Kick them away and then quickly open fire to shoot them out of the air for an Oakley ribbon.

SHISH-KASHOT: Kill at least two enemies with a single OneShot round.

NOTHIN' BUT BITS: Kill multiple enemies with a single Sawed-Off Shotgun blast.

OAKLEY: Kick a Ticker and shoot it out of the air.

CLASSIFIED INTEL

Move past the flaming car and take cover at the corner entrance to the gardens. Target the very first Kantus that appears. Then work your way in and out of cover to avoid the OneShots on the balcony.

Grab the Longshot and snipe the Drones with the OneShots on the balcony. Make sure the last grenade type carried was a Frag Grenade when picking up the Onyx Ammo Cache so you don't replenish it with Ink Grenades—those Frags will be needed to close several E-Holes soon enough.

Move to the balcony and finish off the remaining Locust. The battle may appear over, but several E-Holes are about to open below. Use the OneShot to pick the Kantuses and Boomers off as they charge forth. Keep your head down and, if you're not worried about the Star rating, use Frags or the nearby Mortar to close the E-Holes as quickly as they appear.

DECLASSIFIED: THREE-STAR TACTICS

Grab the Lancer and chainsaw through the wooden door to escape the room Kilo Squad fled into. Round the corner and consider this mission's Declassified option—it makes it much tougher.

DECLASSIFY

USE HAMMERBURSTS, SAWED-OFF SHOTGUNS, AND ONESHOTS ONLY

Kilo Squad utilized a prohibited Locust weapon and claimed it was effective.

Difficulty Increase: Moderate

Star Multiplier: 2.69x

Accepting these conditions matters in so much that you won't be able to use Frag Grenades against the numerous Drones and Kantuses at the start of the mission. It also rules out closing the E-Holes that appear at the end of the mission, as you won't have Frags or the use of the Mortar either. This forces you to deal with numerous Kantuses and Boomers at the end of the mission. Fortunately, the Onyx Ammo Cache can fully replenish Sawed-Off Shotgun ammo (it's the only ammo box that can) and there are eight rounds in an unused OneShot awaiting your arrival on the balcony. Use the Hammerburst to drop the Kantuses from afar, and then move in for multi-kills with the Sawed-Off Shotgun.

L. Gaffney, PFC, Halvo Bay

K.I.A. in Locust ambush, was first to die.

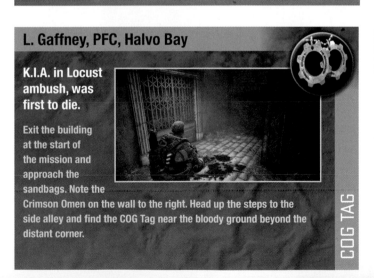

Exit the building at the start of the mission and approach the sandbags. Note the Crimson Omen on the wall to the right. Head up the steps to the side alley and find the COG Tag near the bloody ground beyond the distant corner.

COG TAG

Round the corner past the car engulfed in flames and watch as the first of several Kantuses launches out of the ground. That Kantus isn't alone; numerous Drones and Kantuses are set to attack in the gardens outside the museum. You need to kill each one of them and make it to the museum entrance atop the balcony. To do this, stay in cover near the planters to avoid the Drones with the OneShots on the balcony. Use the Hammerburst and target the Kantuses that appear to keep them from reviving downed Drones. Avoid their Ink Grenades and loop around to the right or left to flank them.

Use the Hammerburst to take down the Kantus on the far left as soon as it appears. Then sprint into cover.

With the Kantuses downed, it's time to look for any opportunities to use the Sawed-Off Shotgun against the Drones. Try to lure the Drones into close proximity and wait to fire until two can be killed with one shot for a Nothin' But Bits ribbon.

Stay in cover to avoid the OneShots on the balcony and wait with the Sawed-Off Shotgun until a multi-kill opportunity arises.

The Onyx Ammo Cache in the middle of the gardens represents your only source of additional Sawed-Off Shotgun ammo. Try to hold off picking it up until you're nearly dry. Fight up the stairs on either side of the balcony and quickly duck into the back hallway to avoid gunfire from the balcony. Keep your head down and move to the ammo crate that exists in each of these rooms. You'll likely be in position to snag another Nothin' But Bits ribbon from this location or, at the least, down a lone Drone and get an execution bonus.

The upper balcony will be crawling with Drones and Kantuses. Try to get in close with the Sawed-Off Shotgun if you can risk it!

The battle might feel like it's won after the last of the Locust are killed, but that couldn't be further from the truth. Numerous E-Holes are about to open across the gardens and a steady stream of Kantuses, Tickers, and Boomers are about to emerge. Grab the OneShot leaning against the statue, take cover near the wall, and open fire! Focus on the Kantuses and Boomers at the rear of the gardens, between the planters, and wait for two or more to line up single file. The OneShot can pierce multiple enemies and net an invaluable Shish-Kashot ribbon. At least two of these are likely needed to earn a three-Star rating on this mission.

Two Kantuses walking in single file is a perfect Shish-Kashot opportunity!

The Boomers do a terrific job of arcing their Boomshot rockets up and over the wall you're using for cover. Be sure to get your head down whenever you hear one of them yell, "Boom!" Your squadmates will do an admirable job of gunning down any heavies that make their way up the steps towards your position, but you'll need to watch out for Tickers. Drop the OneShot and quickly roll out of the way if shooting them isn't an option. Swap the OneShot for the nearby Mortar if the enemies reach the stairs.

SECTION 4: GREAT HALL

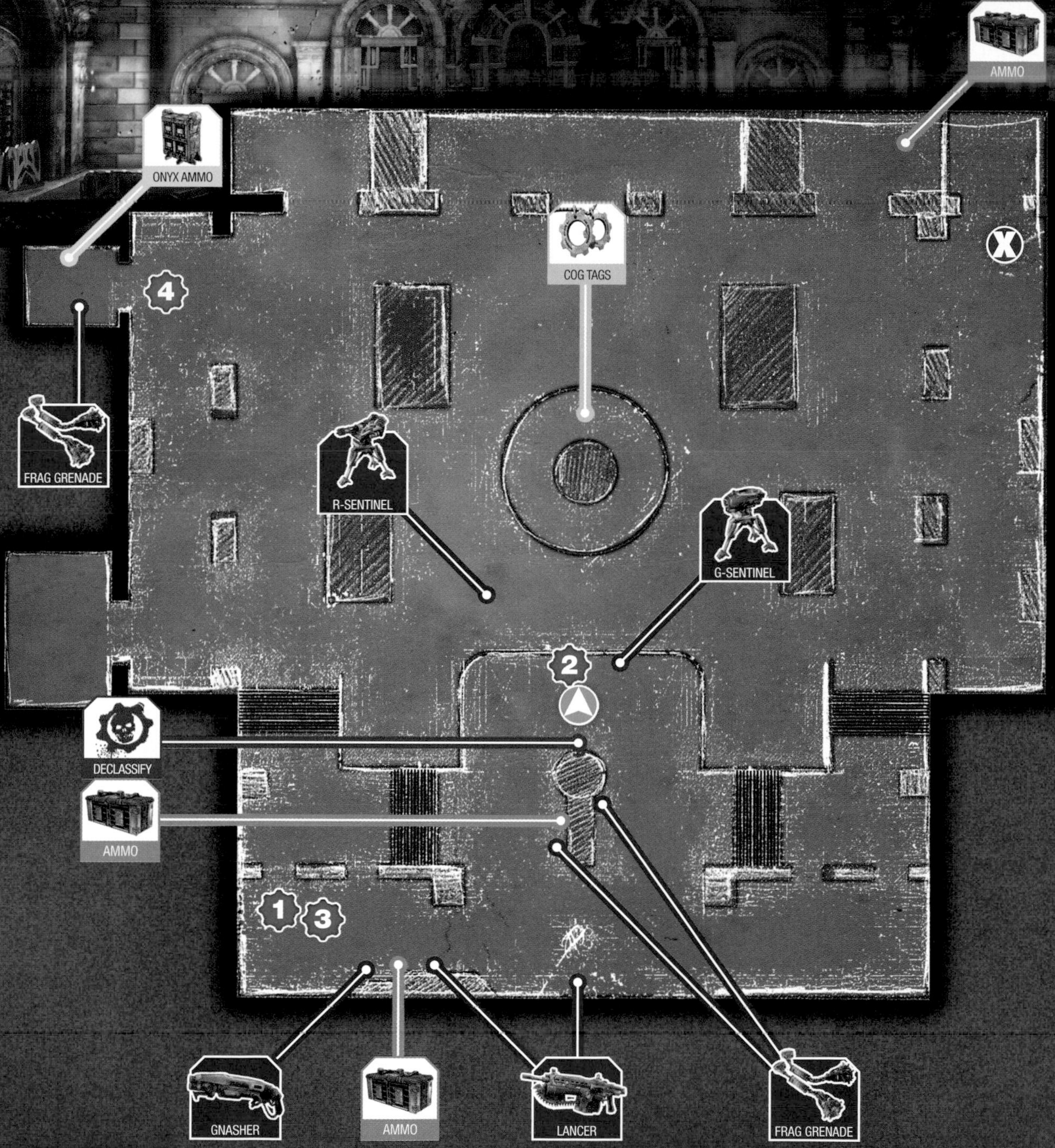

AMMO

ONYX AMMO

④

COG TAGS

ⓧ

FRAG GRENADE

R-SENTINEL

G-SENTINEL

❷

DECLASSIFY

AMMO

① ③

⊕

GNASHER

AMMO

LANCER

FRAG GRENADE

MISSION OBJECTIVES

> Survive the attack.
> Get to the East Wing.

HOSTILES ENCOUNTERED

WRETCH	DRONE	THERON W/ CLEAVER	FLAME BOOMER	BOOMER	MAULER	NEMACYST*
3	3	8	9	11	15	-

☆ = Star Score
*Declassified Mission only.

"WE'RE THE FIRST LINE OF DEFENSE FOR THE ONYX GUARD. LET'S SHOW THEM WHAT REGULAR SOLDIERS CAN DO, KILO!"

RIBBONS AND SCORING

One of the primary challenges in this mission is simply staying on your feet. The Stars will come so long as you don't hurt your cause by getting downed too often. With the Nemacysts flying around, that's easier said than done. Use your Frags early on to get at least one Plug That Hole ribbon. Then focus on killing and gibbing as many enemies as possible while keeping your sentries loaded so they can help protect your upper vantage point. Use the intermission between the waves to scavenge a Boomshot (if possible) and make a point of trying to earn a Boombardier ribbon or two in the second wave. Finally, put your Lancer's chainsaw to use at the end of the battle, when it's only Drones and Wretches left, in an attempt to earn a Lumberjack ribbon or at least a couple of execution bonuses.

CLUSTERLUCK: Kill multiple enemies with one grenade.

PLUG THAT HOLE: Close an E-Hole with explosives.

BOOMBARDIER: Kill multiple enemies with a Boomshot blast.

LUMBERJACK: Chainsaw 3 enemiess in a row.

CLASSIFIED INTEL

Set up the Range Sentinel on the one side of the upper platform, near the hole closest to the wall. Then set up the Gnasher Sentinel in the corner at the base of the stairs on the other side to shoot enemies that walk past.

Stand at the front of the upper platform, where the Sentinels were, and ready a Frag Grenade to throw at the first of the E-Holes as soon as the battle begins.

Stick close to the Range Sentinel throughout the battle and trust the Gnasher Sentinel and the rest of Kilo Squad to defend the other side. It's vital to keep the Range Sentinel loaded.

Use the time in between waves to quickly look for a Boomshot. Then get to the Frag Grenades and Onyx Ammo Cache in the back left corner of the Great Hall. Hurry back to the upper platform and continue the fight!

DECLASSIFIED: THREE-STAR TACTICS

The Locust are mounting an attack set to begin in 1:30, but you needn't handle it alone. Not only will the rest of Kilo Squad be by your side, but the Onyx Guard have also left two Sentinels behind. Once placed, these auto-targeting devices swing into action and can rotate and fire in a 360-degree circle, provided they stay loaded with ammo.

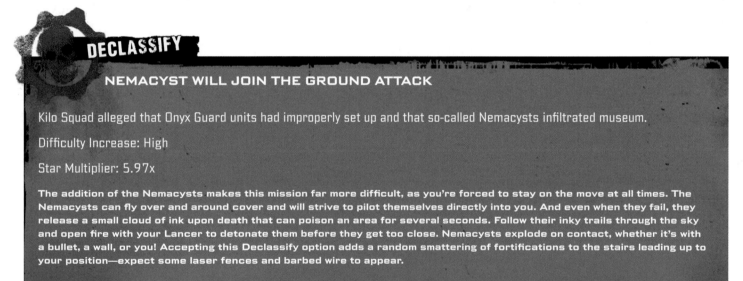

DECLASSIFY

NEMACYST WILL JOIN THE GROUND ATTACK

Kilo Squad alleged that Onyx Guard units had improperly set up and that so-called Nemacysts infiltrated museum.

Difficulty Increase: High

Star Multiplier: 5.97x

The addition of the Nemacysts makes this mission far more difficult, as you're forced to stay on the move at all times. The Nemacysts can fly over and around cover and will strive to pilot themselves directly into you. And even when they fail, they release a small cloud of ink upon death that can poison an area for several seconds. Follow their inky trails through the sky and open fire with your Lancer to detonate them before they get too close. Nemacysts explode on contact, whether it's with a bullet, a wall, or you! Accepting this Declassify option adds a random smattering of fortifications to the stairs leading up to your position—expect some laser fences and barbed wire to appear.

Place the Range Sentry to the left (facing into the Great Hall) on the upper walkway, near the gap in the wall. It can shoot anything that approaches the stairs from the left and is very well protected in this position. Place the Gnasher Sentry on the landing to the right, where fortifications are often less adequate. It can blast enemies from this side at close range. While the rest of Kilo Squad plants Frag Grenades throughout the area, gather the Frag Grenades from the crates up top, acquire ammo, and step to the front of the balcony.

The laser fence will automatically deactivate when a COG walks through, so don't worry about carrying the Gnasher Sentinel to the corner.

Two E-Holes open in the floor beyond the fountain. Carefully lob a Frag into each of them to claim two Plug That Hole ribbons and maybe a Clusterluck. Open fire on the Locust that make it out of the E-Holes, or that start to enter from the rooms on the side. Turn your attention skyward and back away from the front of the balcony while targeting any Nemacysts flying in through the windows.

Have a pair of Frag Grenades ready to close the E-Holes that open beyond the fountain.

The Range Sentinel does an excellent job of shooting Nemacysts out of the air, especially if you're close by it. This allows you to focus on any Drones, Theron Guards armed with Cleavers, or the inevitable Boomers carrying Boomshots or Scorchers. Hold the higher ground and blind-fire over cover for maximum protection from the Nemacysts while targeting the heavies. Continue to watch for Drones, but focus on the heavy units. Pay extra attention to what they drop when they die. Some Boomers will drop ammo but others may drop a Scorcher or Boomshot. If the coast is clear, switch to the Gnasher and grab the Boomshot or Scorcher as soon as the first wave ends.

Stick close to the Range Sentinel so you can reload it when the ammo icon appears. Both Sentinels need ammo but that heavy with a Scorcher takes precedent!

There is a 0:30 intermission between the two waves. Try to swap out your Gnasher for a power weapon. Then head to the far left room and find an Onyx Ammo Cache and a Frag Grenade. Be sure to pick the power weapon up first then the Onyx Ammo Cache to max out your ammo supplies! Both Sentinels will automatically reload during intermission. Consider planting a Frag or two along the columns near the sides of the room. Then return to the upper level and ready yourself for the second wave.

The Nemacysts will keep on coming throughout both waves, so don't take your eyes off the sky.

Expect to encounter several more heavies during the second wave and quite a few Drones. The wave often culminates with a surge of Drones and Wretches. If you're close to getting three Stars, but haven't filled that third Star yet, consider using the Lancer's chainsaw for a chance at earning the Lumberjack ribbon. Either way, resist the temptation to head down the stairs and engage the enemies at close range. It's just too dangerous. If you get downed, you'll be too far from the rest of your squad to be revived before losing much of your Star credit.

S. Paturo, PFC, Llima

K.I.A. from Locust grenade trap.

The COG Tag is inside the fountain in the center of the room, near where the E-Holes appear. Get it after defeating both waves of enemies. Though it can be collected prior to the initial attack, or between waves, that time would be better spent prepping your defenses.

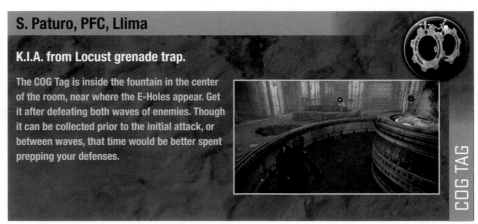

COG TAG

SECTION 5:
KASHKUR WING

FRAG GRENADE

AMMO

LANCER

SAWED-OFF

X

3

2

COG TAGS

T

ONYX AMMO

MISSION OBJECTIVES

Get to the East Wing.

Finish off the Locust attackers.

HOSTILES ENCOUNTERED

3	3	15
WRETCH	DRONE	MAULER

☆ = Star Score

LONGSHOT

1

BOOMSHIELD

BOLTOK

FRAG GRENADE

DECLASSIFY

GNASHER

"BLACK-4 SAID THEY WERE LOSING THE EAST WING. HE DIDN'T SAY THEY LOST EVERYTHING ON THE WAY THERE."

RIBBONS AND SCORING

The best way to assure a three-Star ranking on this mission is to make use of the Boltok Pistol lying in the foyer where you begin. Accept the Declassify option, kick open the door, and use the Boomshield and Boltok against the Drones and Maulers that attack. Aim for headshots whenever possible, but keep on using the Boltok to rack up multiple I'm Your Huckleberry and Hat Trick ribbons. There's a Longshot off to the far right that can also be used to gain the Hat Trick ribbon later in the fight when the last wave of enemies attacks. Use the Frag Grenades against softened Maulers that are near other enemies for a quick Clusterluck ribbon. The final group of Wretches that attacks can each be killed with a single Boltok shot and help to earn additional ribbons. You may also choose to swap the Boltok for the Sawed-Off Shotgun for use against the Wretches that attack last, as it can earn a Nothin' But Bits ribbon.

HAT TRICK: Score 3 headshots in a row without dying.

I'M YOUR HUCKLEBERRY: Kill 5 enemies in a row with any type of pistol without dying.

CLUSTERLUCK: Kill multiple enemies with one grenade.

CLASSIFIED INTEL

1 Grab the Boltok and the Boomshield and take up position behind the large column to the right. This will lure most of the enemies down the right-hand aisle and provide protection from the turret in the distance on the left.

2 Clear the enemies along the right side of the hall. Then advance to the Frag Grenades near the turret in the center. Plant Frags near either staircase. Then man the turret yourself, or, if a squadmate is using it, target the Wretches and Drones that come rushing across the room with your pistol or Lancer.

3 The final attack will originate from the locked doors nearest the turret. Keep clear of this area while finishing off the enemies coming from the south end, or else you could find yourself on the wrong end of a Mauler's flail!

DECLASSIFIED: THREE-STAR TACTICS

The Boltok is your ticket to earning three Stars on this mission (and many more if you hold onto it). Grab it and the Frag Grenades as soon as you enter the Kashkur Wing. The Declassified condition for this mission is one of the easier ones to overcome in Baird's testimony, so make sure to accept it right away.

DECLASSIFY

LANCER WIELDING CYCLOPS DRONES IN THE AREA

Kilo Squad observed Locust equipped with new COG Mk 2 Lancer Assault Rifle.

Difficulty Increase: Low

Star Multiplier: 2.20x

This effectively replaces the Drones' Hammerburst rifles with Lancers, making them able to fire more rounds, faster, with fewer reloads. In short, it means there's going to be more bullets flying your way. It also makes being chainsawed a distinct possibility. Nevertheless, this is a relatively mild difficulty increase and shouldn't impact your tactics.

Equip the Boltok, grab the Frag Grenades, and kick the door open to initiate the battle. Sprint straight into cover and grab the Boomshield lying near the display to avoid the turret fire coming from the distance. The majority of the Drones and Maulers that attack are going to first come from the far end of the hall, but will likely approach on the right. Put the Boltok to use and start firing off as many headshots as possible for a Hat Trick ribbon.

Use the Boomshield and the pillars for cover and aim for as many headshots as possible with the Boltok.

Watch for the slower Maulers to finally make their way to your position. Plant the Boomshield in the ground for cover—this gives you the freedom to quickly lob a grenade or switch weapons without having to toss the Boomshield away. You won't want to lose it in the chaos. Toss a grenade at any softened Maulers, particularly if they're bunched together with a Drone or two. Then go back to using the Boltok for headshots.

Planting the Boomshield in the ground allows you to lob Frag Grenades and switch weapons without dropping your shield.

Hold this position until there's a lull in the battle. Then cut across to the right to get the Onyx Ammo Cache and, if you prefer, the Longshot. Fight up the right side of the hall, towards the turrets at the far end. Keep on using the Boltok and locate the Frag Grenades on the upper landing near the turret.

The final large wave of enemies comes from the locked door adjacent the one first entered. Additional Drones emerge from the floor, while a batch of Wretches attacks on foot. The Boltok can kill Wretches with a single shot, provided it's loaded. Take out as many as possible with the Boltok, and then consider switching to the Sawed-Off Shotgun if you grabbed it.

The Onyx Ammo Cache will replenish your Boltok and keep you pumping Wretches full of six-shooter lead till the last one drops.

The final enemy—a Mauler no less—bursts through the door nearest the turret on the upper platform. It's easy to have this guy appear right alongside you while fending off what you think is the final wave of Drones and Wretches. Make a point of staying clear of all locked doors, as they are little more than monster closets just waiting to be burst open.

A. Guinot, MSgt, Jacinto

K.I.A. from Corpser attack, was impaled.

This COG Tag is on the floor, directly beneath the turret opposite the doors first entered through. The Crimson Omen is visible on the wall to the right of the COG Tag.

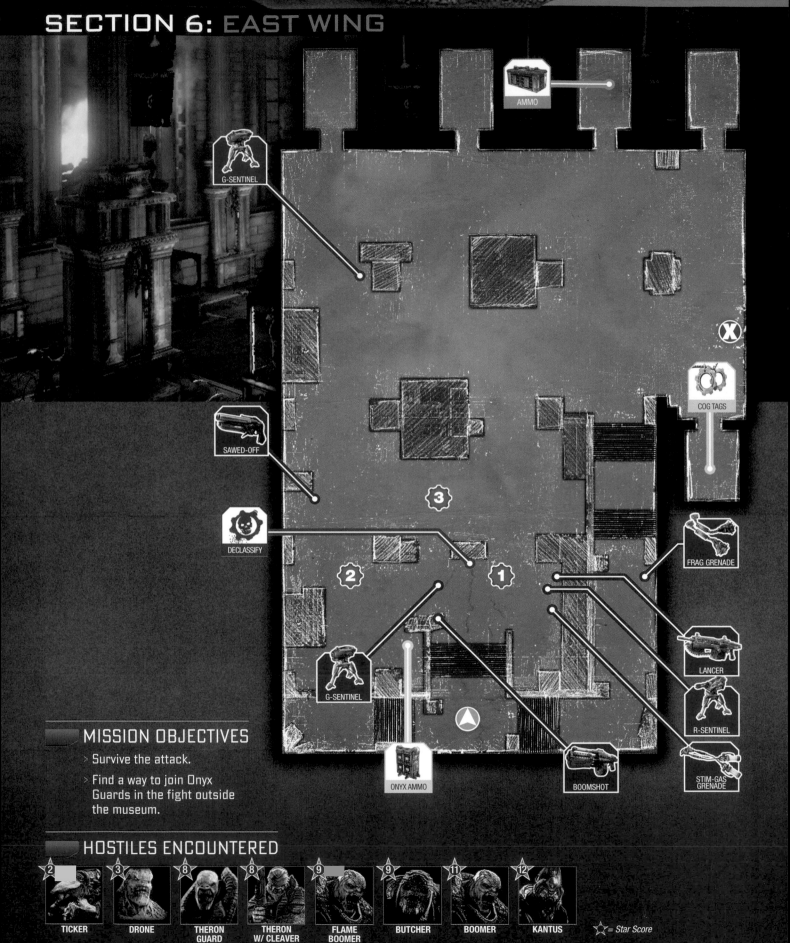

SECTION 6: EAST WING

AMMO

G-SENTINEL

SAWED-OFF

DECLASSIFY

3

2

1

G-SENTINEL

COG TAGS

FRAG GRENADE

LANCER

R-SENTINEL

STIM-GAS GRENADE

BOOMSHOT

ONYX AMMO

MISSION OBJECTIVES

> Survive the attack.

> Find a way to join Onyx Guards in the fight outside the museum.

HOSTILES ENCOUNTERED

2	3	8	8	9	9	11	12	
TICKER	DRONE	THERON GUARD	THERON W/ CLEAVER	FLAME BOOMER	BUTCHER	BOOMER	KANTUS	☆ = Star Score

"WE WERE ALMOST TO THE EAST WING. I WANTED TO BELIEVE WE WERE IN TIME TO SAVE BLACK-4. I WANTED VERY MUCH TO BELIEVE THAT."

RIBBONS AND SCORING

Earning three Stars is going to require the Declassified option, plenty of Clusterluck ribbons, not getting downed more than ever so briefly, and use of the Sawed-Off to get a Nothin' But Bits or Oakley ribbon. The Sawed-Off Shotgun is not needed to get the Oakley ribbon, but it makes it a lot easier. The main thing is just planting Frags around the rooms at the north end of the hall, where the Locust originate, to get Clusterluck ribbons as they spawn. Then you can focus on reloading the Sentinels and staying upright. Another tactic is to use the Lancer's chainsaw to get execution bonuses and possibly a Lumberjack ribbon.

CLUSTERLUCK: Kill multiple enemies with one grenade.

NOTHIN' BUT BITS: Kill multiple enemies with a single Sawed-Off Shotgun blast.

OAKLEY: Kick a Ticker and shoot it out of the air.

LUMBERJACK: Chainsaw 3 enemies in a row.

CLASSIFIED INTEL

1

Even without the need to protect the armor, it's a good idea to set up the three Sentinels close to the stairs where the Mulcher is located. Place the Gnasher Sentinels in front of the stairs, facing left and right on a slight angle. Place the Range Sentinel to the left. This allows it to intercept any enemies coming down the left-hand aisle.

2

Stick close to the Sentinels near the fortifications and focus your firepower on the enemies nearest them. The longer you can keep both Gnasher Sentinels and the fortifications in place, the easier things will be during the second wave.

3

Scavenge for dropped Ink Grenades or Torque Bows between waves and don't pick up the Onyx Ammo Cache until after you've secured a power weapon (or while you're holding the Boomshot or Sawed-Off Shotgun). The second wave features numerous Theron Guards, Butchers, and Tickers. Don't underestimate the threat posed by the little guys. Tickers tend to swarm the area and it only takes one to detonate nearby while you're DBNO to kill you. Drop a Stim-Gas Grenade whenever a large number of Tickers is nearby.

DECLASSIFY

STOP LOCUST FROM DESTROYING NASSAR EMBRY'S ARMOR

> Lt. Baird claimed Kilo Squad defended Nassar Embry's armor with no additional Onyx support.

> Difficulty Increase: Low

> Star Multiplier: 2.07x

This Declassify option adds a valuable asset to protect. Nassar Embry's Armor is inside a display case near the glowing Crimson Omen. Provided all three Sentinels are placed to maximize the armor's protection and plenty of Frags are forward enough to intercept the Tickers destined for your barbed wire fortifications, defending it shouldn't prove that difficult. Though you will need to stay closer to the armor and intercept any enemies that reach it. In some ways, adding this challenge makes the battle easier on the whole (though you do fail the mission if the armor is destroyed) since it distracts the enemies and provides increased fortifications. It's arguably easier to stay alive when this option is accepted, but you may still fail the mission.

Accept the Declassify option on the base of the statue and immediately begin setting up the Sentinels to protect the armor. Place the Gnasher Sentinel directly in front of the armor, facing slightly to the right. Grab the Range Sentinel and carry it to the left, towards the Sawed-Off Shotgun pickup, and position it facing north, beyond the fortifications. Sprint to the far left corner of the room to find a second Gnasher Sentinel and position it next to the other one, on an angle to protect the other side. It's highly unlikely that Locust will make their way up and around the walkway on the right side of the room, so don't worry about them attacking the armor from the south.

Place the Range Sentinel near the bodies on the left side. Then place the two Gnasher Sentinels directly in front of the armor.

Grab the extra Frag Grenades located on the walkway to the right of the armor. Plant them on pillars and sandbags in front of the Sentinels. They will serve to intercept the Tickers that race across the East Wing to take down your fortifications. It might seem like a waste to plant Frag Grenades that you know will be triggered by Tickers, but it's important to protect the fortifications for as long as possible.

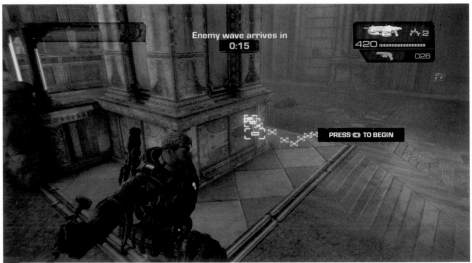

Plant Frag Grenades on the sides of the columns, near the main corridors where the Locust will be walking.

Target the Tickers and Kantuses first. Then turn your attention to whatever the nearest threat is. Use the Boomshot from behind the crates in front of the armor to cut down the enemies as they pour forth from the doors at the far end of the room. It's also worth using the Lancer to chainsaw Drones for the execution and Lumberjack bonuses. Be sure to pick up the Sawed-Off Shotgun as well, especially if playing Declassified. It helps against enemies bunched up near the display case and can earn you the Nothin' But Bits ribbon.

There's a thirty second break between waves. Use this time to scrounge for a Torque Bow or other power weapon. Otherwise stick with the Lancer and Sawed-Off Shotgun. The Sawed-Off Shotgun is particularly useful against the Butchers that march forward with Cleavers. Quickly plant your Frag Grenades again, and then look for an Ink Grenade one of the Kantuses may have dropped. Do this before picking up the Onyx Ammo Cache (located near the entrance to the room) in order to max out your ammo and grenades.

Stick close to the fortifications and the Gnasher Sentinels, not only for your own safety but also to keep them reloaded.

The second wave is quite intense and typically features numerous Theron Guards armed with Cleavers and Torque Bows. Keep close to the Gnasher Sentinels to ensure the protection of the armor during the initial assault. As long as the Sentinels are kept loaded, the armor should survive the assault. Advance out in front of the armor to distract any remaining enemies if the armor's damage indicator drops into the orange or red.

W. Carmine, SPC, East Timgad

K.I.A. by Locust OneShot.

The COG Tag is in the small room to the right of the exit to the archives. The Crimson Omen is on the column near the door. Though it can be collected during setup before or between waves, it's best to collect this item before exiting the East Wing once the fighting is done.

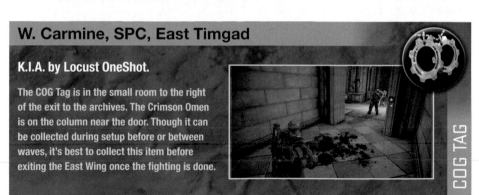

COG TAG

SECTION 7: ARCHIVES

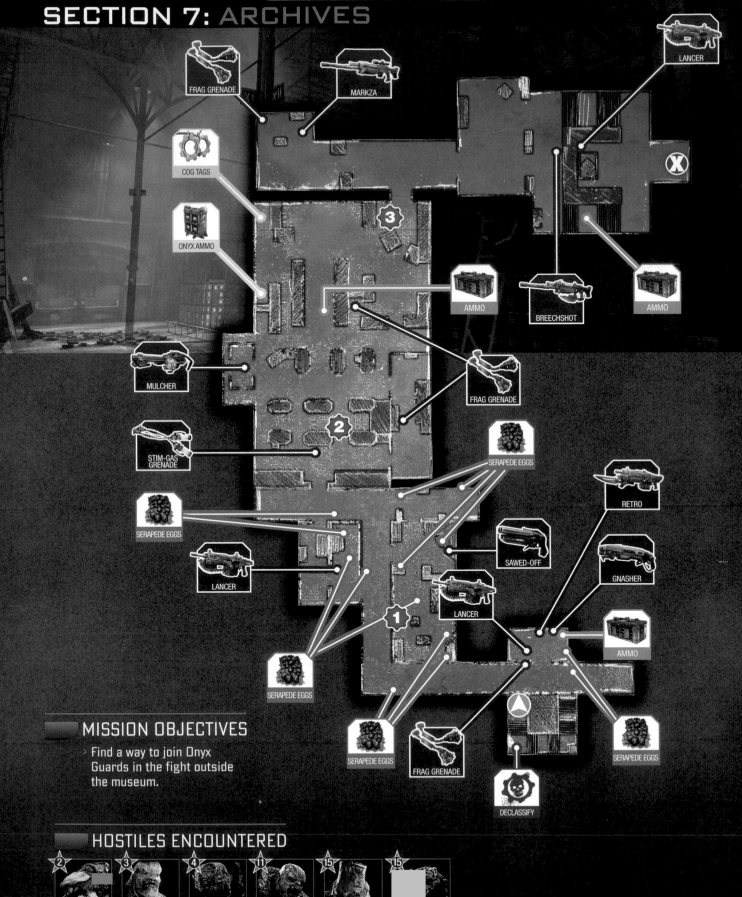

FRAG GRENADE

MARKZA

LANCER

COG TAGS

ONYX AMMO

X

3

AMMO

BREECHSHOT

AMMO

MULCHER

FRAG GRENADE

STIM-GAS GRENADE

2

SERAPEDE EGGS

RETRO

SERAPEDE EGGS

SAWED-OFF

GNASHER

LANCER

LANCER

AMMO

1

SERAPEDE EGGS

SERAPEDE EGGS

SERAPEDE EGGS

FRAG GRENADE

DECLASSIFY

MISSION OBJECTIVES

> Find a way to join Onyx Guards in the fight outside the museum.

HOSTILES ENCOUNTERED

2	3	4	11	15	15	
TICKER	DRONE	LAMBENT WRETCH	FLAME BOOMER	GRINDER	SERAPEDE	☆ = Star Score

"WHILE THE QUICKEST WAY OUT WAS THROUGH THE ARCHIVES, I LEARNED A LESSON: IF YOU'RE TRYING TO AVOID LOCUST, DON'T GO DOWNSTAIRS."

RIBBONS AND SCORING

The key to getting three Stars in this mission is to accept the Declassify option, but not follow through with complete extermination of the egg clutches in the first room. Leave at least one of the 10 clutches intact. This provides more Serapedes to fight in the second room, thus yielding plenty of extra points to earn in the larger warehouse area. Should you get the Tickers, be sure to kick as many of them as possible for the And the Kick is Up ribbon. Then hip-fire the Gnasher or Lancer at them as soon as you kick them to get multiple Oakley ribbons as well. Lastly, aside from staying alive, have a Frag Grenade ready to Plug That Hole when the E-Hole opens. Alternatively, if you target the fuel tanks on the back of the Flame Boomers as soon as they emerge, you can detonate their explosive backpacks and plug the hole that way.

OAKLEY: Kick a Ticker and shoot it in the air.

AND THE KICK IS UP: Kick 5 small enemies.

PLUG THAT HOLE: Close an E-Hole with explosives.

CLUSTERLUCK: Kill multiple enemies with one grenade.

CLASSIFIED INTEL

1 Let the Serapede chase after the other members of Kilo Squad while using the Retro Lancer to gun it down from the rear. Serapedes are only vulnerable to attacks from their last segment.

2 Try to fight the two Serapedes that attack in the warehouse near the door you enter through. It makes it harder for the Lambent Wretches or Tickers to surround you while you fight the larger beasts.

3 Toss a Frag Grenade to close the E-Hole that opens. Then quickly ready another one to take out the Flame Boomers that come through the hole in the wall. Lob the Frag and then turn and fire on the barrels on the walkway to kill the Grinder above.

DECLASSIFIED: THREE-STAR TACTICS

Descend the stairs to reach the dark, dusty maintenance section of the Archives room and accept the Declassify option. This requires seeking out and destroying the Locust eggs scattered throughout the maintenance area. There are 10 total clutches of eggs, located in any of 14 possible locations. The accompanying map shows all of the possible locations of the eggs, and an in-game counter helps you keep track of how many you've destroyed.

DECLASSIFY

SERAPEDE EGGS LEFT INTACT WILL HATCH, SPAWNING MORE SERAPEDES TO FIGHT

> Kilo Squad claimed to have found and destroyed Locust eggs of unknown origin.

> Difficulty Increase: Moderate

> Star Multiplier: 2.16x

Serapedes attack in the main warehouse regardless, but you only have to fight two or three if you destroy all of the eggs. If you choose to Declassify this information, then you have to fight additional Serapedes if you don't find and destroy all 10 clutches of eggs. The eggs are scattered across 14 possible locations. The members of Kilo Squad alert you if there are any remaining eggs before you leave the first section and continue to the warehouse.

One of the clutches of eggs is always located at the base of the stairs, directly in front of you as you finish the descent. Open fire with the Lancer to destroy it. Then enter the room on the right to gather up some Frag Grenades and ammo. Another batch of eggs may be in this room as well.

Move down the hall to the second doorway and head inside. There are multiple egg locations in this room, but that's not all! The first of two Serapedes attacks. Get behind it and shoot the glowing end of its tail—it is bulletproof elsewhere on its body. This first Serapede tends to target the other members of Kilo Squad, thus giving you the opportunity to stay behind it and attack it from the rear. Serapedes typically focus their attention on whoever has shot and ruptured three of their body segments. Don't be surprised if this one turns towards you once you start shortening its length.

The locations of the eggs rotate between 14 possible locations, so consult the map.

Multiple egg clutches are located throughout this area. Look in the hole on the floor, on the ceilings, and all around the map. A second Serapede attacks from the far end of this area. This one will likely come straight for you. Lead it away from your squad so they can get a clean shot at its tail. Try to loop around to get a clean shot on the glowing bits and don't get downed! Though it is possible to shoot the glowing end of its body while backing away from its pinchers, this isn't advised in tight spaces.

Target the glowing end of the Serapede as it chases after your squadmates.

For the best chance at earning three Stars, consider leaving one of the clutches of eggs intact. Head through the door to the warehouse, despite Kilo's warnings of other eggs remaining. Note the location of the Stim-Gas Grenades near the corpse and get ready for a fight. Multiple Serapedes weave through the stacks along with Tickers or Lambent Wretches. It's possible to kick the Tickers and snag a number of ribbons, making it easier to three-Star this level, provided they don't detonate alongside you. There aren't many ribbons to earn against the Lambent Wretches unless you manage to get a Clusterluck ribbon. Use Frag Grenades against the Lambent Wretches and focus on not getting downed.

Stay on the move and keep near your squad so you can open fire on the tail of any Serapedes that are pursuing them. Watch for the lesser enemies hopping around and lob grenades at any groups of foes. There are additional Frag Grenades off to the right and also to the north, in the center of the Archives room.

It's best to shoot from the hip when dealing with this many Serapedes, in order to maintain your field of vision.

R. Wood, 2LT, Vonner Bay

K.I.A. by Kantus when she attempted to take it hand-to-hand.

Kill off the Serapedes and other enemies in the warehouse, but don't head to the far right corner just yet! First follow the left wall past the Mulcher to the Crimson Omen. The COG Tag is near the corpse to the right of the Crimson Omen and an Onyx Ammo Cache is to the left.

COG TAG

Advance to the far right corner and listen for a rumbling. Ready a Frag Grenade if you have it and aim it at the floor, below the tanks. An E-Hole appears along with multiple Flame Boomers. A Grinder also attacks from the catwalk above. Quickly target the red explosive barrels on the walkway to the left of the Grinder. Then take cover and open fire on the backpacks of fuel the Flame Boomers are wearing. You have to face multiple heavy Locust here, including those who attack from the hallway beyond the hole in the wall. Hold your ground and gun them down as they stomp towards your position.

Have a Frag Grenade ready for as soon as the E-Hole opens in the right corner of the warehouse.

Exit through the hole in the wall and collect the Frag Grenades down the hall to the left. There's a Markza in the corner, but you're best leaving it behind. Instead, collect the Breechshot down the hall to the right. The un-scoped Breechshot will serve you well in Vaults.

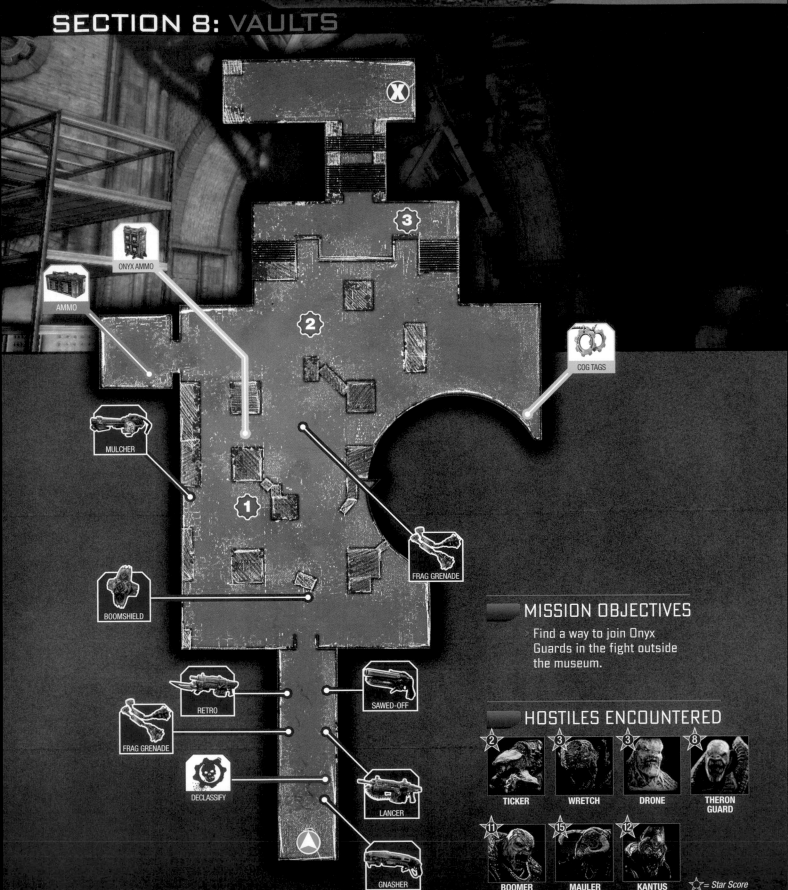

X

3

ONYX AMMO

AMMO

2

COG TAGS

MULCHER

1

FRAG GRENADE

BOOMSHIELD

MISSION OBJECTIVES

> Find a way to join Onyx Guards in the fight outside the museum.

RETRO

SAWED-OFF

FRAG GRENADE

DECLASSIFY

LANCER

HOSTILES ENCOUNTERED

2	3	3	8
TICKER	**WRETCH**	**DRONE**	**THERON GUARD**

11	15	12	
BOOMER	**MAULER**	**KANTUS**	☆ = Star Score

GNASHER

THREE-STAR TACTICS

This can be a tough mission to earn three Stars largely due to the difficulty in staying upright. The need to get close enough to earn Lumberjack ribbons makes you susceptible to Cleaver attacks that can all but down you in a single swing. Fortunately, it's possible to earn Lumberjack ribbons against Wretches. Try to down the occasional Theron so you can use it as a meatshield and then perform a "bag & tag" for a Special Delivery ribbon. Simply press Up on the D-pad while holding an enemy as a meatshield to plant a grenade in its back and kick it towards other enemies. Earning a Clusterluck or Plug That Hole ribbon isn't necessary to earning three Stars, but it certainly helps offset any lost Stars should you be downed. Take your time in the dust and let the targeting reticle help pinpoint the enemies for you—don't fire unless it turns red!

LUMBERJACK: **Chainsaw 3 enemies in a row.**

PLUG THAT HOLE: **Close an E-Hole with explosives.**

"OUR COMMS WERE SPUTTERING BACK TO LIFE. WHATEVER WAS BLOCKING THE SIGNAL MUST HAVE MOVED ON."

CLUSTERLUCK: **Kill multiple enemies with one grenade.**

SPECIAL DELIVERY: **Kill an opponent with a bag & tag.**

CLASSIFIED INTEL

Grab the Boomshield at the start of the battle and use it with the Breechshot from the previous mission if you have it. Another option is to sprint for the Mulcher and set it on top of the crates to open fire on the enemies as they round the corner from the right.

Advance to the Frag Grenades in the center of the room, pick up any dropped Boomshots or Torque Bows, and take cover behind the toppled column. Ready a Frag Grenade for the E-Hole that opens far to the right, just past the collapsed portion of the floor. Don't advance beyond these columns until the majority of the enemies have been slain.

DECLASSIFIED: THREE-STAR TACTICS

The entrance to the Vaults contains a wealth of ammo for the Lancer and Gnasher, as well as some Frag Grenades, a Sawed-Off Shotgun, and a Retro Lancer. If you brought the Scorcher or Breechshot from the previous mission, you'll want to replace at least one of them with the Lancer so you can earn Lumberjack ribbons. Both the Scorcher and Breecher can be used effectively in the dust, as they excel at close and medium range targets. Enemies aren't visible across the map in the dust so having a Markza won't be of help unless you plan to decline the Declassify option.

Several Locust will likely be hiding beyond the doorway at the top of the stairs, waiting for you to ascend the stairs before they attack. Don't let your guard down once the floor is clear. Keep your guns loaded and ready to fire until the chime signals the mission is over.

HEAVY DUST WILL REDUCE VISIBILITY

Kilo Squad alleged dust in Archives reduced its combat efficacy.

Difficulty Increase: Moderate

Star Multiplier: 1.01x

At first glance it would seem that accepting the reduced visibility option wouldn't change the battle much, but it does. Rather than facing enemies with ranged weaponry, you're far more likely to encounter Cleaver-wielding Therons and several Maulers. You're not likely to see any Boomers or Torque Bow-wielding Therons with the dust, nor any Tickers. Instead, you face plenty of Wretches. This may seem like it makes things easier, but Wretches and Therons are quite fast and they can swarm you in seconds, especially under the cover of the dust. Furthermore, the intense dust makes targeting enemies very difficult.

The first wave of attackers consists of Wretches and Cleaver-wielding Therons. Have your Lancer's chainsaw ready and hang back near the first barrier so you can force the Locust to funnel towards you without being surrounded. Go for a Lumberjack ribbon and saw through several of them. Toss a lone grenade if you get a chance to kill two or more at once, but don't plant any Frags early on, as they will likely be triggered by a passing Wretch.

Ready the chainsaw. The Therons will be coming fast!

Put the chainsaw and your shotgun to use against the first wave. Then move further into the dust-choked room. There's a Mulcher on the left, a Frag Grenade pickup in the center, and an Onyx Ammo Cache to the left of the grenades. Numerous Maulers and Therons start to attack. Some launch from the floor, while others emerge from E-Holes. Listen for the sounds of opening E-Holes and lob grenades into the dust around the corner to the right to close them.

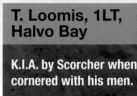

Use the Mulcher to cut down the Locust that attack near the Frag Grenades before stepping out into the open to pick them up.

Fall back to the area just beyond the Frag Grenade pickup and monitor your grenade tally. Pick up the ones in the center if you have two grenades (to bring your total to four), but opt for the Onyx Ammo Cache if you still have three Frag Grenades in order to not waste one.

Things are going to get crazy, but resist the urge to advance too far. The Therons and Maulers can drop you quite easily if they connect, and they attack in tight packs. Aim for long-distance grenade tags to earn a Clusterluck ribbon and switch to a Gnasher. Keep your eyes peeled for any downed Therons and try to pick one up for use a meatshield. This will help protect from Cleaver attacks and, if you have a Frag Grenade, give you a chance to earn a Special Delivery ribbon.

The final moments of this battle are intense. Switch to the Gnasher and start firing as fast as possible. Aim a little high on the Theron Guards in an effort to get headshot bonuses. Fight to the stairs and follow your squad up the steps to the doorway. One final group of Wretches and Therons will attack from the hallway so don't let your guard down until you hear the familiar chime and instructions from Cole about where to go next.

T. Loomis, 1LT, Halvo Bay

K.I.A. by Scorcher when cornered with his men.

The COG Tag is on the far right corner of the main level of the Vaults. There is a Crimson Omen on the right wall, in the opposite corner from where you enter. You can wait to get the COG Tag until after the area is clear of Locust. Head up the stairs to end the dust storm effect, and then turn back to the Vault and search for it at that point once the dust has settled.

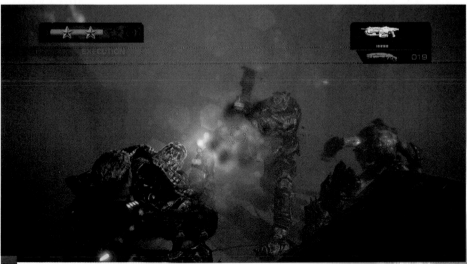

Kilo Squad can use two-handed weapons even when manipulating a meatshield or Boomshield.

COG TAG

HALVO BAY MILITARY ACADEMY

SOFIA'S TESTIMONY
SECTION 1: ENFIELD BRIDGE

"WE FOLLOWED THE MAIN SEWER LINE FROM THE MUSEUM TO THE ACADEMY. IT WAS THE ONLY WAY TO GET THERE ALIVE. IF I WAS GONNA DIE, I'D RATHER DO IT INSIDE THE ACADEMY."

SOFIA HENDRICK, ONYX GUARD CADET

Sofia enlisted in the COG only hours after E-Day began. This surprised many, as she had previously established herself as a shrewd critic of the COG while covering the Pendulum Wars for *The New Ephyran*.

Sofia didn't jump right in as a Private, however. Her intellect and journalistic curiosity made her a prime candidate for the prestigious Onyx Guard Academy in Halvo Bay. She was excelling in her studies until the Locust attacked the region, cutting short her officer training, and thrusting her into direct combat as a member of Kilo Squad. Sofia is an ardent follower of the rules and serves as the ethical compass for Kilo Squad.

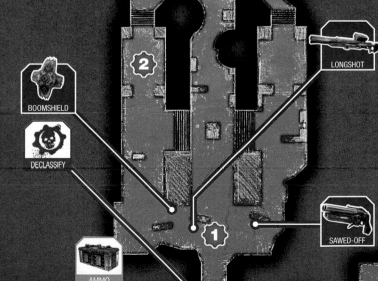

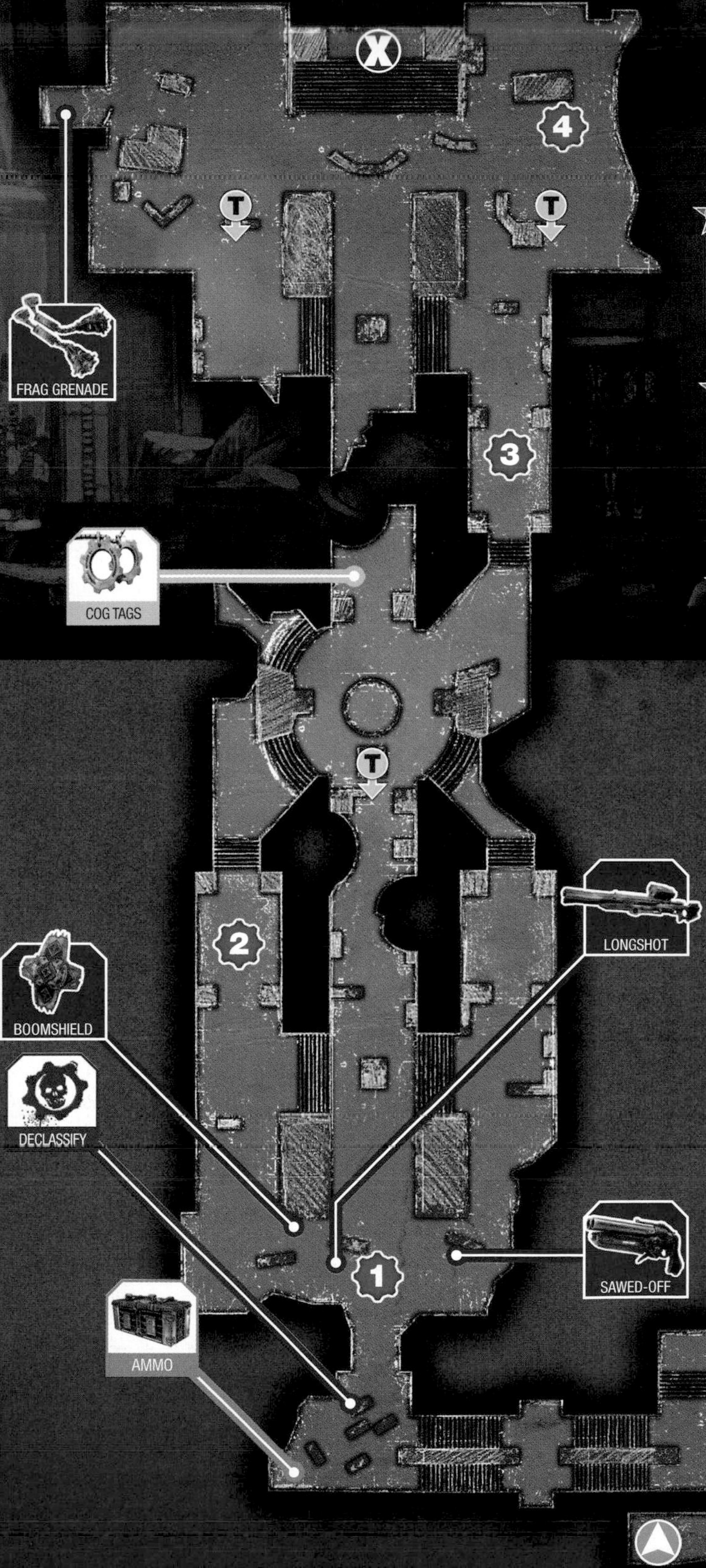

MISSION OBJECTIVES

> Reach Enfield Bridge.

> Get to the Academy Gate.

HOSTILES ENCOUNTERED

WRETCH ③	**DRONE** ③ ★	**DRONE (GRAPPLER)** ③ ★	**SNIPER** 6
THERON (REAVER DRIVER) 7	**THERON GUARD** 8	**FLAME BOOMER** 11	**REAVER** 25 ★

★ = Star Score

RIBBONS AND SCORING

Provided you don't get downed and can make the most of your Longshot and Frag Grenades, this is arguably one of the few missions in which it's possible to get three Stars without accepting the Declassify option (though doing so is very hard). The Declassify option makes it impossible to use the Longshot, so rule out getting any Hat Trick ribbons. Instead, conserve ammo by using Frag Grenades to earn a Clusterluck ribbon and put the Lancer's chainsaw to use. Spot every enemy and immediately turn your guns towards a different foe, leaving the Spotted target to be killed by your squadmates. Do this enough times and you earn the Military Intelligence ribbon, if not two of them. Lastly, utilize the available cover and strive to avoid the Reaver's rockets with all of your evasive skill. You'll be hard-pressed to get three Stars if you get downed for long.

LUMBERJACK: Chainsaw 3 enemies in a row.

CLUSTERLUCK: Kill multiple enemies with one grenade.

MILITARY INTELLIGENCE: Spot 5 enemies ending in kills.

FRAG GRENADE

COG TAGS

BOOMSHIELD

DECLASSIFY

LONGSHOT

SAWED-OFF

AMMO

CLASSIFIED INTEL

1

Descend the stairs to the bridge and immediately take cover near the Longshot. Begin sniping the Drones and Snipers in the distance, near the turret in the center of the bridge. Try to snipe through the blast shield on the turret by aiming for the slit in the shield, just above the turret's barrel.

2

Advance up the left side of the bridge to the covered portico and watch for the first of two Reavers. Use the available cover to fire on the soft underbelly of the Reaver. A Reaver will either land right behind you or on the center of the bridge, near the turret, giving you a clean shot at it from this position.

3

Cross the center of the bridge, past the turret to the right side, and advance to the next covered area. Ignore any Reaver sightings for now and focus on taking out the Locust ahead. Snipe them if you can and look for a Torque Bow or Scorcher to swap out your spent Longshot. Listen for the clanging sound of a Locust grappling onto the bridge and immediately shoot the hooks.

4

Clear out the enemies near the right-hand turret and advance to the relative safety of the truck beyond the turret (only use the turret if no Reavers remain). Use this position to pick off any remaining Locust, or to simply avoid any remaining Reaver's rockets. Sprint across to the far left to snag the Frag Grenades before leaving the area.

DECLASSIFIED: THREE-STAR TACTICS

Kick open the door at end of the alley to spot the picturesque Enfield Bridge. Descend the stairs on the left to the ammo crate and glowing Crimson Omen. Don't bother picking up ammo if you're going to accept the Declassify option, as it's going to be taken from you anyway.

DECLASSIFY

REDUCED AMMO, NO LONGSHOTS, AND ADDITIONAL REAVERS TO FIGHT

Kilo Squad claimed to take Enfield Bridge, and defeat several Reavers, without additional support and despite lack of supplies.

Difficulty Increase: High

Star Multiplier: 1.35x

Accepting this Declassification makes this mission significantly more difficult. There are no longer any weapon pickups on the map and ammo supplies for your Lancer and Gnasher are slashed. Furthermore, the enemies you encounter won't drop weaponry, only small batches of ammo. You gain plenty of ammo from killing Drones and other Locust, but you have to deal with four Reavers instead of the normal two. Accepting this option leaves you with four Gnasher shells and 30 bullets for the Lancer, in addition to two Frag Grenades.

Run up the far right side of the bridge to the first turret and lob one of your two grenades at the feet of the Locust manning the stationary gun. They'll likely be focused on the rest of Kilo Squad and this flanking maneuver allows you to secure a foothold halfway across the bridge without so much as taking a single bullet. Watch out for any Theron Guards that are also in the area.

Toss a grenade at the Locust near the turret, but have your gun ready in case there are any Therons in the area too!

The rest of Kilo Squad will meet you near the turret, just in time to alert you to an incoming Reaver. Immediately fall back to the covered portico on the right side of the bridge, the one that you just ran through. Take cover and dodge any Reaver rockets until it lands on the bridge, usually near the turret. Lean out of cover and open fire. Spot the Reaver to focus your squad's fire on it.

Retreat back the way you came to get a clean, safe shot at the Reaver that lands near the turret.

Additional Reavers come in from the right and a second one lands where you just were. Try to use what little ammo you have left to take it down. If you're out of Lancer ammo, try to get under it and use the Gnasher at close range on its pink soft underbelly. You may get downed doing this so make sure your squad is close by and able to revive you. Dodge-roll often to avoid incoming Reaver rockets as you take the second Reaver on.

Many more Locust swarm the bridge after the second Reaver is dead. Hold the center and use the Gnasher to blast them apart and gather up ammo from their drops. Advance along the right side of the bridge and Spot the Locust near the turret straight ahead. Stay in the second covered section until it's killed so you have cover. Many more Locust come rushing in from the gate ahead. Advance into cover near the turret and take out any Scorcher-wielding Boomers, Therons, or Drones. A third Reaver will attack here, so be ready. Stick close to your squad and continue to Spot enemies, utilizing the available cover while firing on the Reaver. Don't be tempted to use a turret; being locked into place against the Reavers is a recipe for disaster. Hold your ground near the truck to the right of the gate and brace for one final Reaver.

Use the columns for cover until all visible Locust near the turret are killed.

Sprint past the turret to the armored truck in the distance and take out the final two Reavers from behind cover.

W. Felhofer, PFC, Hanover

K.I.A. by Boomshot round while attempting to draw enemy fire.

The COG Tag is on the center of the bridge, just beyond the large circular railing near the first turret. The crumbling structure forces you to the right to continue towards the gate. But you can find the COG Tag by continuing along the middle and then turning to the left. It's best to either get this COG Tag while playing without the Declassify option or after you've killed the last of the Reavers.

COG TAG

RETRO

GNASHER

FRAG GRENADE

DECLASSIFY

MULCHER

BOOMSHOT

SCORCHER

1

2

LONGSHOT

ONESHOT

T

3

BREECHSHOT

AMMO

COG TAGS

4

SAWED-OFF

X

MISSION OBJECTIVES

> Locate Professor Elliott's laboratory.

HOSTILES ENCOUNTERED

2	**3**	**3**	**8**
TICKER	WRETCH	DRONE	THERON GUARD
8	**11**	**15**	**15**
RAGER	BOOMER	MAULER	GRINDER

 = Star Score

"MY FELLOW CADETS WERE THE SMARTEST, THE TOUGHEST, THE BEST THE COG HAD TO OFFER. THE NEXT GENERATION OF OFFICERS. KARN MOWED THEM DOWN LIKE DAISIES."

RIBBONS AND SCORING

It's not enough to be quick; you're going to have to be accurate as well. Accept the Declassified option if the Boomshot is present. Otherwise, restart the mission via the Pause Menu. Sprint straight for the Longshot/OneShot pickup and look for opportunities to either earn a Boombardier or Shish-Kashot ribbon. If present, take the Longshot back down the stairs and carefully line up shots for a Hat Trick ribbon. Move fast through the upstairs of the Academy and save at least one Frag Grenade for the area near the loading dock. Lob it over the stacks of materials to get a Clusterluck ribbon before you fight to the back of the area where the mission ends. Speed and precision have to come together perfectly in order to slip in before the gas deploys.

CLUSTERLUCK: Kill multiple enemies with one grenade.

SHISH-KASHOT: Kill at least two enemies with a single OneShot round.

HAT TRICK: Score 3 headshots in a row without dying.

BOOMBARDIER: Kill multiple enemies with a Boomshot blast.

CLASSIFIED INTEL

1

Grab the Boomshot on your way out of the starting area and move to the Mulcher on the left as you enter the gardens. Put the Mulcher to use in cutting down the enemies from the left. Then loop around the perimeter of the gardens in a counter-clockwise direction to the OneShot/Longshot pickup.

2

Temporarily swap out your Lancer or Gnasher for the Longshot (or pick up the OneShot) and continue up the steps and into cover overlooking the center of the gardens. This provides a relatively safe vantage point from which to snipe or use your Boomshot, though you need to watch for Wretches and other small enemies.

3

Plant Frag Grenades on the terrace outside the door and stand back—a Rager is about to burst through, drop its Breechshot, and enter its enraged state. Kill it with your standard weaponry, then switch to the Boomshot, and lob a few rockets at the other Ragers inside the room. At least two are behind the table on the right and as many as two more are off to the left.

4

Pick up the Sawed-Off Shotgun on the way down the stairs and use it to finish off the Drones and Wretches in the storage yard out back. You may encounter some additional Ragers in this area too, so it's worth holding onto one or two Frag Grenades. Climb onto the loading dock to complete the mission.

DECLASSIFIED: THREE-STAR TACTICS

The initial starting area contains either a Scorcher or Boomshot on rotation. Swap out the Lancer in favor of the Boomshot if it's present; otherwise, stick with your Gnasher and Lancer and leave the Scorcher behind. Make sure to grab the Frag Grenades on the floor before exiting the room.

DECLASSIFY

FINISH BEFORE POISON GAS DEPLOYS

Cadet Hendrick alleged that Academy's proximal defense system was activated during Locust attack.

Difficulty Increase: High

Star Multiplier: 4.29x

Countdown to Poison Gas Deployment

CASUAL	NORMAL	HARDCORE	INSANE
5:20	4:00	3:30	5:15

This Declassified option adds a timed poison gas deployment, forcing Kilo Squad to kill all of the Locust forces and exit the area in a hurry. Consider restarting the mission if the Boomshot is not present at the start, as you need it to make quick work of the initial wave of heavies. Ignore the Mulcher and head straight for the OneShot/Longshot and set to sniping. Stick with the larger capacity Gnasher as you fight your way through the interior—aim high against the Ragers with the Gnasher and try to headshot them before they enrage. Lob a Frag Grenade or two into the rear of the loading dock area as soon as you descend the stairs to eliminate the bulk of the remaining Locust.

Step out into the gardens and take a brief moment to survey the area. Multiple heavy enemies—Maulers, Grinders, and Boomers—are marching across the gardens to your position. They are coming from the opposite side and also from the left. There are no weapon pickups to the left, so immediately sprint straight ahead to the planter near the stairs to find a rotating Longshot/OneShot pickup. If the OneShot is there, immediately grab it and set to taking out as many heavy enemies as possible. Listen for the sounds of your squad, the Boomer's shouts, and the clashes of the Mauler's flail. Hold your ground near this position and duck down while reloading. Look left and right to make sure no smaller, quicker enemies are coming up on your flank.

The OneShot can make quick work of the heavy Locust units.

If the Longshot is present, and you happen to have the Boomshot, kill as many as possible with the Boomshot from this position. Then swap out the empty Boomshot for the sniper rifle. Quickly move back down the stairs to the narrow edge of that same wall. This position provides a good clean shot at the Therons and other heavies near the door to the Academy.

Take the Longshot back down the stairs for an excellent sniping position with full-height cover.

Once ready to advance, switch to the Gnasher (or swap the spent Longshot for a dropped Boomshot) and move up the right side and cut through the small corner room to flank the Therons at the turret. Toss a Frag at the Theron or Drone manning the turret and hopefully earn a Clusterluck ribbon.

Once the squad regroups in front of the doors, a Rager bursts through and attacks. Reactionary gunfire from your squad sets it into its enraged mode in which it becomes much, much harder to kill. Aim for the head or toss a grenade at it. You can chainsaw the Rager from behind while it's raging, but it's best to stay far away from it on the harder difficulty modes. Ideally, you want to have killed this initial Rager and be inside the Academy with at least a minute left on the timer.

Stand back and let the Rager charge your squadmates while you ready a Frag from a safe distance.

There are three more Ragers inside the building: one is often just to the left of the door, and two are behind the tables on the right. Toss a grenade behind the tables (or fire the Boomshot), grab the Gnasher (or swap to the dropped Breechshot), and aim for their heads. It's important to not wound them, as they'll transform and be much harder to kill. Aim a little high, get in close, and blast away with the Gnasher for a headshot!

Numerous Tickers or Wretches run up the hall that leads to the final area where the door to the lab entrance is located. Kick the Tickers out of the way and use the Gnasher to detonate them, or use the Gnasher to blast through the Wretches. Get to the room at the bottom and quickly lob a Frag Grenade or two across the room, behind the various obstacles scattered about the area. There are several Drones and additional small enemies. You must kill them all before you can leave.

A. Sullivan, SSGT, Andius

K.I.A. by multiple Tickers in coordinated attack.

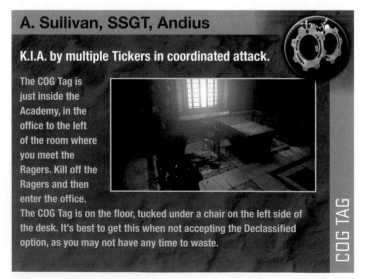

The COG Tag is just inside the Academy, in the office to the left of the room where you meet the Ragers. Kill off the Ragers and then enter the office.

The COG Tag is on the floor, tucked under a chair on the left side of the desk. It's best to get this when not accepting the Declassified option, as you may not have any time to waste.

COG TAG

Visibility will diminish as the gas begins to leak, so lob your remaining Frags and use the Gnasher to shoot anything that moves.

Climb onto the platform on the left and quickly tap Up on the D-pad to end the mission before the poison gas is emitted. You'll likely be cutting it pretty close, so don't delay!

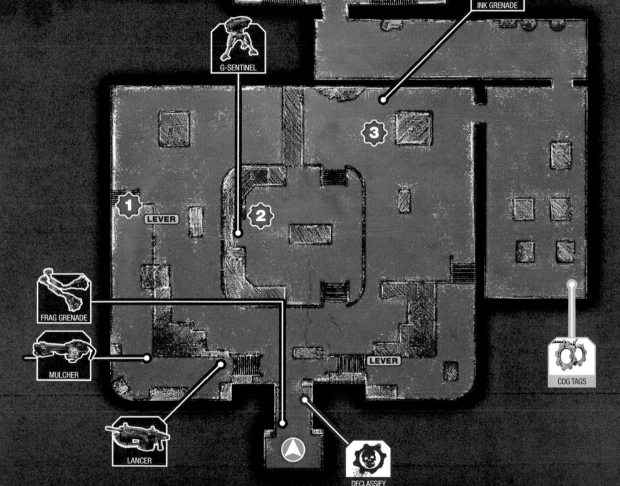

GNASHER

RETRO

BOOMSHOT

INK GRENADE

FRAG GRENADE

G-SENTINEL

FRAG GRENADE

MULCHER

LANCER

LEVER

LEVER

COG TAGS

DECLASSIFY

X

4

3

1

2

MISSION OBJECTIVES

> Find the beacon.

> Escape the Academy.

HOSTILES ENCOUNTERED

3	**9**	**11**	**12**	**15**
DRONE	BUTCHER	BOOMER	KANTUS	GRINDER

 = Star Score

"NO GETTING INTO THE LAB UNTIL YOU CLEARED SECURITY. UNLESS YOU'RE A GRUB. THEN YOU JUST TUNNEL IN."

RIBBONS AND SCORING

This can be a hard mission to earn three Stars. The reduced visibility and weapon availability can make it hard to earn many ribbons. Spot as many enemies as you can—particularly the heavies, Kantuses, and Drones on the catwalk—to maximize your chance of earning a Military Intelligence ribbon. Use your Frag Grenades to close the E-Hole in the back-left corner in the main room and the one that opens inside the server room on the right. These two Plug That Hole ribbons are all but vital to your cause. Lastly, try to get at least one or two headshots with the Gnasher and/or a chainsaw execution with the Lancer to fill more of your Stars than you would with a simple gib kill.

CLUSTERLUCK: Kill multiple enemies with one grenade.

PLUG THAT HOLE: Close an E-Hole with explosives.

MILITARY INTELLIGENCE: Spot 5 enemies ending in kills.

CLASSIFIED INTEL

1 Grab the Mulcher up the stairs to the left and carry it around the corner to the lever controlling the rear shock apparatus. Lob a Frag Grenade at the E-Hole that opens below. Then open fire with the Mulcher on the Locust in the rear of the lab and those coming across the catwalk as they rappel into the lab.

2 Wait for a lull in the action and carry the Gnasher Sentinel around towards the side of the central pit nearest the stairs. It can target the Locust that exit the adjacent room. Use the central column for cover against the Kantus.

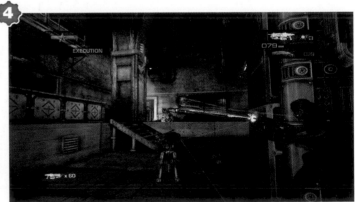

3 Ready a Frag Grenade and approach the door on the right to the server room. Lob the grenade at the E-Hole that opens inside the room, and then back away into cover. This lures the enemies out of the dangerously small room and into range of the Gnasher Sentinel.

4 Descend the stairs in the rear lab to find the beacon. Collect the Boomshot on the right, and then pull the lever to release the beacon.

DECLASSIFIED: THREE-STAR TACTICS

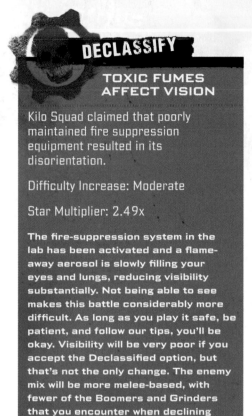

DECLASSIFY

TOXIC FUMES AFFECT VISION

Kilo Squad claimed that poorly maintained fire suppression equipment resulted in its disorientation.

Difficulty Increase: Moderate

Star Multiplier: 2.49x

The fire-suppression system in the lab has been activated and a flame-away aerosol is slowly filling your eyes and lungs, reducing visibility substantially. Not being able to see makes this battle considerably more difficult. As long as you play it safe, be patient, and follow our tips, you'll be okay. Visibility will be very poor if you accept the Declassified option, but that's not the only change. The enemy mix will be more melee-based, with fewer of the Boomers and Grinders that you encounter when declining this option.

Grab the Frag Grenades on the ground to the left and accept the Declassify option. Enter the main laboratory room and immediately open fire on the Grinders or Kantuses that are attacking at close range. Spot them both while hip-firing the Lancer as you move up the steps on the left. Collect the additional Lancer ammo and sprint past the Mulcher—don't pick it up—and round the corner to the far end of the walkway, near the lever controlling the shock device. Toss a Frag Grenade into the E-Hole that opens on the floor below.

Stay in cover to the left of the lever and use your Lancer and Frag Grenades to beat back the Locust that attack below.

Hold this position and use the Lancer to gun down any Drones that appear. Many will take cover behind the computer terminal in the rear of the lab. Pull the nearby lever to electrocute them (a second lever, to the right of the entrance, emits an electrical shock in the center of the lab).

Maintain this position as another wave of Drones runs across the catwalk and rappels into the main area. Gun them down and use a grenade if you want, but be sure to keep one or two Frag Grenades in reserve.

Descend into cover near the terminal at the rear of the room. Either blind-fire your shotgun over it at the enemies or back off and blast their heads as they mantle over the cover. Whatever you do, don't stay in cover if it appears like the Locust are moving into cover against the other side of the terminal. They're likely going to mantle-kick you.

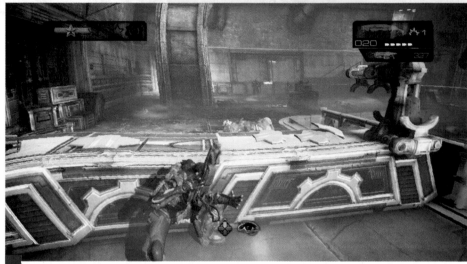

Switch to the Gnasher and blind-fire over the terminal to headshot the Drones that congregate there after rappelling.

Your attention will be drawn to the small lab in the far right corner. Use this as your cue to get the Gnasher Sentinel in the central pit (under the left-hand walkway) and position it facing the stairs pointing towards the room where the next wave of Scorcher-wielding Boomers and Grinders are located.

Maneuver the Gnasher Sentinel into position near the stairs on the left so it can target enemies as they exit the server room on the side.

Take out the Drones and heavies that emerge and, once the coast is clear (don't let your squad get all of your kills), approach the door with a Frag. Another E-Hole will open in the left corner of the side room, straight ahead from the doorway. Plug the hole and kill a few Drones with your grenade.

The E-Hole that opens in the server room is straight across from the door.

Your squad is going to hang back near the entrance from the start of the mission so be very careful when you advance. Help is *not* just around the corner. If you get downed across the room or in the small server room, chances are good there won't be anyone around to revive you.

Clear the area of enemies and exit through the door in the small side room. Proceed down the hall to the secure access door. Sofia has clearance since she used to work here. Head down the stairs, grab the Frag Grenades and Boomshot, and pull the lever to remove the clasps holding the beacon.

G. Bixhorn, MAJ, Jacinto

K.I.A. after Reaver attack, took several hours to expire from injury.

The COG Tag is located inside the small server room off to the right of the main lab. Enter the room and note the Crimson Omen on the wall to the far right. The COG Tag is on the floor, to the left of the Crimson Omen.

COG TAG

Pull the lever to release the bot from its clamps.

BOOMSHOT

AMMO

X

4

R-SENTINEL

BOOMSHOT

3

2

COG TAGS

GORGON

MULCHER

1

SAWED-OFF

DECLASSIFY

LONGSHOT

MISSION OBJECTIVES

> Escape the Academy.
> Protect the beacon.

HOSTILES ENCOUNTERED

2
TICKER

3
WRETCH

3
DRONE

3
DRONE (GRAPPLER)

9
FLAME BOOMER

11
BOOMER

12
KANTUS

15
GRINDER

NEMACYST*

 = Star Score

*Declassified Mission only.

"FROM THERE WE HAD TO FOLLOW THE BOT OFF CAMPUS— AND MAKE SURE NO ONE DAMAGED HIM."

RIBBONS AND SCORING

Stars accumulate more than three times as fast when the Declassified option is accepted. This is fortunate, as Nemacysts yield no individual points when shot. A Range Sentinel will help keep the bot safe from the Nemacysts, allowing you to focus on earning as many ribbons as possible. Much of your scoring opportunity comes once you reach the outside area. Use the available Boomshot to close Emergence Holes as the enemies clamber out to gain both a Plug that Hole and Boombardier ribbon with a single rocket! Use the Lancer's chainsaw to execute any stray Wretches or Drones in the area for additional points, but don't take any unnecessary risks. Keep close to the bot and the Range Sentinel and rely primarily on the Boomshot and Frag Grenades when going on the offensive.

CLUSTERLUCK: **Kill multiple enemies with one grenade.**

PLUG THAT HOLE: **Close an E-Hole with explosives.**

BOOMBARDIER: **Kill multiple opponents with a Boomshot blast.**

CLASSIFIED INTEL

Pick up the Mulcher around the corner from the start and mount it on top of the cover facing the door. Wait to see if the bot goes into its protective stance here. If so, use the Mulcher and the Sawed-Off Shotgun to the right to pick off the Drones and Wretches that attack.

The bot is attacked while cutting through the door leading out to the gardens. Down the first Drone to climb out of the floor and grab it for use as a meatshield. The enemies will grapple up through holes in the floor. Many will come from the area to the right (as viewed with your back to the bot).

The Locust attacks the bot at least twice as it makes its way through the gardens, often right outside the door. Quickly locate the Range Sentinel and place it in front of the bot for protection. Use the Boomshot to quickly close any E-Hole that opens.

Follow behind the bot with the Range Sentinel to see which direction it goes at the fork. Once again, place the Range Sentinel down in front of it and stay between it and the bot. Watch for enemies sneaking up behind the bot from the other direction.

DECLASSIFIED: THREE-STAR TACTICS

DECLASSIFY

NEMACYSTS ATTACK BEACON

Cadet Hendrick alleged that Kilo's support bot was attacked repeatedly by so-called Nemacysts.

Difficulty Increase: Low

Star Multiplier: 3.29x

Nemacysts have found their way to Monroe Commons and are determined to stop the bot before it can lead the squad any further. The Nemacyst make their first appearance as the bot works to cut the door to the outside. Then it is a constant bombardment whenever Locust are in the vicinity. Fortunately, the presence of a Range Sentinel makes defending the bot easier than it would be otherwise. Keep the Range Sentinel in working order and the bot should be just fine.

Accept the Declassified option and head up the stairs towards the Mulcher. Pick up the Mulcher and take cover near the railing around the corner, prior to exiting the hallway. The bot might beep loudly and announce an attack. If so, ready the Mulcher for what will likely be an assault by Drones and Tickers or Wretches.

Use the Mulcher from within the hallway to cut down any attackers without fear of being flanked.

If the bot continues through the hallway and out into the main room without stopping, throw down the Mulcher and consider picking up the Sawed-Off Shotgun or Longshot on the right. If you still have the Boomshot from the previous mission, keep the Boomshot alongside your Lancer and carry on.

T. Perham, PFC, Hatton

K.I.A. during encounter with Ragers, was beaten to death.

Exit the hallway and run straight across the main hall to the library room (where the flames are) to find the Crimson Omen. The COG Tag is actually in the room to the left. Run up the sloping debris pile to the left of the Crimson Omen and follow the right-hand wall to the COG Tag on the floor near the large table.

COG TAG

Escort the bot through the main hall until it stops, and defend it from the Drones and Wretches that attack. You may see some Tickers and it's not unheard of to encounter a Flame Boomer in this area. Many of the Drones grapple into the room from holes in the floor, but an Emergence Hole may open. Some Locust even rappel in. Stick close to your squad and defend the bot.

The bot beeps again while trying to cut through the door to alert you to an incoming Nemacyst attack. Use your Lancer to gun down the Nemacysts as they fly through the air towards the bot. These creatures erupt in an inky explosion so try to destroy them before they get too close. Nemacysts explode with a surprisingly wide blast radius and can down you on harder difficulties without even securing a direct hit.

Use the Lancer to shoot as many of the Nemacysts out of the air as possible before they dive towards the bot.

Follow the bot through the door and immediately grab the Boomshot on the landing. Sprint down the steps and turn to the right to pick up the Range Sentinel. Carry the Range Sentinel towards the bot and proceed after it until it beeps an alert and puts up its defenses. Position the Sentinel in front of the bot, with a clear line of sight towards the oncoming crush of Locust.

This large exterior area forks around the bend to the left and converges in the distance, near the Atrium entrance. The bot leads the way and, depending on how soon the next attack comes, the bot will either go left or right. Typically, if an attack is initiated while the bot is still on the landing where you found the Boomshot, then the bot will travel the right-hand path. If the bot makes it off the landing without interruption, expect it to head to the left at the fork. Regardless when the first attack comes, the bot enters its protective stance twice as it moves through the gardens.

Stick close by the bot and the Range Sentinel, regardless the path the bot takes.

Continue to position the Range Sentinel in a safe and effective manner—don't leave it out in the open where it can be quickly destroyed by Boomers or Nemacysts—and keep it full of ammo. The Range Sentinel is practically indispensable against the Nemacysts, particularly on Insane difficulty.

Advance along with the bot and try to scavenge as many explosives as you can. Use the Boomshot to close the E-Holes if you have no Frag Grenades; otherwise, save them for groups of enemies to earn the Boombardier ribbon. As long as you don't get downed too often, you can earn your three Stars relatively quickly thanks to the numerous enemies and abundant ribbon-earning opportunities. Another way to boost your score is by using the Lancer's chainsaw for executions.

Wait to close the E-Hole until multiple enemies try to climb out to get two ribbons at once!

Beware that it's quite common for there to be one final attack on the bot just as you reach the steps leading to the Atrium door on the far side. Most of the enemies come from the left fork (as viewed en route to the Atrium) but some will also attack from atop the stairs, on the landing near the door. Watch the bot's health meter closely (the green number starting at 100) and try to keep it in the green. Be sure to give the bot even greater attention if its health meter drops into the orange or red numbers.

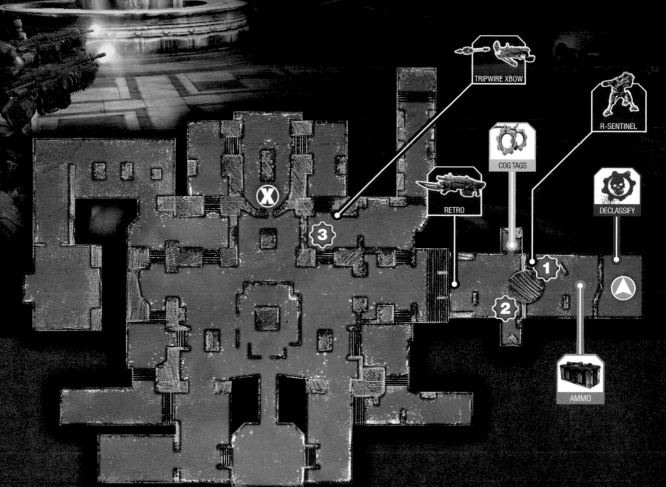

TRIPWIRE XBOW

R-SENTINEL

COG TAGS

RETRO

DECLASSIFY

X

3

1

2

AMMO

MISSION OBJECTIVES

> Escape the Academy.
> Protect the beacon.

HOSTILES ENCOUNTERED

3
WRETCH

3
DRONE

11
BOOMER

15
GRINDER

☆ = Star Score

"I WAS BEGINNING TO WONDER IF THAT BOT REALLY KNEW THE BEST WAY OFF CAMPUS. BUT WITH NO ONE BACK AT CONTROL TO TALK TO, OUR ONLY CHOICE WAS TO FOLLOW HIM."

RIBBONS AND SCORING

Accepting the Declassify option means you'll be fighting with pistols only. It also means you have no chance to earn Boombardier or Clusterluck ribbons and can ill-afford to allow the Range Sentinel to accumulate too many gib kills on your behalf. Use the Snub Pistol and constantly Spot and fire. Don't try to execute or melee until you get at least one I'm Your Huckleberry ribbon. The Snub Pistol doesn't have the firepower of the other weapons, but it has a large clip and can be fired quickly. Just keep Spotting Drones and Wretches and squeezing that trigger. Watch closely to ensure you've earned at least one Military Intelligence ribbon. The Boomers and Grinders are worth a lot of points, so be sure not to allow your allies to get the kill. One final way to boost your Star count is to take advantage of downed enemies and move in for the execution. But only after you've just earned an I'm Your Huckleberry ribbon, as the execution will end the streak.

MILITARY INTELLIGENCE: Spot 5 enemies ending in kills.

I'M YOUR HUCKLEBERRY: Kill 5 enemies in a row with any type of pistol without dying.

CLASSIFIED INTEL

1

Eliminate the initial attackers. Then quickly pick up the Range Sentinel and position it on the left side of the room, behind the sandbags flanking the fountain. Be sure to place it so it can't be kicked by Locust mantling over the barrier.

2

Stay behind the sandbags until the initial horde of Drones has been beaten back. Then scavenge a Boomshot, Retro Lancer, or Gnasher and focus your attention on the doors leading outside, mainly the one on the right. Gun down the Boomers as they march through the door in single file.

3

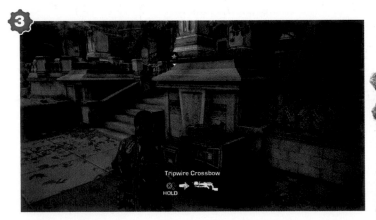

The battle is over before you know it, but you still need to get to the crash site. Be sure to stay to the right as you move through the gardens and pick up the Tripwire Crossbow sitting on the crate.

DECLASSIFIED: THREE-STAR TACTICS

DECLASSIFY

FIGHT WITH PISTOLS ONLY

Kilo Squad claimed to have successfully defended support bot using only pistols.

Difficulty Increase: Moderate

Star Multiplier 2.40x

Fighting with pistols only means there is no opportunity to scavenge for any Boomshots or Gnashers. You can still make use of the Range Sentinel to help keep the Locust at bay, but doing so may hinder any attempts to earn three Stars. Having to face Grinders and Boomers with merely a Snub Pistol is going to be tough on the harder difficulties. Make sure to grab any downed Drones for use as a meatshield when you start to see the heavies coming.

This is a very short mission and plays much like a continuation of the previous one. The bot is going to stop immediately after you enter the Atrium, as a response to a large number of Locust heading towards you. Many will rappel from the balconies and others will march in from the courtyard exterior. There aren't any E-Holes in this area, so don't worry about holding onto your Frag Grenades.

A Range Sentinel is on the right side of the room, in front of the second sandbag wall. Set it up near the bot, but aim it so its laser can detect any Locust mantling the sandbag to the left of the fountain. Be sure to place it far enough back so it doesn't get kicked over when Drones mantle the sandbags. On the other hand, you may wish to place the Range Sentinel back even further so it serves only as a last resort and doesn't hinder your chances at earning three Stars.

Start Spotting enemies immediately and try to quickly rack up a string of five kills against the Wretches.

The battle begins with either a large wave of Wretches or a mix of Drones and heavy units with a few Wretches mixed in. The Drones rappel, whereas the Wretches seem to come from everywhere. Focus on killing as many of the lesser enemies as you can as quickly as possible with the Snub Pistol to optimize your I'm Your Huckleberry ribbons. Be careful not to mantle-kick or execute any downed enemies. Killing an enemy in this manner ends the streak counter for the I'm Your Huckleberry ribbon, forcing you to start a new streak.

Make sure the pistol is fully loaded before taking on a Boomer!

One way to help ease the strain on your trigger finger is to Spot an enemy, and then target the one next to it. By instructing the rest of Kilo Squad to focus on several of the Drones, you can be sure to not only get the points for killing the Boomers and Grinders, but also earn a Military Intelligence ribbon.

Don't advance beyond the sandbags without the protection of a meatshield.

Grab the ammo crate near the bot once you're about a third full. But avoid advancing beyond the second wall of sandbags, or else you could get downed and have little chance of being revived.

D. Andrade, 1LT, Montevado

K.I.A. after he fell into an Emergence Hole.

The COG Tag is in the small room on the right side of the main hall, beyond the second sandbag. It's on the floor behind the door, so you may have to enter the room and turn around in order to find it.

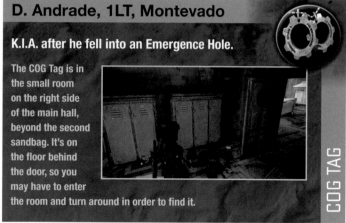

Once the coast is clear, exit the Atrium and follow the squad and the bot to the Tripwire Crossbow on the crate to the right. Pick it up and carry it with you to the crash site.

COG TAG

SECTION 6: CRASH SITE

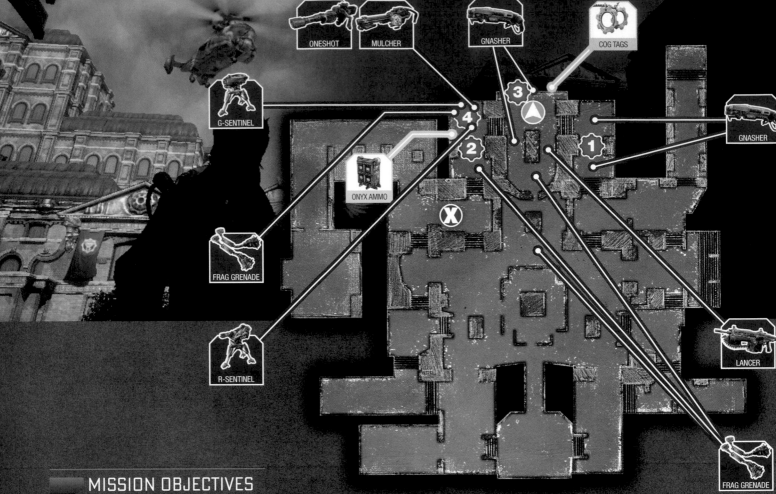

ONESHOT

MULCHER

GNASHER

COG TAGS

G-SENTINEL

GNASHER

ONYX AMMO

FRAG GRENADE

R-SENTINEL

LANCER

FRAG GRENADE

MISSION OBJECTIVES

> Escape the Academy.

> Protect the beacon and
  survive the attack.

HOSTILES ENCOUNTERED

★2	★3	★3	★8	★8	★8
TICKER	WRETCH	DRONE	THERON GUARD	THERON W/ CLEAVER	RAGER
★11	★12	★15	★15	★15	★25
BOOMER	KANTUS	GRINDER	MAULER	SERAPEDE*	CORPSER*

 = Star Score

*Declassified Mission only.

"I FOLLOWED BAIRD TO THE ACADEMY TO FIND OUT WHAT HAPPENED TO MY FELLOW CADETS. I FOUND OUT. THEY WERE ALL GONE. THE MONSTER THAT KILLED THEM HAD TO PAY."

RIBBONS AND SCORING

Earning three Stars on this mission basically boils down to your ability to stay alive without jeopardizing the bot's safety. Accept the Declassify option to gain the additional fortifications. Then set about planting Frag Grenades out in front of them to not only keep the fortifications safe, but to also hopefully earn a Clusterluck ribbon as well. Similarly, you can use the Tripwire Crossbow to earn the It's a Trap ribbon, though you may want to double up the tripwire charges so even larger enemies are killed in the blast. Stick close to the bot and the rest of Kilo Squad and keep the Sentinels loaded. Though you may find a Boomshot or Boltok Pistol and be able to earn a Boombardier or I'm Your Huckleberry ribbon, the OneShot will most likely be your source of additional ribbons. Use it early in the battle to earn a Shish-Kashot ribbon, while the fortifications are still holding the horde at bay.

IT'S A TRAP: Kill multiple enemies with a single Tripwire Crossbow shot.

CLUSTERLUCK: Kill multiple opponents with one grenade.

SHISH-KASHOT: Kill at least two enemies with a single OneShot round.

CLASSIFIED INTEL

Use the Tripwire Crossbow to place traps near the stairs that lead up to the crash site on either side. But only fire three of the four bolts. Pick up the Onyx Ammo Cache before firing the final shot to replenish the Tripwire Crossbow's reserves. Spread the tripwires out so one detonation doesn't trip all of them. Plant Frag Grenades in the ground several steps in front of the tripwires to intercept Tickers or Wretches that may attack first.

Place the Gnasher Sentinel on the steps behind the bot, at the starting point. Here, it can fire on attackers coming from either side but can maintain out of the line of fire. Position the Range Sentinel behind your tripwires on the right or left side, aiming down the aisle into the gardens.

Use any available long-range weapons to gun down the Locust heavies before they get too close. A single tripwire may not be enough to kill them.

Wait to use the Mulcher until the second wave. Bring it to the steps beside the Range Sentinel and mow down the stream of Locust running towards your position from the doors in the rear of the courtyard. Even a string of Cleaver-wielding Therons will be no match for the combined firepower of a Range Sentinel and the Mulcher!

DECLASSIFIED: THREE-STAR TACTICS

The Bot takes position atop the stairs, near the crash site, and almost immediately raises its protective shields. A massive army of Locust is due inbound in 1:30. The upcoming battle features dozens of enemies from various Locust species. Though the Declassified option adds Corpsers and Serapedes to the battle—two of the most fearsome units in the Locust army—it also adds several fortifications and replaces the Mulcher with the OneShot. It's a fair tradeoff and one that makes for a very entertaining fight.

It's important to make good use of the 1:30 setup phase to effectively position the Sentinels, tripwires, and Frag Grenades. There are numerous Frag Grenades scattered throughout the area, but there's no need to use them all at once. Plant just a few of the Frag Grenades at the start of each of the two waves. Place them in the floor out in front of each of the most forward fortifications you have. The idea is to position them in front of the defenses in order to intercept any Tickers that might target the fences. Set up a Gnasher Sentinel on the stairs behind the bot and the Range Sentinel off to the right, behind the second row of defenses. This helps protect the defenses for a while. Be sure to move it nearer the bot once the fortifications on that side have been compromised.

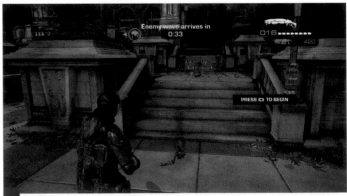

Wait to close the E-Hole until multiple enemies try to climb out to get two ribbons at once!

Fire the Tripwire Crossbow at the planters and at the base of the stairs in pairs, with one bolt on each side of the walkways so enemies have no choice but to be bombarded with blasts from each side. Consider placing both pairs of tripwires on the side of the stairs opposite where you place the Range Sentinel. You can also place individual tripwires far enough forward to intercept Tickers and/or Wretches in an effort to earn the It's a Trap ribbon.

Keep the Gnasher Sentinel loaded at all times, as that's your key to victory. Though it's okay to advance a bit early on to try and protect your defenses, you really must fall back to the main upper platform once the fortifications are down. You need to be around your squad and close by the bot to offer support. It's not a bad idea to hold your ground atop the stairs behind the bot, as it gives you plenty of good angles.

Keep the action in front of you from atop the stairs behind the bot.

The first wave likely starts with plenty of Tickers and Drones, followed by a number of Theron Guards. The Serapedes attack before long. Use the Lancer or Mulcher (if present, as it rotates with the OneShot) on the Serapedes and save the OneShot for the Corpsers. You might have to face a few Boomers or Maulers during or shortly after the Corpser attack—try to line up one or two enemies at a time for a Shish-Kashot ribbon whenever possible, but don't wait for the perfect shot. This battle turns rather chaotic and you'd be fortunate enough to get an accurate shot off before having the enemy on top of you. Luckily, there are plenty of high value targets on the battlefield and earning three Stars is not that difficult, provided you stay alive.

Use the OneShot against the Corpsers, before they destroy all of your fortifications.

There is a brief 0:30 break between waves. Use this time to gather Frag Grenades and to hopefully pick up the OneShot with one round remaining or the Tripwire Crossbow if you still have it. Collect the Onyx Ammo Cache to top off the ammo of this special heavy weapon. This is a major bonus!

The second wave gets very intense because of the numerous Cleaver-wielding Theron Guards, the many Kantuses, and the constant march of Maulers and other heavy enemies. Stick close to your squad and keep the Gnasher handy. Keep on the lookout for weapons to scavenge, particularly the Torque Bow or Boomshot. Hold your ground atop the stairs behind the bot, preferably alongside the two Sentinels, until there are only a few enemies remaining. Even then, don't take any chances! Hunt the remaining foes with a scavenged Boomshield and Lancer.

Use the Boomshield for mobile cover when mopping up the few remaining heavy units.

SEAHORSE HILLS

PADUK'S TESTIMONY

SECTION 1:
AMADOR PARK

"GROWING UP IN THE UIR, OF COURSE I'D HEARD OF THE FABLED MANSIONS IN HALVO BAY. BUT I NEVER IMAGINED I'D SEE THEM LIKE THIS."

GARRON PADUK, COG PRIVATE

Paduk was fished from COG waters after the destruction of the Union of Independent Republics (UIR) by the Locust. Putting aside everything he believed in, he volunteered to fight against the Locust with his former enemies.

Born in Gorasnaya, Garron Paduk served as a Major in the Pendulum Wars, fighting against the Coalition of Ordered Governments. His decision to join the COG in the battle with the Locust wasn't purely out of vengeance, but also a means of getting him out of prison. Gorasni veterans like Paduk were personae non gratae with the COG due to their region's refusal to sign the armistice treaty.

MISSION OBJECTIVES

> Locate the professor and the launch codes.
> Break through the Locust frontlines.

HOSTILES ENCOUNTERED

3 WRETCH	3 DRONE	7 GRENADIER	12 BLOODMOUNT
12 KANTUS	15 ELITE MAULER	25 CORPSER	

⭐ = Star Score

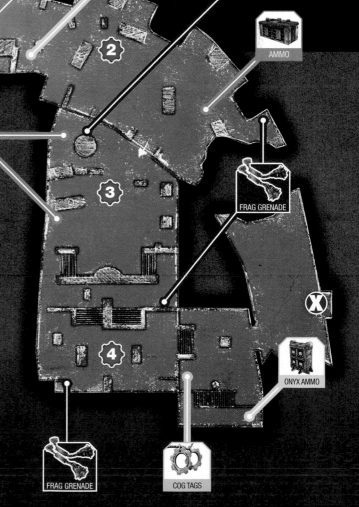

DECLASSIFY

BOOMSHOT

BOOMSHOT

TRIPWIRE XBOW

BOOMSHIELD

1

BOOMSHOT

AMMO

ONYX AMMO

2

AMMO

AMMO

3

FRAG GRENADE

4

FRAG GRENADE

COG TAGS

ONYX AMMO

RIBBONS AND SCORING

A number of ribbons can be earned while playing without the Declassified option accepted. The presence of the Boomshot and Tripwire Crossbow, along with two Onyx Ammo Caches, makes earning the Boombardier and It's a Trap ribbons very likely. There are far fewer opportunities to earn ribbons when playing with the Declassified conditions active. Fortunately, earning three Stars is essentially a matter of surviving without spending too much time on your knees. Use the Sawed-Off Shotgun against the Wretches and Drones to earn Nothin' But Bits ribbons, and use the Gnasher to, potentially, earn a Hat Trick ribbon. You're unlikely to earn many execution bonuses while playing with just the shotguns, but the Gnasher is quite capable of earning a headshot bonus.

IT'S A TRAP: Kill multiple enemies with a single Tripwire Crossbow shot.

CLUSTERLUCK: Kill multiple enemies with one grenade.

BOOMBARDIER: Kill multiple enemies with a single Boomshot blast.

NOTHIN' BUT BITS: Kill multiple enemies with a single Sawed-Off Shotgun blast.

CLASSIFIED INTEL

1

Pick up the Boomshot to the left and loop past the gate to the road ahead. Use the Boomshot to repel the Bloodmounts or Maulers that attack on the road. Then switch to the Gnasher or Lancer to finish them and any nearby Grenadiers off. Hold onto the Boomshot for replenishment later and carry the Tripwire Crossbow up the road.

2

Carry the Tripwire Crossbow up the road to where several Drones burst from the ground. Quickly set up three Tripwire Crossbow traps. Then grab the Onyx Ammo Cache to replenish the Tripwire Crossbow along with your Boomshot and other weapons. Use your remaining Tripwire Crossbow bolts here, as you won't be able to take the weapon to the next area.

3

Use your additional Boomshot ammo against the Corpser beyond the gate. Roll to avoid its attacks and fire on its body or at the ground beside its legs whenever possible. With any luck you'll catch a Wretch with the splash damage. Depending on the difficulty setting, you may encounter two Corpsers here.

4

Hold onto any remaining Boomshot ammo and attack the two Kantuses on the terrace with your Lancer or Gnasher. Several Drones are all that stand between you and the exit. Use your remaining Boomshot ammo on the group of Drones atop the stairs to the left. Retrieve the Onyx Ammo Cache from the balcony before you complete the mission.

DECLASSIFIED: THREE-STAR TACTICS

DECLASSIFY

USE GNASHERS AND SAWED-OFF SHOTGUNS ONLY

Pvt. Paduk claimed that Kilo Squad subdued armored enemies using only shotguns.

Difficulty Increase: Moderate

Star Multiplier: 2.61x

Accepting this option automatically equips each member of Kilo Squad with a Gnasher and a Sawed-Off Shotgun, but with no available weapons to pick up. Getting in close enough to battle Elite Maulers with just a shotgun makes this battle much more difficult than normal. The Elite Maulers rotate with Bloodmounts—consider restarting the mission if you are unhappy with your draw. Make certain to collect the Onyx Ammo Caches on this map; they are the only way to replenish the Sawed-Off Shotgun's ammo supply.

Mantle the low wall on the right to bypass the locked gate and immediately brace for combat. The initial enemy encounter consists of either three Elite Maulers or a pair of Bloodmounts accompanied by Wretches and Drones. Though the Bloodmounts are a bit easier to kill with just shotguns, both can be put down with the right weapon.

Opt for the Gnasher against the Elite Maulers. Its longer effective range helps to keep you out of harm's way—there is no deadlier enemy at close-range than an Elite Mauler! Unlike most other enemies, an Elite Mauler is not happy to have downed you; the fatal blow comes quickly. Use the Gnasher against them, but go to the Sawed-Off for use against Bloodmounts should you encounter them instead. Aim slightly high and fire twice quickly. The first shot weakens the Bloodmount; the second kills it and the Drone riding it, if applicable. Look for opportunities like this to use the Sawed-Off Shotgun and earn a Nothin' But Bits ribbon.

Flank the Elite Maulers with your Gnasher when they target other members of Kilo Squad.

Continue up the road and use the two different shotguns to work over the Drones and Wretches. The Onyx Ammo Cache on the right will replenish your Sawed-Off Shotgun, as it's the only way to get extra ammo for it. Try to use the Sawed-Off Shotgun when engaging multiple enemies; otherwise, use the Gnasher and aim high for headshots.

The Corpser is most vulnerable in its backside, but don't get too close!

Interact with the lock on the gate to continue to a small courtyard playing host to a Corpser and several Wretches. Use the Gnasher, stay on the move, and focus on the Corpser's blindside. Ignore the Wretches unless directly threatened.

The two Kantuses on the terrace occasionally lob Ink Grenades into the battle, but ignore them for the most part until the Corpser is dead. Head up the stairs and take out the Kantuses, again with headshots from the Gnasher. Locate the ammo crate on the right. Then advance towards the squad of Drones and Grenadiers. Beware that the Drones on the balcony near the Onyx Ammo Cache often carry Scorchers.

Consider staying near the Kantuses to draw the Locust down the stairs in smaller numbers.

Use the Sawed-Off Shotgun to earn additional Nothin' But Bits ribbons, or go for headshots with the Gnasher if at all possible. As long as you avoid being downed while separated from your squad, you should have no trouble earning three Stars.

M. Reid, PFC, Ephyra

K.I.A. when a Boomshot round exploded his transport.

Approach the final group of enemies atop the stairs at the end of the area. Notice the Crimson Omen on the wall to the right, near the stairs leading up to the Onyx Ammo Cache. The COG Tag isn't up those stairs, but rather to the right of the Crimson Omen. It's on the landing adjacent the stairs you ascend from the road to reach this area.

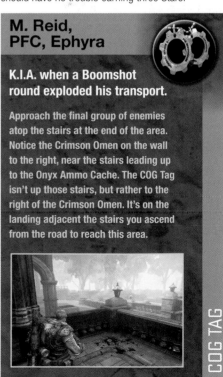

COG TAG

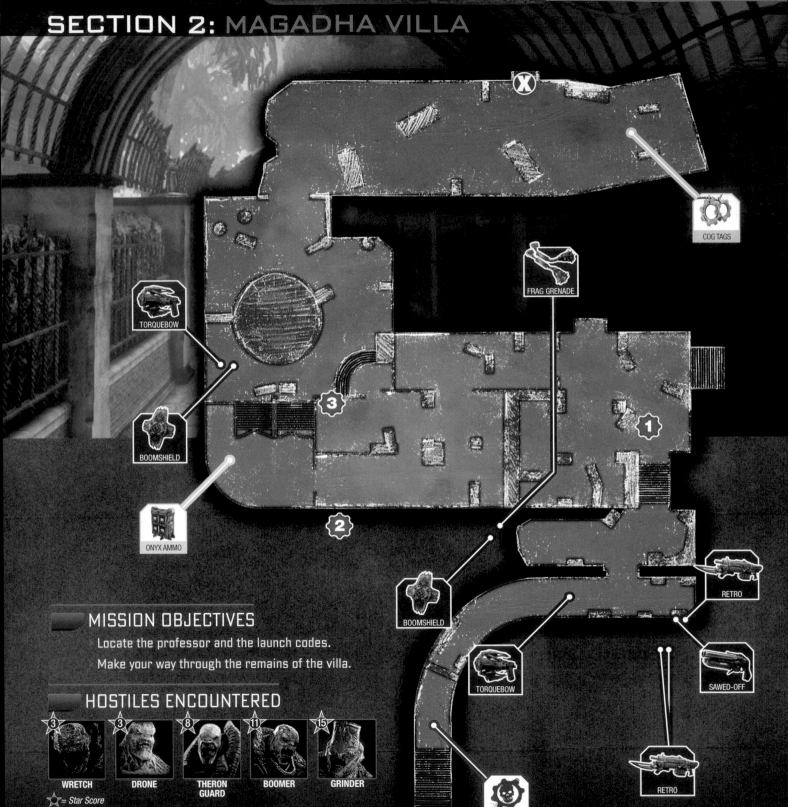

SECTION 2: MAGADHA VILLA

X

COG TAGS

FRAG GRENADE

TORQUEBOW

3

BOOMSHIELD

1

2

ONYX AMMO

RETRO

BOOMSHIELD

SAWED-OFF

TORQUEBOW

RETRO

MISSION OBJECTIVES

Locate the professor and the launch codes.

Make your way through the remains of the villa.

HOSTILES ENCOUNTERED

★3	★3	★8	★11	★15
WRETCH	DRONE	THERON GUARD	BOOMER	GRINDER

★ = Star Score

"WE NEEDED TO GET THE LAUNCH CODES FROM THIS PROFESSOR ELLIOTT. BAIRD AND SOFIA BOTH SAID HE WAS A DECENT MAN. MAYBE HE WAS. I TRIED TO FORGET THAT HIS WEAPON BURNED OFF HALF MY FACE."

RIBBONS AND SCORING

The heavy reliance on the Torque Bow and Frag Grenades recommended for this mission reduces the amount of ribbons you may earn. Though it is possible to earn a William Tell Overture or Hat Trick ribbon on this mission, you're best served focusing on the Clusterluck and Plug That Hole ribbons. Additionally, those who grab the Sawed-Off Shotgun at the start of the mission can look for opportunities to earn a Nothin' But Bits ribbon as well. Fortunately, skillful use with the Torque Bow and Frag Grenades against the Boomers and Grinders can get you plenty close to three Stars without many ribbons. As long as you don't neglect the Wretches and avoid being downed more than ever so briefly, you should score well. One way to help bolster your chances is to aim for the heads of your targets when using the Torque Bow. Despite being an explosive weapon, the Torque Bow is plenty capable of delivering a headshot bonus.

PLUG THAT HOLE: Close an E-Hole with explosives.

CLUSTERLUCK: Kill multiple opponents with one grenade.

CLASSIFIED INTEL

1

Pick up the Torque Bow from outside and melee through the Wretches to the back-right corner of the interior room. Stay in cover and use the Torque Bow to take out the Grinders and Boomers that come in from the outside.

2

Slowly approach the swimming pool in the back corner of the property with a Frag Grenade and lob it as the E-Hole opens. Look for any dropped Torque Bows, grab the Onyx Ammo Cache, and exit the pool to the right.

3

Hold your position between the pool and the fountain, and quickly toss a Frag Grenade to the far right corner to close the E-Hole there. Another E-Hole opens on the street beyond the property, but it can be difficult to reach without a Boomshot. Finish off the remaining Therons and Grinders with the Torque Bow while taking cover against the fountain's base.

DECLASSIFY

LOCUST USE SMOKE GRENADES TO REDUCE VISIBILITY

Kilo Squad reported unlikely tactical use of Smoke Grenades by Locust forces.

Difficulty Increase: Low

Star Multiplier: 2.04x

This mission's structure and recommended tactics are much the same with the Declassified option accepted, though visibility is certainly reduced. The presence of the Smoke Grenades may not sound like much, but the constant bombardment also makes it harder to keep your footing, and aiming precision weapons is more difficult as well. That said, heavy use of the Torque Bow and Frag Grenades will carry you a long way towards earning three Stars on this mission.

Accept the Declassify option and advance to the gate. Multiple Retro Lancers and a Sawed-Off Shotgun are on the ground ahead, but your primary acquisition should be the Torque Bow inside the gate on the left. Swap it with the Lancer, as the Gnasher will certainly come in handy. Or, if you prefer, equip the Torque Bow and either the Sawed-Off Shotgun or Retro Lancer. The goal is to wield a longer range explosive weapon and a short-range weapon like the Gnasher or Retro Lancer.

Fight past the Wretches near the door, either with Torque Bow melee strikes or by using the Sawed-Off Shotgun for a Nothin' But Bits ribbon. Take cover behind the furniture in the back-right corner. The Smoke Grenades detonate all over the room, but this position should keep you out of the reach of their concussive force.

Drones or Wretches attack first, followed immediately by a number of Boomers or Grinders. Keep your head down, listen for the Boomer's telltale shout, and use the Torque Bow against the heavies. Switch to your close-range weapon whenever the Drones or Wretches get near. Continue to use the Torque Bow while also looking for an opportunity to toss a Frag Grenade for a Clusterluck bonus.

Kill the first three Grinders or Boomers. Then move closer to the door you came in through to get a sneak shot on the last heavy while it's still in the other room. Shoot through the hole in the wall on an angle to get it. Remember that you can score a headshot with the Torque Bow and you just might get it to stick in the head of a second enemy.

![Take cover in the back corner of the room with the Torque Bow.](image)

Take cover in the back corner of the room with the Torque Bow.

Shoot through the hole in the left wall to pick off enemies before they march down the hallway.

Finish off any stragglers with your other weapon. Then grab the Frag Grenades in the room to the left. It's also worth swapping the Torque Bow for a Boomshot if there is one lying around. The rest of Kilo Squad then exits via the upper door on the right, where one of two E-Holes is going to emerge outside. Don't follow them!

Instead, descend the ramp to the dilapidated swimming pool and ready a Frag Grenade for the Therons that escape a short-lived E-hole. The E-Hole won't stay open so it doesn't need to be plugged, but you can get a Clusterluck with a well-timed throw. Better still, you can pick up the Onyx Ammo Cache to replenish your Torque Bow and gain another grenade.

Toss a Frag Grenade to kill the Therons that emerge in the swimming pool.

Exit to the yard and quickly head to the right. Toss a Frag Grenade into the E-Hole in the far corner. Circle back to the left, past the Torque Bow and Boomshield near the fountain, and toss another Frag into the street beyond the yard to close the second E-Hole.

A scavenged Boomshot makes it even easier to close the E-Holes in the yard and street!

D. Carmine, PVT, East Timgad

K.I.A. when a stray bullet ricocheted.

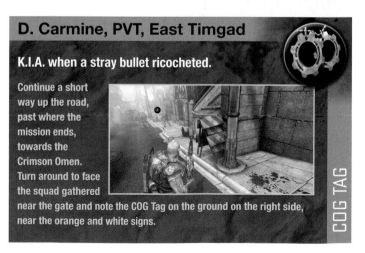

Continue a short way up the road, past where the mission ends, towards the Crimson Omen. Turn around to face the squad gathered near the gate and note the COG Tag on the ground on the right side, near the orange and white signs.

COG TAG

Resist the temptation to pick up a Boomshield, as you lose accuracy with the Torque Bow unless crouching. Instead, take cover against the side of the fountain and continue to use the Torque Bow to eliminate the remaining Therons and Grinders in the area.

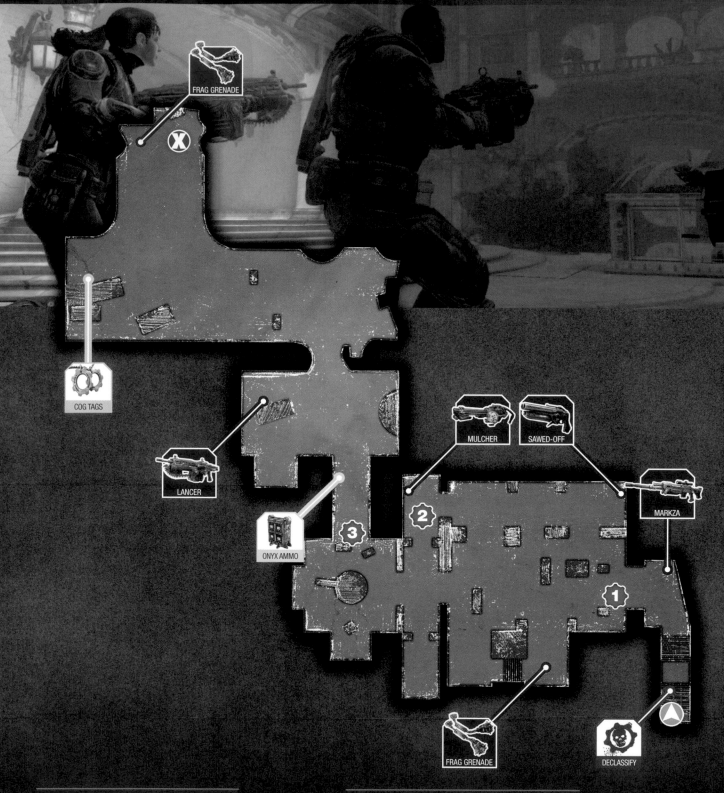

FRAG GRENADE

X

COG TAGS

LANCER

MULCHER

SAWED-OFF

MARKZA

ONYX AMMO

3

2

1

FRAG GRENADE

DECLASSIFY

MISSION OBJECTIVES

> Locate the professor and the launch codes.

> Eliminate both Kantuses on the balcony.

> Clear the area of Locust.

HOSTILES ENCOUNTERED

3	8	8	12	15
DRONE	RAGER	THERON W/ CLEAVER	KANTUS	ELITE MAULER

☆ = Star Score

"STEP BY STEP, WE WERE GETTING CLOSER TO ELLIOTT'S MANSION. I KEPT THINKING, WHO COULD LIVE THROUGH ALL THIS?"

RIBBONS AND SCORING

The combination of distant Kantuses, Elite Maulers, and Ragers combines with a time limit (Declassified only) to curb your ribbon-earning opportunities, but earning three Stars will not be a problem. Use the Markza early in the mission to snipe the twin Kantuses on the balcony, and then take out one additional foe for a Hat Trick before switching to the Sawed-Off Shotgun and Frag Grenades. Use either of these weapons for another multi-kill on your way to the Mulcher. Another Clusterluck opportunity presents itself beyond the gate as you fight your way down the slope towards the Ragers and Drones. Enraged Ragers are tough to kill with a single shotgun blast so try softening them up with the Markza. Then switch to the Sawed-Off Shotgun for a Nothin' But Bits ribbon, if the chance arises. The presence of so many high-value targets makes this a relatively easy mission to earn three Stars, provided you stay alive.

HAT TRICK: Score 3 headshots in a row without dying.

CLUSTERLUCK: Kill multiple enemies with one grenade.

NOTHIN' BUT BITS: Kill multiple enemies with a single Sawed-Off Shotgun blast.

CLASSIFIED INTEL

Quickly grab the Markza from behind the crate straight ahead. Then duck into cover behind the stone column on the left. This provides a solid piece of tall cover from which to snipe the two Kantuses on the balcony. Kilo Squad can keep the Drones at bay, but you must watch out for Cleaver-wielding Theron Guards. If they approach, drop back and use the Gnasher or stick them with a Frag Grenade.

Hurry to the opposite corner, to the right of the gate, and grab the Mulcher before the Elite Maulers break into the villa. Squat down with the Mulcher and open fire from their flank. Hold onto your remaining Frag Grenades, but continue to watch for additional Therons. Expect no fewer than three Elite Maulers to attack in this area.

Collect the Frag Grenades before leaving the main courtyard. Then hurry to the right of the statue and lob them down the road, past the Onyx Ammo Cache, at the Ragers. These Ragers immediately enrage and charge up the hill. Others emerge from an Emergence Hole alongside additional Drones or Therons. Continue to toss Frag Grenades in between bursts of gunfire from the Gnasher and Markza. Maintain the elevated position until the last of the Locust are dead.

FINISH BEFORE EXPLOSIVES DETONATE

Pvt. Paduk alleged that military-grade explosives had somehow been made available to wealthy civilians.

Difficulty Increase: Low

Star Multiplier: 2.59x

Countdown to Explosives Detonate

CASUAL	NORMAL	HARDCORE	INSANE
5:35	4:15	3:30	5:15

The villa that Kilo Squad broke into is rigged with very powerful explosives set to detonate in just a few minutes. Fortunately, the explosives have a relatively slow fuse. There's little time for exploration and you must not waste any time in dealing with the Kantuses and Elite Maulers, but you don't need to rush either. Allow the enemies to come as they will, take them out efficiently, and keep moving. The presence of the detonation timer does make this mission more difficult, but you need not charge into a dangerous situation.

Most timed missions force the player to rush into combat faster than it's normally safe to do. But the nature of the mission at Soleno Villa allows the same basic strategies to work for Declassified and otherwise. Nevertheless, you certainly want to make sure your shots count in order to not waste precious seconds.

Rush into the courtyard where the two Kantuses appear on the balcony. Immediately equip the Markza behind the crate on the right. Then move into cover near one of the columns to the left. Let the rest of Kilo Squad deal with the Drones while you focus on the Kantuses. Immediately snipe one of the two Kantuses—it takes two clean shots to the head to eliminate a Kantus on Hardcore difficulty. Eliminate one Kantus, then the other. Hold onto the Markza but consider grabbing the Sawed-Off Shotgun on the right after earning a Hat Trick ribbon.

The Kantuses are sometimes accompanied by a squad of Theron Guards armed with Cleavers instead of Drones. This presents a far more difficult situation for Paduk. Consider equipping the Markza and Sawed-Off Shotgun immediately and switch between them as necessary to defend yourself. Kilo Squad is unable to prevent the Therons from swarming your position while you snipe the Kantuses, so you must defend yourself against them.

Continue using the Markza to pick off another enemy after killing the Kantuses to get the Hat Trick ribbon. Then toss a Frag Grenade to help eliminate the stragglers. Run down the right-hand alley to the Mulcher and move into cover near the column facing the gate. Three Elite Maulers burst through the gate and march straight towards the other members of Kilo Squad. Open fire on their flank with the Mulcher, but switch your aim to the Therons should they attack as well.

Use the Markza to snipe the Kantuses while the rest of Kilo takes care of the Drones.

Use the Mulcher to eliminate the Elite Maulers and then sprint for the Frag Grenades in the alcove.

Drop the Mulcher after the lull. Run to get the Frags in the alley in the center of the courtyard before exiting the area. Go through the gate and quickly toss two or even three Frag Grenades down the hill to the right at the Ragers that erupt from the ground. Snipe any that you can, but switch to the Sawed-Off Shotgun the moment they start charging up the slope in their enraged state.

Stick close to the squad so they can revive you quickly and fight your way down the hill towards the Onyx Ammo Cache.

Hang back near the top of the slope and snipe the Ragers if you have more than 1:15 remaining on the timer.

Pop a few more rounds at the un-enraged Ragers beyond the tunnel and then push forward for the Onyx Ammo Cache. Hold onto one last Frag Grenade in case you spot an E-Hole that can be closed; otherwise, grab the COG Tag and the Frag Grenades before ending the mission.

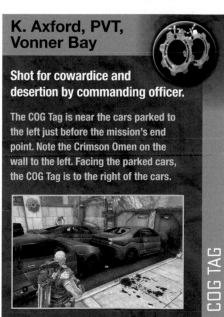

K. Axford, PVT, Vonner Bay

Shot for cowardice and desertion by commanding officer.

The COG Tag is near the cars parked to the left just before the mission's end point. Note the Crimson Omen on the wall to the left. Facing the parked cars, the COG Tag is to the right of the cars.

COG TAG

ONYX AMMO

FRAG GRENADE

AMMO

4

3

LONGSHOT

MORTAR

ONYX AMMO

2

FRAG GRENADE

AMMO

DECLASSIFY

BOOMSHOT

1

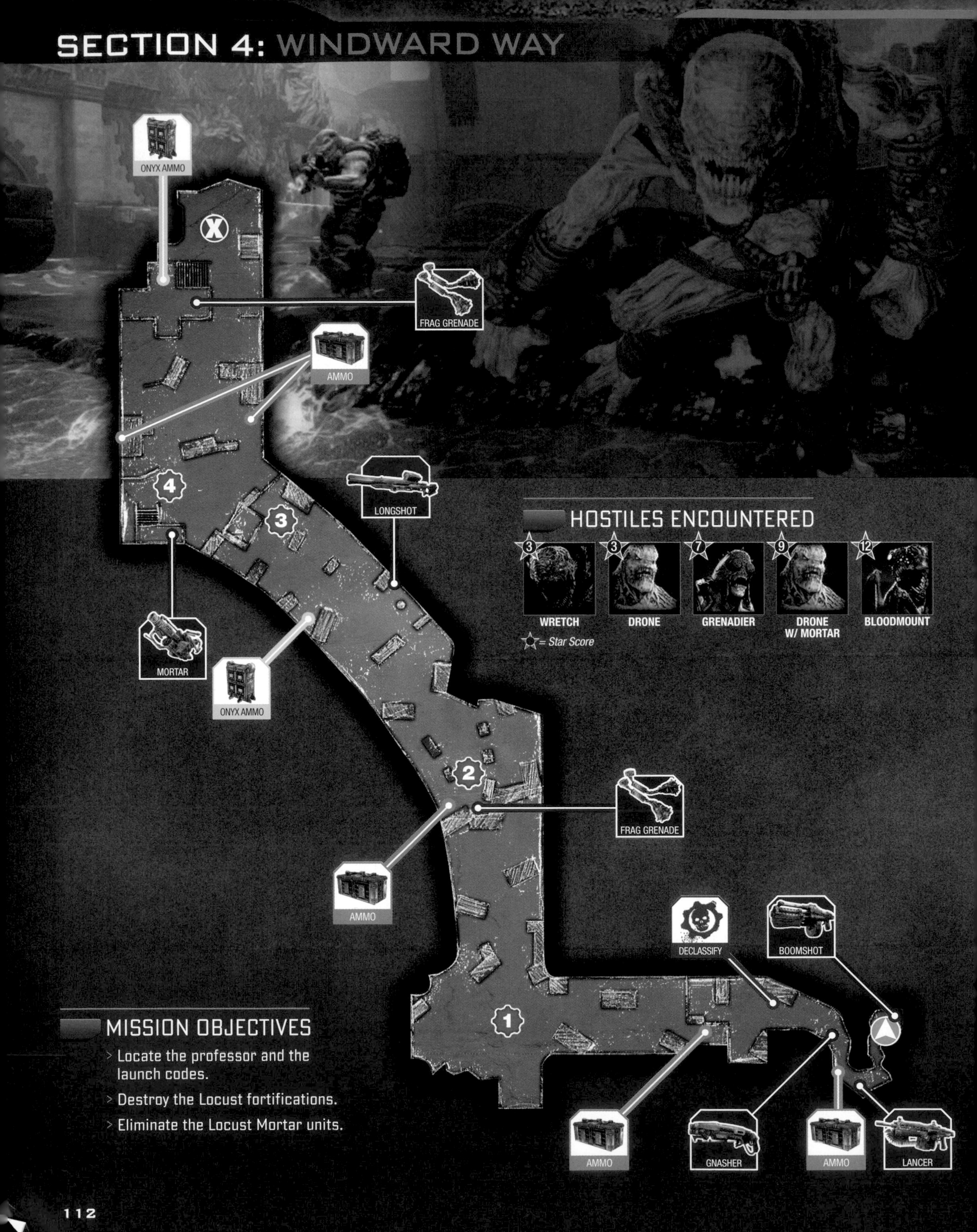

HOSTILES ENCOUNTERED

3	3	7	9	12
WRETCH	DRONE	GRENADIER	DRONE W/ MORTAR	BLOODMOUNT

☆ = Star Score

MISSION OBJECTIVES

> Locate the professor and the launch codes.

> Destroy the Locust fortifications.

> Eliminate the Locust Mortar units.

AMMO

GNASHER

AMMO

LANCER

"AFTER A LITTLE PUSH ON SOME ABANDONED COG HARDWARE, WE WERE THAT MUCH CLOSER TO THE PROFESSOR'S MANSION."

RIBBONS AND SCORING

Earning three Stars in this mission can be difficult, even with the Declassified option accepted. The only way to guarantee three Stars is by earning as many ribbons as possible with the Boomshot and Frag Grenades, even if it means putting down the Mortar. There are several key opportunities to earn an explosive multi-kill and you need to take advantage of them: the first encounter in front of the gate, when the Bloodmounts knock down the wall, and the Locust climbing out of the E-Hole just beyond the fallen wall. The Mortar can help kill the point-heavy Bloodmounts that approach from the rear when accepting the Declassified option, but remember that the Bloodmounts with riders all but guarantee a Boombardier ribbon if you land a direct hit. Lastly, though there are plenty of opportunities for earning ribbons on high-value targets, there are also plenty of opportunities to be downed as well. Stick close to Kilo Squad and make sure you take out the elevated Mortar nest as quickly as possible. If you sense it getting its shot off before you, sprint down the steps and into the blue container for cover.

PLUG THAT HOLE: Close an E-Hole with explosives.

CLUSTERLUCK: Kill multiple enemies with one grenade.

BOOMBARDIER: Kill multiple enemies with a single Boomshot blast.

CLASSIFIED INTEL

①

②

Pick up the Boomshot behind you at the start and then grab the Lancer on your way onto the road. Use the Boomshot against the Scorcher-wielding Drone and its accompanying Wretches to earn a Boombardier ribbon. Switch back to the Lancer and shoot your way past the barricades and fortifications on the road to the right.

Shoot and melee past the fortifications blocking the road to the right. Round the corner to the left and immediately chainsaw or shoot the Drone with the Mortar. A Scorcher-wielding Drone bursts from the ground the moment the other Drone is killed, so watch out. Use the Mortar to clear the road ahead of its fortifications, but leave the heavy weapon behind.

③

④

Two Bloodmounts are in the process of breaking through the gate ahead. Stand off to the side, Boomshot in hand, and fire at the Bloodmounts the instant the gate is toppled. Time this well and you just might rack up the Boombardier ribbons!

Lob a Frag Grenade at the E-Hole beyond the gate. Then hurry up the steps to the left, grab the Mortar, and fire it as far as it can go. There's another Drone with a Mortar on the elevated platform in the distance. The Drone is going to be raining fire all over Kilo Squad if you don't take it out at once! Continue using the Mortar to eliminate the remaining Locust in the street leading to the mission end.

DECLASSIFY

EXTRA LOCUST WILL ATTACK FROM BEHIND

Kilo Squad's testimony on enemy behavior contradicts COG estimates concerning the Locust ability to flank, think strategically.

Difficulty Increase: Moderate

Star Multiplier: 1.58x

Ezra Loomis and the rest of the COG brass continue to discount Locust intelligence, but the soldiers in the field know better. In addition to learning how to erect barricades and fortifications, the Locust have also begun using flanking maneuvers. The road ahead is littered with barricades whether you accept the Declassified option or not. But those who accept this additional challenge have to deal with a battalion of Bloodmounts and Drones approaching from the rear, just as Kilo Squad finds themselves in the middle of a Mortar battle.

Grab the Boomshot behind you at the very start of the mission and continue along the path of rubble to the Lancer ahead. Equip the Lancer alongside the Boomshot, grab the ammo, and continue up the slope to the Locust fortifications. Shoot fortifications with the Lancer, as it has the largest ammo capacity and is largely unneeded for offensive purposes in this mission.

Fire one or two shots from the Boomshot at the Scorcher-wielding Drone and Wretches ahead. Be sure to save at least two Boomshot rockets for use later on. Use the Lancer to finish off this early encounter unless you have an opportunity to earn a Clusterluck ribbon with a Frag Grenade. Sofia notices the professor's mansion's security system beyond the gate—you have to find a different way in.

Always use the Lancer to shoot through the fortifications to conserve more valued, rarer ammo.

Shoot through the fortifications to the right in time to hear the sound of a Mortar unit. Run up behind the Drone on the left and chainsaw it, but beware of the Scorcher-wielding Drone that bursts out of the ground to claim revenge. Clear the immediate threat and then use the Mortar to destroy the fortifications further up the road and in the distance.

Grab the Frags and Ammo near the Mortar and continue up the road towards the gate. Grab the Onyx Ammo Cache on the left to replenish your Boomshot and then cut across to the right. Two Bloodmounts will break through the wall and attack alongside several Wretches and Drones. Fire the Boomshot at the Bloodmounts as soon as the wall falls for a chance to earn multiple Boombardier ribbons.

Be ready with the Boomshot for the moment the Bloodmounts knock the wall down.

You've seen that the Locust are capable of erecting fortifications, now it's time to experience their ability to flank. Drones, Grenadiers, and Bloodmounts are on their way up the road behind you. You must move quickly here! The only reason to hesitate is if you're completely out of Boomshot ammo and Frag Grenades. If so, grab the Longshot, climb onto the fallen wall, and immediately snipe the Drone with the Mortar in the distance.

Climb over the wall and ready a Frag Grenade for the E-Hole that opens beyond the car directly ahead. Toss another at the Locust attacking from the rear and then quickly dash left and up the stairs to an abandoned Mortar. Canvas the area ahead with the Mortar including the Mortar location in the distance on the left side of the road. Hold the Fire button down for as long as possible to ensure you fire the Mortar far enough to hit the elevated platform in the distance. The Mortar you just commandeered has plenty of artillery shells, but you must not stay in this position for long, as the reinforcements are almost here.

Roadie Run along the left side of the road, through the blue container, to the Onyx Ammo Cache in the distance. Head up the stairs to the third Mortar and aim it back the way you just came. Fire the Mortar at the Bloodmounts and Drones attacking from the rear, but mind your Star count. If you are still shy of three Stars, switch to the Boomshot and try to earn a Boombardier ribbon as you finish off the remaining foes.

Sprint along the left side of the road to get the third Mortar and fire it back the way you came.

Fire the second Mortar as far as it will go to eliminate the Mortar nest on the platform in the distance.

J. Carlson, CPT, Halvo Bay

K.I.A. when he sacrificed himself by leaping upon an enemy grenade.

The COG Tag is on the left side of the road, between the second and third Mortars, near the blue container with the ammo crate. It's on the far side of the container and can be hard to see if you don't go through the container and then stop and turn around to find it.

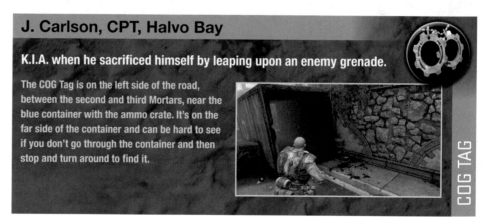

COG TAG

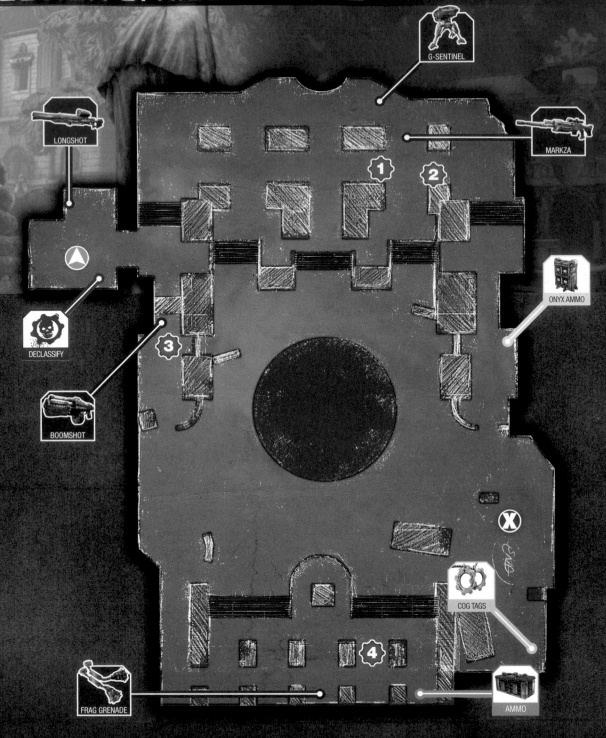

G-SENTINEL

LONGSHOT

MARKZA

1

2

ONYX AMMO

DECLASSIFY

3

BOOMSHOT

X

COG TAGS

4

AMMO

FRAG GRENADE

MISSION OBJECTIVES

> Locate the professor and the launch codes.

> Eliminate all the Locust Mortar units.

HOSTILES ENCOUNTERED

6	6	9	9	11	15	15
CYCLOPS	SNIPER	DRONE W/ MORTAR	BUTCHER	BOOMER	MAULER	GRINDER

☆ = Star Score

"WE COULDN'T GET INTO THE PROFESSOR'S HOUSE UNTIL WE ELIMINATED THOSE MORTAR SQUADS. EVERY MORTAR SQUAD."

RIBBONS AND SCORING

Despite the presence of so many high-value targets at Risea Estate, you'll likely find it moderately challenging to earn three Stars in this mission. This is largely due to the relatively scarce opportunities for earning ribbons. Though it's well worth killing one or two heavy enemies if you can, it's important to not interrupt your string of headshots, or else you may miss out on a Hat Trick ribbon. Use the Lancer to spray a crowd of enemies with bullets before tossing a Frag Grenade to increase your chances of getting the multiple kills needed for a Clusterluck ribbon. Lastly, don't overlook the Boomshot off to the right of the fountain, as it can make it possible to earn a Plug That Hole and Boombardier ribbon with a single shot, provided the Locust are near enough to the hole.

HAT TRICK: Score 3 headshots in a row without dying.

PLUG THAT HOLE: Close an E-Hole with explosives.

CLUSTERLUCK: Kill multiple enemies with one grenade.

CLASSIFIED INTEL

1

Grab the Longshot and sprint for the Gnasher Sentinel outside to the left. Position it under the overhead cover, but between the columns near the Markza so it's not in the way. Take cover near either column and snipe the two Drones with the Mortars. One is above the flaming garage to the left; the other is high atop the roof in the center.

2

Maintain this position and continue sniping the Boomers or Grinders on the lower balcony of the estate. Watch for Maulers and Butchers moving towards you and quickly switch to the Lancer or Markza and take them out. A well-timed Frag Grenade can be a life-saver here.

3

Sprint for the Boomshot to the right of the fountain and use it to close the Emergence Hole just beyond its position. Fire its remaining rockets into the crowd of Locust on the other side of the fountain and near the garage where a second Emergence Hole opens.

4

Hold onto the Boomshot and run under the balcony to get the Frag Grenades and ammo. Close the final E-Hole if it's still open and mop up any remaining Locust from their flank. Collect the Onyx Ammo Cache before exiting the estate.

DECLASSIFY

LOCUST USE ONESHOTS TO PROTECT MORTARS

Kilo Squad claimed to witness sophisticated defense tactics, despite COG intel to the contrary.

Difficulty Increase: Moderate

Star Multiplier: 2.37x

Activating the Declassified option on this mission replaces the Grinders and Boomers normally positioned on the balcony (beneath the upper Mortar unit) with three Snipers manning OneShots. Their presence gives the Locust a way to kill you while peering out of cover to snipe the Mortar units—the OneShot is lethal with even a glancing blow! Rather than target the Mortar units first, you must time your sniping attempts between Mortar volleys and target those with the OneShots first.

Swap out the Gnasher for the Longshot on the left and accept the Declassify option before mantling over the wall. Immediately sprint to the left and grab hold of the Gnasher Sentinel. Move the Gnasher Sentinel slightly forward, under the overhead protection, but between the columns so it's out of the way. Position the Gnasher Sentinel quickly, as the OneShot-wielding Snipers will be aiming this way any moment.

Take cover to the left of the Markza, shoulder the Longshot, and immediately scan the balcony of the building for the three OneShot enemies. Ignore the two Mortar units for now and focus on sniping all three OneShots for a Hat Trick ribbon. You're safe from the Mortar units' bombardment as long as you stay under the overhead cover, but it can be difficult to snipe with the shells going off all around you. Try to time your shots while the Mortars are being reloaded.

Snipe the enemies with the OneShots before aiming for the Drones manning the Mortar.

Keep an eye out for any Maulers or Butchers approaching at close range—you'll no doubt hear their footsteps getting closer. Try to stay under the covered walkway and cover swap to get away from them. Switch to the Lancer if you must, but the Gnasher Sentinel and other members of Kilo Squad should be able to dispatch them. It's best to not interrupt your attempt at a Hat Trick ribbon.

Watch out for Maulers trying to flank you while you snipe.

Return to that same left-hand position and snipe the two Mortar units with the Longshot. One is on the lower flaming part of the roof to the far left side of the large estate. It's hard to spot (and may drop its Mortar onto the street below, but ignore it if it does). The second Mortar unit is atop the roof, in the dead center of the house.

One of the Mortar units is high atop the center of the roof—use the Longshot!

With the Mortar units defeated, all you need to do is clear out the remaining Locust. That means destroying a couple of E-Holes and a large quantity of Drones and heavies.

Swap the Longshot for the Markza and grab the Gnasher Sentinel. Sprint to the right, around the fountain, and place the Gnasher Sentinel down looking at the E-Hole. Toss a Frag in it (or use the Boomshot to the right), and then sprint for the Frag Grenades under the balcony.

Head left to the Ammo Crate and lob an explosive to destroy the E-Hole at the top of the slope. Now you just have the remaining heavies and Cyclops to deal with. Switch to the Markza to rack up some more headshots if the opportunity presents itself, or put the Boomshot or Frag Grenades to use in an attempt to earn a Boombardier or Clusterluck ribbon. Grab the Onyx Ammo Cache and the COG Tag before ending the mission.

Use the Frag Grenades under the balcony to close the remaining E-Hole.

K. Sutton, PVT, New Sherrith

K.I.A. by Mortar round while trying to revive a downed comrade.

The COG Tag is at the bottom of the slope, in the fiery garage under the lower of the two Mortar units. The COG Tag is off to the far left amidst the flaming wreckage inside the building.

COG TAG

TRIPWIRE XBOW

ONYX AMMO

FRAG GRENADE

G-SENTINEL

FRAG GRENADE

DECLASSIFY

LANCER

BOOSHKA

SAWED-OFF

COG TAGS

ONYX AMMO

MORTAR

FRAG GRENADE

MISSION OBJECTIVES

> Locate the professor and the launch codes.

> Eliminate the last Locust Mortar unit.

> Stop the Locust counterattack.

HOSTILES ENCOUNTERED

3	5	7	7	8	8	9	12	12	25
DRONE	DRONE (REAVER DRIVER)	GRENADIER	THERON (REAVER DRIVER)	THERON GUARD	THERON GUARD W/ CLEAVER	DRONE W/ MORTAR	BLOODMOUNT	KANTUS	REAVER

 = Star Score

"THERE WAS ONE LEFT, WHICH WAS GOOD. I WAS GETTING SICK OF THE SOUND OF INCOMING."

RIBBONS AND SCORING

There are plenty of enemies to kill in this mission, but earning three Stars could be difficult if you don't earn those Clusterluck ribbons when you have the chance. Accept the Declassify option and try to take out the first wave of Locust with a Frag Grenade for a Clusterluck ribbon. Fire the Tripwire Crossbow in the bungalow at the door and at the stairs to trap approaching Bloodmounts. Consider firing the explosive traps at the floor near the door for use as mines, which may help earn the It's a Trap ribbon. Use the Lancer's chainsaw to execute any stragglers and move up the stairs to the Mortar unit. Chainsaw the Drone manning the Mortar and watch for the counterattack to start. Rather than grab the Mortar right away, first lob any remaining Frag Grenades down at the Drones and Therons that emerge for a chance at a final Clusterluck ribbon.

IT'S A TRAP: Kill multiple enemies with a single Tripwire Crossbow shot.

CLUSTERLUCK: Kill multiple enemies with one grenade.

NOTHIN' BUT BITS: Kill multiple enemies with a single Sawed-Off Shotgun blast.

CLASSIFIED INTEL

1

Equip the Booshka and Sawed-Off Shotgun and advance across the gardens towards the statue in the distance. An E-Hole opens directly underneath it, allowing several Therons with Cleavers or a large group of Drones to attack. Time your Frag Grenade well to close the hole before too many of them are able to escape. You can use the Booshka to close an E-Hole, but it can take two grenades to guarantee its closure.

2

Run up the steps to the house and grab the Tripwire Crossbow near the window. Several Bloodmounts are fast approaching and they're likely going to come right through the front door! Quickly fire three Tripwire Crossbow bolts into the doorway, either at the door jamb or on the floor as mines. Set up the final bolt on the stairs in case any of the Bloodmounts use the lower entrance.

3

Descend the stairs to the garage and set up the Gnasher Sentinel just under the overhead coverage. Finish off any attackers with the Sawed-Off Shotgun. Then grab the Onyx Ammo Cache and wait for the Mortar unit to have to reload. Reposition the Gnasher Sentinel out into the street, grab the Frag Grenades, and sprint for the small room to the right of the curved stairs dead ahead.

4

Fight up the stairs with the Sawed-Off Shotgun and kill the Mortar unit. Pick up the other Mortar—not the one the Drone was using—and use it to bomb the Drones, Grenadiers, and Therons below. Continue the bombardment until even the Reaver is destroyed. Use the Booshka to finish it off if you run out of ammo.

DECLASSIFIED: THREE-STAR TACTICS

DECLASSIFY

SENTRY GUNS AND LASER FENCES GUARDING THE AREA

Kilo Squad alleged that COG hardware was being used by residents of Seahorse Hills area for personal defense.

Difficulty Increase: Moderate

Star Multiplier: 2.56x

This option forces Kilo Squad to deal with a half dozen sentries scattered across the gardens, the bungalow, and the garage. They also have to contend with multiple laser fences as well. For this reason, it's best to pair the Booshka with the Lancer instead of the Sawed-Off Shotgun. The Lancer's extended range makes it easier to destroy fortifications and sentries from afar.

Equip the Booshka and the Lancer at the start of the mission if you're going to accept the Declassified option. Immediately mantle over the crates on the right and take cover near those facing the sentry to the left. Blind-fire at the laser fence directly ahead while the rest of Kilo Squad deals with the sentry off to the left.

Stay in cover and blind-fire the Lancer to destroy the laser fences and sentry in the garden.

Swap to the Booshka or ready a Frag Grenade for the Grenadiers, Drones, or Cleaver-wielding Therons emerging from the E-Hole ahead. The hole will close automatically so don't worry about trying to get a Plug That Hole ribbon, though it is possible if you hurry. Use the Lancer to destroy the laser fences near the sentries and on the stairs (while staying out of sight of the two sentries in the house). Then use a Frag or Booshka to destroy the two sentries inside. Shoot the laser fence near the stairs inside the house before you enter, as a number of Bloodmounts will attack as soon as you enter the bungalow.

Toss a Frag Grenade into the house to quickly eliminate the two sentries set up inside.

Shoulder the Tripwire Crossbow and fire two Tripwires at the doorway to the left of the weapon and one or two at the wall near the stairs leading down to the garage. Several more home-defense sentries are in the basement. Head down the stairs and use your remaining explosives to clear them out. Quickly set up the Gnasher Sentinel in the garage if any of the Bloodmounts are still on the prowl.

Set up additional Tripwire Crossbow traps in the garage if it appears more of the Bloodmounts are attacking from that direction.

Move the Gnasher Sentinel to the entrance of the garage and watch for the incoming Mortar fire. Fire the Booshka at any approaching enemies, wait for a lull in the Mortar fire, and then sprint across the driveway to the room directly ahead, beneath the Mortar unit. Grab the Frag Grenades and COG Tag inside this room. Then lob a grenade at the enemies coming down the stairs. The Mortar units may be protected by multiple Kantuses, so be careful.

Have a Frag Grenade ready to toss in case there's a Kantus on the steps leading up to the Mortar unit.

I. Hogina, PFC, Autrin

K.I.A. during ferocious Locust firefight, apparent battlefield suicide.

The COG Tag is inside a small room at the base of the curving stairs. Sprint across the street to the room for cover from the Mortar fire. Pick up the COG Tag while gathering the Frag Grenades in this room.

COG TAG

Run up the curving stairs to the platform above and take out any remaining Drones to silence the Mortars. Locate the Mortar lying in the center of the balcony. This Mortar is fully loaded with eight shells, and you're going to need every one of them. But don't grab it just yet. Numerous Locust waves burst from the ground as a counterattack. The members of Kilo Squad on the ground distract them from climbing the stairs to attack, and they are mere fodder for the Mortar. Nevertheless, it pays to lob a Frag Grenade or two down at them in an effort to earn a Clusterluck ribbon before you start the Mortar bombardment.

Grab the Mortar and start firing explosive shells down onto the next wave and, finally, the Reaver that lands in the middle of the street. You don't need to fire as far as you may think. Just two or three clicks on the rangefinder is all it takes to cover the area below with Mortar fire.

Sprint along the left side of the road to get the third Mortar and fire it back the way you came.

The mission ends when you follow Sofia down the path to a gate. Break the chain off the gate and descend the steps to the canal. Cross the waterway to the door and watch Sofia deactivate the security door.

SECTION 7: ELLIOTT'S MANSION

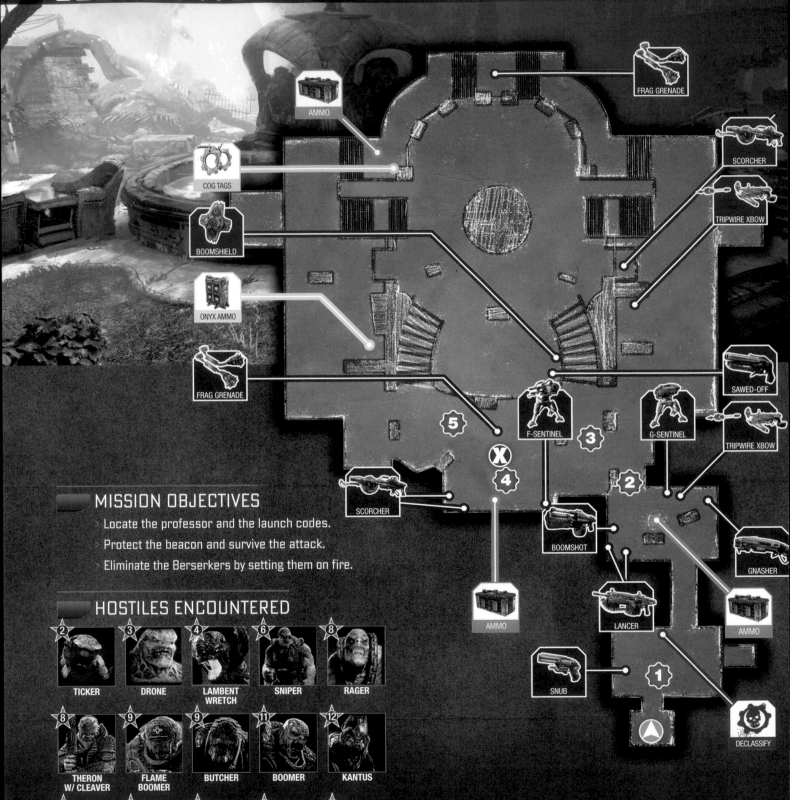

FRAG GRENADE

AMMO

SCORCHER

COG TAGS

TRIPWIRE XBOW

BOOMSHIELD

ONYX AMMO

SAWED-OFF

FRAG GRENADE

TRIPWIRE XBOW

5

X
4

F-SENTINEL

3

G-SENTINEL

2

SCORCHER

BOOMSHOT

LANCER

GNASHER

AMMO

AMMO

SNUB

1

DECLASSIFY

MISSION OBJECTIVES

> Locate the professor and the launch codes.
> Protect the beacon and survive the attack.
> Eliminate the Berserkers by setting them on fire.

HOSTILES ENCOUNTERED

★2 TICKER	★3 DRONE	★4 LAMBENT WRETCH	★6 SNIPER	★8 RAGER
★8 THERON W/ CLEAVER	★9 FLAME BOOMER	★9 BUTCHER	★11 BOOMER	★12 KANTUS
★12 BLOODMOUNT	★15 SERAPEDE	★15 MAULER	★15 GRINDER	★20 BERSERKER

★ = Star Score

"THE TRUTH IS, NONE OF US CARED HOW WELL SOFIA KNEW THIS PROFESSOR. BUT I THINK WE ALL KNEW BY THEN THAT WE WEREN'T GOING TO LIKE WHAT WE FOUND INSIDE HIS MANSION."

RIBBONS AND SCORING

Those who manage to avoid being downed for lengthy periods of time while completing the Declassified option should have little trouble earning three Stars on this mission. Skilled use of the Tripwire Crossbow and Frag Grenades after the 1:30 intermission should enable you to earn Clusterluck and It's a Trap ribbons. Plant Frag Grenades in the floor at the base of the stairs to take out the Tickers that inevitably scurry along in front of the other Locust. Align your Tripwire bolts in tight groups of two or more to ensure the blast is strong enough to kill multiple Locust, especially if playing on Hardcore or Insane difficulty. You aren't likely to earn a Flamebroiled ribbon while playing the Declassified option, but the OneShot Snipers offer opportunities for earning a Boombardier ribbon instead.

IT'S A TRAP: Kill multiple enemies with a single Tripwire Crossbow shot.

CLUSTERLUCK: Kill multiple enemies with one grenade.

BOOMBARDIER: Kill multiple enemies with a single Boomshot blast.

FLAMEBROILED: Kill 3 enemies in a row with the Scorcher.

CLASSIFIED INTEL

1

Break through the gate near the canal and walk with Sofia and the rest of Kilo Squad to the secret "friends and family" entrance to Professor Elliott's estate. Ride the elevator up to his lab to see if he's still alive

2

Place the Gnasher Sentinel in the middle of the doorway to help guard the bot while it hacks into the system to unlock the mainframe door. Leave the Tripwire Crossbow where it is and take the Boomshot and Lancer into the main hall. Stand atop the stairs nearest the bot and gun down the small wave of Therons, Drones, and Grinders that emerges from the hole in the far wall.

3

Use the 1:30 interlude to set up a more robust defense of the bot. Grab the Tripwire Crossbow and set traps across the top of the stairs and on the sides of the column near the door where the Gnasher Sentinel is. A second Tripwire Crossbow down the hall on the right can be used to add additional traps. Consider planting Frag Grenades at the base of the stairs to intercept the Tickers, and swap the spent Boomshot for the Sawed-Off Shotgun. Stick close to the Gnasher Sentinel.

There is just 0:30 to prepare for the next wave. Carry the Gnasher Sentinel to the mainframe and position the Flame Sentinel directly next to it. Equip a Lancer, Scorcher, and Frag Grenades and stick close to the Sentinels. Keep them loaded and do your best to guard the bot from the army of Serapedes, Butchers, and Therons headed your way.

The Locust send two Berserkers after the bot in a final attempt to stop it from getting the launch codes. Berserkers are relatively impervious to damage except when set on fire. Use the Scorcher (and the Flame Sentinel) to engulf them in flames, and then switch to the Lancer while they're glowing red. Pour as many rounds as possible into the Berserker before it cools off. Then switch back to the Scorcher and repeat the process.

DECLASSIFIED: THREE-STAR TACTICS

DECLASSIFY

LOCUST USE ONESHOTS

Kilo Squad claimed to have overcome powerful Locust siege using only scavenged flame weapons.

Difficulty Increase: High

Star Multiplier: 2.54x

There are two major differences in this mission when playing Declassified, and the presence of Locust with OneShots is actually the lesser of the two. The Snipers with the OneShots can be easily flanked and present minimal trouble. The primary challenge lies in having to scavenge for Scorchers. Those playing Declassified have to go without the Flame Sentinel and use two Scorchers located inside the mainframe area. Make sure to save the Onyx Ammo Cache for when you have a Scorcher, or you may find yourself having a hard time against the Berserkers.

Lead Kilo Squad past the gate and across the canal to the secret elevator leading up to Professor Elliott's lab. The bot can retrieve the launch codes in the professor's absence, but it must first hack into the system to unlock the mainframe's secured door. The bot's efforts unfortunately cause the power to go out, allowing the Locust a chance to breach the estate's walls.

Gun down the three Lambent Wretches that break into the library—there are many, many more where they came from! Move quickly to set the Gnasher Sentinel up in the doorway but leave the Tripwire Crossbow for later. Top off your Lancer ammo and grab the Boomshot and head into the main hall.

▶ Position the Gnasher Sentinel on a slight angle facing the column so it can target any approaching Locust.

The Locust begin the attack with a small band of Grinders and Drones to test the estate's interior defenses. Use the Boomshot and a Frag Grenade during the early part of this attack to rack up Clusterluck and Boombardier ribbons while holding the upper balcony near the Gnasher Sentinel. Listen for the telltale sound of a OneShot's targeting system and duck into cover on the right. Move across the upstairs walkway to flank the two enemies with the OneShots. It only takes one Frag or Boomshot rocket to kill them both. Get the Frag Grenades they drop and regroup with the others.

Sprint along the upper walkway to flank the Snipers with the OneShots and arc a Boomshot rocket right into them!

You now have 1:30 to prepare for the Locust's full-scale assault. Grab the Tripwire Crossbow from the library and set up an array of traps atop the stairs and around the sides of the column near the Gnasher Sentinel. A second Tripwire Crossbow is on the right-hand walkway—use this one to set up additional traps near the left-hand stairs if you have the time. Whatever you do, do *not* pick up the Onyx Ammo Cache. It's very important that those playing with the Declassified option active save the Onyx Ammo Cache for later.

This large wave of enemies consists of all manner of Locust including Boomers, Kantuses, Therons with Cleavers, and Tickers. Use the Lancer and target every Ticker you see. Not only might their detonations soften up those around them, but it's also important to destroy the Tickers before they scurry in front of the other Locust and trigger your Tripwire traps.

Take cover atop the stairs and look for opportunities to earn Boombardier ribbons.

The bot moves to the mainframe in the center hall, and you now have 0:30 to set up its protection. Continue to hold onto the Boomshot but *do not* pick up the Onyx Ammo Cache—don't even think about it! Quickly move the Gnasher Sentinel to the bot's new location and scavenge for dropped Boomshots or, if none are available, swap it out for a Sawed-Off Shotgun.

Position the Gnasher Sentinel off to the side of the bot, so it's not directly in the line of fire.

This next wave consists of a random assortment of all manner of Locust including Maulers, Bloodmounts, Serapedes, and Ragers. Additionally, two Snipers armed with OneShots have returned to the far balcony. Use any grenades you find and try to eliminate as many enemies as possible until you hear the OneShots begin to hum. Flank the two Snipers just as you did previously, and then return to protect the bot. Do your best to lure any Serapedes or Ragers away from the bot while keeping the Gnasher Sentinel loaded so it can gun down the others.

The Serapede will follow whoever last destroyed three of its segments—try luring it away from the others!

Eventually, there's a crash at the back of the mansion and two Berserkers, some Ragers, and, most importantly, Flame Boomers attack. The Flame Boomers are your only source of Scorchers, and you're going to need them for the Berserkers that attack last. Spot the Flame Boomers so all of Kilo Squad focuses on them—you want them dead while their Scorchers still have plenty of ammo. Pick up the Scorcher, note the location of the other one that was dropped, and switch back to the Lancer to finish off the remaining Locust.

G. Frost, SPC, Jacinto

K.I.A. while trying to prevent Locust from killing civilian families.

The COG Tag is on the upper level, in the opposite corner from the door where you first enter the main house. This is where the Lambent Wretches break through. It's on the balcony in the corner near the blue ammo box. Be sure to pick it up during the battle or *immediately* after killing the Berserkers, or else you'll miss your chance.

The Berserkers aren't interested in going after the bot, so don't be afraid to spend much of the fight up top near the mainframe. Keep some obstacles or half-walls between you and the Berserkers and use the Scorcher to light them on fire—they take far more damage while they're smoldering and glowing red. Switch back and forth between the Scorcher and Lancer to maximize the damage you inflict. Use the Onyx Ammo Cache to replenish the Scorcher's ammo supplies if necessary, but only fire the Scorcher at the Berserkers until they turn red. Once they start to glow, immediately Spot the molten Berserker for your allies and open fire with the Lancer. The blue ammo crate near the mainframe respawns approximately every minute, so you should never run out of Lancer ammo.

Burn the Berserkers with the Scorcher and then switch to the Lancer and open fire!

ONYX POINT

COLE'S TESTIMONY

SECTION 1: FORTRESS

> "NEXT WE HEADED FOR ONYX POINT. I TOURED HALVO A FEW YEARS BACK. ONE OF YOUR GENERALS WAS A BIG FAN. TOOK ME ON A TOUR."

AUGUST COLE, COG PRIVATE

Cole walked away from a legendary Thrashball career to enlist in the COG—a decision he's still struggling with. It remains to be seen whether Cole will become an effective frontline Gear.

Despite having no prior military experience, Cole's fitness and never-quit attitude quickly proved invaluable to the COG. With Baird by his side, Cole found himself on the front lines of every major COG operation from the Lightmass Offensive to the sinking of Jacinto, and countless others. Despite the numerous accolades, Private Cole has refused promotion at every turn. The man, who lived his life in the spotlight of the adoring Cougar fans, is more than happy letting others seek recognition in this arena.

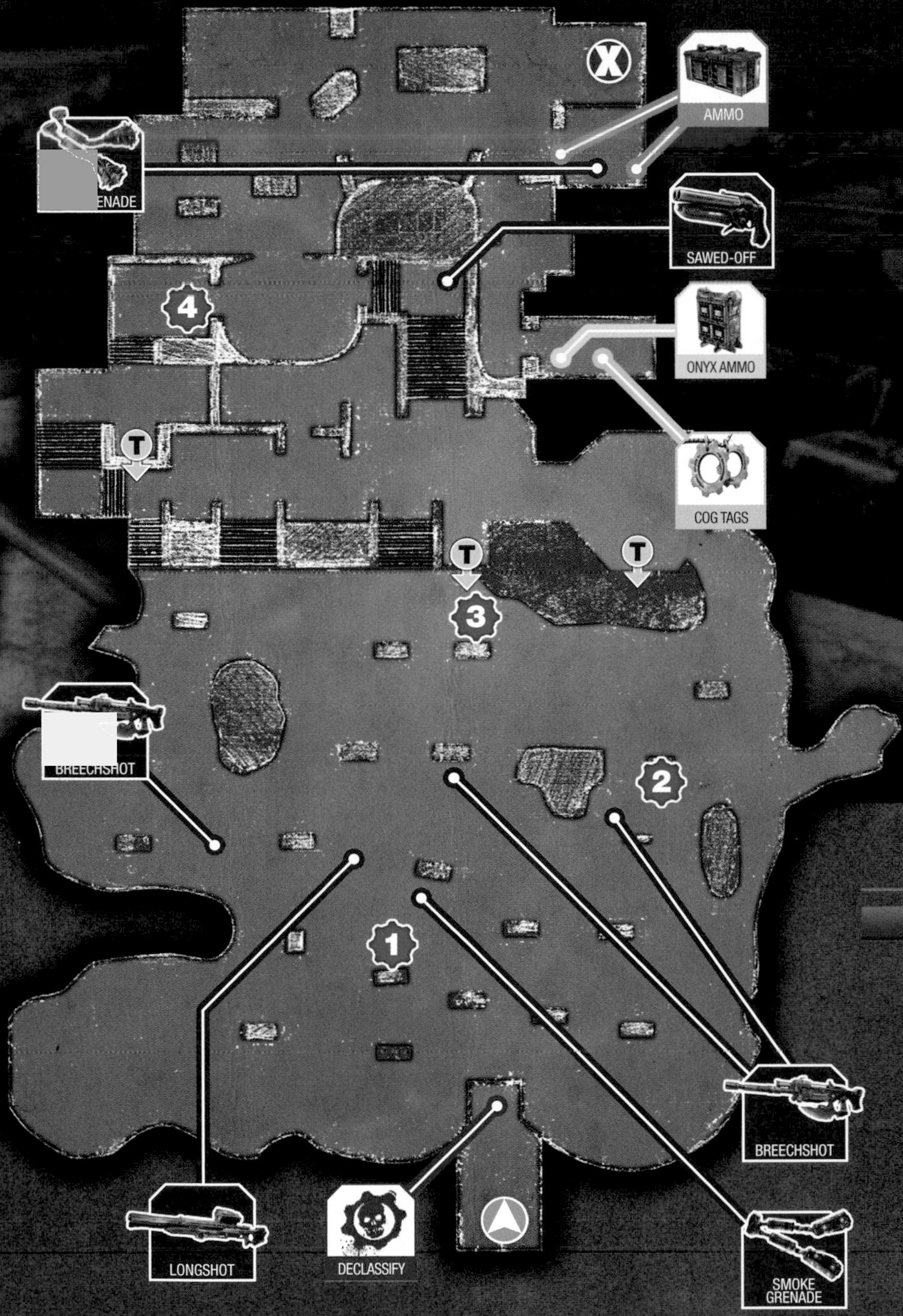

AMMO

SAWED-OFF

ONYX AMMO

COG TAGS

GRENADE

BREECHSHOT

BREECHSHOT

SMOKE GRENADE

LONGSHOT

DECLASSIFY

RIBBONS AND SCORING

The Stars come quick in this mission, which is good because you're bound to have a hard time staying on your feet due to the enemy Mortar fire. Move swiftly from cover to cover to reduce being downed and resist the temptation to try and snipe the Drone manning the Mortar, as it presents a very small target. Use the Longshot to take out the three Drones manning the turrets for a Hat Trick ribbon and then switch to the Breechshot. By using the Breechshot continuously to the end of the mission you should be able to net yourself at least one additional Hat Trick ribbon and also the Once More Unto the Breech ribbon. There aren't any E-Holes to close and the enemies tend to avoid bunching together. That said, you may be able to score a Clusterluck ribbon early in the assault on the fortress. Try not to let this come at the expense of a Breechshot kill-streak, though.

HAT TRICK: Score 3 headshots in a row without dying.

ONCE MORE UNTO THE BREECH: Kill 5 enemies in a row with the Breechshot without dying.

CLUSTERLUCK: Kill multiple enemies with one grenade.

MISSION OBJECTIVES

> Conquer the beach.
> Reach the interior of Onyx Point Fortress.

HOSTILES ENCOUNTERED

| DRONE | THERON GUARD | DRONE W/ MORTAR | MAULER |

 = Star Score

1

Exit the landing craft and sprint straight for the Smoke Grenade behind the tank trap beyond the water's edge. Toss the two Smoke Grenades towards the Longshot to the left, grab your Frag Grenades, and then swap out the Gnasher for the Longshot. Immediately fall back into cover and snipe the Drones manning the two Troikas on the right.

2

There's little time for additional sniping thanks to the Mortar unit blanketing the beach with explosive rain. Cover swap between the tank traps to avoid incoming explosives and try to snipe the Drone on the third Troika as you advance towards the rocks on the right. Swap out the Longshot for a Breechshot and use it and your Frags to take out the Mauler.

3

Move into cover against the rocks to the right of the center stairs, and use the Lancer to destroy the spiked fortifications. Switch to the Breechshot and set to sniping as many of the Drones and Theron Guards in the area as possible. The Breechshot is a very potent weapon and can be quite lethal at close to medium range. Sweep across the lower level of the fortress from right to left, passing under the third Troika.

4

Ascend the stairs on the left to the upper level and continue to use the Breechshot to kill the Drones near the turret. Be careful, as one may have a Scorcher. Let the Drones in the area behind the left bunker come to you. Stand back and play the angles to continue racking up the headshots with the Breechshot. The Sawed-Off Shotgun on the stairs to the right can be used if you prefer.

DECLASSIFIED: THREE-STAR TACTICS

DECLASSIFY

FRAG GRENADES PLANTED AROUND THE BEACH LANDING WITH REDUCED ACCESS TO LOCUST DEFENSES

Pvt. Cole claimed to have witnessed advanced Locust tactics that run counter to established COG intel.

Difficulty Increase: Low

Star Multiplier: 2.61x

Your assault on the beach goes a bit slower when playing the Declassified option. Many of the tank traps available for use as cover on the beach have been adorned with Frag Grenades. You must delay your rush for the Longshot and instead use the Lancer to clear out the planted Frag Grenades. You can also use the concussive force of the Smoke Grenades to detonate the planted Frags in addition to using them for a smokescreen.

The Locust were expecting your arrival and have lined the beach with Frag Grenades, many of them placed precisely where you need to take cover! Exit the landing craft and immediately shoot the Frag Grenade on the nearest tank trap. Duck into cover and target Frags near the Longshot and Smoke Grenade pickup, directly ahead. The Lancer is well-suited for detonating planted Frag Grenades. You can also use the Smoke Grenades behind the central tank trap to clear out other nearby Frag Grenades.

Head straight into cover, watch for a Locust near the Longshot directly ahead on the sand, and kill it. Wait for a lull in the Mortar activity, and sprint for the Longshot. Then retreat to the tall two-block piece of cover furthest from the sand, near where you exited the boat.

Use the Lancer and Smoke Grenades to clear out the Frags and then fall back and start sniping.

The first order of business is to snipe any Drones manning OneShots and the two Drones manning the two Troikas to the right. Try to stay in this position and collect as many headshots as possible, at least enough for one Hat Trick ribbon. If you're able to snipe the Mortar unit, then go ahead and stay in this position until you run out of targets.

Try sniping some of the Therons in the area to ensure at least one Hat Trick ribbon before advancing.

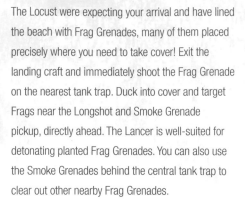

Switch to the Lancer and push forward to the next closest center cover. Use the Lancer and detonate the planted Frags on all of the cover near the nearest Breechshot. Swap the spent Longshot for the Breechshot and advance to the large boulder. From here you can get an ironsights shot on the left turret if it's being used. Clear out the fortifications and advance to the center wall between the stairs leading up to the fortress. Target the Frag near the stairs on the right, and then destroy the spikes at the base of the stairs.

Don't forget to target the Frag Grenade on the wall above the spikes!

There are a number of ways to sweep through the fortress, now that you've made it up the beach. One way is to use the Breechshot exclusively in an attempt to earn the Once More Unto the Breech ribbon. Another option is to pick up the Sawed-Off Shotgun and wrangle a Nothin' But Bits multi-kill ribbon. Lastly, you can put your Frag Grenades to use in clearing out the bunkers for a Clusterluck ribbon. Our advice is to let the enemy positioning determine your approach.

There are likely three to four more enemies in the back area. Depending on your Star situation, you should try to either look for an opportunity to get the Clusterluck or Hat Trick ribbon with the Frag Grenade or Breechshot, respectively. If two or fewer enemies remain and they're too close to use the Breechshot, switch to the Lancer and chainsaw them for the execution bonus.

Toss a Frag Grenade into the upper pillbox if you see two or more Drones inside.

B. Michandani, PFC, Lake Station

K.I.A. during Locust attack on Onyx Point, was attempting to protect a weapons cache.

The Crimson Omen is on the wall to the right of the mission end. The COG Tag is in the room to the far right of it, with the Onyx Ammo Cache. Raid the area for Frags and ammo and get the COG Tag before ending the mission.

SECTION 1: FORTRESS

COG TAG

COG TAGS

X

3

2

1

MULCHER

SILVERBACK

DECLASSIFY

MISSION OBJECTIVES

> Reach the interior of Onyx Point Fortress.
> Break through the Locust ranks.

HOSTILES ENCOUNTERED

2
TICKER

3
DRONE

11
BOOMER

12
KANTUS

15
GRINDER

⯪ = Star Score

"FIRST TIME I WAS AT ONYX POINT,
MY TOUR GUIDE WAS DRUNK.
SO WAS I! EVEN BACK THEN,
THE PLACE HAD BAD SECURITY."

RIBBONS AND SCORING

The Silverback makes completing the mission with the Declassified option a relatively straightforward affair, so be sure to accept it for the faster Star accumulation. Use the Silverback exclusively during the mission for two Nice Suit ribbons. Use the Silverback's rockets whenever encountering a group of two or more enemies in order to earn Boombardier ribbons (the Silverback is outfitted with Boomshot-like rockets as a secondary weapon). Lastly, halt your advance as soon as the gate opens and fire several rockets into the distance beyond the large truck to earn one or more Hail Mary ribbons. There are plenty of opportunities to earn three Stars in this mission, provided you don't get knocked out of the Silverback far from your squadmates. Give the Ink Grenades a wide berth!

NICE SUIT: Kill 10 enemies with a Silverback.

BOOMBARDIER: Kill multiple enemies with a single Boomshot blast.

HAIL MARY: Boomshot kill from over 100 feet.

CLASSIFIED INTEL

Toss a Frag Grenade or two at the first few Drones and climb aboard the Silverback. Immediately set to gunning down the Drones to the right. A Boomer or Grinder emerges under the canopy in the center of the yard. Switch to the Silverback's rockets (press the A button) and blow it up.

Advance until the large gate opens. Then quickly return to rocket mode and fire several long-range rockets at the numerous Drones and Locust heavies in the distance. With any luck, you'll earn at least a Hail Mary ribbon or Boombardier ribbon. Switch your attention to the enemy bursting through the room on the right.

Cross the bridge on the right to slip through the building near the terminal's edge to get in a proper flanking position. Use the guns to eliminate the remaining Locust nearest the gate. Reload the rockets while still out of sight of the Boomers further ahead, then round the corner, switch to rockets, and let them have it. Continue to use the Silverback to wipe out the remaining Locust.

DECLASSIFIED: THREE-STAR TACTICS

DECLASSIFY

FINISH BEFORE ARTILLERY STRIKE HITS

Kilo Squad alleged they were fired upon by off-shore COG artillery.

Difficulty Increase: Low

Star Multiplier: 2.12x

Countdown to Artillery Strike

CASUAL	NORMAL	HARDCORE	INSANE
5:10	4:00	3:30	4:45

Accepting this Declassify option adds a timed element to the mission, but one with a considerable margin for error. The presence of the Silverback allows you to cut through the enemy forces with relative ease, provided you employ flanking maneuvers and make an effort to avoid direct hits from enemy Boomshots and Ink Grenades. Time should not be an issue, even if you have to abandon the Silverback at some point.

Mantle over the wall and ready a Frag Grenade. Baird spots the Silverback straight ahead just as a number of Drones sprint into cover from the left. Toss the Frag at the Drones near the small camp in the center of the yard to possibly snag a Clusterluck ribbon. Then hop into the Silverback and immediately open fire with its chainguns.

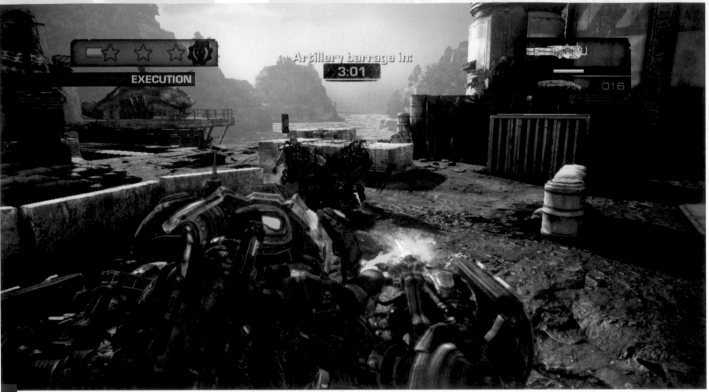

Hurry to the Silverback before your squad starts killing the Drones before you can.

Strafe to the right while firing the machine guns and clear out the Drones in this area. A lone Boomer or Grinder emerges under the netting in the center, so don't turn your back on this area just yet. Slowly advance until the gate is opened. Then quickly fire a pair of rockets at the enemies far off beyond the large military truck. With any luck, you'll snag a Boombardier and two Hail Mary ribbons!

Though you can certainly advance along the main road, it's safer to cross the bridge on the far right of this area and fight through the small building off to the side. This affords you a prime flanking opportunity. Watch for a Locust to blow open the wall, and then fire a pair of rockets into the room. Fire a third if the reticle is still red amidst the cloud of smoke and debris. Reload the rockets before moving on.

Switch to rockets once the gate opens and aim at the furthest targets you can spot.

Much of the action in this mission takes place beyond the large truck parked near the gate. Use the guns against any Drones or Tickers near the truck and advance just far enough to aim over the walls. Don't activate cover mode if any Kantuses or Tickers are around, as you will be a sitting duck for their Ink Grenades and suicide detonations, respectively.

Stick to the side of the road to avoid being caught in crossfire.

A Nice Suit ribbon is earned for every 10 enemies killed in the Silverback, so do your best to not let your squadmates steal any kills. Keep moving and use the rockets for any groups of Drones or Boomers; otherwise, stick to the machine guns. Try to keep at least partially behind cover, angling yourself in such a way that tall cover shields you from one side of the yard while you fire on the other. Half-walls offer some protection but you may have trouble aiming rockets over them in cover mode, especially if the enemies are at close range.

It's easier to arc rockets over cover the further away you are. Cover mode lowers your stance.

The final batch of Locust is back near the entrance to the motor pool. If you've already earned three Stars, play it safe. If not, get in front of the rest of Kilo Squad and get those kills. Watch out for Frag Grenades, and avoid the middle to ensure you don't get knocked out of the Silverback. Getting knocked out of the Silverback too many times or, even worse, allowing it to be destroyed certainly hinders your chance at earning three Stars, but it's still possible.

T. O'Neill, CW2, Andius

K.I.A. by sniper while trying to radio back to mainland for reinforcements.

The COG Tag is on the walkway on the right side of the terminal, just before you reach the mission end. Locate the Crimson Omen on the column and follow the smeared trail of blood into the distance to find the COG Tag.

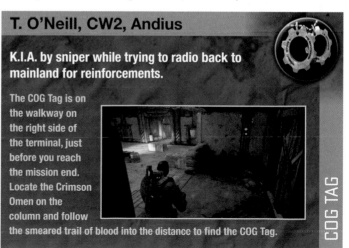

COG TAG

FRAG GRENADE

FRAG GRENADE

X

3

ONYX AMMO

2

COG TAGS

1

LONGSHOT

GNASHER

AMMO

BOOSHKA

LANCER

DECLASSIFY

FRAG GRENADE

MISSION OBJECTIVES

> Reach the interior of Onyx Point Fortress.

> Deal with the Locust outpost.

HOSTILES ENCOUNTERED

WRETCH	DRONE	THERON GUARD	BOOMER	GRINDER
3	3	8	11	15

☆ = Star Score

"WE MADE IT OUTTA THERE IN NO TIME. NOT SURE WHAT WOULDA HAPPENED IF WE DIDN'T, BUT WE DID. THE DOORS WERE UNLOCKED. WE HOPED THAT KEPT UP UNTIL WE FOUND THE MISSILE."

RIBBONS AND SCORING

The only chance to earn any ribbons is while playing without the Declassified option active. It's possible to earn three or more Hat Trick ribbons while using the Longshot, provided you don't take out too many enemies with the Booshka or other weapon. There are also several opportunities in which a well-tossed Frag Grenade can earn a Clusterluck ribbon. As for earning three Stars, you need only accept the Declassify option, follow the strategy outlined here, and avoid getting downed. You won't earn any ribbons, but there are enough enemies to earn three Stars as long as you suffer no DBNO penalties.

HAT TRICK: Score 3 headshots in a row without dying.

CLUSTERLUCK: Kill multiple enemies with one grenade.

CLASSIFIED INTEL

1

Equip the Longshot and Booshka and exit the garage. Take immediate cover and use the Longshot to snipe the Drones and Therons atop the hill in the distance. Take out the one manning the Troika first. Then follow the glow of the Therons' Torque Bows for subsequent targets. Continue sniping until out of ammo and blind-toss a Frag Grenade at any enemies that get too close.

2

Switch to the Booshka and advance up the hill, from cover to cover. Duck into the doorway on the right to find an Onyx Ammo Cache that fully replenishes your Longshot. Take cover against the taller rock outside the door and use the Booshka to eliminate any remaining Locust where the trail leads up the hill towards the Troika.

DECLASSIFIED: THREE-STAR TACTICS

3

Sprint around the corner and past the Troika to the tall cover on the left. The final group of Locust is holed up inside the flaming garage down the hill. The group may consist of Therons or a number of Drones. The Drones are more likely to charge your position. Use the Longshot to snipe as many as possible before the rest of Kilo Squad takes them out. Act fast and you can snag another Hat Trick ribbon.

DECLASSIFY

USE BOOMSHIELDS AND LANCERS ONLY

Kilo Squad made use of Locust shields, disobeying direct orders to avoid enemy equipment.

Difficulty Increase: Low

Star Multiplier: 3.92x

This option limits you to a Lancer and Boomshield, with no chance at even tossing a Frag Grenade. The Boomshield used in the Declassified option does not fall out of your hands, even if you are downed. You can melee with it, but cannot plant it in the ground for stationary cover. The Lancer is one of the better guns to wield with the Boomshield, but you are unable to use its chainsaw feature. All melee attacks are performed with the Boomshield.

Exit the starting area and immediately angle to the right and shoot the spike fortifications at the base of the stairs. Shoot the next set atop the stairs to reach the Onyx Ammo Cache, but don't grab it just yet. Kill as many enemies as possible from this flanking position while staying away from windows or doorways so you can't be shot back. Grab the Onyx Ammo Cache once you're ready to advance, and watch out for Grinders or Boomers. Hold the Boomshield out in front of you for maximum protection and continue a slow push up the hill.

Cut across the map to take cover by the far left corner, beyond the stone column. Sweep through the room with the Troika and continue your march on the garage in the distance. You won't earn any ribbons while playing the Declassified option, but you needn't worry about this provided you don't get downed. Slowly forge ahead towards the flaming garage at the bottom of the hill while continuing to shoot enemies. Try to down enemies when you can and, if possible, move in with the Boomshield for an execution bonus.

Shoot the spikes on the stairs and duck inside for a perfect flanking maneuver!

The Locust are no match for Cole's steady march forward!

Use the cover of this room for protection from the Therons up the hill while you clear the lower hill.

C. White, CPT, Halvo Bay

K.I.A. by Cleaver-bearing Theron Guards.

The COG Tag is on the grass directly above the Crimson Omen. Walk up the hill and around to the grass directly above the wall where the Crimson Omen is to find the COG Tag. It's tucked in the weeds on the left and can be hard to spot, but it's there!

COG TAG

SECTION 4: THE CLIFFS

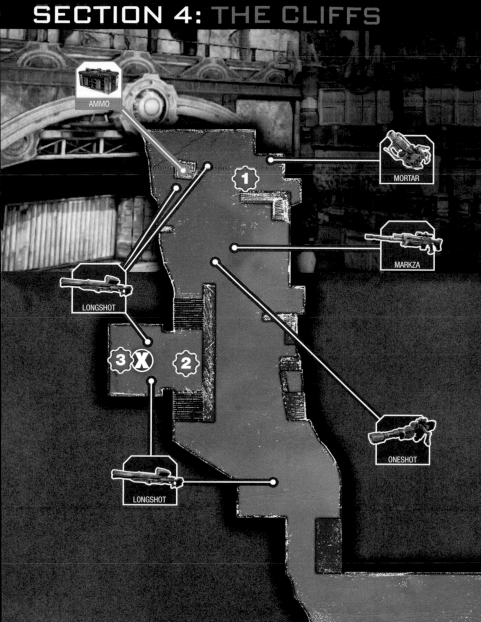

AMMO

MORTAR

MARKZA

LONGSHOT

① ③ Ⓧ ②

LONGSHOT

ONESHOT

DECLASSIFY

COG TAGS

MISSION OBJECTIVES

> Reach the interior of Onyx Point Fortress.

> Eliminate the Locust snipers.

HOSTILES ENCOUNTERED

DRONE

SNIPER

THERON GUARD

⭐ = Star Score

"WE DIDN'T SEE ANY OTHER GEARS. THAT'S THE PROBLEM WITH A TOP-SECRET BASE: REGULAR GEARS DON'T KNOW HOW TO FIND IT WHEN THERE'S TROUBLE."

RIBBONS AND SCORING

The ribbon you'll be earning on this mission depends entirely on whether you select the Declassified option or not. Those who forego the additional challenge are able to use the Longshot throughout the mission and accumulate a vast number of Hat Trick ribbons. On the other hand, those who opt for the Declassified option have to get their headshots with the scope-less Breechshot. Though far more challenging, this also allows you to earn the Once More Unto the Breech ribbon for every five consecutive kills with the Breechshot. It's possible to earn a Hat Trick ribbon with the Torque Bow, but you risk killing other enemies with splash damage. This, in turn, limits your ability to earn additional Hat Trick ribbons. Try using the Breechshot throughout the entire mission to maximize your ribbon tally and earn three Stars.

HAT TRICK: Score 3 headshots in a row without dying.

ONCE MORE UNTO THE BREECH: Kill 5 enemies in a row with the Breechshot without dying.

CLASSIFIED INTEL

1

2

3

Gather all of the Longshot ammo you can carry and duck into cover in the far left corner, nearest the cliff. Man the Mortar and begin canvassing the opposing cliff with Mortar fire. Let the OneShot targeting lasers be your guide if you're unsure of the Locust's positions.

Take cover on the raised platform in the center near the elevator and start sniping. Aim to target the enemies with OneShots first, and then move on to the Theron Guards. The glow of their Torque Bows tells you where to aim, but this is a blessing and a curse: a direct hit from a taut Torque Bow downs you on Hardcore mode, and likely kills you on Insane. The Locust manning the Troikas are an easy target and pose little threat at this range. Keep on sniping until there are no more enemies.

Use a Frag Grenade or other weapon to kill the two Drones descending on the elevator. No additional Locust attack until you press the button on the lift, so gather as much ammo as you can carry. Continue sniping as many Locust as possible during the slow elevator ride up the side of the cliff. Consider standing slightly behind the rest of Kilo Squad and move side to side to avoid incoming Torque Bow and OneShot projectiles.

DECLASSIFIED: THREE-STAR TACTICS

H. Molnar, SGT, Ephyra

K.I.A. while trying to set a grenade trap.

Exit the garage and immediately head up the steps on the left to find the COG Tag. The Crimson Omen is near the corner of the building, past this small landing, but the COG Tag is right here. This is a rare COG Tag that is hidden before you can even spot the Crimson Omen.

COG TAG

DECLASSIFY

USE TORQUE BOWS AND BREECHSHOTS ONLY

Kilo Squad admitted to using Theron Guard weaponry, despite explicit battlefield orders not to.

Difficulty Increase: Low

Star Multiplier: 1.96x

It may sound difficult to engage in a sniping duel across a canyon without a scoped weapon, but it's actually easier than it sounds. The Breechshot is a terrific weapon at range, thanks to its precision aiming and the red glow of the targeting reticle. Aim high on an enemy, watch for the reticle to turn red, and then squeeze the trigger. You won't always kill the enemy with a perfect headshot, but it only takes two or three clean hits to drop a Locust even on the hardest settings. You can replenish the Breechshot at the large pile of ammo to the left.

Move onto the cliffs, where Cole recognizes an elevator that should lead up to the base. The elevator is currently up top, and the only way to get it to descend is to lure some Locust down on it. First, fend off an onslaught of Drones and Therons armed with Longshots, OneShots, Torque Bows, and even a Troika. They're across the chasm on an opposing cliff, so you're entirely reliant on sniping.

The ammo cache in the distance replenishes your Breechshot ammo, but you have to make do with the Torque Bow ammo that you have from the start. We recommend only using the Torque Bow in a pinch, so this limitation shouldn't factor into the outcome (though the Torque Bow does a great job of detonating the fuel barrels scattered around the enemy cliff).

The Breechshot is quite powerful, particularly with a perfect active reload. Reload every chance you get, whenever there's a lull in the action or you're trying to spot your next target. Don't pull the trigger unless the reticle is red, and use the sniper trails, Torque Bow glow, and OneShot lasers to pinpoint your targets. Always aim for the head, even if you can't completely make it out in the distance.

It's possible to accumulate a number of Hat Trick ribbons with the Breechshot. Watch the locations of enemies, position the reticle ever so slightly above the railing or cover they're ducking behind, and then pull the trigger as soon as they raise their heads. Use the barrels to detonate nearby enemies, and always take out the enemies with OneShots and the Torque Bow first.

Always keep your head down when reloading—you never know when a Torque Bow is going to detonate.

Keep the gun aimed just above cover and wait for the enemy to stand up.

143

It should be possible to get at least one Hat Trick and one or two Once More Unto the Breech ribbons before the elevator starts to descend. Move off the raised platform near the elevator for a better angle and work fast to headshot the two enemies on the lift before your squad fires a Torque Bow and steals your kill. Return to the ammo cache and collect some additional ammo before boarding the lift.

Let the glow of the Torque Bows and OneShot lasers guide you to the enemy.

Track how many headshots or kills you have and try to get another Hat Trick or Once More Unto the Breech ribbon before switching to the Torque Bow if you feel so inclined. It's not easy, but you can get to three Stars without even using the Torque Bow. You can do it with the Torque Bow as well, but it's going to require some very good shooting. The mission ends once the elevator reaches the top, but don't discount the threat the Locust pose while you're on the lift. You're far more exposed during the ride up the side of the cliffs than before. Strafe back and forth to avoid being shot and try to stay at least partially behind your squadmates for cover.

Consider switching to the Torque Bow once the elevator is halfway to the top.

SECTION 5: CENTRAL BASE

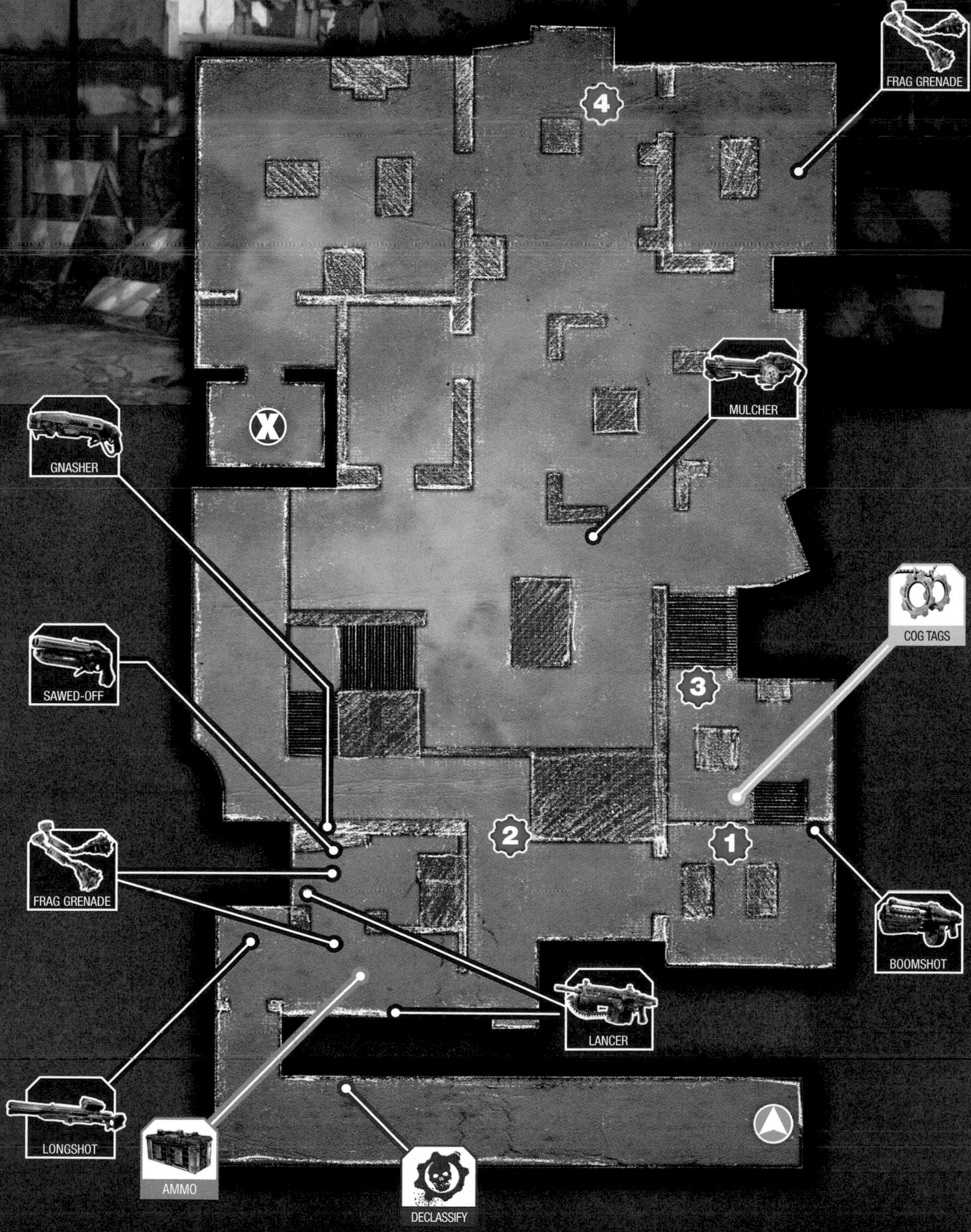

FRAG GRENADE

4

MULCHER

GNASHER

X

COG TAGS

SAWED-OFF

3

FRAG GRENADE

2

1

BOOMSHOT

LANCER

LONGSHOT

AMMO

DECLASSIFY

MISSION OBJECTIVES

> Find and arm the Lightmass Missile.

HOSTILES ENCOUNTERED

2	3	8	11	15
TICKER	DRONE	THERON W/ CLEAVER	BOOMER	GRINDER

☆ = Star Score

"WE COULDN'T BELIEVE HOW MANY GRUBS WERE IN THE FORT WAITING FOR US. WHAT IF THEY'D ALREADY FOUND THE LIGHTMASS MISSILE?"

RIBBONS AND SCORING

Those playing without the Declassified option are in a much better position to earn a Hat Trick ribbon, but that's likely to be the only difference in terms of ribbons. The presence of ample Frag Grenades, a Boomshot, and the Sawed-Off Shotgun makes earning Clusterluck and Boombardier ribbons relatively common. Though there's never a guarantee that you'll earn a Nothin' But Bits ribbon, you're not any more or less likely to depending on the Declassify conditions. The presence of so many Therons makes this mission conducive for scoring a lot of points very quickly. In fact, it's not uncommon to earn your third Star well before approaching the final group of enemies, as long as you avoid being downed for long.

HAT TRICK: Score 3 headshots in a row without dying.

CLUSTERLUCK: Kill multiple enemies with one grenade.

NOTHIN' BUT BITS: Kill multiple enemies with a single Sawed-Off Shotgun blast.

BOOMBARDIER: Kill multiple enemies with a single Boomshot blast.

CLASSIFIED INTEL

1 Equip the Longshot, Sawed-Off Shotgun, and all the Frag Grenades you can carry before heading outside. Immediately sprint across the deck to the right and plant a Frag Grenade near the stairs leading down from the Boomshot, and then plant another closer to the entrance from the deck. Plant yet another Frag on the left side of the deck to cover your blindside.

2 Take cover on the center of the decking and use the Longshot to snipe as many enemies as you can, focusing on the Kantuses and Boomers when possible. Toss any remaining Frag Grenades at any bunches of enemies that appear. Keep your ears open for the sounds of a Cleaver being swung or of a Lancer's chainsaw, as this is your cue that there's a Theron at close range—your planted Frags won't last forever. Immediately switch to the Sawed-Off Shotgun and blast any enemies on the deck.

3 Continue sniping for as long as the Longshot ammo lasts. Then swap the exhausted weapon for the Boomshot off to the right. Descend the stairs and use the Boomshot to clear a path directly across the paved area to the building in the back-right corner. Switch to the Sawed-Off Shotgun as you get close to the Frag Grenades and hold off the remaining Locust from within this structure.

4 Multiple enemies pour out of the left corner building, but two Boomers likely remain inside. They guard the elevator you need to access. Hang back until all the other enemies are killed and then use the Frags and Sawed-Off Shotgun to eliminate the heavyweights inside.

DECLASSIFIED: THREE-STAR TACTICS

STRONG WIND AFFECTS MOVEMENT

Pvt. Cole claimed that adverse weather conditions affected Kilo Squad's combat efficiency.

Difficulty Increase: Moderate

Star Multiplier: 3.24x

Adverse weather conditions may not sound like much, but that's just Private Cole's way of understating the situation. Kilo Squad doesn't just have to deal with high winds, but fog and snow as well. Though you can take cover on the upwind side of heavy objects and walls to keep from being blown across the map, there isn't anything you can do about the poor visibility. The Longshot is all but useless in these conditions, so opt for the Lancer and the Sawed-Off Shotgun instead.

Sprint across the deck to the building on the right and wait for the first two Therons to rush in. Toss a Frag at their feet and then double-back the way you came to assist the rest of Kilo Squad on the deck. Use the Lancer's chainsaw whenever possible to gain an execution bonus. Put down as many enemies as possible from the center of the deck before swapping the Lancer out for the Boomshot, but keep the Sawed-Off Shotgun on hand. Enemies can get the drop on you in the limited visibility and you don't want to fire the Boomshot at close range in a moment of panic.

B. Newman, PFC, Port Caval

K.I.A. during Ink Grenade attack, suffocated.

The COG Tag is in the building across the deck to the right, at the base of the steps near the Boomshot. The Crimson Omen is on the wall not far from the Boomshot, but the COG Tag is on the floor, to the right of the stairs when facing the Crimson Omen.

COG TAG

Work your way from cover to cover and try to keep on the upwind side—the wind largely blows from the right—of cover as you move from the building with the Boomshot to the one with the Frags. Visibility is much better while looking out from the building with the Frags towards the one in the back-left corner, where the enemies are coming. Plant a Frag or two near the entrance and fire a Boomshot at any groups that appear.

▶ Use the available cover and the power weapons to fight your way to the shed with the Frag Grenades.

Reload the Sawed-Off whenever possible so you always have two shells ready to fire. Cautiously approach the final building, where the elevator to Central Control is located. Two Boomers hunker down inside, standing guard over the elevator. Kill all other Locust before heading inside. Resist the urge to blind-toss a Frag Grenade through the windows at the Boomers. The windows are very narrow and unusually shaped. Blind-throwing a Frag is highly risky, as it's very likely to bounce back towards your feet.

▶ Plant some Frag Grenades to either side of the deck and try to absorb the initial rush of enemies from up top.

▶ Take shelter from the elements in the building with the Frags and draw the Locust to their death.

Use the Boomshot or your Sawed-Off Shotgun to take the Boomers out. If timed right, and the two Boomers are standing close enough, you just might earn a Nothin' But Bits ribbon. Board the lift to complete the mission.

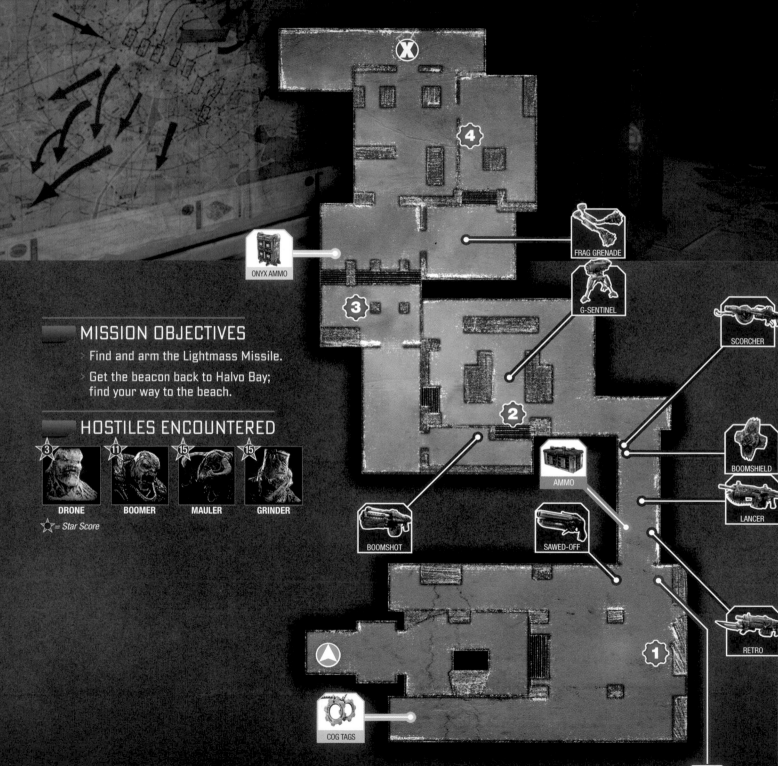

MISSION OBJECTIVES

> Find and arm the Lightmass Missile.

> Get the beacon back to Halvo Bay; find your way to the beach.

HOSTILES ENCOUNTERED

DRONE	BOOMER	MAULER	GRINDER
3	11	15	15

☆ = Star Score

ONYX AMMO

FRAG GRENADE

G-SENTINEL

SCORCHER

BOOMSHIELD

LANCER

AMMO

BOOMSHOT

SAWED-OFF

RETRO

COG TAGS

DECLASSIFY

RIBBONS AND SCORING

Despite this mission's short length, it's possible to earn a number of ribbons regardless of classification. Take advantage of the Drones that attack early and earn a Flamebroiled ribbon before the heavy units start to attack. The Boomshot and Frag Grenades combine well with the tight confines of this area to make earning a Boombardier or Clusterluck ribbon a sure thing. As long as you avoid being downed, it's possible to earn three Stars with just two or three ribbons. It will likely come down to the final group of enemies. Wait for them to bunch together before using your explosives, unless it looks as if the other members of Kilo Squad are moving in with their chainsaws.

FLAMEBROILED: Kill 3 enemies in a row with the Scorcher.

CLUSTERLUCK: Kill multiple enemies with one grenade.

BOOMBARDIER: Kill multiple enemies with a single Boomshot blast.

CLASSIFIED INTEL

Cross the floor of the Central Base to the computer terminals overlooking the Lightmass Missile. Press the button to check the comms. Baird takes it from there. Exit the room via the door on the left when the time comes, but make sure to get the COG Tag first.

Use the Boomshield and the Scorcher to push across the first room, where the initial wave of Drones attacks. Get at least two kills with the Scorcher, ignore the Gnasher Sentinel in the center, and cut across to the left to get the Boomshot on the walkway. Keep using the Scorcher and Boomshield combo until earning a Flamebroiled ribbon.

Switch to the Boomshot and clear the room ahead of Drones and whichever heavy attacks, either a Mauler or Boomer. Pick up the Onyx Ammo Cache to the left to replenish your Scorcher and Boomshot reserves. Take advantage of any Boombardier opportunities in the room to the left.

Never walk through the center of a room when you can move along the perimeter! Grab the Frag Grenades and proceed along the elevated walkway on the right. Use the Frags and Boomshot to clear out the remaining Locust before exiting through the door to the beach.

L. Zhang, 2LT, Jacinto

K.I.A. after ordering a retreat back to Central Base.

The Crimson Omen is nowhere to be seen, but you can find the COG Tag in the room with the missile controls, just steps from where you exit the lift. Enter the missile control room, turn to the right, and head up the steps on the right side. Follow the walkway all the way back towards the lift to find the COG Tag. You can do this before approaching the control terminal.

COG TAG

Kilo Squad exits the lift in a room refreshingly devoid of Locust. Collect the COG Tag around the corner to the right, and then approach the computer terminal in the distance. Press the button to activate the radios. After a few tense moments, the decision is made to return to the beach in order to try and rescue Omega Squad.

A decision has been made…

The lack of lights and slower health regeneration make it necessary to play this mission with some sense of caution when accepting the Declassified option. Though it's still not necessary to use the Gnasher Sentinel, those playing on Insane difficulty should do so. But don't leave it in the first room; carry it with you and set it up perpendicular to the direction the enemy will be coming from.

Those playing on Hardcore and below aren't likely to need the Gnasher Sentinel's assistance. Instead, grab the Scorcher and follow the left wall around to the stairs, where you can take cover overlooking the room where the first Locust appear. Toss a Frag Grenade at the first group of Drones to earn a Clusterluck ribbon and use the Scorcher on any that approach individually. Collect the Boomshot atop the steps on the left but continue using the Scorcher in an effort to earn a Flamebroiled ribbon.

DECLASSIFY

HEALTH REGENERATION SLOWED AND LIGHTS ARE OUT

Pvt. Cole claimed that Kilo Squad fought in darkness while alleged chemical spill adversely affected squad ability to recuperate from injury.

Difficulty Increase: Moderate

Star Multiplier: 2.68x

The lack of visibility isn't too much of an issue since the area is rather compact and you'll be relying on close- to medium-range weaponry anyway. The diminished healing ability is, however, a much more serious challenge. It shouldn't change your overall strategy, but you do need to be careful. Be aware of any and all damage you take and immediately find cover. Though we don't recommend using the Boomshield in this situation because of its interference with throwing grenades and weapon swapping, do consider using it if the slower health regeneration proves problematic.

Can't tell if they're friend or foe? Light 'em up!

The Scorcher works well against shielded enemies like the Mauler, so try to save some fuel for it when it approaches. Otherwise, wait for it to draw near other Locust and use the Boomshot or Frag Grenade for another multi-kill ribbon.

Don't fire the Boomshot if the Mauler gets in too close; switch to the Scorcher.

Stay to the left, clear the area immediately beyond this doorway, and mantle over the cover on the left to get the Onyx Ammo Cache. Immediately sprint all the way to the right to get the Frag Grenades in the next room. This sets you up nicely to advance along a slightly elevated walkway and flank the final gang of Locust. Toss the Frag Grenades over the railing at the Drones and heavy Locust unit in the room below. Keep your head down and blast them as they try to fend off the rest of Kilo Squad moving in on the lower level.

Lob Frag Grenades over the walkway's railing for a mission-ending Clusterluck!

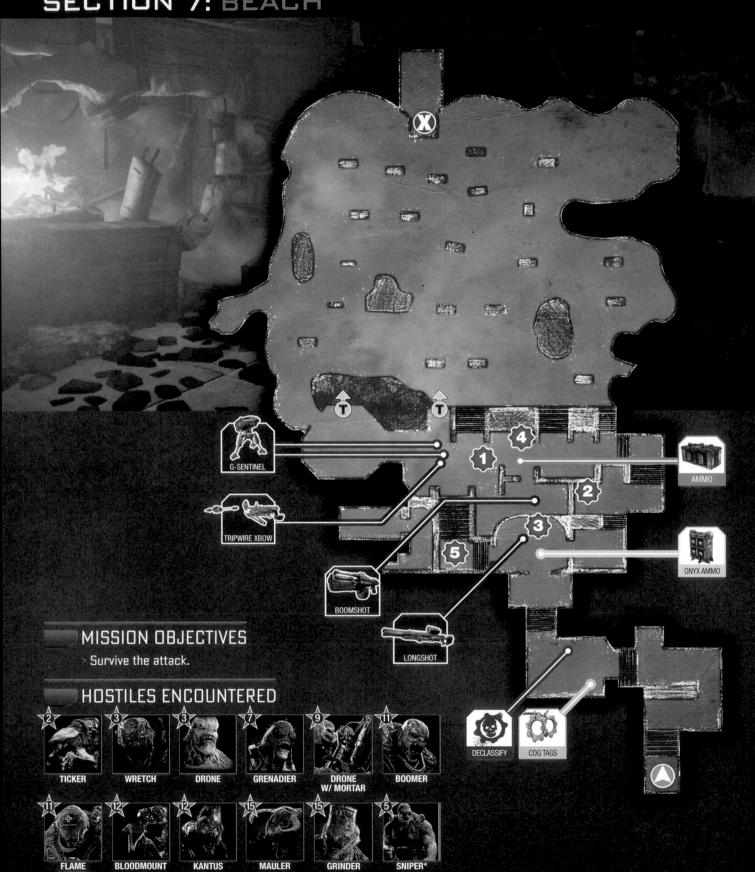

G-SENTINEL

TRIPWIRE XBOW

AMMO

ONYX AMMO

BOOMSHOT

LONGSHOT

DECLASSIFY

COG TAGS

MISSION OBJECTIVES

> Survive the attack.

HOSTILES ENCOUNTERED

2 TICKER	**3** WRETCH	**3** DRONE	**7** GRENADIER	**9** DRONE W/ MORTAR	**11** BOOMER
11 FLAME BOOMER	**12** BLOODMOUNT	**12** KANTUS	**15** MAULER	**15** GRINDER	**5** SNIPER*

"THE DOOR WAS THE ONLY WAY BACK TO THE MISSILE LAB. AND NOW IT WAS SHUT UP TIGHT. IT WAS TIME TO GET BACK TO THE BEACH."

RIBBONS AND SCORING

There are seemingly countless ways to earn ribbons during this mission thanks to the length of the fight and the variety of weapons at your disposal. The accompanying list mentions the ones you're most likely to obtain following the tactics detailed here, but earning a Flamebroiled, Shish-Kashot, or Lumberjack ribbon isn't out of the ordinary. Suffice to say, earning three Stars on this mission is all but certain provided you don't get killed by a OneShot. Take advantage of your elevated position, the overhead cover afforded by the upper bunker, and the long-range weapons at your disposal. At the very least, you shouldn't have much trouble earning multiple Hail Mary and Clusterluck ribbons. Good luck!

HAT TRICK: Score 3 headshots in a row without dying.

IT'S A TRAP: Kill multiple enemies with a single Tripwire Crossbow shot.

CLUSTERLUCK: Kill multiple enemies with one grenade.

BOOMBARDIER: Kill multiple enemies with a single Boomshot blast.

HAIL MARY: Boomshot kill from over 100 feet.

CLASSIFIED INTEL

Exit the base and immediately pick up the Boomshot just outside the door. The bot detects an incoming Locust attack and you have 1:30 to prepare for it! Tuck one of the Gnasher Sentinels into the corner facing the stairs coming up from the beach, and position the other in the very center of the lower platform facing the ammo crate. Use the Tripwire Crossbow to set traps on each set of stairs coming from the beach.

Get the Longshot in the upstairs bunker, but leave the Onyx Ammo Cache for later. Descend the right-hand steps to where the third Troika used to be and get ready to snipe. The Locust arrive in three waves aboard their very own landing craft. Snipe as many as possible while they're far away. This first wave consists primarily of Drones, Wretches, and Boomers. Let your traps and Gnasher Sentinels take care of the Locust that make it up the beach. Save your Boomshot ammo for the next wave.

You have just 0:30 to prepare for the second wave. Gather any Frag Grenades you can find and plant them along each of the stairs leading up from the beach. Use the remainder of your Longshot ammo, and then use the Boomshot from that same position to earn a Hail Mary ribbon. Keep this up until you hear Mortar fire. Run to the Onyx Ammo Cache, replenish your ammo reserves, and finish this wave from the safety of the upper bunker. Pay close attention to where the Drone with the Mortar is when he dies.

There's another short break before the third wave. Sprint onto the beach to pick up the Mortar and carry it back to the lower platform, near your Gnasher Sentinels. Plant any grenades you have on the stairs and near the cave off to the left, and get ready for the Locust. Fire the Mortar as far as it will go as soon as you see the Locust craft start to deploy their troops. This wave usually consists of numerous Bloodmounts that can get up the beach in a hurry!

Finish off the visible Locust, reload the surviving Gnasher Sentinels, and head up the stairs to the right of the upper bunker. You should still have plenty of Longshot or Boomshot ammo. The remaining Locust likely target the other members of Kilo Squad below you. Stand your ground on the corner of the stairs and gun them down with your remaining ammo. If forced to scavenge for weapons, be sure to grab a Boomshield for protection. Board the Locust boat once the beach is cleared of Locust.

DECLASSIFIED: THREE-STAR TACTICS

S. Garooon, 2LT, Soteroa

K.I.A. after successfully locking down elevator to Onyx Point's main armory.

Follow the path as it curves around from the start to the staircase near the small fire. Climb the stairs and immediately turn left to find the COG Tag. If you reach the Crimson Omen, you've gone too far.

COG TAG

LOCUST USE ONESHOTS

Pvt. Cole claimed to have defended Onyx Point beach against OneShot-wielding Locust.

Difficulty Increase: High

Star Multiplier: 2.35x

The addition of OneShot-wielding Locust makes this battle considerably more difficult. Their presence forces you to manage your Longshot ammo more carefully and deal with them first. This allows the other Locust to advance further up the beach and close on your position before being targeted. The risk of being hit by a OneShot is quite substantial, especially on the harder modes, and you must respect their presence. Crouch out of sight between shots and try to use taller cover whenever possible.

Exit the base interior, pick up the Boomshot, and immediately approach the two Gnasher Sentinels on the left. You have 1:30 to set up for the first of three waves of Locust assaults on the beach. Just as you fought your way up the beach at the start of Cole's testimony, so too will the Locust.

Tuck the two Gnasher Sentinels into the center of the fortress's lower level, facing the main stairs leading down to the beach, and beside the stairs leading up to the bunker. This keeps them out of the direct path of enemies. Use the Tripwire Crossbow to set traps along the stairs leading up from the beach. You may want to save the Tripwire Crossbow until prior to the second or third wave, but you have much less time between subsequent waves so we recommend using the Tripwire Crossbow before the first wave. You can scavenge Frag Grenades for use before the other waves.

Set up two Tripwires on the main stairs, and then one each on the two other sets of steps leading down to the beach.

Pick up the blue ammo crate if you're carrying a Lancer and then swap it out for the Longshot in the upper bunker. Leave the Lancer on the ground near the Onyx Ammo Cache so you can return to it later if necessary. Start the battle armed with the Boomshot and Longshot.

Take position down the right-hand stairs from the upper bunker and start sniping as soon as the enemies exit their landing craft. The first wave typically consists of Drones, Boomers, Grinders, and Wretches. Target any Snipers with a OneShot first, and then scan the area to make sure there aren't any Kantuses. Try to make it through this first wave relying entirely on your Longshot.

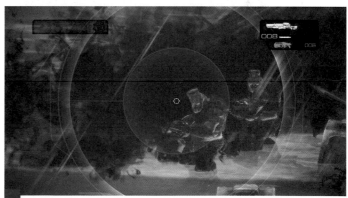

Snipe any heavy units that appear when the wave begins, and then scan for OneShot and Mortar units.

You have just 0:30 before the second wave arrives. Quickly scavenge the area for Frag Grenades and Boomshots. Plant Frag Grenades on the stairs leading up from the beach and grab a OneShot if one is close by. The Gnasher Sentinels reload automatically between waves.

The second wave likely contains a Drone with a Mortar. Use the OneShot (if you have it) from the middle platform and then switch to your Boomshot as soon as it's out so you can snag some Hail Mary ribbons and fend off the Maulers and Boomers before they get too far up the beach. If you don't have a OneShot, return to where you were sniping during the first wave and use the rest of your Boomshot and Longshot ammo as soon as the wave begins. Return to the upper bunker once you hear the sounds of a Mortar and grab the Onyx Ammo Cache. Snipe the Mortar unit on the beach, but try to leave one other enemy standing so you can work your way onto the beach before the intermission begins. This gives you enough time to grab the Mortar and carry it back to the fortress deck before the third wave starts.

Use the Mortar to bombard the Locust as soon as they emerge from their landing craft.

Fire the Boomshot into a crowd of Drones for a Hail Mary bonus!

The third wave is far longer and contains numerous Bloodmounts. Use the Mortar to take out the initial fray. Then fire your Boomshots for more Hail Mary ribbons. Look around for fallen grenades and place them on the steps leading up to the bunker to cover your blindside as you return up the stairs to resume sniping duties. Watch for additional Mortars and OneShot units on the beach. Always aim to target the OneShots first, especially if you're under overhead cover.

Snipe the Mortar unit and then send a partner to fire the Mortar back at the fortress for a surprise attack!

There is a brief lull, and then a second assault within this wave commences. Make sure your Gnasher Sentinels are loaded and let the squad take the brunt of the enemy attack on the middle platform while you fire down from above. Focus on sniping the Kantuses while they scream, turn white, and resurrect their downed comrades.

If playing with a partner, send one member of your party onto the beach to claim one of the abandoned Mortars or OneShots and fire it back at the fortress while the rest draw the Locust's attention. Don't worry about harming your friends with the Mortar fire, as there's no friendly fire. Another advanced tactic to try, if you have the time, is to place Boomshields near the stairs and plant Ink Grenades near them to snare the slowed Locust in the toxic cloud.

Plant an Ink Grenade and Boomshield next to one another atop the stairs to give the Locust a nice slow death.

With the Locust dead, it's time to leave the beach for good. Make your way to the water and board the Locust craft marked on-screen.

DOWNTOWN HALVO BAY

BAIRD'S TESTIMONY

SECTION 1: WHARF DISTRICT

"THE LIGHTMASS MISSILE WAS READY TO LAUNCH. WE NEEDED TO FIND KARN, GET THE BEACON CLOSE TO HIM, AND FIRE. AND WHERE WAS KARN? WELL, OMEGA KNOCKED OUT HIS SEEDERS AT THE MUSEUM. I FIGURE HE'D WANT TO DEAL WITH THAT PERSONALLY."

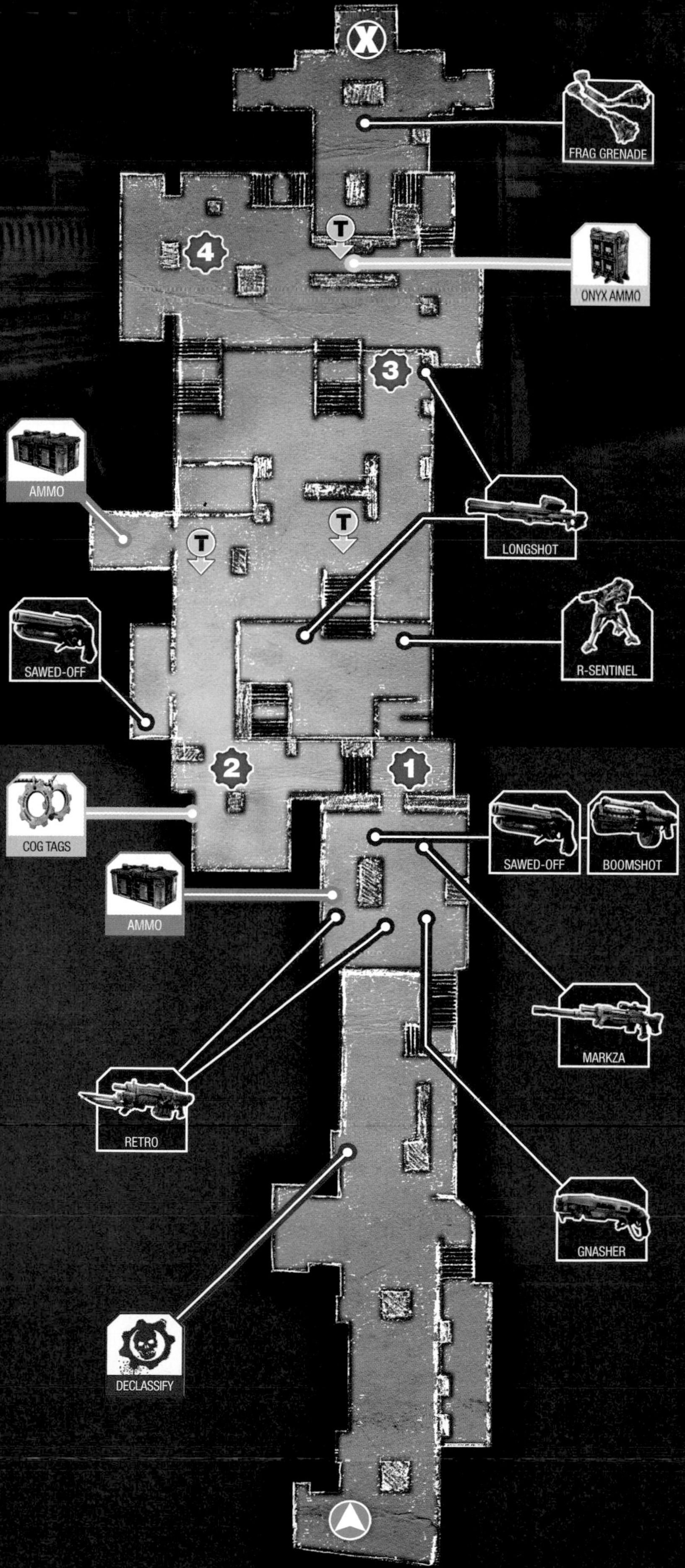

FRAG GRENADE

ONYX AMMO

AMMO

LONGSHOT

SAWED-OFF

R-SENTINEL

COG TAGS

AMMO

SAWED-OFF **BOOMSHOT**

MARKZA

RETRO

GNASHER

DECLASSIFY

MISSION OBJECTIVES

> Get to the museum.
> Make your way through the wharf.

HOSTILES ENCOUNTERED

DRONE

SNIPER

FLAME BOOMER

DRONE W/ MORTAR

BOOMER

MAULER

GRINDER

☆ = Star Score

RIBBONS AND SCORING

Any ribbons you earn in this mission are going to come from sniping and skilled use of the Boomshot, should you get it instead of the Sawed-Off Shotgun. It's best to tackle enemies from afar in this mission. Approaching them at close range usually forces you to cede the elevated advantage to the Locust. Instead, use the Markza, Longshot, and Boomshot to attack across the trenches for Hat Trick and Boombardier ribbons. You may even get a Hail Mary ribbon if you fire at an angle across the wharf. Use the Range Sentinel for protection while you snipe to avoid being downed. Stay on your feet and earn at least two ribbons (and several other headshot bonuses) to earn three Stars.

HAT TRICK: Score 3 headshots in a row without dying.

CLUSTERLUCK: Kill multiple enemies with one grenade.

NOTHIN' BUT BITS: Kill multiple enemies with a single Sawed-Off Shotgun blast.

HAIL MARY: Boomshot kill from over 100 feet.

CLASSIFIED INTEL

Equip the Boomshot and Markza and kick open the gate. Immediately drop into cover against the wall in front of the gate and attack the Locust across the trench. Use the Markza against the lone Drones, but look for an opportunity to lob a Boomshot rocket for a Boombardier ribbon.

Move to the left, past the stairs, and into cover at the corner. Multiple Boomers emerge from the small room ahead, to the left. Use the Boomshot to put them down. Then rush ahead and collect their dropped weapons to replenish your own. Grab the COG Tag behind you before advancing.

Descend the stairs into the trench. Ignore the Longshot here and pick up the Range Sentinel. Carry the Range Sentinel up the stairs and over to the Longshot leaning against the railing. Set it down under the roof—there's a Mortar unit ahead—and temporarily swap out the Markza for the Longshot. Take cover against the column and start sniping the enemies with OneShots and Mortars in the distance. The Range Sentinel does a fine job as your personal bodyguard while you snipe.

Pick up the Markza and carry the Range Sentinel down the stairs to the far left side. Set it between the two pieces of tall cover, on an angle facing the stairs to where the Mortar units were. Grab the Onyx Ammo Cache. Then fall back into cover and take care of the Drones as they try to fend off the Range Sentinel's steady fire.

DECLASSIFIED: THREE-STAR TACTICS

DECLASSIFY

EXTRA LOCUST RESISTANCE IN THE AREA

Kilo Squad claimed to overcome a number of coordinated Locust defensive positions.

Difficulty Increase: Moderate

Star Multiplier: 2.30x

Accepting this additional challenge adds numerous spiked fortifications to the map as well as three enemy Troikas and additional Locust forces. You're far more likely to encounter Grinders and Maulers when playing the Declassified option. The rest of Kilo Squad does a fine job of using their Lancers to destroy the fortifications, but you may want to lend a hand with a Sawed-Off Shotgun if the Boomshot isn't present.

Collect the Markza and either the Boomshot or Sawed-Off Shotgun (they rotate randomly). The Sawed-Off Shotgun is excellent for blasting away the spiked fortifications. Kick open the gate and immediately duck into cover against the wall and start sniping with the Markza. Move far to the right to get a slight angle on the Locust manning the Troika in the opposite corner. Maintain this position, wait for the Locust to bunch up, and launch a Boomshot rocket into the crowd for multiple Hail Mary and Boombardier ribbons.

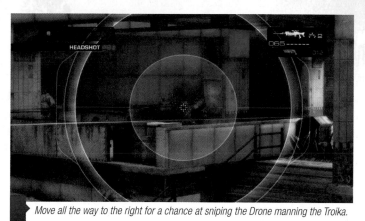

Move all the way to the right for a chance at sniping the Drone manning the Troika.

Continue to snipe as many enemies as possible with the Markza until it seems that no more are coming. Head left and duck behind cover in time for a Mauler or Grinder to emerge at close range. Toss a Frag or use your Boomshot to kill it and any additional Locust in the distance, near the Troika. Eliminate any remaining floor spikes and commandeer the Troika. Open fire on any remaining Locust off to the right, near the other Troika.

D. Yalovsky, SPC, Halvo Bay

K.I.A. from enemy fire while attempting to prevent a civilian from falling into an Emergence Hole.

The COG Tag is on the floor at the turn to the right, but in the shadows to the left of the Crimson Omen. Notice the Crimson Omen on the wall as you approach. Look on the floor beneath the bulletin board to find the COG Tag.

COG TAG

Hurry to the Troika in the corner and put it to use against the remaining Drones near the other turret.

Descend the stairs into the trench you just skirted and locate the Range Sentinel to the right. Carry it to the area between the second Troika and the Longshot leaning against the railing. Position the Range Sentinel here and swap the Markza for the Longshot. Take cover against the column, making sure to stay under the protective roof. In addition to a third Troika, the Locust's final line of defense also contains several Mortar units and Snipers armed with OneShots. Some additional Drones charge your position but the Range Sentinel takes care of them.

Target the OneShot units first, and then any Drones manning the Troika. The Mortar units keep their heads down and are very hard to see. If you look for the mortar tube and pan the Longshot's reticle just above the tile of the ledge they're behind, you should see the reticle turn red. This is their head. Fire to headshot them, and then search for more OneShots or a second Mortar unit.

The Range Sentinel watches your back while you snipe the Mortar units in the distance.

Swap back to the Markza, grab the Range Sentinel, and loop around to the left to assist the squad with the final push up the stairs. Don't attack the remaining Locust head-on; come at them from the left side instead. There are several spikes on the floor here and the squad likely bursts through them with grenades or Lancer fire, but you may need to help. Place the Range Sentinel near the base of the stairs and then grab the Onyx Ammo Cache. Much of the action takes place to the left of the stairs, leaving you with a perfect flanking opportunity to the right. Lob a Frag Grenade onto the landing for a Clusterluck attempt and look for isolated Drones to gun down from the right.

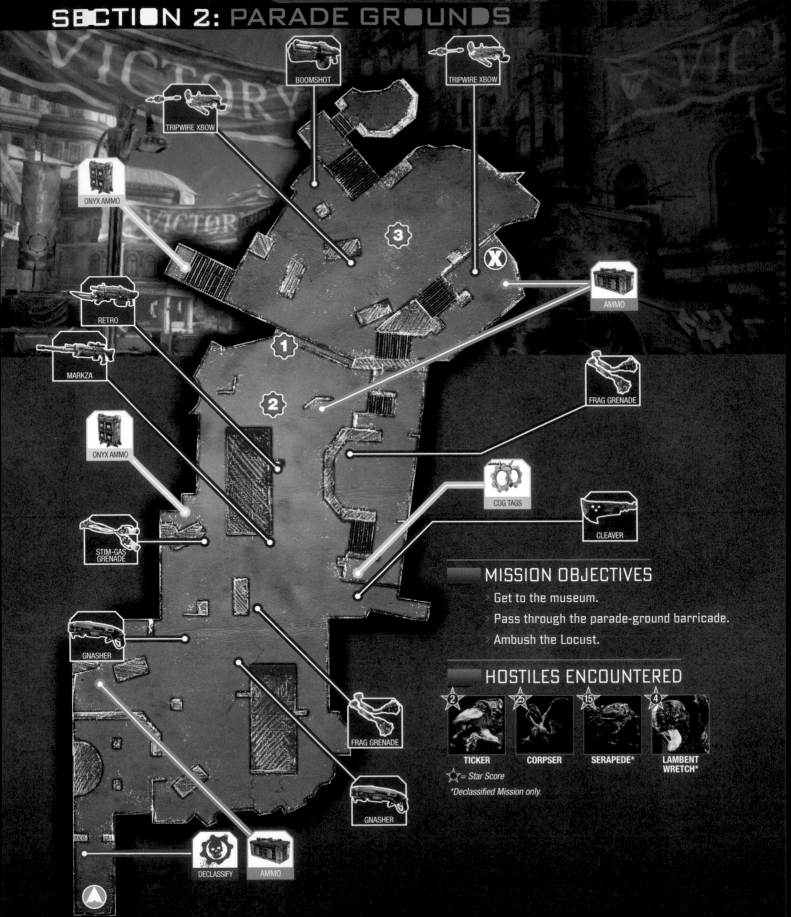

TRIPWIRE XBOW

BOOMSHOT

TRIPWIRE XBOW

ONYX AMMO

③

AMMO

RETRO

①

②

FRAG GRENADE

MARKZA

ONYX AMMO

COG TAGS

CLEAVER

STIM-GAS GRENADE

MISSION OBJECTIVES

> Get to the museum.

> Pass through the parade-ground barricade.

> Ambush the Locust.

GNASHER

HOSTILES ENCOUNTERED

FRAG GRENADE

⭐2	⭐25	⭐15	⭐4
TICKER	CORPSER	SERAPEDE*	LAMBENT WRETCH*

⭐ = Star Score

*Declassified Mission only.

GNASHER

DECLASSIFY

AMMO

"COLONEL LOOMIS, KARN HAD ALREADY WIPED OUT SEVERAL ONYX COMPANIES. DID YOU REALLY THINK YOU HAD THINGS UNDER CONTROL? THESE GRUBS ARE SMARTER THAN WE THINK."

RIBBONS AND SCORING

Of all the missions in the game, this is the most conducive for earning three Stars *without* accepting the Declassified conditions. Simply use the Gnasher and focus your attention on kicking the Tickers that attack. Shoot as many as you can out of the air for a string of Oakley ribbons. Ignore the Corpser and continue kicking the Tickers for the And the Kick is Up! ribbon. The Stars don't accumulate much faster with the Declassified option (only 7% faster) but the addition of a Serapede and numerous Lambent Wretches helps you earn even more points. Use your Frag Grenades to earn a Clusterluck ribbon. Otherwise, just keep firing that Lancer.

OAKLEY: **Kick a ticker and shoot it in the air.**

AND THE KICK IS UP!: **Kick 5 small enemies.**

CLUSTERLUCK: **Kill multiple enemies with one grenade.**

CLASSIFIED INTEL

Load up on Gnasher ammo, find the COG Tag, and move past the parade floats to the gate at the end of the road. Detonate the clutch of eggs on the right to remove the Lambent hazard, and then turn the wheel to open the gate. Baird automatically stops turning the wheel once the Tickers start streaming in.

Immediately start meleeing the Tickers to kick them into the air where you can then shoot them with the Gnasher for an Oakley ribbon. Continue kicking the Tickers and shooting to earn numerous Oakley ribbons and the And the Kick is Up! ribbon. A Corpser attacks as well, but you can effectively ignore it. The rest of Kilo Squad inflicts enough damage that it will likely die in a Ticker explosion, perhaps of your doing. By focusing entirely on the Tickers, you can earn three Stars without even accepting the Declassified option.

Open the gate the rest of the way in time to see a large army of Locust heading your way. You have 0:45 seconds to prepare for their arrival. Swap out the Gnasher for the Boomshot to the left (leave the Onyx Ammo Cache until the next mission) and use the Tripwire Crossbow to set traps in the middle of the street. Aim directly into the ground, in the middle of the street, to ensure that the blast is close enough to the Locust when they pass through. Head up the stairs on the right to end the mission.

DECLASSIFIED: THREE-STAR TACTICS

MORE POWERFUL LOCUST RESISTANCE

Kilo Squad claimed to have encountered numerous Locust beasts in Parade Grounds area.

Difficulty Increase: Moderate

Star Multiplier: 1.07x

The Declassified option adds a Serapede to the battle and replaces the Tickers with Lambent Wretches. The Serapede slithers under the gate at the start of the combat and the Lambent Wretches follow shortly after. You have roughly thirty seconds to kill the Serapede before the Corpser attacks.

The enemies here are worth so many points that it only takes a single Clusterluck ribbon to provide enough of a bonus to earn three Stars on this mission when playing Declassified.

Use the Lancer to gun down the Corpser from afar. Give it your full attention to avoid being downed.

Exit the hotel and grab both Gnashers in the street beyond the first parade float. Pick up the Frag Grenades, but leave the other weapons behind. Move to the gate ahead and plant a Frag Grenade on each of the concrete barriers flanking the gate.

Turn the wheel to partially open the gate; Baird automatically backs away when a Serapede slithers in from under the gate. Open fire on its tail with the Lancer and try to back away from where you planted the Frag Grenades. Multiple Lambent Wretches enter the area within moments so be ready for them.

Stay on the move to avoid the Corpser's attacks and continue to pepper it with your Lancer and the occasional Frag Grenade. Additional Frag Grenades are on the balcony to the right, should you need them. Swap out the Lancer for the Markza if you prefer. Then grab the Onyx Ammo Cache before turning the wheel to open the barricade.

A large army of high-powered Locust are heading your way and you have just 0:45 to prepare (the battle actually takes place in the next mission). Swap out the Gnasher for the Boomshot and grab the Tripwire Crossbow leaning against the vehicle in the center of the road. Use the latter to set traps in the middle of the road. The wide boulevard means that enemies might be well out of range of the explosive when they trip the laser, so fire the Tripwire Crossbow at the street to set mines instead. Refrain from picking up the Onyx Ammo Cache until after the assault, during the following mission.

Back away from your planted Frag Grenades and open fire on the Serapede's tail.

Keep your attention on the Serapede to make sure it's dead before the Corpser attacks. The Corpser appears roughly 30 seconds after the Serapede first attacks. Watch for opportunities to lob a Frag Grenade at groups of Lambent Wretches.

Use the four Tripwire Crossbow shots now and leave the Onyx Ammo Cache until after the fight.

This mission automatically ends when the timer reaches zero, but it's best if you work fast and get to the tower on the right before it does. Pick up the second Tripwire Crossbow and step into the blue ring of light to end the mission.

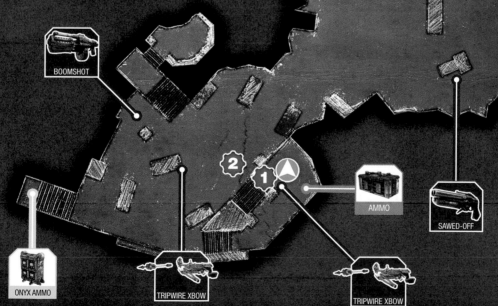

R-SENTINEL

DECLASSIFY

AMMO

ONESHOT

AMMO

BUUSHKA

ONYX AMMO

MARKZA

❌

④ ⑤

③

COG TAGS

MISSION OBJECTIVES

> Get to the museum.
> Ambush the Locust.
> Access the rooftops to reach the museum.
> Defend the beacon.

FRAG GRENADE

BOOMSHOT

②

① ▲

AMMO

SAWED-OFF

ONYX AMMO

TRIPWIRE XBOW

TRIPWIRE XBOW

HOSTILES ENCOUNTERED

⭐3	⭐3	⭐8	⭐11	⭐12	⭐15	⭐15	⭐15	⭐5
WRETCH	DRONE	THERON W/ CLEAVER	BOOMER	KANTUS	MAULER	GRINDER	ELITE MAULER	RAGER*

 = Star Score
*Declassified Mission only.

RIBBONS AND SCORING

Most of your ribbon-scoring opportunities come during the ambush phase of the mission, before you're even presented with the option to Declassify or not. Skilled use of the Tripwire Crossbow nets an It's a Trap ribbon early on (with another to come later). Lob Boomshot rockets from the balcony to earn a Boombardier ribbon if you see groups of enemies; otherwise, wait for the Wretches that attack in the second wave. Though it's not impossible to earn a Hail Mary or Plug That Hole ribbon while defending the bot, it's better to simply focus on killing the enemies as fast as possible and let the ribbons come accidentally if playing Declassified. The Stars accumulate so much faster with the Declassify conditions activated that you're all but certain to earn three Stars if you avoid being downed more than once or twice and earn just two ribbons.

IT'S A TRAP: Kill multiple enemies with a single Tripwire Crossbow shot.

CLUSTERLUCK: Kill multiple enemies with one grenade.

BOOMBARDIER: Kill multiple enemies with a single Boomshot blast.

SHISH-KASHOT: Kill at least two enemies with a single OneShot round.

CLASSIFIED INTEL

1

Fire down on the Locust as they march towards your Tripwire Crossbow traps (set up from the previous mission). Use the Lancer and Boomshot to eliminate the initial wave of Maulers and Drones from this elevated position. Only pick up the Tripwire Crossbow on this platform if you are starting this mission fresh and don't have traps already in place. Otherwise, save it until this battle is over.

2

Head down the stairs and prepare for the onslaught of Theron Guards and Wretches. Use the Boomshot for any clusters of Wretches. Otherwise, use the Lancer and its chainsaw to kill the Wretches. You can replenish the Boomshot with the Onyx Ammo Cache after the ambush is over, so don't hesitate to use it against the Cleaver-wielding Therons.

3

Pick up the second Tripwire Crossbow and the Onyx Ammo Cache to replenish your Boomshot. Continue down the street to the blown-out building on the left. You must protect the bot while it cuts through a door to the elevator. Don't approach that door without first setting up. Place Tripwire Crossbow traps throughout the rubble, plant Frag Grenades out in front of them on the ground, and set up the Range Sentinel to the right of the elevator door.

4

Take position in the room to the left of the elevator, near the Markza, and prepare for the next attack. Use the Boomshot to eliminate as many Maulers and Boomers as possible while they're at a distance. Then switch to the Markza to snipe them as they get closer. Your defenses should hold off the initial crush of Locust, but it's going to get much more challenging.

5

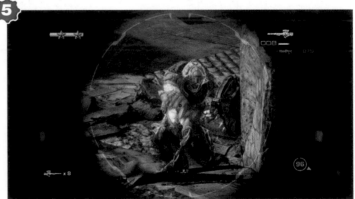

Scavenge for additional Boomshot ammo while you can. Then grab the OneShot and start targeting the Elite Maulers, Boomers, and Drones heading your way. Try to line up two or more Locust whenever possible, but don't wait for a shot that might not come. Use up the OneShot's available ammo and then grab the Booshka if more Locust are on the march.

DECLASSIFIED: THREE-STAR TACTICS

This mission picks up exactly where the last one left off. We highly recommend playing them back to back without stopping so the defenses you set up at the end of the previous section are in place at the start of the ambush. You need to quickly lay down some defenses (or go without) if you are loading a game save or restarting the mission anew. Quickly grab the Tripwire Crossbow on the upper right balcony where you start alongside Paduk and start setting traps in the street below. Plant a Frag Grenade near the steps and use your Lancer to fire at enemies in the street. Lob another grenade at the Cleaver-wielding Therons that bring up the rear.

Maintain the higher ground and cut down the Locust as they enter the ambush site.

The ambush begins with a Kantus, Maulers, and some Grinders. A wave of Cleaver-wielding Therons and Wretches are close behind. Use the Boomshot if you have it from the previous mission; otherwise, make do with the Lancer and Gnasher as best you can. Finish off the ambush and outfit yourself with the Lancer, Boomshot, and the second Tripwire Crossbow. Collect the Onyx Ammo Cache from the stairs near the gate and then continue down the road.

N. Vietzen, SGT, Andius

K.I.A. when a makeshift bridge across two adjacent rooftops collapsed.

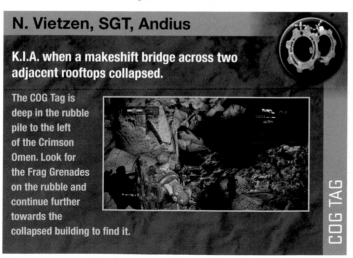

The COG Tag is deep in the rubble pile to the left of the Crimson Omen. Look for the Frag Grenades on the rubble and continue further towards the collapsed building to find it.

COG TAG

Follow the blood-streaked arrows on the side of the van towards the bombed-out building. Locate the Frag Grenades on the left and use them in conjunction with the Tripwire Crossbow to set as many traps and defenses as you can. Try to spread them out so one explosion doesn't cause multiple detonations. Kilo Squad needs the bot to cut through the elevator door inside the building, but don't approach the door just yet! First accept the Declassified option and position the Range Sentinel to the right of the elevator.

HEAVY LOCUST AND RAGER OFFENSIVE

Kilo Squad claimed to have fought additional units of exceptional ferocity.

Difficulty Increase: High

Star Multiplier: 3.59x

You encounter more heavy units during the mission, namely Elite Maulers and a greater number of Boomers, but the main challenge is dealing with the Ragers. The Ragers' speed can make it quite difficult to fend off the Elite Maulers. It's important to immediately target the Ragers as they enrage; this is the only way to keep the battle in the street. If not, the Ragers force you to deal with them at close range, allowing the other heavy units to march right on up as well. You can get by with the Markza and a Boomshot for much of this battle normally, but the Declassified option all but requires using the OneShot from the beginning.

Swap out your Lancer for the Booshka (to go along with the Boomshot) on the right and note the OneShot in the center of the building. Approach the elevator door to trigger the next phase of the mission. Then hurry to the OneShot and train it on the road, where you just came from. The battle begins with multiple Elite Maulers leading the charge—just the type of enemy to use the OneShot on! Try to get a perfect active reload each time, as their shields are tough!

Use the OneShot early in the battle so the Elite Maulers don't take out all of your defenses.

Take aim on the Elite Maulers with the OneShot before they lower their shields and try to get a Shish-Kashot if possible. Many more enemies emerge from E-Holes and some simply burst from the ground. You're going to face many enemies in this battle, including an onslaught of Ragers.

OneShot a Rager if you can catch it while it's enraging. Otherwise, switch to the Boomshot.

Make sure to be out of the general path towards the beacon when the Ragers come so you can fire at them from the side with the Boomshot or Booshka. Ideally, you want to rack up a Boombardier or Clusterluck ribbon and then sprint into the main room to reload your Range Sentinel before slipping out of the way again. The Ragers typically move too fast for the OneShot to be of much use, so you better get them before they enrage or as they exit the E-Hole. If you have a clear shot, try closing the Emergence Hole with the Boomshot.

Use the Onyx Ammo Cache if you haven't already (it's great for replenishing the Boomshot and Booshka during the Rager ambush). Finish the battle and collect any fallen ammo or grenades you want, particularly the Markza, as you're unlikely to have used it. Then approach the bot to exit to the rooftops.

Don't end the mission without first scouring the area for valuable munitions.

SECTION 4: STATE STREET ROOFTOPS

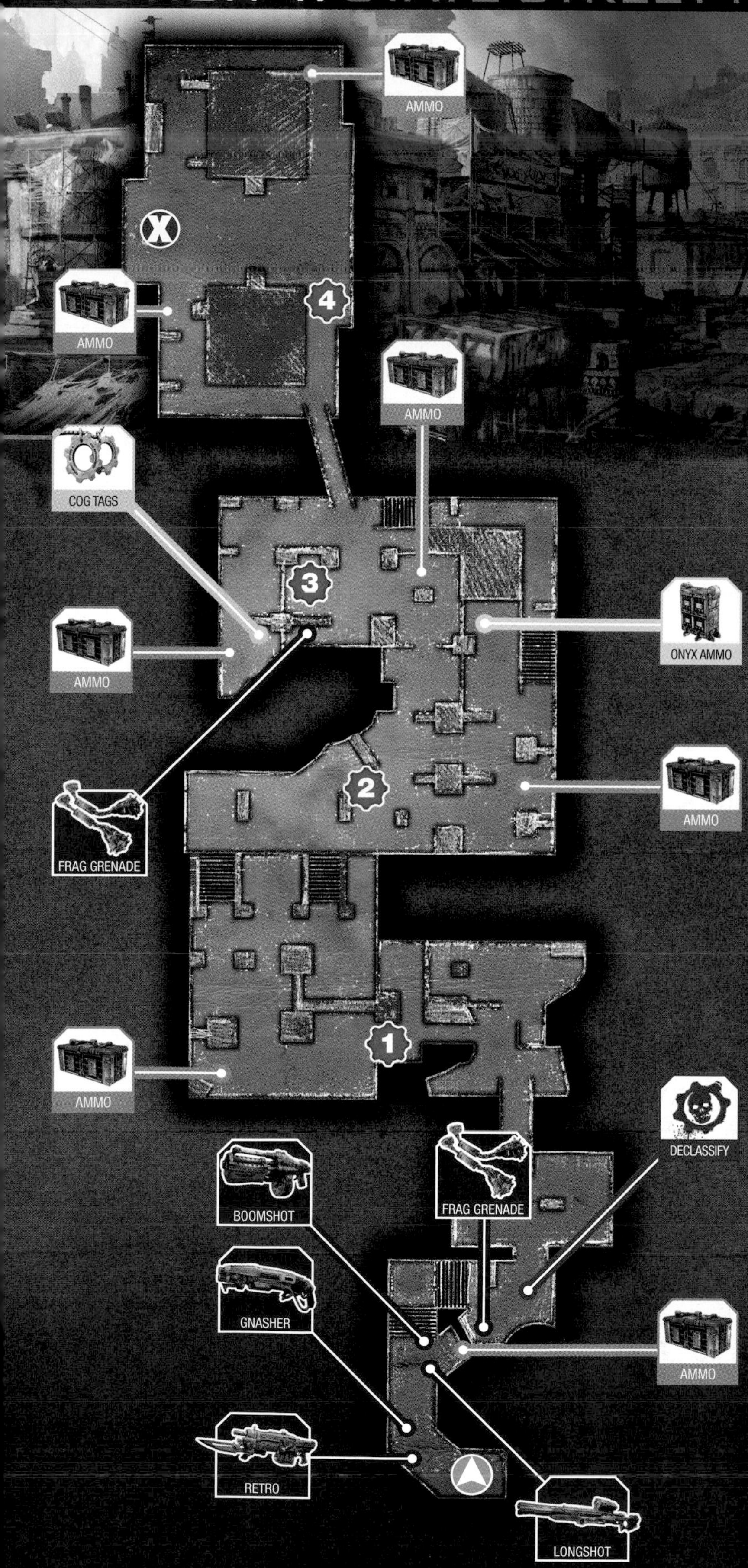

AMMO

X

AMMO

4

AMMO

COG TAGS

3

AMMO

ONYX AMMO

2

AMMO

FRAG GRENADE

AMMO

1

FRAG GRENADE

DECLASSIFY

BOOMSHOT

GNASHER

AMMO

RETRO

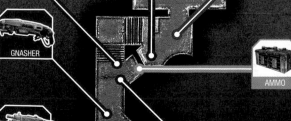

LONGSHOT

MISSION OBJECTIVES

> Get close to the museum.

HOSTILES ENCOUNTERED

⭐3 DRONE	⭐3 DRONE (GRAPPLER)	⭐5 SNIPER	⭐5 DRONE (REAVER DRIVER)

⭐7 THERON (REAVER DRIVER)	⭐7 SHRIEKER	⭐25 REAVER

⭐ = Star Score

RIBBONS AND SCORING

A number of ribbons are possible on this mission depending on whether you play with or without the Declassified option. Those foregoing the additional challenge have their pick of numerous weapons. We recommend using the Boomshot and Retro Lancer. Put the latter to use to down an enemy, grab a meatshield, and then bag & tag it for a Special Delivery ribbon. It's possible to send a bag & tagged foe into a group of other Drones for multiple Special Delivery ribbons and a Clusterluck ribbon too! Three Stars come fast to those who make extensive use of the Boltok when accepting the Declassified option. Watch the I'm Your Huckleberry and Hat Trick ribbons pile up as you blast away the Drones with Boltok headshots. It's not uncommon to earn three Stars before the Reaver makes its appearance!

SPECIAL DELIVERY: Kill an enemy with a bag & tag.

BOOMBARDIER: Kill multiple enemies with a single Boomshot blast.

HAT TRICK: Score 3 headshots in a row without dying.

I'M YOUR HUCKLEBERRY: Kill 5 enemies in a row with any type of pistol without dying.

CLASSIFIED INTEL

1

Equip the Boomshot and Retro Lancer at the start of the mission and be sure to grab the Frag Grenades. Sprint across the first bridge, turn left, and open fire with the Retro Lancer as you charge up the ramp to the higher roof. Numerous Drones move across the roof and many more grapple up on the left. Shoot the grappling hooks off the side of the roof if you can; otherwise, stay in cover and use the Boomshot. Grab any downed enemies and perform a bag & tag maneuver for a Special Delivery ribbon.

2

Duck into cover atop the stairs to the right and immediately target the Shriekers flying in from the distance. Shriekers dive-bomb the nearest living creature—friend or foe—upon death, so keep away from them. Fire the Retro Lancer in short bursts to down them while they fly over the Drones. Collect the Onyx Ammo Cache on the upper roof to the right and target enemies from this elevated position.

3

Cross the main roof towards the Frags and Cog Tag while listening for the sound of grappling hooks. Several Drones climb onto the catwalk that wraps around the right corner of the building. Hit them with a Boomshot or Frag Grenade as soon as they bunch up near the top of the metal stairs. Scavenge fallen Hammerbursts if you wish to use a more precise rifle than the Retro Lancer.

4

A Reaver swoops by, knocking a bridge into place as it touches down on the far side of the next rooftop. Sprint across the bridge, take cover, and advance along the side of the building as safety permits. Use the Boomshot to target the two Reaver Drivers. Then open fire on the Reaver's soft underbelly to finish the fight.

DECLASSIFIED: THREE-STAR TACTICS

DECLASSIFY

USE BOLTOKS AND LONGSHOTS ONLY

Lt. Baird claimed to have led Kilo Squad to victory despite lacking adequate supplies and weapons.

Difficulty Increase: Moderate

Star Multiplier: 3.36x

Being limited to Boltoks and Longshots may reduce your firing rate, but this pairing of weapons packs a tremendous punch. Consider sticking with the Boltok exclusively, as it's potent enough to down Shriekers with just one or two rounds. Using the Boltok also helps earn both Hat Trick and I'm Your Huckleberry ribbons. Additional Longshots appear on the map near each of the ammo crates to ensure you have plenty of ammo for that weapon.

Rather than charge up the ramp with guns blazing, it's much safer to cross the wooden bridge at the start and take cover behind the sandbags. The first wave of Drones attacks, several from the right and a few more near the top of the ramp. Fend them off from this spot with the Boltok. Then ascend the ramp just enough to see over the edge and continue to use the Boltok. Shoot the grappling hooks if you want or continue racking up headshots for a Hat Trick ribbon.

Deadliest pistoleer since Wild Bill, they say.

Grab the ammo crate in the corner and head up the stairs into cover. Shoot any Shriekers and Drones that pose an immediate threat and gradually cover-swap your way to the right. The slightly raised section of roof on the right has plenty of ammo and affords a covered elevated position from which to flank the other enemies. Put your Boltok and Longshot to use near the Onyx Ammo Cache and target the Shriekers as they fly over the Drones.

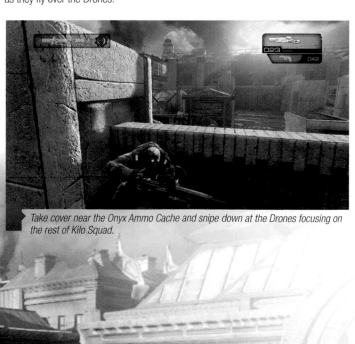

Take cover near the Onyx Ammo Cache and snipe down at the Drones focusing on the rest of Kilo Squad.

The Boltok is perfect for knocking Shriekers out of the air.

Shriekers can typically withstand being hit three times before entering their kamikaze dive, but the Boltok and Longshot are both powerful enough to drop them in just one or two bullets. The Shriekers dive towards whoever is closest to them upon death, so be sure to keep out from under them!

Loop up and around the catwalk in the far right corner, in a counterclockwise direction. Three Drones grapple up from below. Shoot their grappling hooks if you have time; otherwise, stand back and snipe them.

S. Bishop, COL, Gerrenhalt

K.I.A. by Torque Bow round while trying to divert civilians toward better cover.

The COG Tag is near the end of the first large building, before you cross the overturned bridge to battle the Reaver. Note the Crimson Omen on the left and loop up and around to the slightly raised portion of roof directly above it. An Ammo Box is back there too.

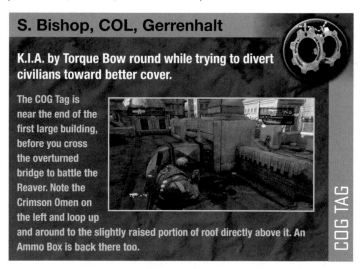

COG TAG

A Reaver swoops in and knocks over a bridge, allowing you to advance to the next building. Move into a covered sniping position and take out the Reaver Riders to reduce the threat. This calms the Reaver somewhat and likely gives you a chance to either snipe its red underbelly or get in close enough to blast it with the Boltok.

Several additional Drones may attack near the Reaver, but you can leave them to the other members of Kilo Squad until you've dealt with the Reaver.

Don't get any closer than you have to!

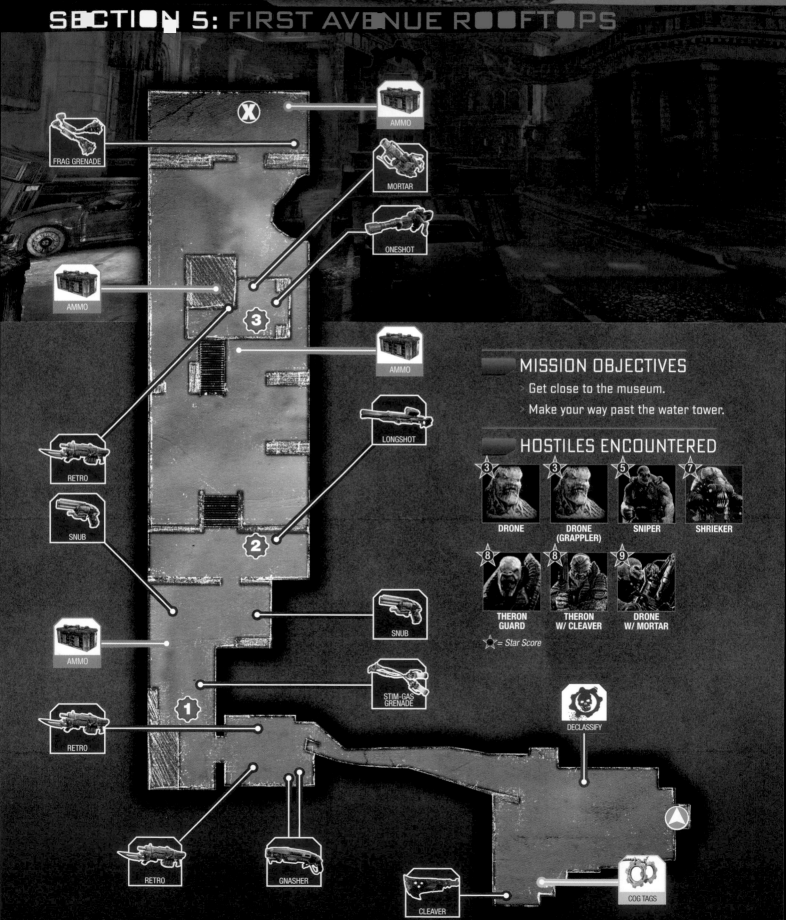

FRAG GRENADE

AMMO

MORTAR

ONESHOT

AMMO

AMMO

RETRO

LONGSHOT

SNUB

SNUB

AMMO

STIM-GAS GRENADE

RETRO

DECLASSIFY

RETRO

GNASHER

CLEAVER

COG TAGS

MISSION OBJECTIVES

> Get close to the museum.

> Make your way past the water tower.

HOSTILES ENCOUNTERED

DRONE (3)

DRONE (GRAPPLER) (3)

SNIPER (5)

SHRIEKER (7)

THERON GUARD (8)

THERON W/ CLEAVER (8)

DRONE W/ MORTAR (9)

☆ = Star Score

"THE CLOSER WE GOT TO KARN, THE MORE FEROCIOUS THE FIGHTS. AND EVERYTHING ON THOSE ROOFTOPS STUNK OF DEATH."

RIBBONS AND SCORING

The latter half of this mission is heavily reliant on the Mortar and OneShot. This makes the early encounters most conducive for earning ribbons. If you choose to decline the Declassified option, you can put the Longshot to use and earn a Hat Trick ribbon. On the other hand, those playing with the Declassified option can potentially use the Snub Pistol to earn an I'm Your Huckleberry ribbon with some considerable effort. Fortunately, it's possible to earn three Stars on Declassified without earning any ribbons, provided you don't get downed before the third Star is awarded.

HAT TRICK: Score 3 headshots in a row without dying.

I'M YOUR HUCKLEBERRY: Kill 5 enemies in a row with any type of pistol without dying.

CLASSIFIED INTEL

1 Cross the bridge to the shelter—the first Stranded camp—and load up on Retro Lancer. Take a moment to eavesdrop on the conversation through the air vent. Then move towards the door leading outside. Equip the weapon you'd like to swap out before exiting.

2 Drop into cover on the right and equip the Longshot leaning against the wall. Keep your head down to avoid the two Therons manning OneShots on the water tower's platform. Wait for them to reload, and ready your shot. Snipe the enemies on the water tower. Then switch to the Retro and shoot your way past any of the Cleaver-wielding Therons that charge your position.

3 Roadie run up the stairs to the water tower platform and man the Mortar in the corner. A large number of Theron Guards and Drones have moved in to defend the exit off this rooftop. Canvas the area with Mortar fire. Aim three clicks on the rangefinder and angle your shots to the left and right to blanket the area. A second wave attacks with a Mortar unit in their midst. Switch to either of the OneShots and take out the Mortar unit as soon as possible.

DECLASSIFIED: THREE-STAR TACTICS

START WITH NO AMMUNITION FOR BOLTOKS AND LONGSHOTS

Kilo Squad claimed to have crossed downtown rooftops carrying virtually no ammunition.

Difficulty Increase: Moderate

Star Multiplier: 3.84x

Starting off with no ammo would be a frightening predicament if not for the Cleaver on the left. Use it to fight your way to the Snub Pistols inside. From there, you need only use the Snub Pistol until you gain the Mortar and OneShots on the water tower platform. Then it's business as usual.

J. Corbin, 1LT, Jacinto

K.I.A. by enemy fire as she was escorting civilians toward higher ground.

The COG Tag's Crimson Omen hint is on the left at the start of the mission, directly opposite the glowing Declassify Crimson Omen on the right. The COG Tag itself is to the small Crimson Omen's right, near the scaffolding around the corner, by the Cleaver stuck in the crate.

COG TAG

Grab the Cleaver on the left and cross the bridge to the refugee shelter inside the building across the way. Multiple Cleaver-wielding Therons attack as you reach the interior; consider waiting outside for them to funnel through the doorway. Try to stick close by the other members of Kilo Squad (they have Cleavers too) and just keep swinging.

Make sure Kilo Squad is close by when you engage these three Cleaver-wielding Therons.

Slash through the Therons as best you can. Then grab the two Snub Pistols inside. You may luck into some Boltok ammo, but probably no more than six rounds. You can't carry two pistols, so ditch the Boltok in favor of the 72 rounds provided by the two Snub Pistols. Pick up the Stim-Gas Grenades on the right.

Keep your head down until just after the OneShot is fired. Then rise up and take out that Theron!

Kick open the door and duck into cover. Use the Snub Pistol to down the Therons with the OneShots on the water tower platform while they prepare their shot. Be sure to duck if their lasers swing your way.

Several Theron Guards charge your position with Cleavers, but the other members of Kilo Squad do their best to defend you. Back away from the rail and fire the Snub Pistol as quickly as you can to aid in your own defense. Lob a Stim-Gas Grenade at your feet if you end up in a close-range fight with a Cleaver-wielding Theron—you're going to need it.

Sprint up the ramp to where the Therons were, pick up the Retro Lancer for defense, and grab the unused Mortar in the corner. Numerous Therons, Drones, and Snipers are scattered across the further terrace with more coming in droves. Blanket the area with Mortar fire, making sure to target the Therons with the Torque Bows, as they pose the most threat. Listen closely for enemies coming up the ramp to your position and quickly back away, drop the Mortar, and open fire with the Retro Lancer.

Fire off as many Mortar shots as you can before the Therons finally charge your position.

Pay attention to the area above the doorway, as the final wave of enemies contains a Mortar unit. Quickly grab a OneShot and take it out. You're completely exposed to Mortar fire on the water tower platform, so act fast. With the Mortar unit dead, you can take your time picking off the rest of the Therons with the OneShot. Advance to the doorway to finish the mission.

Switch to the OneShot to finish off the enemy Mortar unit and any remaining Therons.

AMMO

X

AMMO

4

3

COG TAGS

ONYX AMMO

T

T

AMMO

2

SAWED-OFF

FRAG GRENADE

BOOSHKA

FRAG GRENADE

1

DECLASSIFY

RETRO

GNASHER

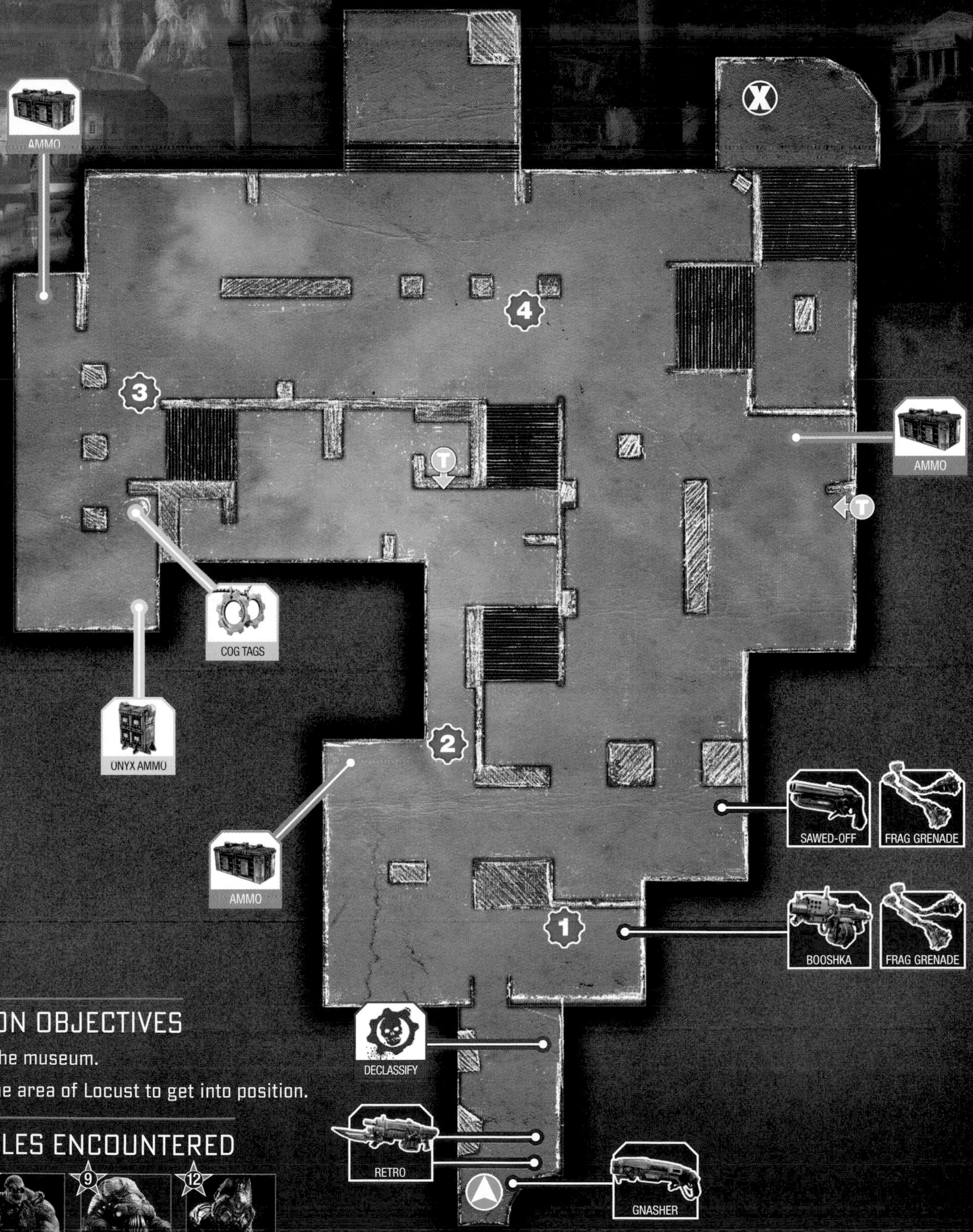

MISSION OBJECTIVES

> Get to the museum.

> Clear the area of Locust to get into position.

HOSTILES ENCOUNTERED

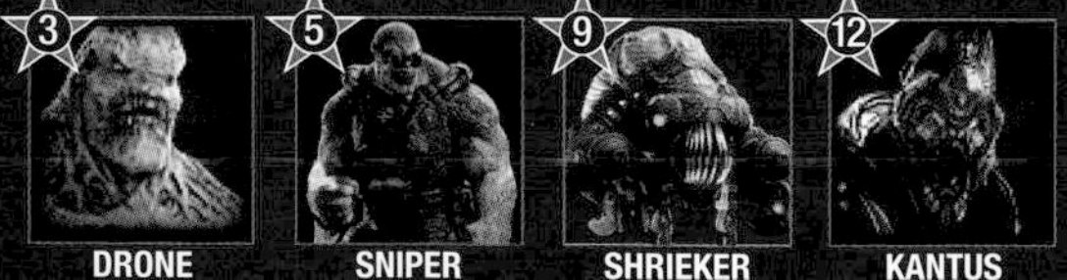

3	5	9	12
DRONE	SNIPER	SHRIEKER	KANTUS

"WE WERE VERY CLOSE NOW. THE ONLY THING I REGRETTED WAS HAVING TO SACRIFICE THE BOT TO KILL KARN. LITTLE GUY HELPED US OUT. BUT WE ALL HAD A JOB TO DO."

RIBBONS AND SCORING

The only ribbons you're likely to earn on this mission, given the available weapon supply, are related to Frag Grenades (unless you opt to use the Sawed-Off Shotgun). There are multiple opportunities to earn a Clusterluck ribbon whether or not you accept the Declassified option. Also, thanks to the power of the Retro Lancer, it's quite easy to down a Drone and use it to earn a Special Delivery ribbon. This is a particularly useful technique as you make your way from the Onyx Ammo Cache towards the stairs where the four rappelling Drones attack. Earning at least one Clusterluck ribbon goes a long way towards getting that third Star. If you find yourself well shy of a third Star as you take on the final group of Drones, turn to the Retro Charge or Lancer's chainsaw to gain execution bonuses. Another option is to use the Sawed-Off Shotgun in hopes of earning a Nothin' But Bits ribbon.

CLUSTERLUCK: Kill multiple enemies with one grenade.

SPECIAL DELIVERY: Kill an opponent with a bag & tag.

CLASSIFIED INTEL

Load up on Retro Lancer ammo and kick open the door to head onto the roof. Grab the Booshka or Frag Grenades (they alternate at random) and duck into cover. Use the Booshka to take out the Troika in the distance on the left, beyond the stairs. It's a long shot, but you can reach it from here. You have to move closer if the Frag Grenades were there instead.

Round the corner to the left and take cover near the ammo crate. Multiple Drones and Kantuses approach from the stairs next to the Troika. Lob a Frag for a chance at the Clusterluck ribbon. Then take cover near the short wall. Use the Booshka, if you have it, to take out the Troika to the right. Otherwise, use the Lancer or leave it for the rest of Kilo Squad to deal with. Fight along this upper walkway towards the first Troika and turn left.

Collect the COG Tag en route to the Onyx Ammo Cache around the corner to the left. Stay on the road and move to the far right corner of the rooftop. Use the Retro Lancer to gun down any remaining Kantuses and look for a downed Drone to grab as a meatshield. Use the Frag Grenade from the Onyx Ammo Cache to bag & tag a Drone for a Special Delivery ribbon.

One final gang of Drones rappels down the brick wall atop the stairs, near the mission's endpoint. Fire the Booshka up the stairs if you have it. Otherwise, use the Retro to down the nearest Drone and grab yourself a meatshield. March up the stairs with your Locust shield and show the other Drones what a Retro Lancer at close range feels like.

DECLASSIFIED: THREE-STAR TACTICS

DECLASSIFY

FINISH BEFORE REAVER BARRAGE

Kilo Squad claimed to have seen and avoided Reaver forces using tactics internal COG intel does not support.

Difficulty Increase: High

Star Multiplier: 2.94x

Countdown to Reaver Barrage

CASUAL	NORMAL	HARDCORE	INSANE
3:30	2:30	2:00	3:00

An inbound Reaver assault is going to take place in a few short minutes, meaning you have very little time to get into position to deploy the bot. The mission plays out the same under Declassified conditions, but you need to hurry. Ideally, you want to have the Onyx Ammo Cache with at least half of your available time still remaining. Kilo Squad may encounter Shriekers as they step onto the roof.

Load up on Retro Lancer ammunition before accepting the Declassified option. Kick open the door, switch to the Gnasher, and quickly swap it for the Booshka if it's present. Otherwise, just grab the Frag Grenades. The countdown and potential presence of Shriekers mean you need to move quickly. Loop around to the building on the left and take cover. Use the Booshka (or a Frag Grenade) to take out the Troika straight ahead. Then, if using the Booshka, fire it to eliminate the Drone manning the Troika far off to the right.

Lob some additional explosives towards the Kantuses and Drones massing atop the stairs to the right of the first Troika. Eliminate any that you can. Then round the corner to the left and sprint for the COG Tag and Onyx Ammo Cache at the dead-end.

Finish off any Drones you spot near the sandbags at the top of the stairs. Then sprint for the Onyx Ammo Cache.

Taking out the Troika on the walkway to the left is top priority!

You want to reach the Onyx Ammo Cache with roughly half of the available time still remaining. Double-back past the stairs you just descended and into cover near the exhaust vents. Dispatch any Kantuses you see. Then scan the left and right for isolated Drones—every enemy must be killed before the time runs out. Don't leave any behind!

One final wave of Drones is set to rappel the wall near the stairs leading to your target position. Lob a Frag Grenade up the stairs at the Drones to coincide with them reaching the end of their rope. Take a meatshield for protection if you can, and charge up the stairs under a blaze of Retro gunfire. Tap Up on the D-Pad to end the mission as soon as the last Locust has been slain.

Use the Retro Lancer to down isolated Drones for use as meatshields or to earn a Special Delivery ribbon.

P. Surrs, CPT, Hanover

K.I.A. when an unseen Serapede crept up behind him.

The COG Tag is far to the left, near the Onyx Ammo Cache. Notice the Crimson Omen on the wall above the Onyx Ammo Cache as you approach it. The COG Tag is behind the sandbag on the left nearest the stairs. Though it only takes a second to grab the COG Tag, you can leave it and collect it during the next mission, which isn't under any time constraints.

COG TAG

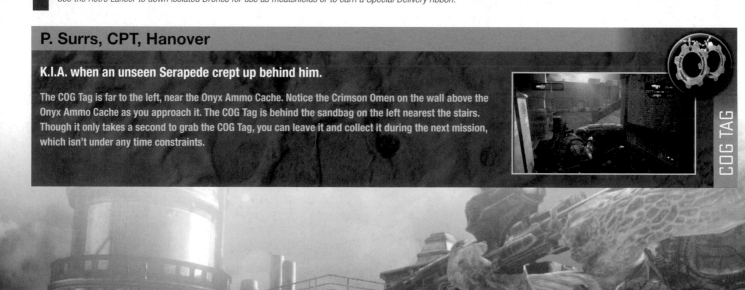

SECTION 7: OVERLOOK

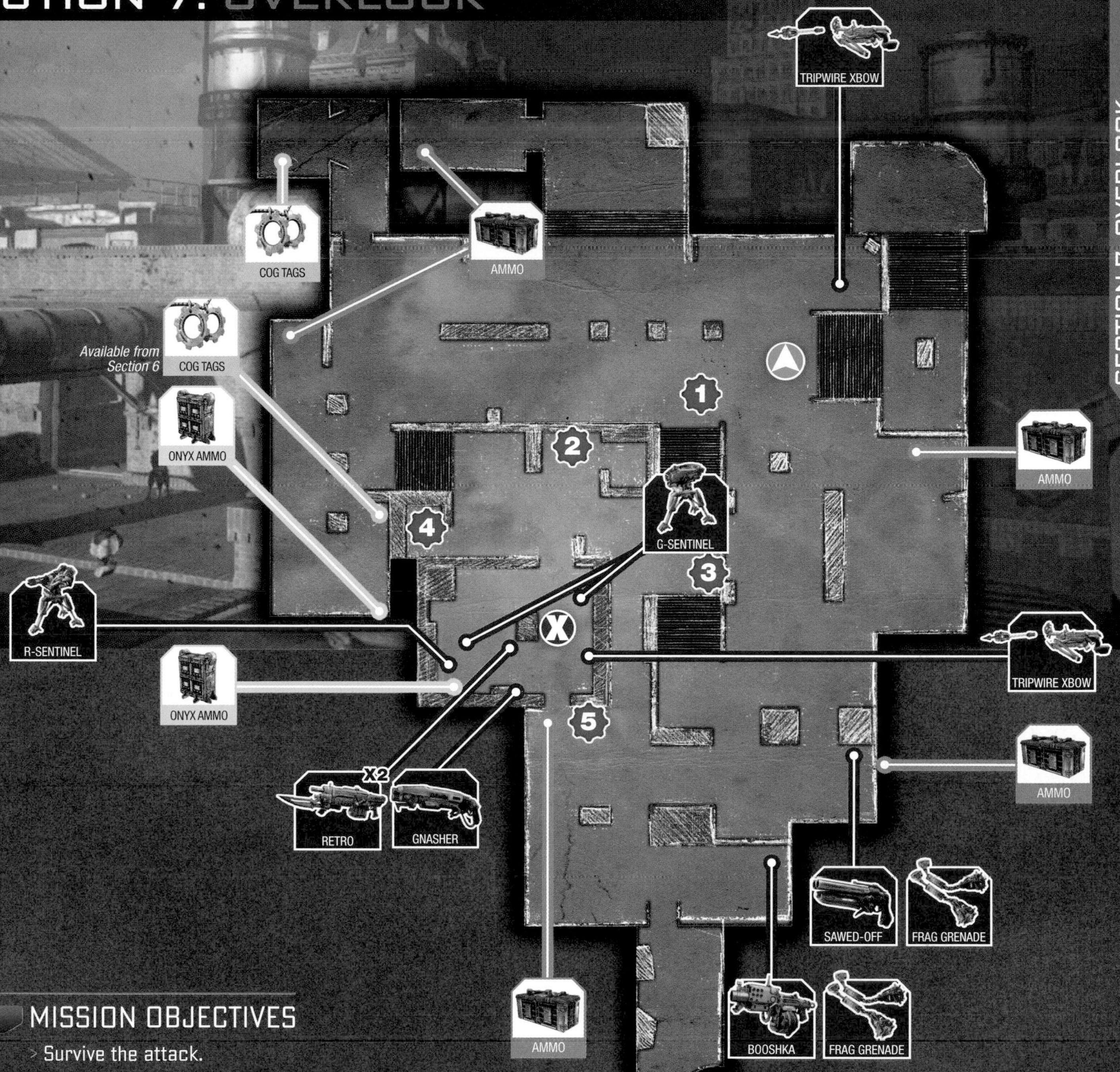
TRIPWIRE XBOW
COG TAGS
AMMO
Available from Section 6
COG TAGS
ONYX AMMO
AMMO
G-SENTINEL
R-SENTINEL
TRIPWIRE XBOW
ONYX AMMO
AMMO
X2
RETRO
GNASHER
SAWED-OFF
FRAG GRENADE
AMMO
BOOSHKA
FRAG GRENADE
1
2
3
4
5
X

MISSION OBJECTIVES

> Survive the attack.

HOSTILES ENCOUNTERED

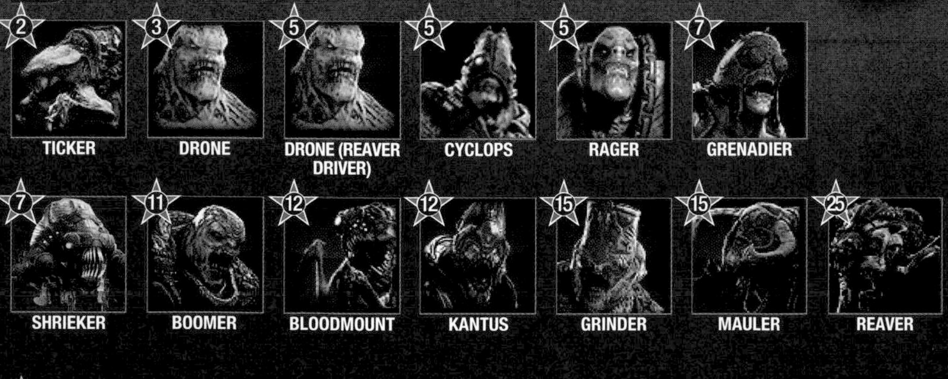
2
TICKER
3
DRONE
5
DRONE (REAVER DRIVER)
5
CYCLOPS
5
RAGER
7
GRENADIER
7
SHRIEKER
11
BOOMER
12
BLOODMOUNT
12
KANTUS
15
GRINDER
15
MAULER
25
REAVER

★ = *Star Score*

"I THOUGHT IF WE KILLED KARN, THE GRUBS WOULD JUST STOP FIGHTING. I GUESS THIS WAR'S GONNA MAKE A PESSIMIST OUT OF ME YET. LOOK, KARN NEEDED TO DIE. IF THAT WAS THE WRONG CALL, COLONEL, YOU CAN GO AHEAD AND SHOOT ME."

RIBBONS AND SCORING

Getting three Stars on this mission with the Declassified option accepted is essentially a matter of staying alive. What makes this mission unique is that it's entirely possible to earn three Stars without the Declassified option, provided you absolutely minimize the time spent crawling around in a DBNO state. Use both Tripwire Crossbows to earn at least one It's a Trap ribbon and seek out a dropped Boomshot during the first wave. Use the Onyx Ammo Cache before the second wave to replenish the Boomshot and keep it on hand for the Bloodmounts that attack. You almost can't help but get a Boombardier ribbon when firing a rocket at a softened Bloodmount. Lastly, remember to Spot as many enemies as you can. Even if you don't get the kill directly, you're at least making progress towards a Military Intelligence ribbon.

CLUSTERLUCK: **Kill multiple enemies with one grenade.**

IT'S A TRAP: **Kill multiple enemies with a single Tripwire Crossbow shot.**

BOOMBARDIER: **Kill multiple enemies with a single Boomshot blast.**

MILITARY INTELLIGENCE: **Spot 5 opponents ending in kills.**

CLASSIFIED INTEL

Kill the three Drones atop the stairs. Then turn and pick up the Tripwire Crossbow beneath where you finished the previous mission. You have 1:30 to prepare for a full-scale Locust counter-assault. Use the crossbow to set Tripwires along the square exhaust vents straight ahead, to the right of the Crimson Omen. Hurry up the stairs to the central building and place the two Gnasher Sentinels in the middle of the platform outside. Tuck them against the sandbags and walls so they're out of the way. Place the Range Sentinel in the corner near the stairs so it can shoot anything that reaches this walkway.

Take cover against the wall looking out past the exhaust vents, as most of the Locust come from that direction. Use the Booshka you're hopefully carrying from the previous mission and/or the Retro Lancer to gun down the first group of attackers, led by Maulers and Grinders. Keep the Sentinels loaded, look for a dropped Boomshot if your Booshka goes dry, and continue to defend this platform against the Cyclops and other Locust that comprise the rest of the first wave.

3

You have just 0:30 to prepare for the second wave, which is much longer and more difficult. Grab the Tripwire Crossbow inside the room and set traps on the stairs leading up to your platform. Set three Tripwires and then grab the Onyx Ammo Cache to replenish the weapon. The second wave often begins with enemies approaching from the right side of the roof and often contains several Shriekers. Be ready to retreat indoors if the Shriekers get too close.

4

The bulk of the third wave is comprised of Ragers and Bloodmounts. This is a great time to rack up some Boombardier ribbons if you have the Boomshot. But your main focus is keeping the Sentinels loaded and staying alive. Stay away from the area near your two Gnasher Sentinels, and avoid the area where the two flights of stairs are. Instead, take cover under the corrugated awning, near the Range Sentinel in the corner. This gives you some cover, allows you to stay close to the Range Sentinel for support, and keeps you on the periphery, where you can inflict optimum damage.

5

Your attention is drawn to two Reavers approaching. Quickly grab one of the fallen Breechshots and replenish it via the ammo supplies inside the room. Stay close to the double door leading to where most of the battle took place just long enough to entice the Reavers to land in that area. Once they touch down, enter the building and start shooting through the windows and doorways. Avoid the Reaver's rockets and retreat out the back side of the room to either the corner of the building or just beyond the door. Fire round after round with the Breechshot into the Reavers until they're both dead.

DECLASSIFIED: THREE-STAR TACTICS

DECLASSIFY

GREATLY REDUCED VISIBILITY

Lt. Baird claimed that Kilo Squad was able to overcome severe operational disadvantages in aftermath of museum destruction.

Difficulty Increase: High

Star Multiplier: 2.27x

The battle plays out the same as it did without the Declassified option, but visibility is greatly reduced. This would be a problem if there were several long-range weapons to rely on, but there aren't. By making use of the Retro Lancer and a scavenged Boomshot and Breechshot, you shouldn't need to adjust your tactics much on account of the smoke and dust. That said, we strongly recommend that you play this mission once without the Declassified option, so you truly know the map and what to expect as the battle gets underway.

Kill the Drones on the stairs. Then turn and grab the Tripwire Crossbow on the ground behind you. Carry it up the stairs to the room near the Crimson Omen and set it down near the wall to the right. You only have 1:30 to set up before the first wave arrives, so hurry. Position two Gnasher Sentinels outside the room, near the sandbags between the overhead pipe and the stairs you just came up. Place the Range Sentinel at the end of the walkway, near the sandbags under the corrugated awning. This provides ample coverage of the walkway and catches enemies in deadly crossfire.

The other members of Kilo Squad plant Frag Grenades around the stairs while you set up the Sentinels.

With the Sentinels in position, it's time to set up some Tripwire traps. Grab the Tripwire Crossbow you carried up earlier and fire each of its four shots at the chimneys in the center of the roof. Fire one into each side of the chimneys so that two detonate simultaneously—you need the extra firepower to kill the Maulers and Boomers that typically lead the initial assault. If you didn't pick up the Onyx Ammo Cache in the previous mission, it is still there and can replenish the Tripwire Crossbow, provided you don't empty it of ammo. You can only have five Tripwires active at once, so wait until one or two have been tripped before firing any additional ones at the columns or at the top of the stairs leading up from below.

Well-placed Tripwires come in handy when you're fighting blind.

Take position near the wall or by the stairs on the right and use your assault rifle to take out any Shriekers that appear. Focus fire on the Boomers or Grinders that are coming forward. Monitor the position of the Boomers and, when the coast is clear, sprint to swap out one of your weapons for the Boomshot, unless you still have Booshka ammo from the previous mission. Hold onto the Boomshot for later if possible, so you can replenish your ammo from the Onyx Ammo Cache inside the armory room.

The remainder of the first wave consists of numerous heavies and some Shriekers, Kantuses, and Drones. Fall back when you need to, either to the interior of the armory or behind the sandbags near the Range Sentinel. Try to hold onto your Frag Grenades for the next wave, but do use up any remaining Boomshot weaponry in an effort to get a Boombardier ribbon.

Take cover near the Range Sentinel and continue to use your Lancer or Boomshot from a safe distance.

You get a brief 0:30 intermission before the second wave begins. The Sentinels automatically reload, giving you time to grab the second Tripwire Crossbow and fire it at the wall between the two sets of stairs to the right. This helps ward off the Ragers and Bloodmounts that comprise most of the second wave.

Stay clear of the fray and attack from the perimeter in order to avoid being trampled under the feet of the Bloodmounts or charged by the enraged Ragers. The Retro Lancer and Gnasher (or Sawed-Off Shotgun if you retrieve it) are good choices should you get caught between the angry horde. The weapons from the previous mission can be found back where you first entered this area, provided you didn't pick them up already.

Clear the deck of Bloodmounts before rushing out to reload the Gnasher Sentinels.

The battle culminates with Kilo Squad having to stave off two Reavers at once. Reload your Sentinels while they circle. Then rush into the room as soon as the Reavers land. They'll likely touch down in the corner near the two sets of stairs. Rush inside and fire at the Reavers through the doors and windows. You're not completely safe inside, as the rockets can still find their way through an opening. Keep as far from the Reavers as you can and use the angles—and available cover—to your advantage. It's even worth exiting the far side of the armory room and shooting the Reavers from the far side of the building. Just be careful not to stray too far; getting downed too far from Kilo Squad is just as deadly as getting impaled at close range.

Stay outside just long enough to bait the Reavers into landing near your Sentinels. Then head inside.

J. Salton, PFC, Autrin

K.I.A. by Reaver-fired rockets while attempting to protect civilians.

This COG Tag is difficult to find, especially with the reduced visibility of playing Declassified. It's deep inside one of the rooms that the Locust open. Access the outer doors, then eventually a pair of double doors inside that hallway. The COG Tag is located in the far left-hand corner inside that second room. You must get it before destroying the Reavers, or else you have to replay the mission. We recommend making a run for it as soon as the Reavers make their appearance.

COG TAG

THE COURTHOUSE
PRESENT DAY

SECTION 1: GRAND COURTROOM

"NOW WE CAN GET BACK TO WORK!"

MISSION OBJECTIVES

> Get out of the courtroom.

HOSTILES ENCOUNTERED

DRONE (3)	WRETCH (3)	RAGER (5)	SNIPER (5)
THERON W/ CLEAVER (8)	GRINDER (15)	MAULER (15)	REAVER (25)

☆ = Star Score

RIBBONS AND SCORING

Stars accumulate dramatically faster when the Declassified option is accepted, and earning even two Stars without it can be a challenge on the harder difficulties. That being said, much of the mission is played before the option to Declassify is reached. Use this time to earn yourself a Clusterluck or Lumberjack ribbon, especially if you draw a larger number of Wretches and Drones than Ragers. The presence of numerous Ragers and lack of sniping weapons makes this mission conducive for earning a Rage Denied ribbon. Pump a few rounds from the Gnasher into the enraged Rager and then dash forward and melee it for a fatal knockout.

CLUSTERLUCK: Kill multiple enemies with one grenade.

LUMBERJACK: Chainsaw 3 enemies in a row.

RAGE DENIED: Kill an enraged Rager with a melee attack.

FRAG GRENADE

COG TAGS

DECLASSIFY

INK GRENADE

AMMO

2

INK GRENADE

1

3

AMMO

STIM-GAS
GRENADE

FRAG GRENADE

1

2

3

The Reaver that attacks at the start of the battle is of utmost concern. Immediately take cover at the fallen pillar ahead and blind-fire your Lancer at the Reaver. Toss a Frag once its position stabilizes and understand that you may get downed by the splash damage, but your squad revives you in short order. Hit it with a second Frag if it's needed. Otherwise, finish the Reaver off with the Lancer and Spot it for the others.

Retreat to the perimeter and begin the clockwise loop around the courtroom. Use the fallen pillars and staircases for cover from the Ragers, Drones, and Theron Guards. Use the Ink Grenades on the Ragers as they stop to enrage and the Therons with the Cleavers as they begin their three-swing attack. This is a good time to try to earn a Lumberjack or Rage Denied ribbon.

Gather up the ammo and Frags atop the stairs leading to where Colonel Loomis was presiding. Kill the Mauler moving up the stairs and commandeer its Boomshield. Advance slowly under the protection of the Boomshield while using the Lancer to cut through the Grinders and other Locust between you and the exit.

DECLASSIFIED: THREE-STAR TACTICS

The Declassified option isn't presented until you are almost to the Grand Courtroom's exit, making it possible to approach this mission the same way right through a final decision.

The Reaver that attacks at the start of the battle is the single biggest threat Kilo Squad faces in this mission. Immediately duck into cover, toss your Frag Grenades at it, and blind-fire with the Lancer. You may get downed by the splash damage, but your Kilo squadmates revive you in a hurry. Those playing on Insane difficulty should take cover against the fallen pillar directly behind the starting position to put a little extra distance between you and the Reaver. The Reaver may retreat to the perimeter in an attempt to circle around to your position.

Quickly back away and circle around into cover to the right. Move in a clockwise direction around the perimeter of the courtroom. Many Ragers, Drones, and even some Cleaver-wielding Therons and Wretches are intent on stopping you. Don't go across the center, as you're just too exposed. Use the many raised pulpits around the perimeter for cover and even run up the steps to the top to gain an elevated advantage.

Take cover against the forward pillar and sink as many bullets into the Reaver as you can.

B. Clarkson, 1LT, Tollen

K.I.A. during Cadet Hendrick's testimony.

The COG Tag is atop the second pulpit from your starting position, the one opposite the flames. It is before the alcove where the Frag Grenades are located. Run up the steps to find it. You might as well sit and shoot from here for a moment, too.

COG TAG

Lob the Ink Grenades at the enemies that are in cover, or wait for a Rager about to enrage or a Cleaver Initiating a melee attack on another COG—always use Ink Grenades when the enemy can't turn and run out of the cloud. Grab the Frag Grenades in the alcove on the left before moving ahead to accept the Declassify option. Hold your ground here and do not push on to the Crimson Omen until all enemies are cleared in this area.

A lot of Ragers, Grinders, and Drones remain between here and the finish, which is just up and over those stairs ahead and down to a pair of doors leading out of the courtroom. Don't be afraid to accept the Declassify option; it's not as tough as it sounds.

Run up the stairs with the Cleaver and immediately kill any remaining Drones milling around. Take cover and wait for the approaching Grinders to go on cooldown and then rush towards them and start swinging. Use cover, and try to stay behind your squad so they absorb most of the Grinder fire. The Cleaver can slash through Grinders with surprising ease. But be careful because you can get overrun by Ragers. Finish off the remaining foes and head to the halls.

You can't use those Frags once you accept the Declassify option, so use them right away.

DECLASSIFY

USE CLEAVERS ONLY

Col. Loomis's report contradicted eyewitness accounts of Kilo Squad having employed melee weapons.

Difficulty Increase: Low

Star Multiplier: 5.90x

Accepting the Declassified option forces Kilo Squad to use nothing but a Cleaver while fighting past the final gang of Grinders, Ragers, and Drones. Thanks to the available cover and the Mulcher's lengthy cooldown, it's not as difficult as it sounds. Swarm the enemies with your squadmates and time your attacks so the enemies are caught while reloading. The only noticeable difference to how the mission plays out is that you won't have to contend with a Mauler when accepting the Cleaver challenge.

Take cover atop the stairs and wait for the Grinder to have to cool his Mulcher before engaging.

Move in a pack with your fellow squadmates—there's safety in numbers!

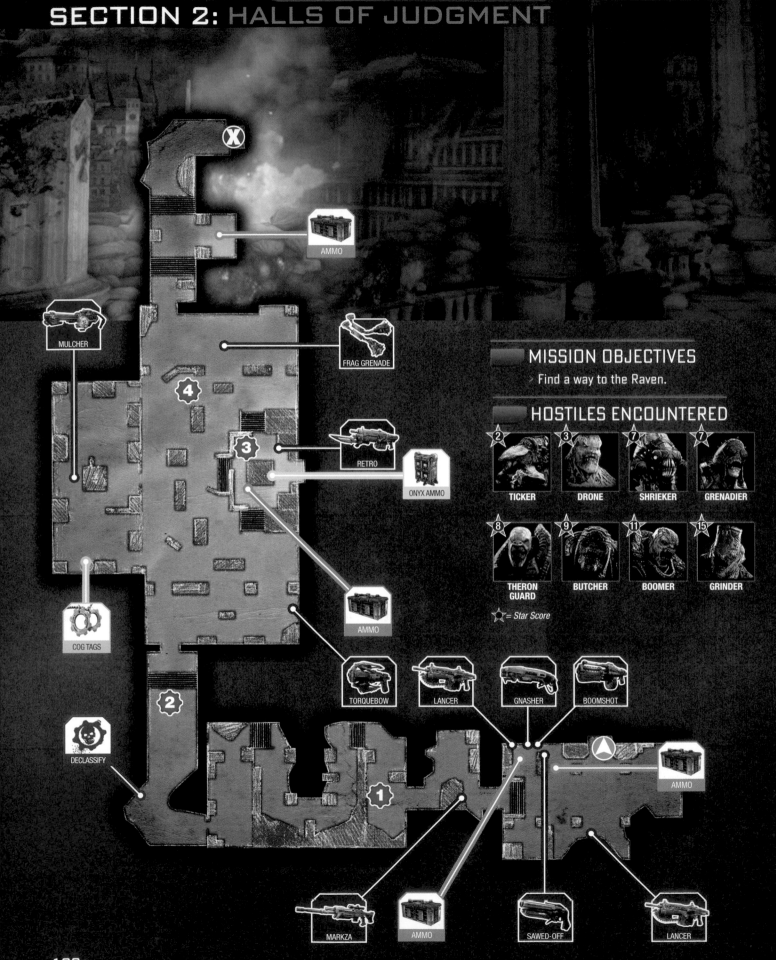

X

AMMO

MULCHER

FRAG GRENADE

MISSION OBJECTIVES

> Find a way to the Raven.

HOSTILES ENCOUNTERED

2	3	7	7
TICKER	DRONE	SHRIEKER	GRENADIER

8	9	11	15
THERON GUARD	BUTCHER	BOOMER	GRINDER

☆ = Star Score

4

3

RETRO

ONYX AMMO

AMMO

COG TAGS

2

DECLASSIFY

TORQUEBOW

LANCER

GNASHER

BOOMSHOT

AMMO

1

MARKZA

AMMO

SAWED-OFF

LANCER

"WE SHOULD HAVE BEEN OUT THERE FIGHTING TONIGHT."

RIBBONS AND SCORING

The Clusterluck and Boombardier ribbons are worth aiming for regardless of classification, as you'll likely be making frequent use of the Boomshot and Frag Grenades either way. Those playing without reduced visibility will likely encounter numerous Tickers that can be struck for the And the Kick is Up! ribbon. Precision weapons like the Markza or a scavenged Boltok can be used in clear air to earn a Hat Trick ribbon, but doing so likely comes at the expense of Boombardier ribbons.

CLUSTERLUCK: Kill multiple enemies with one grenade.

BOOMBARDIER: Kill multiple enemies with a single Boomshot blast.

AND THE KICK IS UP!: Kick 5 small enemies.

CLASSIFIED INTEL

Stock up on Lancer ammo and equip the Boomshot, Markza, or Sawed-Off Shotgun to go along with it. Take cover as soon as you enter the room with the zigzagging path, as dozens of Shriekers are set to attack. Use the Lancer to shoot the Shriekers out of the sky before they get too close. It typically takes three hits to knock a Shrieker into its dive-bomb, so stick with a target before moving to the next. Retreat for more Lancer ammo before continuing.

Tickers, Butchers, and Grinders pour through the doorway ahead. Kick the Tickers out of the way and use your chosen secondary weapon to down the heavy units. Those playing with a Boomshot may run out of ammo before they reach the Onyx Ammo Cache in the next room. If so, consider using the Butcher's Cleaver to cut a path to the center platform in the next room.

Clear the raised platform of remaining enemies and rush to grab the Onyx Ammo Cache before the next wave of enemies bursts through the doors and windows to the left. Take cover and use the Boomshot and Frag Grenades to eliminate the Boomers and Therons that emerge. Time your attacks to earn a Boombardier or Clusterluck ribbon.

Gather the dropped Boomshots or Torque Bows, collect the COG Tag on the balcony, and take cover near the sandbags in front of the door to the right. One final wave of Theron Guards, a Flame Boomer, and Drones burst through that door. Lob a Frag Grenade as the door opens and then ready your Boomshot to take out the rest.

DECLASSIFIED: THREE-STAR TACTICS

Gather as much Lancer ammo as you can carry and swap out the Gnasher for the Boomshot if planning to accept the Declassify option. The Markza is of little help in the thick smoke. Pass through the burned-out room where the Markza is and immediately take cover along the railing in front of the door.

A seemingly endless swarm of Shriekers flies in from the ceiling and bombed-out walls. Stay in cover and shoot them out of the air with the Lancer. Shriekers can withstand up to three hits before finally entering their explosive dive-bomb maneuver. Always target those making the most progress towards your position, but be quick to roll out of the way if one hovers directly overhead. Never shoot a Shrieker that is overhead, as it will only crash down and detonate on top of you.

Pepper the Shriekers with Lancer fire. Then return to the previous room to replenish your ammo supplies.

DECLASSIFY

LOCUST SMOKE-GRENADE TRAPS REDUCE VISIBILITY

Col. Loomis's report made no mention of Locust smoke-grenade traps.

Difficulty Increase: Moderate

Star Multiplier: 3.35x

You've dealt with reduced visibility before, but the amount of smoke filling the Halls of Judgment is unprecedented. Vision is so limited that the COG must consider dispensing with all precision, long-range weapons and opting instead for shotguns, assault rifles, and the Boomshot, which offers a large margin for error. Keep your head down and follow the Locust's muzzle-flash to see where they're located.

Ready the Boomshot and Frag Grenades for the Maulers that attack in the hallway leading to the Hall of Judgment. The Maulers are quick to lower their Boomshields, so aim for their feet or the floor right next to them.

Enter the hall and take cover at once. From cover, eliminate the enemies on the raised platform to the right. Clear the platform with your explosives and claim it for your own. This position has both an ammo crate and an Onyx Ammo Cache and gives you a great view of the heavies set to break through the outer wall on the left. Use this position to launch explosive attacks. Don't grab the Onyx Ammo Cache until you're out of Boomshot ammo, and then use it to replenish your weapon.

T. Carlson, 1LT, Halvo Bay

K.I.A. during Lt. Baird's first testimony.

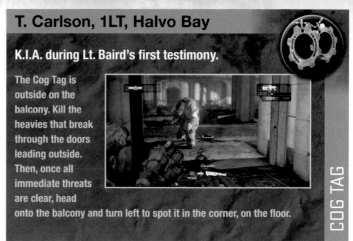

The Cog Tag is outside on the balcony. Kill the heavies that break through the doors leading outside. Then, once all immediate threats are clear, head onto the balcony and turn left to spot it in the corner, on the floor.

COG TAG

Eliminate the Boomers, Grinders, and Therons. Then head outside to where the heavies came from to get the COG Tag and leave any strays for your squad to handle. Gather any dropped power weapons—there will likely be an assortment of Boomshots and Torque Bows with a few rounds left in each—and duck into cover near the sandbags and plinths to the right.

The final enemies come from the doorway opposite where you entered. Use the available cover in the center, near the Frag Grenades, and advance slowly, as they have a Flame Boomer in their midst. They can be very difficult to spot in the thick smoke, so lob a Frag Grenade through the doorway before advancing to make sure the last of them have been killed.

Take cover just inside the hall and lob a Boomshot rocket at the enemies on the platform to the right.

Hold this position as you pinpoint the location of the Locust bursting through the doors and windows from the balcony.

Use the plinths for cover and let the rest of Kilo Squad draw the enemies out of that final hallway.

SECTION 3: TERRACE

X

MISSION OBJECTIVES
> Get to the Raven.
> Find a way to the ground floor.

HOSTILES ENCOUNTERED

3	4	5	8	8
WRETCH	LAMBENT WRETCH	GRENADIER	THERON GUARD	THERON W/ CLEAVER

9	11	12	15
FLAME BOOMER	BOOMER	BLOODMOUNT	MAULER

⭐ = Star Score

COG TAGS

T

LONGSHOT

AMMO

STIM-GAS GRENADE

2

3

SAWED-OFF

GNASHER

LANCER

MULCHER

1

STIM-GAS GRENADE

DECLASSIFY

STIM-GAS GRENADE

STIM-GAS GRENADE

RETRO

AMMO

BOOMSHOT

AMMO

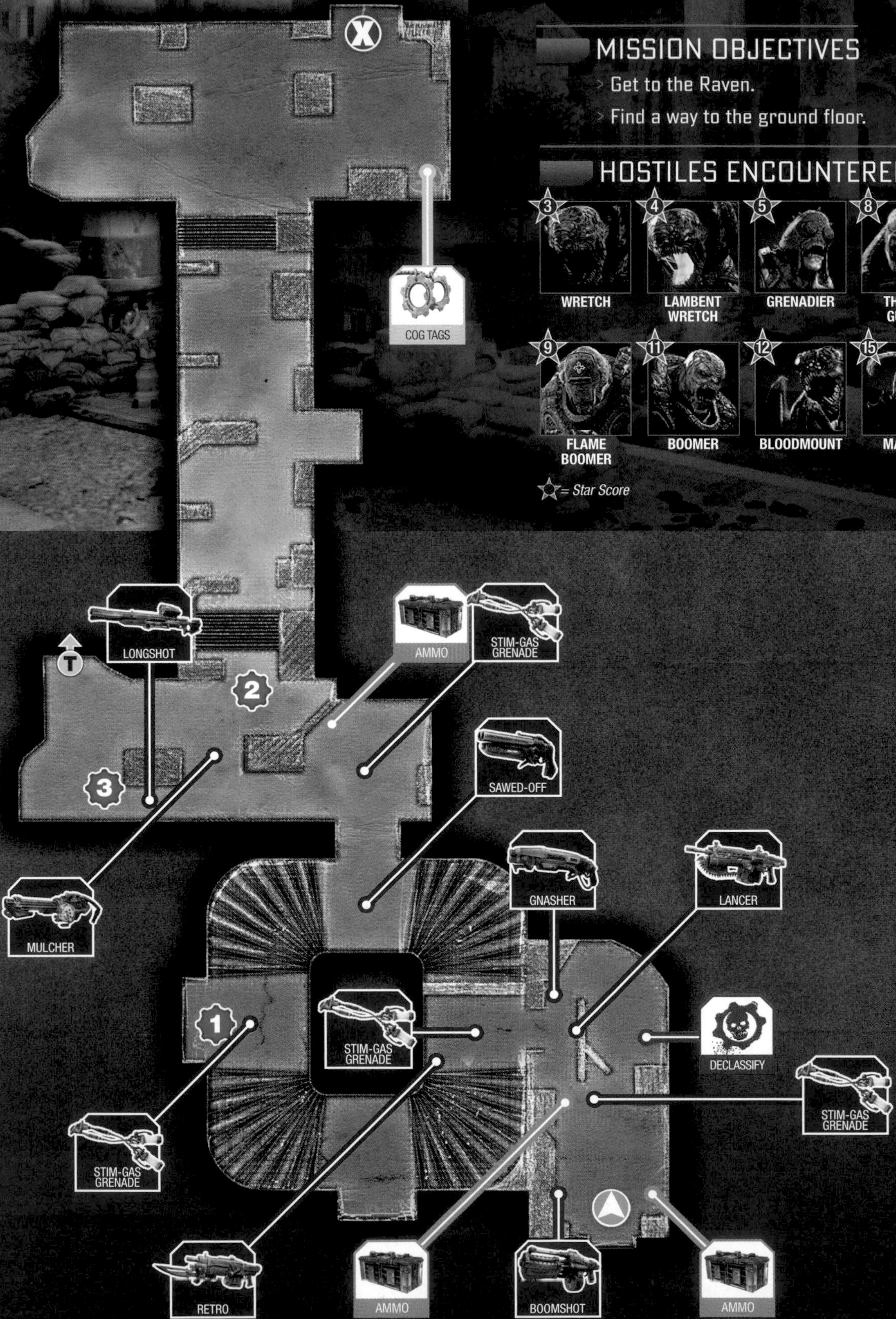

RIBBONS AND SCORING

If playing without the Declassified option active, you can risk using the Lancer's chainsaw throughout the duration of the staircase descent to earn three or more Lumberjack ribbons. Once off the stairs, the potential to earn ribbons is virtually the same regardless of classification. Use the Boomshot and Sawed-Off Shotgun to earn any multi-kill ribbons you can manage. There is an outside chance of earning a None Shall Pass ribbon with the Troika, but the Wretches and Bloodmounts will likely slip past while the turret is on cooldown. You can earn three Stars while playing the Declassified option while just earning a single ribbon if you avoid being downed.

LUMBERJACK: Chainsaw 3 enemies in a row.

CLUSTERLUCK: Kill multiple enemies with one grenade.

BOOMBARDIER: Kill multiple enemies with a single Boomshot blast.

NOTHIN' BUT BITS: Kill multiple enemies with a single Sawed-Off Shotgun blast.

CLASSIFIED INTEL

1 There are a number of ways to approach the fight on the stairs, including using the Gnasher or taking a Theron as a meatshield for the long descent. Here's another way: Load up on Lancer and Boomshot ammo in the room where the mission begins and head onto the spiraling staircase. You must fight through a dozen Wretches and Therons on your way to the bottom. One way to do this is to use the Lancer's chainsaw almost exclusively. Continue chainsawing the Wretches for multiple Lumberjack ribbons. Deploy a Stim-Gas Grenade whenever you start to take damage.

2 Swap out the Lancer for the Sawed-Off Shotgun at the bottom of the stairs and use it and the Boomshot you've been carrying to kill the enemies outside the door. Rush to the Troika if you have time. Otherwise, use the Boomshot against the Therons and Bloodmounts streaming across the walkway ahead. Switch to the Sawed-Off Shotgun as they near and try to get in close enough for a Nothin' But Bits ribbon.

3 Equip the Longshot leaning against the sandbags once the Bloodmounts are slain and start sniping the final wave of enemies. Aim for the Boomers first, and then back away and no-scope headshot the Therons with the Cleavers as they charge towards you. Save the Flame Boomer for last, as it's the easiest to dodge and can be killed with any of the weapons scattered around at the end of the battle.

DECLASSIFY

HEALTH DOESN'T REGENERATE

Col. Loomis's report made no mention of Kilo Squad's reduced recuperative abilities.

Difficulty Increase: High

Star Multiplier: 2.32x

If not for the presence of the Stim-Gas Grenades, this would be one of the most difficult challenges to ever hit Sera. Though still very difficult, it is possible. You must make strategic use of the Stim-Gas Grenades, retreat back up the stairs to collect more, and be very careful about avoiding the ravenous Wretches and Bloodmounts. You can always duck behind cover to avoid a bullet, but a pack of razor-clawed, leaping beasts can be even harder to avoid.

Equip the Lancer and Boomshot at the start of the mission, but refrain from using the latter until outside the tower. Kilo Squad must fight their way down a spiraling staircase, past numerous Wretches and Therons. There are a total of three Stim-Gas Grenade pickups in this tower and they represent your only way to heal once you've taken damage (though you can still be revived when downed).

If you begin the mission with any Frag Grenades, descend to the first groups of Wretches and toss your Frags to get some Clusterluck ribbons. Run back up the stairs and grab the Stim-Gas Grenades from the starting area. Descend with the Lancer in hand and hip-fire at the Wretches and grab more Stim-Gas Grenades. Try to spot one of the Therons before the rest of Kilo does and take it as a meatshield. Having a meatshield goes a long way towards keeping you full of health. On the other hand, any heavy units that make their way into the tower should be introduced to the Boomshot as quickly as possible.

Grab the first Theron you encounter for use as a meatshield.

Continue relying on the Lancer during the descent and try to avoid having to use any Stim-Gas Grenades. Once at the bottom, swap out the Lancer for the Sawed-Off Shotgun and switch to the Boomshot. Fire a couple of rockets through the doorway to clear out the remaining Locust at close range (make sure you're well out of the blast radius).

Run to the Troika on the left and open fire on the Locust that leap up to the walkway. You might encounter Wretches, Lambent Wretches, or Bloodmounts. Back away from the Troika as soon as the Locust get perpendicular to your position. Toss a Stim-Gas Grenade down and resume using the Boomshot and Sawed-Off Shotgun to keep yourself alive while an army of heavy units begins their march across the terrace.

The Sawed-Off Shotgun is perfect for clearing away the normal Wretches, but shouldn't be used against Lambent Wretches on the higher difficulties.

Resist the urge to cross the terrace until you've dealt with every last enemy, including the Theron Guards that serve as the final hurdle. Shoulder the Longshot behind the sandbags near the Troika and snipe your way to the end of the mission.

Those Therons are all that stand between Kilo Squad and the North Entrance.

S. Mograbi, PFC, Jacinto

K.I.A. during Private Cole's testimony.

The COG Tag is located in the far right-hand corner, near the door leading out of the mission area. Don't end the mission without first finding it in the corner.

COG TAG

SECTION 4: NORTH ENTRANCE

MISSION OBJECTIVES

- Get to the Raven.
- Reach the main entrance.

HOSTILES ENCOUNTERED

② TICKER	③ WRETCH	③ DRONE
⑧ THERON GUARD	⑧ THERON W/ CLEAVER	⑫ KANTUS

☆ — Star Score

X

5

BOOMSHOT

FRAG GRENADE

FRAG GRENADE

GNASHER

R-SENTINEL

DECLASSIFY

AMMO

SAWED-OFF

AMMO

X2

TRIPWIRE XBOW

MULCHER

1

2

4

3

COG TAGS

T

AMMO

LANCER

LONGSHOT

AMMO

RIBBONS AND SCORING

This is the single-best mission in the game for earning It's a Trap ribbons, as there are two Tripwire Crossbows available at the start and narrow staircases that the enemies must proceed along. It's also conducive for earning Plug That Hole ribbons, as there are no fewer than five Emergence Holes that you can close. Though it's possible to earn a Hat Trick ribbon with the Longshot, the rest of Kilo Squad may interfere with your chance if you don't work quickly. Your approach to earning ribbons shouldn't change based on whether you're playing with the Declassified option or not. Earning two Stars without the Declassified option is common; earning three with the blurred vision challenge is just a matter of minimizing your time spent on all fours.

IT'S A TRAP: Kill multiple enemies with a single Tripwire Crossbow shot.

PLUG THAT HOLE: Close an E-Hole with explosives.

BOOMBARDIER: Kill multiple enemies with a single Boomshot blast.

CLASSIFIED INTEL

1

Position the Range Sentinel at the top of the stairs and grab either of the two Tripwire Crossbows. Use the first one to quickly fire Tripwires at the flight of stairs across the room, before the Locust make their descent. Pick up the Frag Grenades behind the pillar atop the stairs.

2

Stand close to the Range Sentinel and defend your stairs with Frag Grenades and the Lancer until there is a brief lull in the fighting. Quickly grab the other Tripwire Crossbow and fire bolts to set traps on the stairs leading up to your position and also near the base of the walls below, where the Emergence Holes are opening.

3

Several Drones and Snipers attack from the opposing balcony. Grab the Longshot where you first entered and take cover behind one of the pillars. Take your time sniping the Locust on that balcony, as reinforcements will not arrive until they've been eliminated.

4

Carry the Range Sentinel down the stairs and approach the statue between the stairs as it starts to fall into an E-Hole. Place the Range Sentinel down and lob a Frag into the hole before the Locust climb out.

5

Replenish your Lancer ammo and equip the Boomshot off to the right, before the stairs. Kilo Squad has one final room to clear and it's infected with Theron Guards, Drones, and a Locust with a Scorcher. Use the Boomshot to clear the platform to the right. Advance to that elevated position and continue to use your explosives to close the E-Holes in the far corners of the room. The sooner you close the E-Holes, the safer you'll be.

DECLASSIFIED: THREE-STAR TACTICS

TAKING DAMAGE IMPAIRS SIGHT

Col. Loomis's report contained nothing about Kilo Squad's impaired vision due to exertion and injuries.

Difficulty Increase: Low

Star Multiplier: 2.00x

Kilo Squad has bounced back from their previous challenge. They're now recuperating their health, but their vision is blurred when injured. Fortunately, it's only blurred at a distance; they can still see close objects just fine. Let the rest of Kilo Squad challenge enemies up close while you stay in cover and attack from afar. That's the key to good eye health!

Quickly set the Range Sentinel on the upper landing, pointing down the stairs. Grab the Tripwire Crossbow, and move towards the Longshot pickup location. Aim through the gap in the railing to fire multiple Tripwires at the wall at the base of the far stairs, low on the wall near the Crimson Omen. Fire the four, and then pick up the second Tripwire Crossbow and move back to that same location to do it again, once the first ones you fired start to get tripped. You can rack up numerous It's a Trap ribbons here—this is a great place to farm that ribbon for the corresponding medal if you so choose. You can also aim the first couple of Tripwire bolts at the base of the column atop the other flight of stairs, directly across from where you pick up the Tripwire Crossbows.

Place multiple Tripwires just under the Crimson Omen on the opposing stairs.

Another good spot for the Tripwires is at the top of the enemy stairs.

Additional Locust emerge from E-Holes in the center of the lower floor, to the left. Grab the Frag Grenades from behind the column atop the stairs where you start and be ready to toss them down for a Clusterluck or Plug That Hole ribbon. Swap out the Gnasher for the Longshot and set to sniping any Kantuses before they can summon too many Tickers. It's also worth sniping any enemies that appear with Scorchers. Try to stay close to the reloaded Range Sentinel and trust it to protect your upper position. The rest of the squad advances down the stairs and draws most of the attention, leaving you to snipe with relative calm.

You can't snipe with blurry vision, so keep your head down when waiting for a shot.

Save one Frag Grenade for the final E-Hole, which opens down the hall on the lower level, closer to the next room you need to reach. Toss the Frag and finish them off.

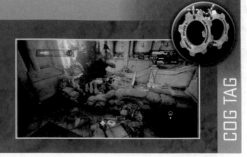
Enter the small room outside of this hall and load up on ammo and weaponry. The next fight can be difficult, as you'll be dealing with many Theron Guards. Take the Boomshot along with the Sawed-Off Shotgun or Gnasher and grab the Frag Grenades.

Kick open the door and quickly move into cover on an angle to the right. Use the Boomshot to take out any approaching Locust from the center and fire again onto the platform on the right to thin the number of Drones and Therons there. Advance with the Sawed-Off, blast any still standing, then quickly switch to the Boomshot and use it to close the E-Hole in the back-right corner.

One well-aimed Boomshot can clear away most of the enemies on the platform to the right.

More Locust may be around, so be careful. They move fast and are very aggressive. A second Emergence Hole opens in the back-left corner, on the raised platforms there. It's possible to close it with a Boomshot or Frag Grenade while standing on the right-hand platform. Stick close to your squad and use your explosives only at a distance. Otherwise, stick to the Sawed-Off Shotgun or commandeer one of the Scorchers that get dropped by the Flame Boomers.

It's a long toss, but it's worth a shot.

FRAG GRENADE

FRAG GRENADE

COG TAGS

AMMO

MISSION OBJECTIVES

> Reach the main entrance.
> Clear the area of Locust.

BOOMSHOT

INK GRENADE

X

3 **1** **2**

AMMO

HOSTILES ENCOUNTERED

 3
 7
 8

DRONE

GRENADIER

THERON GUARD

 9
 12
 15

FLAME BOOMER

BLOODMOUNT

GRINDER

☆ = Star Score

DECLASSIFY

FRAG GRENADE

LONGSHOT

SAWED-OFF

SAWED-OFF

LANCER

GNASHER

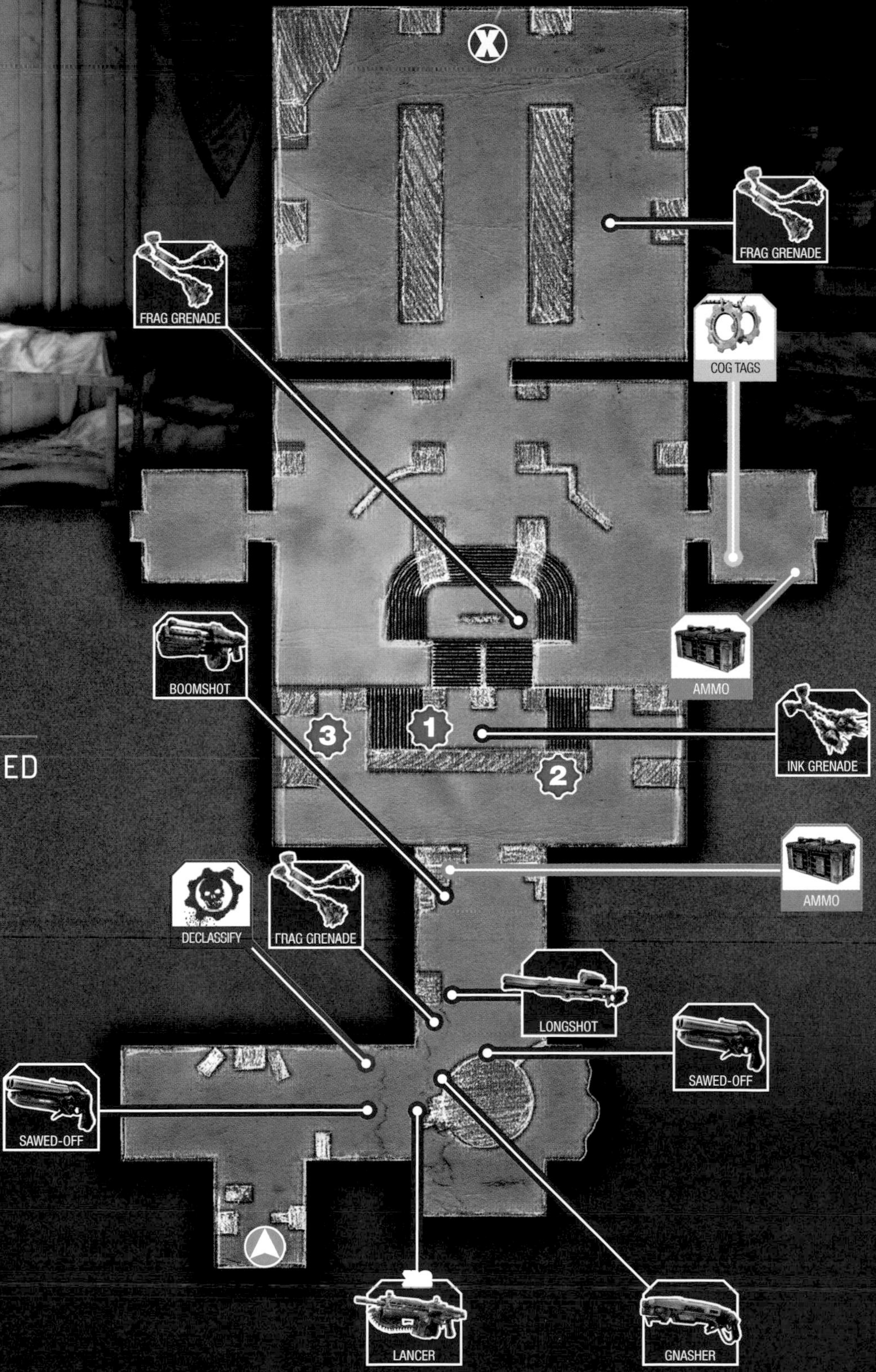

"ALL THAT'S LEFT OF LOOMIS'S GRAND STRATEGY..."

RIBBONS AND SCORING

Though you may earn a Nothin' But Bits ribbon while playing the Declassified option, you'll have to play without it if you want to earn many ribbons on this mission. The presence of a Boomshot and Longshot, as well as so many Frag Grenades, makes this a prime spot to load up on Boombardier, Hat Trick, and Clusterluck ribbons. Earn enough of them while avoiding being downed, and you just might get three Stars without accepting the Declassified option. Earning three Stars with the Boomshield and Sawed-Off is not a problem, as long as you don't let the rest of Kilo Squad do all the work for you.

CLUSTERLUCK: Kill multiple enemies with one grenade.

BOOMBARDIER: Kill multiple enemies with a single Boomshot blast.

HAT TRICK: Score 3 headshots in a row without dying.

NOTHIN' BUT BITS: Kill multiple enemies with a single Sawed-Off Shotgun blast.

CLASSIFIED INTEL

1

2

3

Collect both Sawed-Off Shotguns, the Boomshot, and the Frag Grenades. Then race through the door and down the stairs to the first landing. Plant a Frag Grenade at the base of each set of stairs in case you need to retreat. Use the Boomshot to eliminate as many of the early attackers as you can, making sure to take advantage of Boombardier opportunities. Try to push a little lower to the Ink and Frag Grenades and put them to use as well.

Retreat to the upper hallway and swap the empty Boomshot for the Longshot, hopefully before the Bloodmounts arrive. Grab the Mulcher and carry it a few steps to either side and use it to cut down the Bloodmounts and any Grinders coming up the stairs. The rest of Kilo Squad is likely near the sandbags at the base of the stairs, drawing much of the Locust attention.

A final parade of enemies makes their way from beyond the heavy doors in the center of the hall. Switch to the Longshot and take position off to the side, at the top of the stairs, and start sniping. There's absolutely no reason to descend the stairs until the last Locust body hits the floor.

DECLASSIFIED: THREE-STAR TACTICS

DECLASSIFY

USE BOOMSHIELDS AND SAWED-OFFS ONLY

Col. Loomis's report stressed that no Locust weapons were employed by COG forces.

Difficulty Increase: Moderate

Star Multiplier: 2.56x

This option offers a significant departure from the standard classification. Rather than using Boomshots and Longshots, each member of Kilo Squad is equipped with just a Boomshield and Sawed-Off Shotgun. Keep the shield in front of you at all times and use the architecture's natural chokepoints to your advantage.

Move down the side stairs to the first landing in time to engage the first wave of Locust heavies. You encounter numerous Flame Boomers, Bloodmounts, and Grinders early on, so keep your shield in front of you at all times. Move between the railing and the center column of whatever side the most enemies are coming from and try luring them to you in single file. Ignore the Locust that remain on the upper balconies across the hall, as they eventually jump down to attack up close.

The Boomshield keeps you from getting burned as you wait for the Flame Boomer to get close enough to kill.

Let the rest of Kilo Squad go ahead; hold your ground and let the Bloodmounts funnel towards you.

Maintain your position on the stairs, near the sandbags, until all of the enemies from the side rooms and E-Holes are killed. The final two or three Locust burst through the heavy doors opposite the stairs. Expect some combination of Grinders and Flame Boomers. Stick to one side and circle towards them from the periphery. Do not approach straight-on, as you risk splitting them—your Boomshield can only protect you if both of them are kept in front of you.

Approach the door on an angle to keep both Locust heavies in front of you.

G. Valera, WO1, Ilima

K.I.A. when the final COG lines inside of the Courthouse broke.

Clear the room of Locust. Then enter the room on the right side of the main entrance hall. The doors to this room are locked initially, but Grinders and Bloodmounts break through during the battle. Enter this room to get the COG Tag near an ammo crate on your way to the finish.

COG TAG

MULCHER

COG TAGS

TRIPWIRE XBOW

LONGSHOT

DECLASSIFY

1

2

X

GNASHER X2

AMMO

AMMO

RETRO

FRAG GRENADE

LANCER

BOOMSHOT

3

RETRO

4

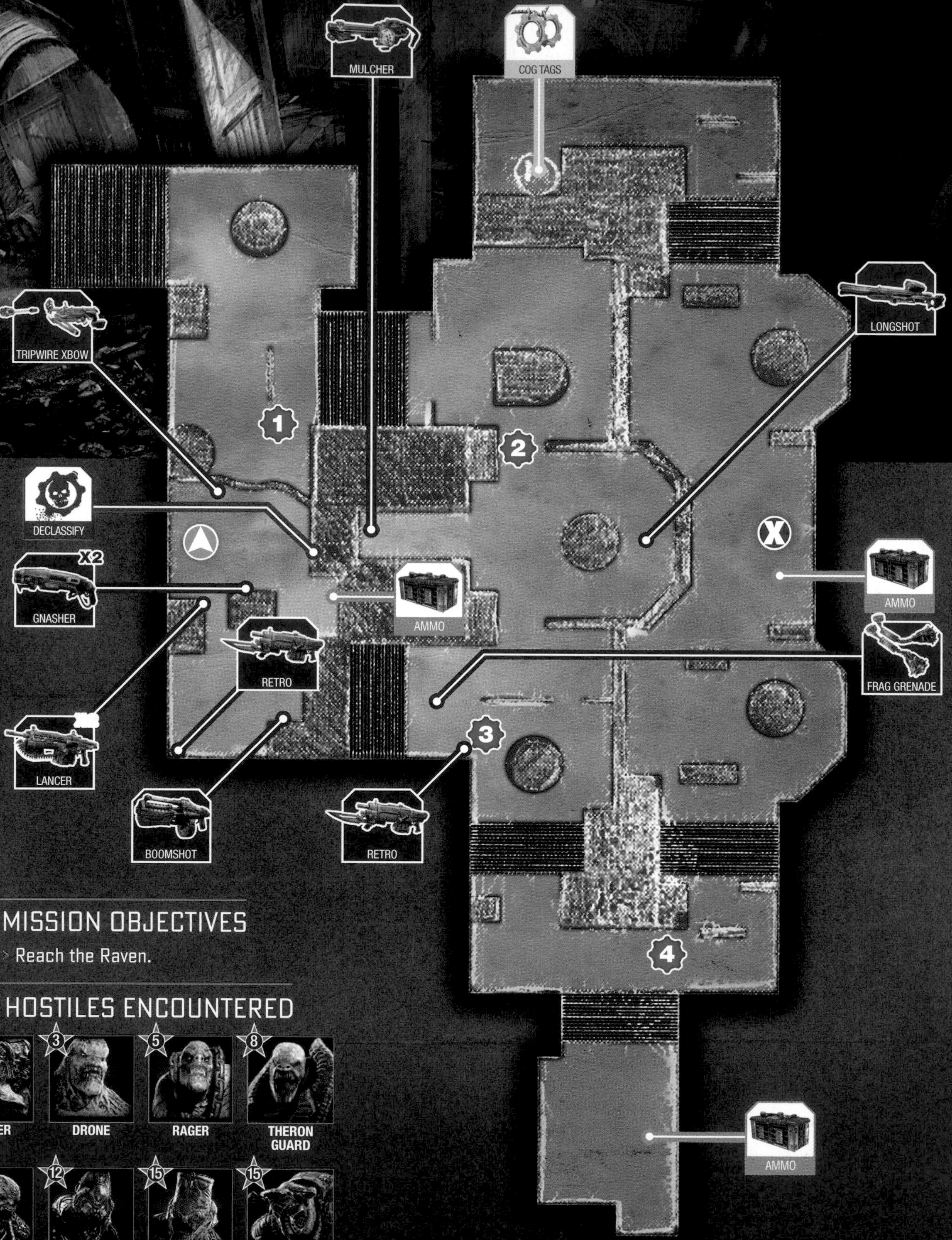

MISSION OBJECTIVES
> Reach the Raven.

HOSTILES ENCOUNTERED

2	3	5	8
TICKER	DRONE	RAGER	THERON GUARD

11	12	15	15
BOOMER	KANTUS	GRINDER	ELITE MAULER

☆ = Star Score

AMMO

"THE RAVEN'S DOWN THE STAIRS TO THE LEFT, KILO!"

RIBBONS AND SCORING

There's almost no limit to the number and variety of ribbons that can be earned on this mission. Frequent use of the Boomshot and Frag Grenades all but guarantees at least a couple of their respective multi-kill ribbons. Similarly, you almost can't help but get a Plug That Hole ribbon at the very start of the mission. There are enough heavy units on the map to Spot that you can still get plenty of kills on your own without worrying about the squad stealing kills. Lastly, numerous enemies of all kinds leap in the air as you reach the turn in the stairs. Use a Breechshot or Longshot to snipe them while they're airborne to earn the Pull! ribbon. Maximize these ribbon-scoring opportunities, rack up as many headshots as possible, and avoid being downed, and you just might earn three Stars without accepting the Declassified challenge.

CLUSTERLUCK: Kill multiple enemies with one grenade.

BOOMBARDIER: Kill multiple enemies with a single Boomshot blast.

PLUG THAT HOLE: Close an E-Hole with explosives.

PULL!: Kill a ground-bursting enemy in the air.

MILITARY INTELLIGENCE: Spot 5 enemies ending in kills.

CLASSIFIED INTEL

Equip the Boomshot and Lancer and pick up the Tripwire Crossbow near the sandbags. Mantle the sandbags and quickly switch to the Boomshot and fire it at the Emergence Hole opening at the base of the stairs. Time this shot well and you can earn multiple Boombardier ribbons and a Plug That Hole ribbon with one shot!

Use the Tripwire Crossbow to set two double-traps on the side of the planter just past the door where Colonel Loomis emerges. Hold this position near the circular planter and use the Boomshot and Frag Grenades to keep the Locust heavies at bay. Scavenge additional Boomshot ammo if you saw one drop. Otherwise, swap out the spent Boomshot for the Longshot and advance to the Frag Grenades ahead on the right.

You need to make a major stand near the second circular planter. Get creative with the weapons you scavenge for use against the numerous Ragers, Therons, and Grinders coming at you. Consider planting an abandoned Boomshield into the ground for mobile cover and use the Longshot or Torque Bow from behind it. There's also a Mulcher in the closet where Loomis was that can come in handy.

A large number of Locust burst from the ground near the turn, so don't rush around the corner just yet. Sweep in wide to ensure none pop up behind you. Then look for a fallen Breechshot or Torque Bow to use against the final group of Locust nearest the Raven.

DECLASSIFIED: THREE-STAR TACTICS

FINISH BEFORE AMMO DUMP EXPLODES

Col. Loomis's report stated clearly that all COG ammunition was stored safely and securely.

Difficulty Increase: High

Star Multiplier: 2.51x

Countdown to Ammo Dump Explodes

CASUAL	NORMAL	HARDCORE	INSANE
6:00	5:20	4:00	6:00

This mission plays much the same way regardless of classification, only you can't afford to be as patient when the ammo dump is going to explode. There's a much smaller margin for error when playing Declassified. You must kill swiftly, constantly scavenge for the most powerful weapons available, and not give up ground.

The key to reaching the Raven before the ammo dump explodes lies in making sure each of your actions is both precise and maximizes your available firepower. A large number of scavengeable power weapons are available as you fight your way down the Great Staircase. You need to make the most of them in order to beat back one of the largest Locust armies the COG has ever encountered.

Get the race to the Raven off to a good start by loading up on Boomshot and Lancer ammo and taking the Tripwire Crossbow as you mantle the sandbags. Quickly switch to the Boomshot and fire a rocket into the E-Hole opening down the stairs. Use the Lancer to finish off any Locust who survive the blast. Then pick back up the Tripwire Crossbow and run down the stairs and around the corner to where Colonel Loomis joins your squad.

Close this E-Hole with the Boomshot and try to meet up with Colonel Loomis in under 30 seconds.

Set several Tripwire Crossbow traps on the planter just past the door Colonel Loomis exited and fall back to the area near the circular planter. Use the Boomshot and Frag Grenades to aid the Tripwire traps in absorbing the combination of Elite Maulers, Boomers, Ragers, and Therons that attack here.

> Don't hesitate to use the Tripwire Crossbow to headshot an enemy if they're not going to hit your traps.

> Aim the Tripwire Crossbow at any smooth surface that you expect the Elite Mauler to walk past.

Your ability to make quick work of the initial crush of Elite Maulers and other units that attack where Colonel Loomis appears goes a long way in determining your success or failure in this mission. Always be on the lookout for fallen weapons and move to procure your favorite one, whether it is the Boomshot, Torque Bow, or Longshot. Those are the three you should be continuing to pair with the Lancer.

The area where the path turns between the two sets of steps is the most dangerous part of the Great Staircase descent. This area should be avoided at all costs until you know there aren't any enemies left to emerge. Advance only so far as the second circular planter. This elevated position gives you a clear view of the enemies bursting from holes in the turn, as well as those marching up the steps from the Raven. Toss the Frag Grenades down the steps towards the turn and then quickly gather any fallen weapons. It's worth grabbing something that you can use to headshot the Ragers before they enrage, even if it's a Torque Bow or Breechshot.

> Put any scavenged Boomshot ammo to use against the Locust bursting from the ground at the turn.

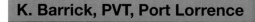

> Spot any remaining heavy enemies to focus your squad's firepower on them to save time.

K. Barrick, PVT, Port Lorrence

K.I.A. during Lt. Baird's second testimony.

The COG Tag is located well past the mission end and can take as much as eight seconds round-trip to get from where you need to beat the ammo depot explosion. Continue past the mission end-point and around the corner to the left to find it. We recommend playing this mission once without the time limit if for no other reason than to get this COG Tag without having to risk failing the mission.

COG TAG

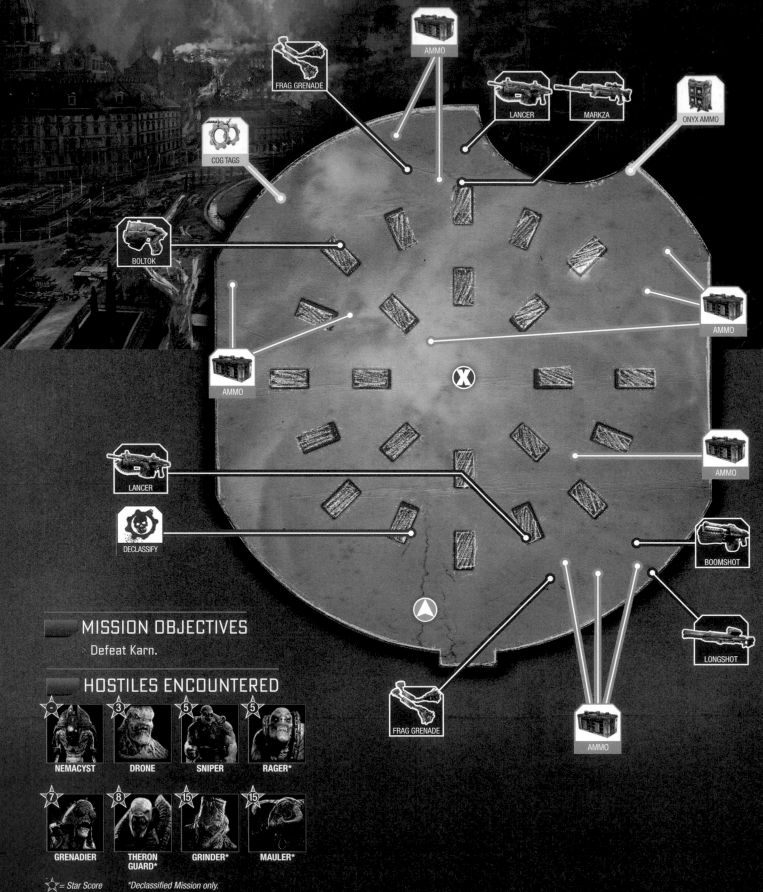

FRAG GRENADE

AMMO

LANCER

MARKZA

ONYX AMMO

COG TAGS

BOLTOK

AMMO

AMMO

LANCER

AMMO

DECLASSIFY

BOOMSHOT

LONGSHOT

FRAG GRENADE

AMMO

MISSION OBJECTIVES

> Defeat Karn.

HOSTILES ENCOUNTERED

NEMACYST	DRONE	SNIPER	RAGER*
3	5	5	

GRENADIER	THERON GUARD*	GRINDER*	MAULER*
7	8	15	15

☆ = Star Score   *Declassified Mission only.

RIBBONS AND SCORING

Those hoping to earn three Stars against Karn must take advantage of the Locust reinforcements and earn as many ribbons off of them as possible. Hold onto your Frag Grenades and Boomshot (or Boltok or Longshot) until Karn calls for support personnel. Use your explosives to take them out as they land from their ground-bursting arrival to earn Clusterluck and Boombardier ribbons. Those playing without the Declassified option will find it easy to use the Lancer's chainsaw for an execution bonus and possibly a Lumberjack ribbon as well. The elite forces that defend Karn on the Declassified setting are generally harder to chainsaw but offer more points upon death. Though the Stars accumulate only marginally faster with the Declassified option accepted, the enemies you encounter are worth many more points. Earning three Stars with the Declassified option accepted is quite a challenge and earning it without the elite reinforcements is all but impossible.

CLUSTERLUCK: Kill multiple enemies with one grenade.

BOOMBARDIER: Kill multiple enemies with a single Boomshot blast.

HAT TRICK: Score 3 headshots in a row without dying.

RAGE DENIED!: Kill an enraged Rager with a melee attack.

MILITARY INTELLIGENCE: Spot 5 enemies ending in kills.

ELITE LOCUST DEFEND KARN

Col. Loomis's report denied arrival of additional elite forces during battle with supposed Locust tactician known as Karn.

Difficulty Increase: High

Star Multiplier: 1.43x

Accepting this challenge effectively replaces the Drones, Snipers, and Grenadiers with a mixture of Grinders, Maulers, Ragers, and Theron Guards. On the one hand, this dramatically increases the difficulty, but it also yields many more points and offers a chance to scavenge some powerful weapons during the fight. Other than this enemy swap, the battle plays out in identical fashion.

KARN

Immediately take cover at the start of the battle to avoid the twin chainguns. Switch to the Lancer, lean out of cover, and target the glowing barrels of the chainguns. You must disable the guns one at a time (the disabled gun tilts upwards, out of commission) to prod Karn into revealing the beast named Shibboleth's weak point. Try to move between pieces of tall cover and visit the ammo cache whenever the Lancer drops below 150 rounds of ammo.

With the guns disabled, Karn has no choice but to lean forward and prepare to attack with an incendiary launcher on Shibboleth's back. Continue shooting the launcher, but monitor it for successful launches. Back away from the incendiary bombs hurtling towards you and fall back into cover. Failure to destroy the launcher before it commences firing allows the beast to once again use its chainguns. Destroy the guns again, reload, and prepare to target the incendiary launcher. You should be able to destroy the launcher during this second cycle and effectively wound Shibboleth.

The Lancer is the weapon of choice for taking out Karn's chainguns.

Target the incendiary launcher on the beast's back once the guns are disabled.

The fire from the incendiary bombs spreads fast and wide, so get clear.

Having lost the incendiary launcher, Karn climbs to the top of one of the buildings flanking the plaza and summons reinforcements. Depending on the classification status, you either face Snipers and Grenadiers or a mixture of elite Locust units. Sprint to the ammo pile to the right of the starting point and swap out the Gnasher for the Boomshot and grab the Frag Grenades. Lob your explosives at any groups of enemies that form after they land from their ground-burst to earn a Clusterluck or Boombardier ribbon. Another option is to equip the Markza or Boltok and try to rack up the headshots for a Hat Trick ribbon. Either way, the Onyx Ammo Cache to the right of Karn's crater is there to replenish your power weapon when needed.

Colonel Loomis gives the squad a fifth member, which helps dramatically with reviving downed teammates.

Karn soon returns to the battlefield and mixes in a trample attack with the chaingun. Take care to avoid being run over and listen for Cole and Sofia's shouts to target the oversized mechanical leg when it starts to glow. Karn uses this leg to fire Diggers through the ground at you. Back away while continuing to shoot the leg with your Lancer. Avoid getting too close to Karn and Shibboleth while they're stationary; they deploy a toxic ink cloud when threatened at close range. Destroying the leg wounds Shibboleth a second time. In pain and angry, the creature speeds across the plaza in fury, attempting to trample you for what you've done. Dodge out of its path and watch as it climbs the side of the other building.

Target the giant glowing leg while backing away from the underground Digger bombs it deploys.

You might notice that the reticle turns red when Karn is targeted atop the building, but save your ammo. There's nothing you can do to him while he's out of the arena recovering for the next wave. Instead, use this time to replenish ammo supplies and ready for the next wave of reinforcements.

Karn summons another wave of reinforcements from atop the building, but not before deploying a small flock of Nemacysts. The Nemacysts soar overhead and dive-bomb Kilo Squad's location. You can generally ignore them if you stay on the move, as they offer no points toward earning a Star.

This second wave of reinforcements is your key to earning enough ribbons to three-Star the battle.

The next wave of reinforcements emerges near the building where Karn is located. The Boomshot and Frag Grenades can once again work wonders against them, but more continue to attack throughout the remainder of the battle. Therons and Grinders are always a threat, but you really need to watch out for an enraged Rager charging up behind you. One way to ensure they don't get a chance to enrage is to use the Lancer's chainsaw to execute them (if you don't have one of the headshot-capable weapons on hand).

The third phase of this battle is similar to the first in that you must disable the twin chainguns to reveal Shibboleth's weakness. The only difference, aside from the presence of other Locust forces, is that trample and Imulsion bomb attacks are now mixed in with the chaingun bullet storms.

Continue to target the chainguns as Karn strafes around the battlefield. Stick to the outside, narrower ends of the taller cover to keep him in front of you and avoid the gunfire. Shibboleth periodically rears back on its hind legs and fires an arcing bomb of Imulsion that can fly up and over cover. Cover-swap laterally around the perimeter of the plaza to avoid this attack when it lifts its legs.

Steer clear of Karn's long distance Imulsion bombs!

You must disable the chainguns to get Shibboleth to finally expose its mouth. This is the final weak point. If you don't destroy it in time, it will reactivate its guns and attack again. It also periodically summons more reinforcements throughout this final third phase. Don't hesitate to unload on Shibboleth's mouth with everything you've got.

Open fire on the beast's mouth to down it and continue firing while the reticle is red.

Hit it with any remaining explosives or power weapons you have. It's essentially defenseless when it squats down and exposes its mouth—finish it!

D. Jones, CPT, Andius

K.I.A. shortly after trying to warn Col. Loomis to postpone Kilo Squad's tribunal.

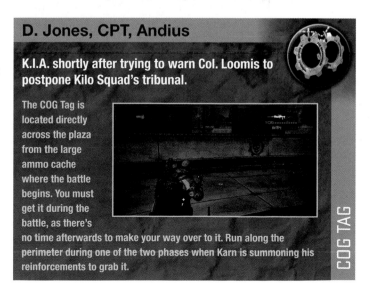

The COG Tag is located directly across the plaza from the large ammo cache where the battle begins. You must get it during the battle, as there's no time afterwards to make your way over to it. Run along the perimeter during one of the two phases when Karn is summoning his reinforcements to grab it.

COG TAG

AFTERMATH CAMPAIGN

AFTERMATH

SECTION 1: REUNION

Halvo Bay
24 Hours Before Adam Fenix Releases the Imulsion Cure

Have you ever wondered where Baird and Cole went while the rest of Delta Squad
was procuring that old submarine from the shipyard? Did you want to know
more about the ship Baird and Cole used to reach Azura? Puzzled over who those
reinforcements were that accompanied them? If so, the Aftermath Campaign is for
you. These six chapters represent a previously unseen Act from *Gears of War 3*,
presented in a style reminiscent of the previous games. There are no Stars to earn
here, nor are there any mission details to Declassify. Just Cole, Baird, Carmine, and
an old friend of Baird's by the name of Paduk. You may have heard of him.

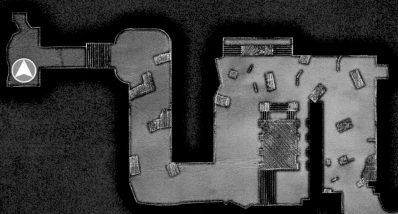

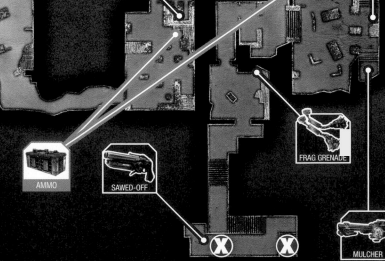

RETRO

AMMO

LONGSHOT

GRENADE

FRAG GRENADE

FRAG GRENADE

AMMO

SAWED-OFF

MULCHER

MISSION OBJECTIVES

> Rendezvous with Paduk's allies.
> Escape the landslide.
> Find your way out of the service station.
> Find a way to open the gate.
> Defend against the ambushing Locust.
> Investigate the shopping center.

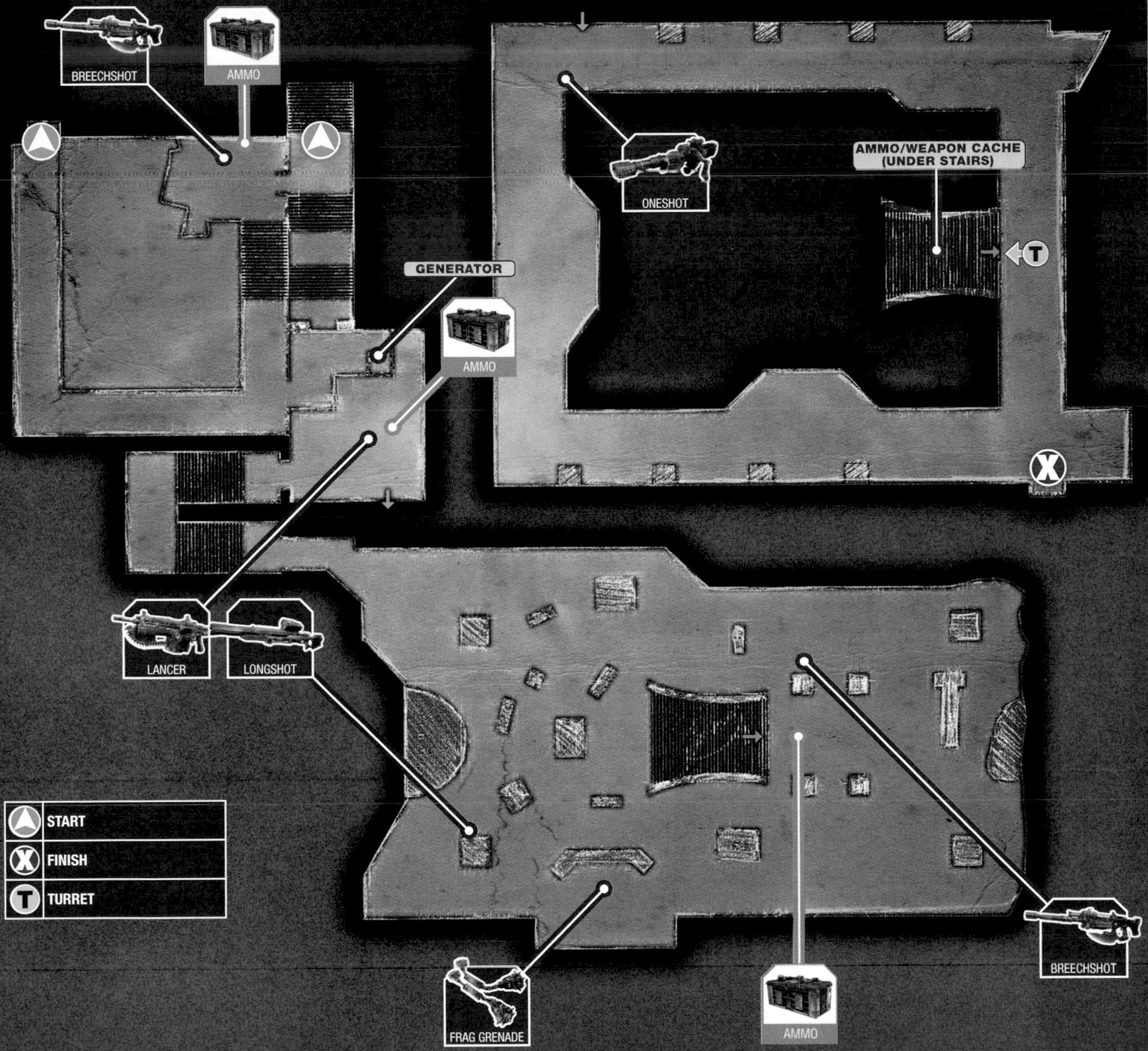

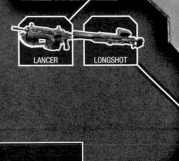

BREECHSHOT

AMMO

ONESHOT

AMMO/WEAPON CACHE
(UNDER STAIRS)

AFTERMATH

GENERATOR

AMMO

T

X

LANCER

LONGSHOT

BREECHSHOT

	START
X	FINISH
T	TURRET

FRAG GRENADE

AMMO

HOSTILES ENCOUNTERED

TICKER	RAGER	SAVAGE BOOMER	SAVAGE DRONE	SNIPER	SAVAGE GRENADIER

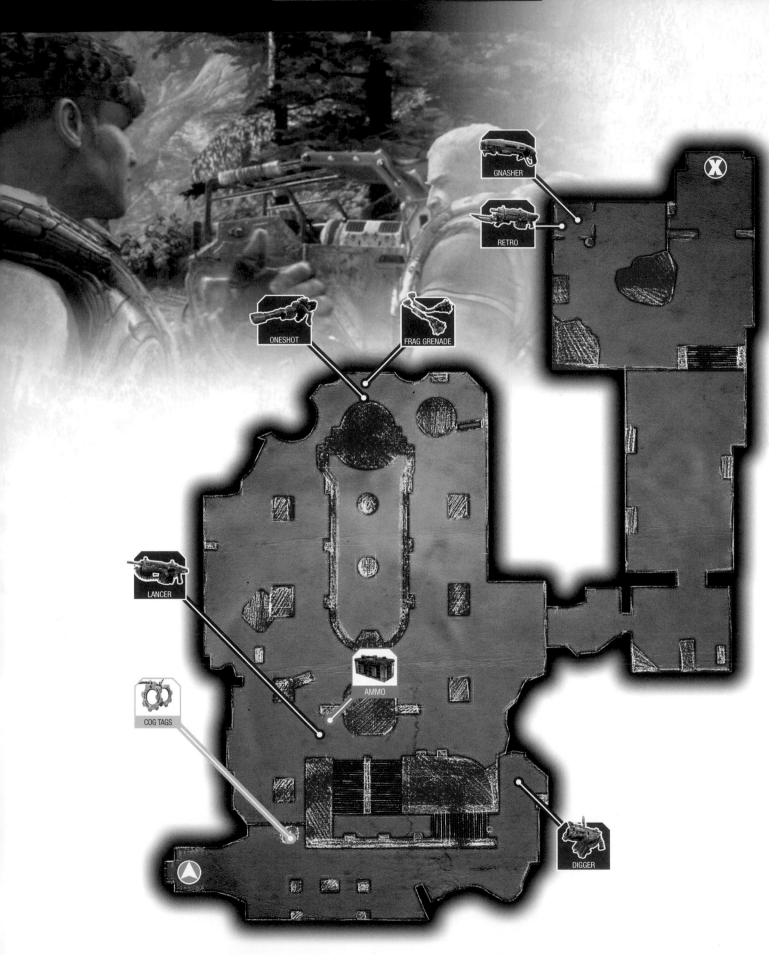

GNASHER

RETRO

ONESHOT

FRAG GRENADE

LANCER

AMMO

COG TAGS

DIGGER

HALVO BAY OVERLOOK

Baird, Cole, and Carmine travel to the one place Baird never wanted to see again: Halvo Bay. If there was any hope of Baird suppressing his memories of leading Kilo Squad here, it quickly vanished when an old friend stepped out of the shadows to greet them. Baird lost contact with Paduk shortly after their battle with Karn, but it looks as if the two old squadmates are set to ride into battle together one more time.

THE ROAD INTO TOWN

Cross the rickety wooden bridge, look to your left to find some viewfinder-style tourist binoculars that allow you to take in what is left of Halvo Bay. Then, descend the hilly road toward what is left of the town. Paduk quickly spots some Locust grubs down the road to the left. Let Cole, Carmine, and Paduk move straight for them while you flank around the building ahead to get the drop on the Locust. Cross the street and head left along the sidewalk behind the building to get a clean shot on the Locust from the rear.

Circle the building and take out the Locust from their flank.

Round the corner to the right and take cover behind the concrete barrier. Several more Locust are heading your way, including two Savage Boomers armed with Diggers. Blind-fire your Lancer and toss a Frag Grenade to eliminate them before they launch too many Diggers. Swap out your Sawed-Off Shotgun for the Diggers they drop.

Take out those Savage Boomers pronto!

A Savage Drone manning a lookout signals for a mortar attack on a nearby hillside just as the squad passes beyond the wooden gate. Sprint down the street to the service station ahead to escape being buried under the crumbling hillside.

The only way out of the service station is blocked by some fallen shelves and the husk of a sports car. To clear the obstacle you must power up the generator in the right corner and then throw the switch controlling the floor lift. The generator is beneath the large sign; follow the yellow power cable to the switch for the floor lift. Kick open the door to the shop, grab the Frag Grenades behind the shelves on the right, and exit through the next door to the junkyard.

Follow the yellow cord from the generator to the switch.

IS THIS FOG NORMAL?

The fog alone would make the junkyard a frightful place, but the telltale noise of approaching Tickers makes it even worse. Normally a few Tickers wouldn't be something to fear, but this is no normal Ticker attack. The junkyard is infested with nearly dozens of them! Keep the Lancer loaded and try to stay behind the others whenever you can. Pepper the Tickers with a few rounds from the Lancer to detonate a Ticker. You need only detonate one Ticker to destroy any others nearby.

The Tickers become much harder to spot as you advance into the junkyard.

Kick away any Tickers that get too close and quickly retreat. A lone Ticker blast isn't fatal except on Insane difficulty, but it will leave you heavily damaged and vulnerable to a second explosion. Advance slowly, watch for the reticle to turn red, and fire a few bullets at anything that glows orange.

Grab the extra Digger ammo to the right of the gate. Then kick open the security shack to the left of the gate. Press the button inside, under the window, to open the gate.

▶ When in doubt, push the button.

Temporarily swap out the Lancer for the Longshot and take cover near the ammo crate in the back of the pickup truck. Snipe the Locusts with the OneShots in the distance before the fog gets even thicker. Numerous Savage Drones burst from the ground as the fog cloaks the area, making it impossible to snipe. Switch to the Digger, move to the concrete barrier to the left, and launch away!

The fog vanishes and several Snipers appear on the upper level of the department store to the right. Take cover beside the pickup truck and use the Longshot to headshot them before they do the same to you. Continue sniping from this vantage point until an explosion rocks the lower level of the store and a number of Ragers and Savage Boomers exit. Quickly switch back to the Digger and launch your remaining Diggers at the Ragers. Grab the Lancer and take off to the left, to the crumbled building opposite the store.

▶ Toss your Frag Grenades at the Ragers if you run out of Digger ammo.

Grab the Frag Grenades and duck into cover amidst the rubble near the Mulcher. Snipe any remaining Ragers before they enrage, then take out the stragglers. Carry the Mulcher to the narrow piece of concrete in the center of the crumbling building and use it to cut down the two Butchers that attack last from within the store.

▶ Save the Mulcher for the Butchers that attack last.

Take a minute to gather all of the ammo and grenades you can carry (we recommend taking the Breechshot). Cut through the store where the Locust were and descend the stairs to the shopping mall outside. There are two ways into the mall: the upper Employees Only entrance, and the lower Security entrance. They both go to the same place, but there's a generator in the upper area that allows you to unlock a secured door to a balcony that can't otherwise be reached.

SHOP 'TIL THEY DROP

Enter the door to the right, beneath the "Employees Only" sign, and follow the catwalk around to the generator in the small office on the side. Fire up the generator to power the secured door in the room below. Then descend the stairs towards the mannequins. The door on the right leads outside to the stairs near the Security entrance. Once inside the security office, you can either descend the stairs on the right to the ground floor of the shopping center or open the security door and head onto the balcony.

▶ Press the green button to unbolt the door to access the balcony and a OneShot.

Take advantage of the elevated position and opt for the balcony, per Paduk's recommendation. Grab the OneShot just outside the door and carry it around the corner to the bench on the right. Take out the Locust near the turret atop the stairs in the distance and any others you see, but listen for the sounds of the door to your right opening. Back away and toss a Frag Grenade as the Locust run out. Many run around the balcony in a counterclockwise direction. Carry the OneShot to the right corner and look for opportunities to use it. Additional Locust rappel from the roof to the ground floor. Maintain this position on the right corner of the balcony and wait for them to ascend the stairs and rush towards you—Shish-Kashots abound!

Carry the OneShot to the balcony's right corner for multi-kill opportunities as the Locust run towards you.

Claim the Longshot on the lower level of the mall and regroup with the rest of your squad in the corner of the balcony opposite where you entered. The sounds of mortar fire have Paduk on edge, and for good reason: the next shell blows apart the hallway connecting this first part of the shopping center with the next wing. Shoulder the Longshot (or Breechshot if you prefer) and slowly advance to the next area of the mall. Approach the railing on your left at your first opportunity and snipe the two Mortar units on the floor below.

Taking out those Mortar units is your top priority!

Locust continue to charge up the steps to battle your squad until the Mortar units are dispatched. The next batch of Locust retreats to the far side of the fountain where they have access to a OneShot. Continue to use the Longshot. Otherwise, sprint down the stairs, claim a Mortar, and canvas the back-left corner

of the area. Additional Locust enter via the doors to the left, so hold your ground until Carmine comments on "that being the last of them."

Use one of the abandoned Mortars to take out the OneShot behind the fountain.

Sprint to the rear of the fountain and grab the OneShot leaning against the blue tile. Multiple Savage Boomers are about to lead a large group of Locust through the door in the side of the mall. Ready the OneShot and start firing. Focus on the Savage Boomers first, and then worry about the Savage Drones and Savage Grenadiers.

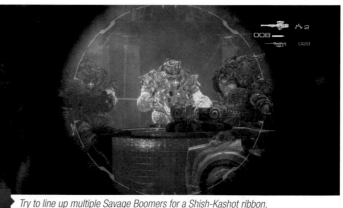

Try to line up multiple Savage Boomers for a Shish-Kashot ribbon.

D. Rovik, BG, Ephyra

K.I.A. during Locust attack on Halvo Bay.

The COG Tag is underneath the walkway where you first entered this portion of the mall. Descend the stairs and loop around to the left side of the fountain to spot the Crimson Omen. The COG Tag is behind one of the columns, directly under the walkway.

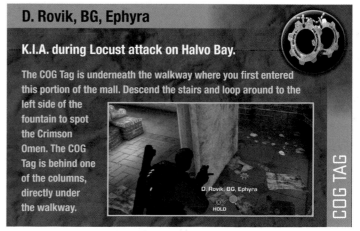

Locate the COG Tag and exit through the door where the last wave of Locust attacked from. Paduk's camp is just beyond the yard outside the storage room. Break through the wooden crates in the shack in the yard's rear-left corner to find the Retro Lancer and Gnasher. Raise the gate to Paduk's camp.

COG TAG

AMMO

RETRO

COG TAGS

AMMO

GNASHER

AMMO

AMMO

FRAG GRENADE

R-SENTINEL

AMMO

GNASHER

RETRO

MISSION OBJECTIVES

> Make your way to the rooftop lift.

HOSTILES ENCOUNTERED

FORMER

PADUK'S CAMP

With no guard manning the gate and the camp a veritable ghost town, Paduk is on edge. A lift on a nearby building's roof can be used to access the beached Imulsion rig, but it's worth taking a look around first. Seek out the Retro Lancer in the garage with the COG Tag if you don't have it—it's going to come in handy.

H. Mahawar, SPC, Soteroa

K.I.A. by Karn during Locust attack on Halvo Bay.

Stick to the left once inside the gate and locate the garage in the far corner, beyond the wall of sideways cars. Find the COG Tag and a Retro Lancer in the back, near a pair of suicide victims. The Crimson Omen is visible on the wall above them.

H. Mahawar, SPC, Soteroa

HOLD

COG TAG

Descend through the terraced encampment towards the lights and growing moans of horror echoing from within the buildings. Spread out a pair of Frag Grenades near the generator as it runs out of fuel and back away, towards the stairs. Be sure to grab the Frag Grenades behind the shipping container on the right before descending the stairs.

The question regarding Paduk's fellow campers has been answered: they've turned into Formers. An angry mob of nearly 50 Formers bursts from the windows and doors and swarms the area. Toss your additional Frags into the fray and then open fire with the Retro Lancer. The Retro Lancer is particularly useful against Formers. You can Retro Charge straight through a multitude of Formers, popping them one by one without stopping for a Charge ribbon. Back away from the Formers to get plenty of room to get up to speed, then Retro Charge across the area to rack up a number of kills without firing a single bullet. Retreat up the stairs if a little breathing room is needed between you and the Formers, as they can down you in a hurry if you get surrounded. They're easy to kill, but don't take them lightly. They're extremely dangerous when traveling in large packs like this.

The Retro Charge attack can kill multiple Formers during a single charge.

HOUSE OF HORRORS

Head up the steps and gather ammo while Paduk enters the code to raise the gate. The hallway ahead is vacant, but numerous Formers are set to burst through nearly every door, ceiling tile, and window. Advance slowly to draw each small group of Formers out one at a time. Open fire, somersault backwards to get away, then reload and advance again. Gradually move down the hall to the room in the corner near the barricade.

Advance slowly, then back away as soon as the Formers emerge.

Another dozen Formers are set to attack as you move in a clockwise loop around the desks and shelves in the corner room. Stick close to your fellow COG soldiers so they can revive you if you get downed. Stick close to the room's entrance until the first batch is killed, and then run to the left corner. Always keep your back against a solid barrier so the Formers can't surround you.

Exit the room and continue down the hall to the next glass window on the left. Kill the Formers that exit this room and locate the Range Sentinel behind the desk in the corner. Carry it out into the hall and set it down near the double doors on the left before the final Former assault. Tens of Formers drop from the ceiling and charge at full-speed from the other end of the hallway. Stick close to the other COGs near the doors and keep the Range Sentinel loaded.

Stick close to the Range Sentinel for protection.

Cut the lock on the door and ascend the stairs to the Onyx Ammo Cache near the roof. Resist the temptation to open fire on the Formers below, where you first encountered them. Instead, climb the final set of stairs to the lift to access the Imulsion rig deck.

Hope you're not afraid of heights…

SECTION 3: DEAD END

FRAG GRENADE

GNASHER

GAS MASKS

AMMO

AMMO

LANCER

RETRO

SAWED-OFF

AMMO

RETRO

AMMO

AMMO

MISSION OBJECTIVES

> Find any survivors.

> Get to the gas mask locker.

> Find your way to the fire escape.

> Make your way to the upper deck.

> Fire the flare.

> Hold out until rescue comes.

> Get to the rescue helicopter.

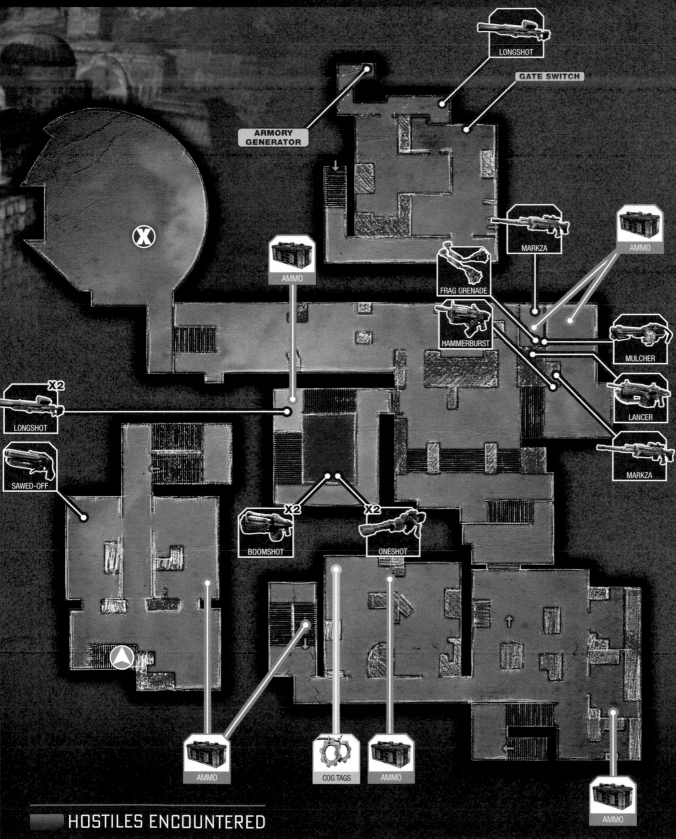

LONGSHOT

GATE SWITCH

ARMORY GENERATOR

AMMO

MARKZA

AMMO

FRAG GRENADE

HAMMERBURST

MULCHER

X2

LONGSHOT

LANCER

SAWED-OFF

MARKZA

X2

BOOMSHOT

X2

ONESHOT

X

AMMO

COG TAGS

AMMO

AMMO

HOSTILES ENCOUNTERED

FORMER

LAMBENT WRETCH

THERON GUARD

BUTCHER

SAVAGE BOOMER

REAVER

SAVAGE DRONE

SAVAGE GRENADIER

BEACHED IMULSION RIG

Paduk wants the group to move to the control room at the top of the rig. Head up the stairs of the shifting, rickety Imulsion rig and step inside. The interior of the rig is flooded with Imulsion—not even the ultra-fit COG can stand breathing this air for long. They need to get to the gas mask locker in the far right corner before they succumb to the fumes!

The upper level of the rig's interior contains a circuitous raised metal path comprised of small panels surrounded by metal railings. The COG must mantle from one section to the next as they loop around the area to the gas mask locker. It doesn't matter which direction you head; the rig shifts once again and a segment of the path collapses, forcing a retreat in the other direction. Unfortunately, the noise of the falling platform has drawn the attention of an endless mob of Formers.

Head back in the other direction and quickly mantle over cover to avoid the Formers.

The toxic fumes cause each of the COGs to suffer temporary, slight damage with every breath. The red indicator in the screen's center seemingly pulses with faint damage as the COGs inhale the gases.

Double-back in the other direction and take off running. Ignore any Formers that don't pose a direct threat to your progress. Use the A button to slam it into cover, mantle to the next section, and sprint to the next railing that must be mantled to continue. Stop and shoot the final three Formers that exit the bulkhead door near the locker.

Loop around to the corner with the 02 and 03 painted on the walls to reach the locker.

The squad must go down before they can go up. Descend the stairs to the lower, Imulsion-flooded area, and start working your way to the fire escape in the far corner. Wind between the tanks to the Retro Lancer and ammo crate and turn to the left, away from the pool of Imulsion. Touching the Imulsion has a similar effect as being set on fire; it's okay to step in a puddle but it's lethal if you wade into it for more than a second.

Round the corner to the right and halt when you hear the moans of the Formers. They attack from the narrow path leading down towards the Imulsion. Hold your ground and open fire as they funnel through the chokepoint. Wait for the chime to sound, signaling you've killed the last of them, then head for the stairs in the corner. Continue past the store rooms to reach the next deck.

Regroup upslope from the Imulsion and let the final wave of Formers attack.

UNLOCKING THE WEAPONS LOCKER

The stairs beyond the store room lead to small room with a couple of cabins on the right, a bulkhead door on the left, and a large bay door up ahead. That large door leads outside, where you eventually need to go, but there's a control room above the nearby sick bay that you can access to unlock a heavy weapons locker outside.

Don't raise the bay door until you've first unlocked the heavy weapons locker.

Kick open the bulkhead door on the left to enter the sick bay, where you can find a COG Tag and several Formers. Continue down the hall to the stairs at the end and ascend to the next floor. Paduk announces the presence of a heavy weapons locker, though he doesn't know where it is.

Enter the control room on the left and press the button straight ahead, near the shuttered windows. This lowers the stairs needed to access the weapons locker. Now you just have to unlock it. Snake your way past the electronics and climb out the window to the catwalk near the Longshot. Grab the rifle, head left, and engage the generator in the corner. This raises the shutters on the locker below, revealing two OneShots and a pair of Boomshots. They will certainly come in handy!

Push the button to lower the stairs outside.

Pull the cord on the generator to open the weapons locker.

AFTERMATH

223

Return the way you came, past the control terminal, to the door atop the steps on the left. Kick the ladder on the small landing to return directly to the area near the bay door and head outside to the top deck.

SIGNALING AN EVACUATION

Shoot the Lambent Wretches charging up the stairs to greet you. Move onto the deck, ignore the flare for a moment, and head left towards the green lights, signaling the way to the weapons locker. Continue around the corner, past the weapons locker, to gather up the additional Longshot ammo at the end of the path. Return to the weapons locker and pick up the two Boomshots and a OneShot. Make your way back towards the flare and set the OneShot down to the left.

> Head up the stairs near the green lights to the weapons locker.

Paduk's UIR comrades return an answering flare—help is on the way—but the flares have alerted every Locust within sight of your location. You must hold them off while the Gorasni chopper makes its way to your rescue.

The first Locust to arrive is a Reaver on the platform beyond the flare. Have the OneShot ready and take it out! Numerous Therons and Grenadiers grapple up to the deck beyond the pipes in front of you. Drop the OneShot and use the Longshot to snipe as many as possible before the next Reaver arrives in the upper left.

> Keep your head down and wait to fire the OneShot until the Reaver is reloading.

Toss a Frag Grenade (or use the Boomshot) at any groups of enemies near the pipes in the center. Not only will the explosion kill the Locust, but it will rupture the bandaged pipes and drain Imulsion onto them. The Locust are susceptible to the liquid Imulsion just like the COG.

Use the OneShot to kill the second Reaver and fend off any other nearby Locust. A Raven soon appears off in the distance, but the pending evacuation has increased the Locust's intensity. Another Reaver lands in the upper left corner just as a gang of Formers attacks from the right and numerous Butchers and other heavy Locust units attack from the center.

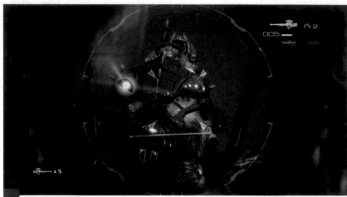

> Use the OneShot to kill the Reaver after you spot the Raven so you can move about the deck safely.

Sprint up the steps to your right and put your Boomshot to use in killing the Reaver off in the distance. Fight down the stairs to the alcove on the right and swap out the Longshot for a Lancer—you're going to need something you can kill the Formers with. Stay in cover to avoid any additional Reaver rockets and use the Boomshot and Frag Grenades to eliminate the Butchers and other bipeds attacking from the middle of the deck.

> Fend off the Formers and make sure none of your squadmates have been downed.

The Raven's searchlight eventually sweeps across the deck and it begins offering some aerial support. Wait for it to land on the helipad. Then sprint through the channel in the deck's center and up the stairs to the helicopter.

SECTION 4: ONE STEP CLOSER

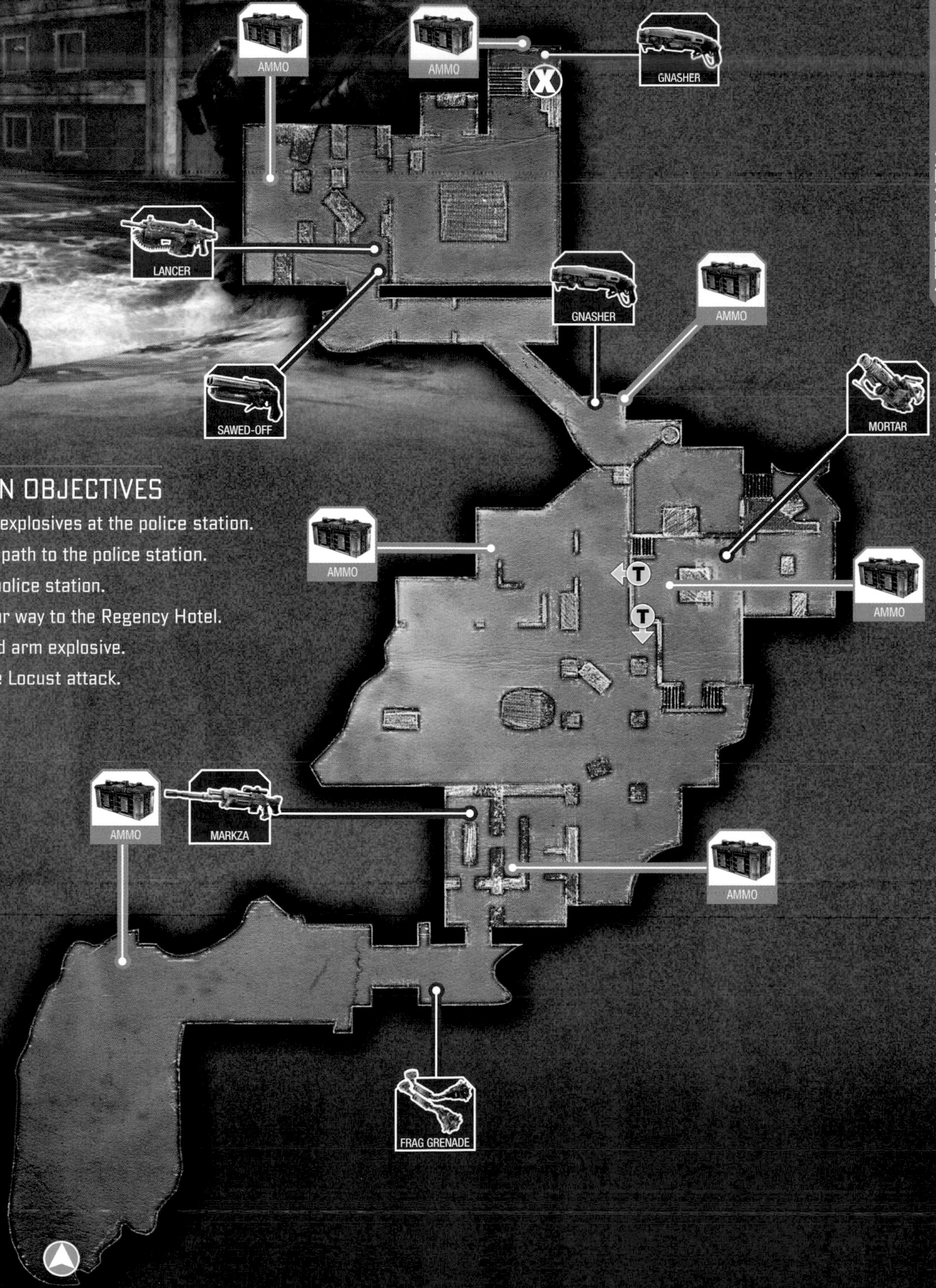

AMMO

AMMO

GNASHER

X

LANCER

GNASHER

AMMO

SAWED-OFF

MORTAR

MISSION OBJECTIVES

> Retrieve explosives at the police station.
> Create a path to the police station.
> Exit the police station.
> Make your way to the Regency Hotel.
> Place and arm explosive.
> Repel the Locust attack.

AMMO

T

T

AMMO

AMMO

MARKZA

AMMO

FRAG GRENADE

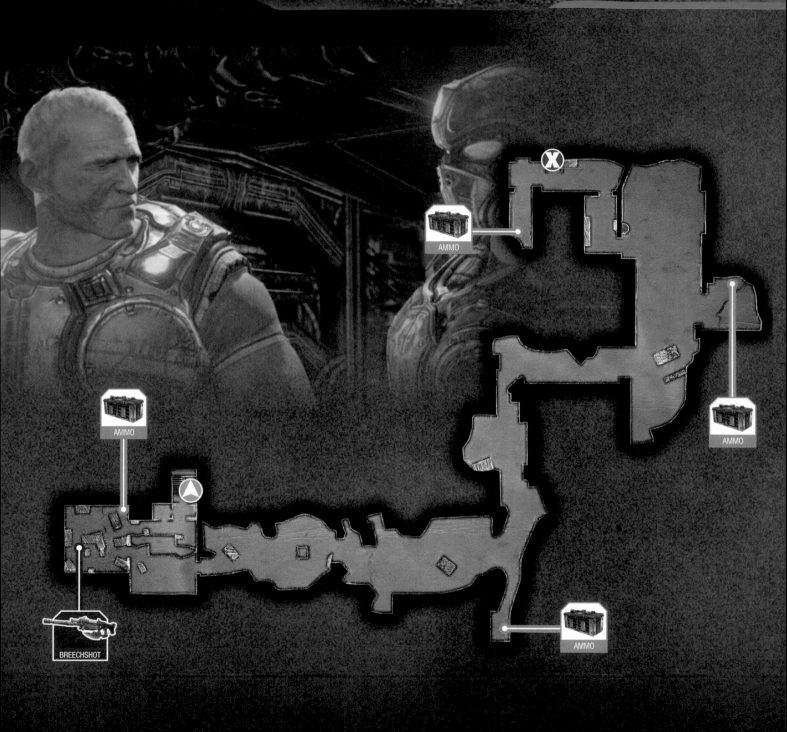

AMMO

AMMO

AMMO

AMMO

BREECHSHOT

AMMO

ONESHOT

EXPLOSIVE

LANCER

EXPLOSIVE

MULCHER

FRAG GRENADE

AMMO

EXPLOSIVE

EXPLOSIVE

AMMO

FRAG GRENADE

AMMO

AMMO

AMMO

ONESHOT

COG TAGS

BOLTOK

LONGSHOT

DOWNTOWN HALVO BAY

The chopper sets your squad down on the shores of the tsunami-ravaged city of Halvo Bay. Paduk believes the nearby police station has enough explosives to topple the building that the ship is resting upon. There's only one way to find out, but Baird has his doubts.

The Sinking of Jacinto wasn't without its side-effects.

Most of the people in the city's downtown core were killed in the tsunami. Those who weren't either fled or were killed by the Locust who have since taken over the area. Before they left, however, the survivors did manage to mark the way to the Regency Hotel with red X's. It can get pretty confusing in the streets of Halvo Bay, but the painted X's can be used as a guide if necessary.

BREAKING AND ENTERING

Move away from the water's edge and kick open the gate near the red X. Grab the Frag Grenades on the right and then duck into the bookshop on the left. Swap out the Lancer for the Markza and collect the ammo behind the counter. The Markza is particularly useful during this section, so hold onto it for the duration.

Exit the bookshop on an angle towards the building with the large patio, but don't go too far. Locust on the patio have a Mortar and are quick to man the Troikas when they see you coming. Duck back inside the bookshop and use the Markza to snipe the Savage Drone on the Troika. Continue shooting the Locust until it's clear that the Mortar stops firing. Race up the stairs towards the terrace in time to lob a Frag Grenade at the Savage Boomer coming over the wall. Then grab the Mortar.

Stay inside the doorway and keep sniping until the Mortar stops firing.

Storm cellar doors open within the shell of the building opposite the terrace. You can bombard the area with a barrage of Mortar fire to kill many of the Locust as they emerge. The numerous Wretches and Savage Locust are ripe for killing with the Mortar. Man the Troika once out of Mortar shells and continue to mow down the Locust as they emerge and climb over the wall. Things get a bit hairier when the Ragers appear. Make sure the Troika is cooled down before starting to shoot a Rager, or they may survive to enrage and charge you before you kill them. It's often safer to use the Markza to snipe the Ragers so they don't even get a chance to enrage.

▶ Take aim with the Mortar on the Locust climbing over the wall.

▶ Man the Troika once out of Mortar shells.

Approach the Imulsion pouring out of the sewer pipe near the police station. Then turn and approach the stairs leading back up to the terrace in time to see a Savage Boomer break through the door. Kill the Locust and loop through the building around to the left to the large truck. Detonate the Imulsion core under the truck's rear tire with a shot from your Markza. Run across the truck and open the garage door to get the explosives.

▶ Knock the truck down into the Imulsion. Then cross over to the police station.

Now that you have the explosives—four canisters to be exact—you need to travel across town to the Regency Hotel. First things first, you need to exit the police station's basement. Grab the ammo on the far left and then make your way to the stairs in the opposite corner. The basement is infested with Tickers but you can keep them at bay with the Markza.

Climb the stairs to the next floor, where several Savage Drones wait. Take cover inside the stairwell, snipe them with the Markza, and push on to the right. Fallen debris forces you to loop around through the adjacent room in a counterclockwise direction. Keep the Markza loaded and be ready for additional Locust rappelling into the room. Take cover near the police trucks, as several enraged Ragers lurk just beyond the exit.

▶ Switch to the Gnasher once the Ragers make their move.

SNIPER'S ALLEY

Advance up the slope, past the rusting cars and piles of debris, to the alley running left towards the ship. A Locust armed with a OneShot appears on the building in the distance—he's just there to serve as a warning and backs away before you can shoot him. Continue up the path and head down the road to the right, to the corner of the building on the left.

The Locust with the OneShot is now on an upper floor in the Regency Hotel, joined by several others. Save your bullets, as there's no eliminating them all. Wait for the OneShots to fire, and then sprint across the street to the pipe. Wait for another round of OneShots to fire, then sprint back across on an angle towards the hole in the building near the vertical column. You can shoot an Imulsion core that's up on a fire escape to drop the pipe down. This helps you cross the alley.

▶ Zigzag your way up the main road in between OneShot rounds.

Exit to the side street and kill the Locust rappelling down to join the Savage Boomer coming around the corner on the left. The main road is blocked by barbed wire so you must cut through the building across the alley. Approach the sound of the OneShots to emerge on a stoop next to a large sinkhole blocking direct access to the hotel.

Wait for the OneShots to pan away from you before making your move.

You can cut through this building's ground level to emerge uphill of the sinkhole, at which point you must sprint back across the street towards the red X. Another—safer—option is to descend the stairs near the Crimson Omen into the basement and cross through the trench where you're safe from the OneShots. Both routes lead to the same spot, but the latter leads you to the COG Tag. Duck into the building with the red X to the right of the door.

D. Strome, PVT, Halvo Bay

K.I.A. by Karn during original Locust invasion of Halvo Bay.

Descend the stairs near the Crimson Omen to the water-logged basement. Loop around the wall directly ahead to find the COG Tag in the water near a stack of ruined washing machines.

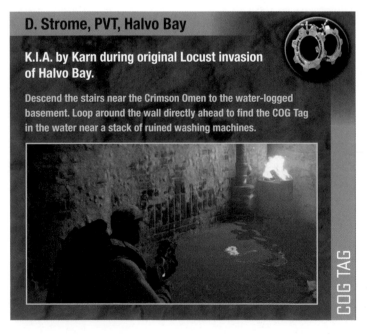

COG TAG

Fight past the Wretches on the stairs to the second floor where the other COGs attack some Locust on the balcony. Continue on your own up to the third floor where a Longshot waits in a perfect sniper's perch overlooking the entrance to the hotel. Shoulder the Longshot and begin sniping. Start with the Savage Drone on the turret before focusing on the two Savage Boomers. Keep sniping until the last of the Locust are dead. Then head back to the second floor and join your squad outside.

Snipe from the third floor while your squad draws their attention down below.

Gather the two Boomshots dropped by the Boomers and head inside. It's time to put this plan into action.

BRINGING DOWN THE HOUSE

Baird wants to place and arm one of the explosives in each corner of the hotel, starting with the one to the left. Approach the column marked with the red icon and press the X button to place the explosive. Then press the A button to begin arming it (the other members of the squad place the other three explosives). The arming mechanism consists of two small white rings, one stationary and one larger one, slowly shrinking towards the thicker one. Press the A button when the two rings overlap; otherwise, you have to start the process over. Do this three times successively to arm the explosive. Then move on to the next column.

Place and arm the explosive in the column to the left. Then mantle over the obstacle and head across to the near right corner to arm the second explosive. Wretches and Drones start to attack during the arming process, but you can ignore any that don't pose a direct threat to your safety. Just melee any Wretches in the area before you start the arming process, or else you may get downed before you can arm the explosive.

Press the button when the outer ring shrinks and aligns with the inner ring.

Advance along the right wall to the third corner and arm the explosive there. Note the location of the OneShot in this corner before running over to the left to arm the final explosive.

A number of Boomers approach the hotel just as the fourth explosive is armed. Take cover near the holes in the wall and use the Boomshot you picked up earlier to eliminate them. A large number of Drones and Therons attack next. Run over to the right corner near the OneShot and use the Markza to headshot as many as possible. Two Reavers and a Boomer attack last. Grab the OneShot from the floor behind you and take them out. Put up a solid defense, or else the hotel will be overrun.

Aim the Boomshot at the ground between the Boomers approaching the hotel entrance.

Hold off using the OneShot until the Reavers show up. Then blow them away!

SECTION 4: STRAIGHT TO THE TOP

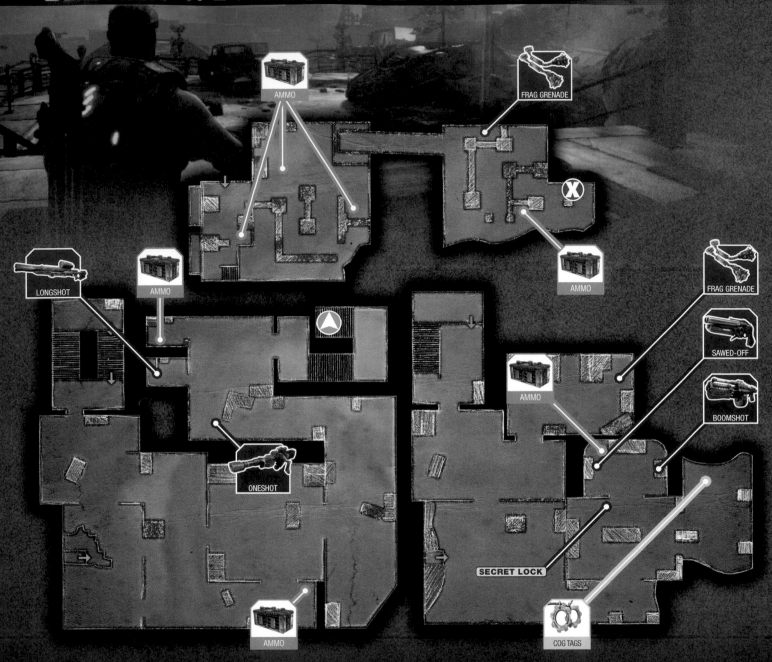

FRAG GRENADE

AMMO

X

AMMO

LONGSHOT

AMMO

FRAG GRENADE

SAWED-OFF

AMMO

BOOMSHOT

ONESHOT

SECRET LOCK

AMMO

COG TAGS

MISSION OBJECTIVES

> Reach the rooftop.
> Secure the rooftop.
> Destroy cables to create bridge.

> Clear restaurant roof.
> Enter restaurant building.

HOSTILES ENCOUNTERED

WRETCH   DRONE   THERON GUARD   SAVAGE BOOMER   REAVER   SAVAGE DRONE

REGENCY HOTEL

The hotel took a jolt, but it's still standing. At least long enough for Baird to give it one final shove. And to do that, the squad must get to the roof of the adjacent building and find a way to cross over. Head up the lengthy flight of stairs to the 20th floor (there's a Torque Bow on the 17th floor) and kick open the door for a scenic view, and a chance-meeting with a Stranded carrying a OneShot.

Use the Longshot from the bathroom to snipe the three Locusts in the other building.

Raid the bathrooms for a Longshot and ammo and duck into cover near where the Stranded was killed. Three Locusts armed with OneShots are in the building across the street and they are deadly accurate. Keep your head down whenever they're in the process of acquiring a target. Then rise up and snipe them once they've fired. Take out the two to the right from the furthest piece of cover. Then advance to the desk on the right and snipe the one on the left for the Hat Trick ribbon.

Swap to the Lancer and open fire on the Savage Boomer that bursts through the door around the corner. Then take aim on the grappling hooks of the Savage Drones trying to climb in through the windows. More grapple up from the hole in the tiled floor and then one final Savage Drone attacks near the door to the stairwell.

The stairs in the corner lead up to the roof, but don't head that way just yet! First drop through the hole in the tiled floor and explore the area directly below you. Kill the Wretches and Drone near the office on the left. Then approach the two Hanover Cougar busts and rotate the one on the left to uncover a secret weapons cache behind the bookshelf. Swap out the Longshot for the OneShot. Kill the other Locust on the 19th floor, get the Frag Grenades near the bunk beds in the corner, and head up the stairs to the roof.

It may not look like you can go down there, but you should.

Rotate the Cougar bust on the left to access a hidden weapons closet.

D. Galvin, CPL, Mercy

K.I.A. during final evacuation of Halvo Bay.

The COG Tag is located in the lower level, accessible only by dropping through the hole in the checker-tiled floor. Enter the office on the left and climb through the window to bypass the debris pile to reach it.

D. Galvin, CPL, Mercy

COG TAG

RUMBLE ON THE ROOF

Follow Carmine onto the window-washing platforms to stay low and flank the Locust coming down the stairs from the upper roof. Gun them down, grab their ammo, and run up the stairs and into cover.

The upper, larger section of roof is where things get tough. You must fend off a large number of Savage Drones and Savage Boomers as they move towards your position from all directions. What makes this more difficult is that you need to hold onto some of your heavy weaponry for the Reaver that attacks last—don't go using up all of your Boomshot rockets on the Savage Boomers!

Pay close attention to the Savage Boomers, as those pipes won't protect you from their Diggers.

Use the metal pipes for cover and look for opportunities to lob a Frag (or one or two Boomshot rockets) at a crowd of Locust or a fast-approaching Savage Boomer. But try to get by with the Lancer as much as possible. Stick to the perimeter, near the stairs you climbed to reach this second section of the roof, and don't stray from your squad. There's a high chance you'll be downed at least once on the harder difficulties, and being around your squad is your only hope for survival.

Use the pipes for cover and try to flank around the side of the Reaver.

Swap your spent Boomshot for an abandoned Digger and approach the tower that Paduk mentions. Target the two cables with your Lancer and shoot them apart to make the leaning tower into a bridge.

Target the cables to make a bridge out of the tower.

The restaurant roof is infested with Therons and at least one Savage Boomer. Use the Digger you scavenged on the previous roof to thin their numbers. Then look to cut down a Theron for use as a meatshield. Use the meatshield for protection while gunning down as many Therons as you can before the Reaver arrives. Ditch the meatshield and circle around to the left corner of the roof, to where the Frag Grenade pickup was. Take cover against the brick structure and open fire on the Reaver's pink underbelly.

It always pays to have a meatshield when going up against Therons.

Lean around this piece of cover for a safe, clear shot at the Reaver.

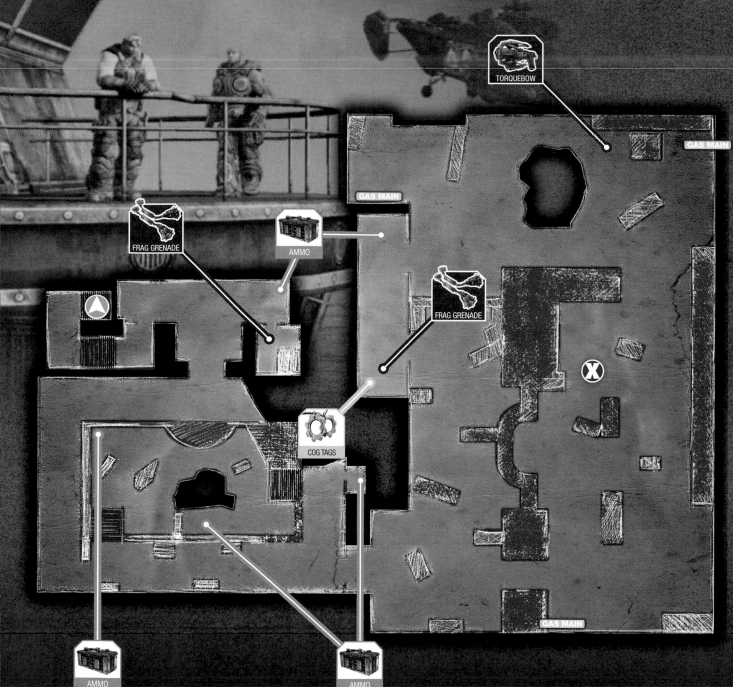

AFTERMATH

TORQUEBOW

GAS MAIN

GAS MAIN

FRAG GRENADE

AMMO

FRAG GRENADE

COG TAGS

X

GAS MAIN

AMMO

AMMO

MISSION OBJECTIVES

> Secure restaurant.

> Search kitchen.

> Open gas mains.

> Clear zipline path.

HOSTILES ENCOUNTERED

DRONE

RAGER

THERON GUARD

ARMORED KANTUS

SAVAGE DRONE

HALVO BAY SEAFOOD RESTAURANT

Descend the stairs from the roof to the restaurant entrance and collect the ammo and Frag Grenades from the bathroom on the left. A large number of Therons, Savage Drones, and Ragers have amassed inside the restaurant—it's as if they know Baird is trying to take the boat to Azura.

Follow the railing around to the left, overlooking the sunken dining area in the middle. Use your Lancer and Frag Grenades to beat down the initial crush of attackers. Then try to claim a meatshield. March across the center of the restaurant (or the right walkway) with a meatshield and gun down the last of the enemies. There should be some good opportunities to claim a Clusterluck ribbon with the Frag Grenades. Keep your eyes peeled for some fallen Torque Bows before approaching the door to the kitchen.

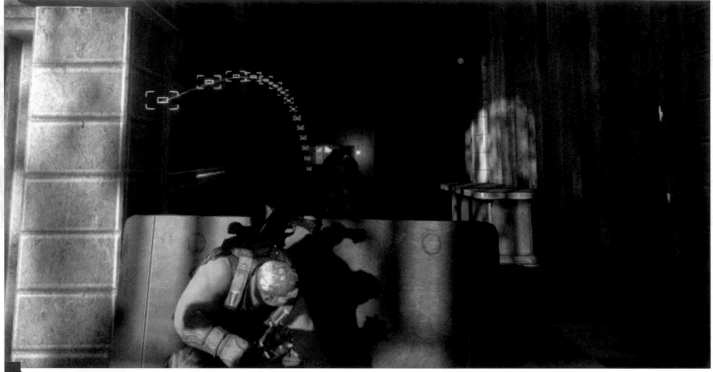

The Savage Drones charge your position at the start; have a Frag ready!

COOKING WITH GAS

Kick open the door to the kitchen and immediately take cover against the tile counter straight ahead. Several Therons are scattered throughout the area, but they're not alone. There's also an Armored Kantus in the kitchen. Hold this position behind the counter and gun down as many Therons as you can before the Armored Kantus makes itself the focal point of the battle.

Be ready to fire on the Armored Kantus' mouth whenever it begins to scream.

True to their name, Armored Kantuses are incredibly resistant to bullets. Though you can eventually wear them down with splash damage and ample gunfire, the most efficient way to defeat these Gorgon-wielding threats is to hit them with explosives and then open fire on their mouths as they scream. Aim for the orange glow of the Armored Kantus' mouth to secure critical hits that are all but guaranteed to prove fatal. Given the weaponry available, a prime tactic for dealing with this Armored Kantus is to hit it with a Torque Bow or Frag Grenade and then quickly switch to the Gorgon Pistol and fire a burst straight through its open mouth.

M. Cohen, 1LT, Ephyra

K.I.A. during Col. Loomis's last stand in Halvo Bay.

The final COG Tag, the 48th in the game, is located in a narrow hall inside the kitchen. It's on the ground near a pair Frag Grenades and just inside the doorway from the Crimson Omen.

The room starts to slowly fill with gas as each gas main is opened.

With the kitchen cleared of the initial wave of enemies, Baird can finally set to the task at hand: open each of the three gas mains! There are a number of pipes and valves throughout the kitchen, but only three are for the gas supply, and the others are for water. Ignore the water mains and pull the levers to open each of the three gas mains. They are located near each of the corners, except for the one nearest the door to the dining area.

Two Armored Kantuses lead the attack as you open the gas mains. Use your Frag Grenades to force them to yell and open fire on their mouths, preferably while Spotting them for the rest of the squad to focus on them as well (relevant only to co-op play). They attack in close proximity to one another so a barrage of explosives can keep them on the defensive and maybe even prove fatal to both.

Numerous other Therons and Ragers grapple into the room from a hole in the floor. Open the remaining gas mains. Then duck into cover and finish off the remaining Locust. Try to focus on the Ragers before they enrage. Many are skilled users of cover—look for opportunities to mantle-kick them, then quickly chainsaw them while they're stunned.

Baird hands everyone a hook to use to zipline off the building before it explodes. Use the Boltok to shoot the gondolas off the cable ahead of you. Don't worry about the gondolas on the other cables—the COGs take care of their own ziplines. Target the hook atop the gondola's bracket where it hangs from the cable and shoot it free. Clear the path of both gondolas to touch down safely alongside the UIR vessel.

Get ready to shoot the gondolas off your zipline path.

Azura, here you come…

MULTIPLAYER COVERAGE

MULTIPLAYER OVERVIEW

Welcome to *Gears of War: Judgment* multiplayer. This chapter covers the basics of multiplayer: differences in gameplay from the previous *Gears of War*, getting started, getting around, weapon basics, and general information on each mode.

DIFFERENCES FROM PREVIOUS *GEARS OF WAR* GAMES

The following table details the changes in the *Gears of War: Judgment* gameplay.

CONCEPT	HOW IT WORKS IN *GEARS OF WAR 3*	HOW IT WORKS IN *GEARS OF WAR: JUDGMENT*
Drop from Heights	Unable to drop from a higher level, just off of short platforms	Run, dive, or vault over cover from a higher elevation to a lower one—taking damage if height is too high
Number of Weapons Carried	Carry two guns along with a pistol	Carry two guns
Loadout	Select a Rifle and Shotgun to go along with the Snub Pistol (3 weapons)	Select a rifle or shotgun to go along with the Snub Pistol
Pistol	Replace Snub Pistol with Boltok or Gorgon when found	Snub Pistol is only handgun in multiplayer
Weapon Select	D-pad selects between three guns and grenades	Y button toggles between your two guns
Perfect Active Reload	Tap the Right Bumper at the right time during a reload to gain bonus damage	No longer in multiplayer
Grenade Control	Press Down to select and then toss with Fire button	Use Left Bumper to toss—no need to select
Starting Grenade	Always start with Smoke Grenade	Start with your choice of grenade except for Incendiary Grenade
Tac-Com	Pressing the Left Bumper brings up the Tac-Com until button is released	Press Down on the D-pad to bring up Tac-Com for three seconds
Grenade Tag	Plant a grenade on another player or the environment	Frag Grenades are now sticky, allowing for tagging from afar
Ammo Crates	Ammo Crates limited to Campaign and Horde mode	Now in Versus modes and all non-OverRun game types, along with Campaign
Picking Up Ammo from Dropped Weapons	After killing an enemy with the same weapon as you, hold X to pick up ammo	Ammo is automatically picked up by running over it
Down But Not Out (DBNO)	Players can be knocked down to DBNO and then revived by teammate or executed/used as meatshield by enemy	No longer in multiplayer—except for Grenadiers in OverRun
Curb Stomp/Execution	Y button performs these moves to an enemy who is DBNO	No longer in the game
Boomshield	Can only be used with a pistol	Can be used with most weapons including all starter weapons
Locust in Versus Modes	One side plays as Locust and the other as COG	Except for OverRun, everyone plays as COG—red or blue side
Mutators	Allows changes to gameplay such as Infinite Ammo	No longer in the game
Versus Mode Rounds	Can play best of three rounds	Games limited to one round

GETTING STARTED

The following chapters cover the Survival co-op and Versus modes. Survival allows you and up to four others to fight against wave after wave of Locust Horde. In Versus, you can join up to nine other players in up to five-on-five competitive multiplayer. Versus modes include OverRun, Free-for-All, Team Deathmatch, and Domination—more on these later.

CHARACTER SETUP

Selecting Character Setup from the main menu gives you the opportunity to change the look of your character and weapons as well as view PrizeBoxes that have been earned.

The first tab displays the unlocked Weapon Skins. This is where you change the look of your weapons. Select the weapon you want to change, highlight your desired skin, and press A to apply it to the weapon. Press Start to apply the skin to all weapons. This page also allows you to equip a weapon and view its information. Press Y to equip and get information on grenades.

The second tab shows the unlocked Characters. Here you can read a short bio on each and select which character you want to use in Versus modes.

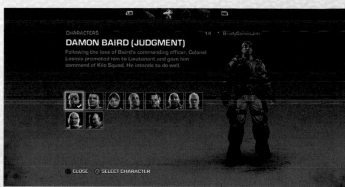

The third tab lists available Character Skins. By selecting a character on the previous tab, you can then highlight a skin on this page and apply it to that character. These can be pretty outlandish—some are even animated. It may add an extra level of satisfaction and fun to taking someone down while dressed as a clown, but it makes tracking you down that much easier. The Appendices at the end of the guide tells how to unlock all of the skins in the game.

Any PrizeBox that you've earned during gameplay is listed on the final tab. Highlight one and press the A button to receive your award. Refer to the PrizeBoxes entry later in this chapter for information on how to earn these awards.

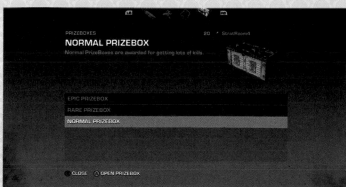

STARTING/FINDING A MATCH

After selecting Survival or Versus, you can then select a Standard or Private match. Standard allows you to play any of the competitive Versus modes online, either in a Ranked or Quick match. This matches you and your party with other online players. Select Private to play with bots and friends. Private is the only option that allows for customized match settings.

Two more types of matches that are also selectable in Versus are Special Event and VIP. Special Event is a match with special rules such as Free-for-All with Gnashers only. VIP allows play of any competitive Versus mode online, either in a Ranked or Quick match. All DLC is used and more XP is awarded than standard playlists. You and all members of your current party must purchase a VIP Pass to participate.

For Private matches, there are options that can be changed to customize your game. The options for each mode are covered later in this chapter. After you've selected the options and a map, you get an opportunity for Character Setup. Use the Shoulder buttons and D-pad to change your weapon, grenade, weapon skin, and character skin.

Even after pressing Start to begin the match, you still have a few seconds to make any final changes to your character as a timer counts down to the start.

While another player in your party sets up a Private match, you have access to the Party Member Menu. Here you can access Character Setup, your Stats & Awards, Options, and Xbox Live Marketplace. You can also leave the party. Additionally, in the pre-game lobby, you can enable Spectator mode by clicking the Right Stick.

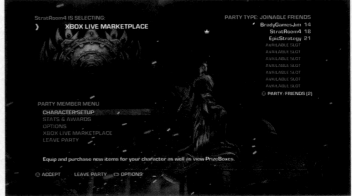

WEAPON SWAP

For the private game host, at the Pregame Lobby, pressing Back allows you to change the Weapon Pick-Ups on the map. Here you can swap out any of the default map-based weapons with a weapon of your choice. After saving this weapon swap, it holds true for all Versus games that you host until you change it again.

Find the Initial Weapon that you want to take off of the map and Replace With… the weapon that you want to take its place. You can also just turn it off by selecting Disabled. On Gondola, you are unable to switch out the Frag Grenades.

LEVELING UP

Performing certain actions in single player and multiplayer nets you experience. Experience points come from killing opponents, completing objectives, and earning ribbons. As your XP goes up, your level increases. Your level is shown in the pre-game lobby and on the scoreboard next to your gamertag.

RE-UP

Once you maximize your experience points and cannot go any further, you have the option of re-upping.

This resets your XP to 0, level to 1, and increases your rank by 1. Select Stats & Awards to get to your character's summary. If your level is now a star, it means that you can re-up. Press the X button, and then say yes to complete the process.

GAME AWARENESS

Being aware of what is going on around the map can go a long way in moving up the leaderboards. Use the following tools to plan out your next move.

SCOREBOARD AND MAP

During a multiplayer game, hold Back to bring up the Scoreboard which shows the current leaderboard along with each player's score. Press B with the Scoreboard up to get an overhead map.

The map shows your location along with any teammates. Map-based weapons, ammo crates, OverRun/Survival objectives, and Domination rings are also shown. Use the map to find your team or plan your route to a power weapon or ring. Be careful not to spend too much time on the map, as you are vulnerable when in a match.

RESPAWNING

After dying, the camera follows your killer as a timer counts down to your respawn. You can watch from another player's view by using the Left and Right Bumpers. Press the Left and Right Triggers to get a view from cameras around the map. By pressing the X button, you can view from wherever you wish with the Ghost Camera. Using these cameras can give you an idea of where others are fighting.

If you're unhappy with your present loadout, your grenade and primary weapon can be changed at this point with the D-pad. Up and Down change the grenade while Left and Right change your main gun. Press the B button to take a peek at the overhead map.

After respawning, a character gets a few seconds of protection. This gives you a little time to get your bearings in case you spawn in a bad spot.

TAC-COM

Press Down on the D-pad to bring up your Tac-Com. This provides a heads-up display showing the location of your teammates, map-based weapons, ammo crates, and the rings in Domination.

WEAPON PICKUP AND KILL NOTIFICATIONS

In the lower-left corner of the screen, messages appear when someone makes a kill or picks up a weapon. Awareness of these notifications combined with map knowledge is almost as useful as the Tac-Com.

GETTING AROUND

Getting around the map in multiplayer uses the same mechanics as single player, but there are some things that can be done to help outlast your opponents.

MOVEMENT

Just as in single player, use the Left Thumbstick to move around the map. This alone is not fast enough in multiplayer, where it is important to dart around the map to make yourself a tougher target. Unless you're firing at a target, try to remain at full speed.

ROADIE RUN

Hold the A button and your character moves forward in a crouched position. This is the fastest way to get around, but it does have drawbacks. You are unable to use a weapon and turning is extremely limited.

You should roadie run whenever you can. But beware, as you are an easy target for an enemy straight ahead. Zigzag when you're under fire to avoid taking too much damage. Learn advance movements such as the wall bounce to make movement more erratic.

Running directly into cover causes your character to automatically assume a cover position. This is great to scan for enemies behind protection, but it's faster to perform a cover slide. More information on this later.

SENSITIVITY

In Options/Controller, you can select the sensitivity for Looking, Targeting, and Zooming. These adjust how quickly you can turn the player, turn the player when targeting your weapon, and turn the player when zoomed in with your weapon, respectively. It is worth bumping these up, as they can give you a definitive advantage over those with lower settings. Try a higher sensitivity for a while to see if you're able to get used to it.

This is critical in close combat when fighting with shotguns and when tracking a fast-moving target. Experiment with the highest sensitivity settings and then lower them down until you're comfortable with them.

CONTROLLER	BradyGamesJim
INVERT Y-AXIS	ON
INVERT X-AXIS	OFF
OMNIDIRECTIONAL EVADE	ON
LOOK SENSITIVITY	+14
TARGET SENSITIVITY	+14
ZOOM SENSITIVITY	+14
VIBRATION	ON
STICKS	DEFAULT
TRIGGERS	DEFAULT
CONTROL SCHEME	DEFAULT

Adjust how quickly you can turn the player when targeting your weapon

DODGE

Press the A button to roll in the direction that you are pressing. Use this to quickly duck behind cover, quickly evade an incoming enemy, or to dodge some weapon fire. Mix up your movements though. Evading in the same way makes your next location more predictable.

Dodging is not as effective against an enemy with a shotgun. A skilled player knows the timing of rolls and will hit you with a shotgun shell in the face.

OMNIDIRECTIONAL EVADE

Select Omnidirectional Evade to toggle this option on or off. By default, it is on and means that you can roll in any direction. Disable this option if you wish to only roll in the four cardinal directions.

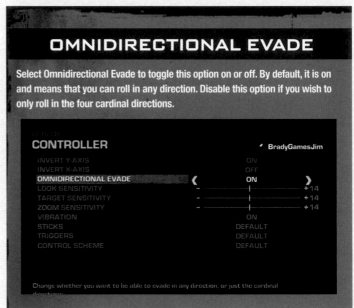

CONTROLLER		BradyGamesJim
INVERT Y-AXIS	ON	
INVERT X-AXIS	OFF	
OMNIDIRECTIONAL EVADE	ON	
LOOK SENSITIVITY		+14
TARGET SENSITIVITY		+14
ZOOM SENSITIVITY		+14
VIBRATION	ON	
STICKS	DEFAULT	
TRIGGERS	DEFAULT	
CONTROL SCHEME	DEFAULT	

Change whether you want to be able to evade in any direction, or just the cardinal directions.

Continuing to hold the A button after a roll along with a direction on the Thumbstick allows you to run instantly, once you're back on your feet. This is another way to switch up your directions quickly.

COVER

Press the A button to duck behind nearby cover. This protects you from most shots from the front and makes you difficult to hit from anywhere on the other side of the wall. You're still just as vulnerable from explosives though. A good sniper can hit any part of you that is exposed.

It is easy when coming from single player to get in the bad habit of hanging out behind cover. Staying in motion is more important in multiplayer than fighting from these positions.

FALLING FROM HEIGHTS

If you are on a higher level, you can run, dive, or vault over cover down to a lower one. This presents the need for a whole new awareness in *Gears* that never existed before. Knowing where you can drop down to ambush an enemy, or where an opponent can do the same to you, is essential. Dropping from small heights appears to cause no damage; falling from greater heights brings up a partial Crimson Omen and makes you an easier kill.

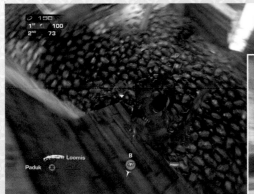

SPOTTING AN ENEMY

While targeting a foe with the Left Trigger, click the Left Thumbstick to mark the target. This allows your teammates to see the enemy's location and can earn you assists and extra points. Make it a habit to do this whenever you aim at an opponent, as it benefits you and your entire team.

ADVANCED MOVEMENT

The following table lists some basic and advanced maneuvers that can help you get around faster and become a tougher target for your opponents.

COMMAND	ACTION
Roadie Run	Hold A
Right-Angle Turn	While Roadie Running, tap and hold A while pointing the Left Thumbstick left or right
180-Degree Turn	While Roadie Running, tap and hold A while pointing the Left Thumbstick down
Cover Slide	Press toward a piece of cover and press A
Cover Slide Cancel	During a Cover Slide, press in the opposite direction of slide
Cover Slip	Press forward with Left Thumbstick while at the edge of cover and press A
Cover Swap	While in cover, point the Left Thumbstick toward another nearby piece of cover and press A
Roll Switch	Continue to hold the A button and a direction on the analog stick after performing a dodge

COVER SLIDE

Press toward a piece of cover as you get close and press A to perform a cover slide. This gets you to safety a little quicker than simply roadie running. You can slip into cover ahead of your character or to the side. You can even slide into cover that you've just passed by pressing back at an angle.

COVER SLIDE CANCEL

Combining the cover slide with other advanced maneuvers allows you to move around the maps much faster than just roadie running. It is also important to master the cover slide cancel. As you slide into cover, press the Left Thumbstick in the opposite direction of your slide to stop your motion. From there you can slide into another piece of cover. Mastering this technique makes you a much tougher target as you fly around the area.

WALL BOUNCING

Wall bouncing is the act of using cover slide cancels to quickly move through a map. Use this to quickly reach an enemy's flank or rear position, making for an easy shotgun kill. This also makes you a more difficult target for longer, more precise weapons.

Practice cancelling cover slides as you move through a map and then start connecting these with other advanced maneuvers. This alone puts you on even footing with most players. Eventually, this becomes more natural and you find yourself doing it all the time.

ROLL SWITCH

As mentioned before, if you continue to press the A button after a dodge, you can instantly run in a different direction. This can save your life when you come under fire, as you run into a new location. Combine roll switches with cover slides to make yourself more difficult to hit.

ROADIE RUN SWITCH

During a roadie run, briefly release and then hold the A button and a direction on the Left Thumbstick to change your run direction. This maneuver is another way to switch up your direction in a hurry and make your movements more unpredictable. Typically, a roadie run does not allow for much turning, but the roadie run switch changes that.

Make quick 90- or 180-degree turns to move around the maps more rapidly and present a challenging target to your opponent. If you realize that you're heading into a bad situation and need to quickly reverse, perform a roadie run switch in the opposite direction to avoid trouble.

MELEE COMBAT

With a possible shotgun in everyone's hands, melee combat is pretty much limited to surprise finishing moves. Press the B button to swing your selected weapon at an opponent. Hold the button down to continually swing it. It takes about three hits with the pistol and two with other guns to take down an opponent. Though by this time, chances are you'll be shot to death.

LANCER FINISHING MOVES

With the Lancer or Retro Lancer equipped, you can finish off opponents with an attached melee weapon. This method is best saved for unsuspecting foes because you are vulnerable during the attack.

With the Lancer, hold the B button to rev the chainsaw. It takes a little while to get it going, and if you are damaged during this time, the chainsaw is automatically lowered. You move slowly with the chainsaw revved, so use this when close to an opponent. If an opponent brings out a chainsaw at the same time, a chainsaw duel ensues. Jam on the button to win this battle and take down your foe.

Holding the B button with the Retro Lancer selected initiates a retro charge with its bayonet. Once you hit full speed, the blade pierces an enemy and takes them out with one shot. This takes some distance to hit full speed, so an opponent can easily take you down if they're aware of your attack.

MANTLE KICK

With an enemy hiding behind cover, point the Left Thumbstick toward his location and press A to mantle over the ledge and kick the foe. This inflicts a little

damage, so it can down a hurt target. Follow this up with a quick shotgun blast or chainsaw to the face to finish the foe off.

Be careful staying in the same position for long, as the mantle kick just adds to the level of danger. It's easy for someone to sprint in and deliver a quick mantle kick to you if you are focused elsewhere.

WEAPONS

You select a primary weapon and grenade to take with you into a multiplayer match. Your secondary weapon is automatically the Snub Pistol. If you want a more powerful second weapon, pick up an enemy's gun after a kill. We go into more depth on each weapon in the Arsenal section, but the choice for your primary depends on what range you want to fight at and your skills.

SWITCHING WEAPONS

To switch between your primary and secondary weapons, press the Y button. Watch your ammo and switch to your other gun when one runs low. If the Snub Pistol is not meeting your needs as a secondary weapon, pick up a more powerful weapon with the handgun equipped to replace it.

AIMING

Hold the Left Trigger to bring up your weapon and aim down its sights. Aiming your shots gives you improved accuracy. Press in on the Right Thumbstick while aiming to zoom in and get a better view of your target.

It is also possible to shoot from the hip or blind-fire from behind cover. Simply press the Fire button without aiming. Firing blindly results in worse accuracy, but for some weapons it still works — such as a shotgun at short range. Blind-fire is also good for laying down suppression fire while teammates flank an enemy or go for an objective.

RELOAD

At any time when your weapon has less than a full clip, press the Right Bumper to initiate a reload. Tap the button again when the slider passes over the reload bar's sweet spot to reload immediately. The gun automatically reloads when the slider reaches the end of the bar. If you press the button but miss the gray area, the weapon jams and more time is spent to reload.

DROPPED WEAPONS AND AMMO

After killing an enemy, their current weapon is dropped. If you're already carrying that weapon, just running over it picks up the ammo. Otherwise, you can switch out your currently equipped weapon with the dropped weapon by holding down the X button. Be sure that you select the gun that you want to get rid of before swapping.

AMMO CRATES

Ammo crates are found in set locations on each of the four Versus maps. When next to the crate, hold the X button until the white circle fills and the ammo is picked up. This replenishes ammo for any starter weapon (rifles, shotguns, Snub Pistol) and gives one grenade. The amount of ammo varies for each weapon. Refer to our Arsenal chapter for specific ammo counts for each weapon.

Ammo is not given for special weapons when an ammo crate is picked up. You gain one grenade of the type that you chose for your loadout, except for Smoke Grenades that get two from these boxes. Ammo is given for your starter weapons until you reach its maximum amount.

TRADING WEAPONS

To exchange weapons or share ammo in any mode except OverRun and Survival, move within close range of a squadmate. Aim at that player with the Left Trigger and press Y to share ammo, X to swap your primary weapon, or A to trade your secondary weapon. Pistols and grenades may not be swapped. If you have two power weapons, give one to a teammate and share the wealth.

MAP-BASED WEAPONS

For each of the four Versus maps, there are weapons available for pickup from the start. These are made up of the heavy weapons, special weapons, and the Incendiary Grenade. Some of these guns can be a huge game changer, so it's worth noting where they are and roadie running to that spot. Refer to our Versus Maps chapter for all of the weapon locations.

For each map there will be favorite first stops for players and you'll have to be quick to get the better weapons. Use roadie run and wall bouncing to beat your opponents there, or target these hot spots with your grenades for easy kills or to disorient others.

STARTER WEAPONS

You're allowed to select one starter weapon to go along with your Snub Pistol.

RIFLES

The three main rifle choices each have their own advantages and optimal ranges. Choosing between the Lancer, Retro Lancer, and Hammerburst depends on where you are fighting and personal preference. The Classic Hammerburst can also be selected if you pre-ordered the game, and it gives the same benefits as the Hammerburst.

The Markza is a new rifle choice that gives you long-range power with a 1.5x zoom. If you select a rifle as your primary weapon, it is worth your time to pick up a shotgun for your secondary slot if one becomes available.

This way you have the shorter-range and longer-range covered.

SHOTGUNS

The Gnasher and Sawed-Off Shotguns will probably be the most popular choices among most players as their primary weapon. This is why it's good to have your own shotgun to counteract this firepower. This leaves your Snub Pistol as your long-range weapon, so it is good to replace it with a more powerful rifle or heavy weapon.

SNUB PISTOL

Everyone goes into multiplayer matches with the Snub Pistol as their secondary weapon. This is a decent weapon for long-range fighting, but there is much better out there.

HEAVY WEAPONS AND SPECIAL WEAPONS

Heavy and special weapons are located around each Versus map, and it is well worth the extra effort to get them. Make a beeline for their spawn points when the round begins and visit these points to see if they are back. Communicate with teammates when you know a powerful weapon is back at their spawn point.

GRENADES

In *Judgment*, grenades are much easier to toss than in previous games. No longer do you have to select your grenades before using them. Simply tap the Left Bumper to blind-throw the explosive. Hold the Left Bumper to bring up a trajectory arc and aim with the Right Thumbstick. Release the Left Bumper to throw it. Cancel a grenade throw by pressing the Y button to switch to your primary weapon.

When selecting your loadout, you can choose from five different grenades to carry into the fight: Frag, Ink, Smoke, Spot, and Stim-Gas. Each of these has its own uses in battle. Incendiary Grenades are also available as a map-based pick-up.

Frag Grenades can stick to an opponent if they hit them on the fly. If you get stuck with a Frag Grenade, you'll see an onscreen indicator and hear the classic "clank" sound. If this happens, move toward the closest enemy to try and take them down with you.

MULTIPLAYER MODES

Along with the co-op Campaign and Survival Modes, there are four multiplayer modes that can be played with up to 10 players. OverRun and Domination are objective-based modes that require teams to attack or defend points of interest and capture rings. Team Deathmatch and Free-for-All are all about killing. This section of the Multiplayer chapter gives the basics of the five modes and how they work. For strategies and map information, check out the following chapters.

SURVIVAL
Co-Op Mode: Up to 5 Players

Survival Mode is a co-op mode where you and up to four other players or bots defend against 10 waves of Locust Horde. Playing as the COG, each player can select from four different character classes: Baird the Engineer, Cole the Soldier, Paduk the Scout, or Sofia the Medic.

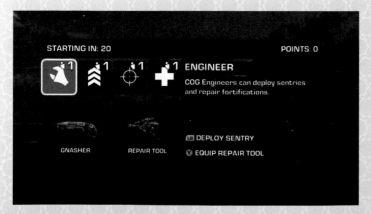

> **Engineer:** COG Engineers can deploy sentries and repair fortifications.

> **Soldier:** COG Soldiers are highly trained weapon specialists. They can deploy ammo for themselves and their teammates.

> **Scout:** COG Scouts can access elevated sniping positions and reveal enemy locations by deploying spotting beacons.

> **Medic:** The COG field Medic can deploy Stim-Gas in order to heal and revive teammates.

The COG attempts to protect three objectives as the Locust attack from their current spawn point. These objectives include two E-Hole covers and a generator. The Locust always start out on the left side of the map as the COG spawn near the first E-Hole cover.

As each objective is taken over by the beasts, the COG are pushed to the next objective. The Locust then spawn at the previous objective. The game ends when the Locust destroy the generator, or once 10 waves of Locust have successfully been defeated.

Each of the four COG classes has its own advantages. We go into more detail on each later in the guide. The 10 waves of Locust Horde gradually get tougher as you progress through the game. The first wave starts out with just Tickers and Grenadiers. By the time you reach the tenth and final wave, you will have faced nine different beast types.

OVERRUN
Versus Mode: Up to 10 Players split into 2 Teams

In OverRun, up to 10 players are split into two teams that take turns attacking objectives as Locust and defending them as COG. Once the objectives are destroyed or time runs out, the two teams switch sides.

The defensive round, played as the COG, is like Survival Mode except instead of waves of Locust, the beasts just keep coming. You must protect the objectives from their attack. Once one goes down, you're moved back to the next objective. There are three objectives in all: two E-Holes and a generator.

The first objective must be defended for six minutes. If it's overtaken, three minutes are added to the clock. If the second E-Hole is destroyed, three more minutes are added to the time. If you're able to defend either point until the clock hits zero, the other team earns a score equal to the number of objectives they destroyed. In other words, they score one point if they only destroy the first E-Hole. The round is over and the teams switch sides when the objectives are defended until the clock runs out or when the generator is destroyed.

The offensive round is played as the Locust in an attempt to destroy the next objective. The objectives and times are the same. As the Locust Horde, you can select from eight different beasts—though some are unavailable until you earn enough points. Each beast has its own strengths and weaknesses. Knowing which one to take is the key to success. Fight your way through the COG defenses and destroy the three objectives.

With the Mercy Rule turned on, the game is over if the Locust get further than the other team in the second round. If both teams successfully defend the same number of objectives, then it goes down to time. The team that spent less time attacking wins the match. If the times are the same, then it ends in a draw.

OPTIONS

For OverRun, you can only change the difficulty of the bots and toggle the Mercy Rule on and off. When this rule is on, the game is over as soon as the second attacking team beats the first team's score. Otherwise, you play until the time is up or the generator is destroyed. In a Private match, all 10 spots are always filled with bots.

OPTION	DESCRIPTION	SELECT FROM
Bot Difficulty	The effectiveness of AI players	Casual, Normal, Hardcore, Insane
Mercy Rule	If the second attacking team beats the first attacking team's score, the game ends	On or Off

DOMINATION
Versus Mode: Up to 10 Players split into 2 Teams

In Domination, two teams of up to five players compete to control the three rings on the map. Points are earned by possessing each ring. The first team to reach the score limit wins the match.

Each player earns a score based on Kills, Deaths, Caps, and Breaks. This is displayed on the scoreboard, but the important numbers show up in the top-left corner during gameplay. This shows how many points each team has received from possessing rings. The goal is displayed above the two team scores. Once a team's score reaches this goal, they win the match.

Enter a ring to start gaining possession of it for your team—blue or red. If an enemy enters the ring with you, progress toward capture is stalled. Enter a ring captured by the other team and you score a Break. Their possession is drained and you start capturing it for your side. The more teammates in a ring, the faster it is captured. A team only scores when they "own" a ring.

OPTIONS

A default game of Domination requires 150 points to win. In a Private match, select Fill to have AI players join until there are 10 players. Friendly Fire can be enabled to really make things interesting.

OPTION	DESCRIPTION	SELECT FROM
Round Score Limit	The number of points needed to win the match	Different increments between 50-425
Number of Bots	How many AI players should join the game	0–8 or Fill
Bot Difficulty	The effectiveness of AI players	Casual, Normal, Hardcore, Insane
Friendly Fire	Weapons deal damage to allies as well as enemies	Off or On

FREE-FOR-ALL
Versus Mode: Up to 10 Players

Free-for-All is survival of the fittest—if it moves, shoot it. The first player to reach the required number of kills wins the match. Once someone gets within three kills of victory, a warning is flashed on the screen to let you know.

Outplaying the other nine players is the key to winning. Map-based weapons litter the maps, and some of these locations become hot spots of activity. Use your full arsenal along with the heavy weapons to top the leaderboard.

OPTIONS

A default game of Free-for-All requires 20 kills to win. In a Private match, select Fill to have AI players join until there are 10 players.

OPTION	DESCRIPTION	SELECT FROM
Goal Score	Number of points needed to win the match	15–99
Number of Bots	How many AI players should join the game	0–8 or Fill
Bot Difficulty	The effectiveness of AI players	Casual, Normal, Hardcore, Insane

TEAM DEATHMATCH
Versus Mode: Up to 10 Players split into 2 Teams

Team Deathmatch pits two teams of up to five players against each other. The first team to reach the goal score wins the match. Just like in Free-for-All, when a team gets within three kills, a warning is given to let people know the match is almost over. Team play is vital to win this mode.

OPTIONS

A default game of Deathmatch requires 20 kills to win. In a Private match, select Fill to have AI players join until there are 10 players.

OPTION	DESCRIPTION	SELECT FROM
Goal Score	Number of points needed to win the match	10–999
Number of Bots	How many AI players should join the game	0–8 or Fill
Bot Difficulty	The effectiveness of AI players	Casual, Normal, Hardcore, Insane
Friendly Fire	Weapons deal damage to allies as well as enemies	Off or On

STATS & AWARDS

RIBBONS

After each multiplayer match, ribbons are awarded based on your performance. Select the Ribbons tab from Stats & Awards to review the ribbons that you have earned, how many times you have received each, and which ones you are missing. Ribbons also get you Epic PrizeBoxes, which in turn unlock skins or give bonus experience.

MEDALS

Medals are long-term achievements, most with four levels to unlock, which correspond to an awarded title. The four levels are Bronze, Silver, Gold, and Onyx. These are a mark of excellence awarded for extraordinary in-game feats or accomplishments.

Equip one to wear during multiplayer matches to flaunt your greatness to other players on Xbox LIVE. Select Stats & Awards from the main menu, press a shoulder button to get to the Medals tab, select an unlocked medal, and press the A button to choose your title. Your selected accolade appears next to your gamertag in the player roster and is viewable in the pre-game lobby. Refer to our Appendices for full lists of ribbons and medals.

PRIZEBOXES

PrizeBoxes are awarded for achieving certain goals. These can be opened by going into Character Setup and selecting the last tab. These give you a little XP toward leveling up or unlock a weapon or character skin.

There are three types of PrizeBoxes: Normal, Rare, and Epic. The following table shows what you need to earn each one and how much XP you can get from them. Each box requires more kills, levels, and ribbons than the previous one.

TYPE	HOW TO EARN	AMOUNT FOR FIRST BOX	XP
Normal	Number of Kills	100	50
Rare	Leveling Up	Level 2	100
Epic	Earning Ribbons	50	150

Once all skins have been unlocked, every PrizeBox nets you XP.

MULTIPLAYER TACTICS

Multiplayer matches played online are always changing, so your tactics need to adapt. There are proven strategies that you can employ to get ahead of the other players and move up the leaderboard. In this chapter, we talk about ideas and strategies that can help achieve this goal.

Map knowledge and game awareness are even more valuable when you're on your own—you can no longer rely on teammates to inform you of what's happening. Getting a powerful weapon also becomes more important. Quickly figure out your location on the map and immediately head for a nearby weapon. If you're more concerned about speed, then avoid heavy weapons that can slow and encumber you.

As a player, you do not take an accuracy penalty when shooting without holding the Left Trigger. The only advantage to holding the Left Trigger is a slight camera zoom and more controlled movement when aiming. It is to your advantage to avoid using the Left Trigger as much as possible so you can continue to move through the map as quickly as possible.

Roadie running whenever possible and making your character a tough target are vital to survival. Work on cover slides and wall bouncing to accomplish this. Getting to the best power weapons is just as important; these can be game changers.

USING COVER

Movement and awareness are the most important concepts that you can work on to improve your game, but using cover is also a valuable asset. This protects you from most shots from the front and makes you difficult to hit from anywhere on the other side of the wall.

However, you are still just as vulnerable from explosives, and a good sniper can hit any part of you that is exposed. Plus, a Scorcher can damage you when fired over low cover. Limit your time behind cover unless you have good protection from your team.

FLANKING

A flank attack takes advantage of a distracted enemy—rushing them from the side in an attempt to catch them by surprise. It's a great strategy that can be employed in almost any mode of *Gears of War: Judgment*. This is very effective, as it takes away an enemy's cover advantage.

It helps to know the maps really well. This allows you to choose the best routes to flank an enemy. If you catch the enemy as they flank your location, slip out the other way or mantle over the cover to escape the attack. It's not worth sticking around, as they already have the jump on you and hold the advantage.

ELEVATION

Another way to get a jump on an enemy is with an elevated level or platform. This gives you a tactical advantage—allowing you to fire down on your opponent. Learning where the best elevation is on each map can help greatly.

You can not only get the advantage over others, but you can also quickly spot enemies who fire down on you.

New to the *Gears of War* series is the ability to fall from higher levels. From these heights, you can run, dive, or vault over cover down to a lower one. This presents the need for a whole new awareness in *Gears* that never existed before. Knowing where you can drop down to ambush an enemy, or where an opponent can do the same to you is essential.

LEARN THE MAPS

Learning the ins and outs of each map goes a long way in achieving success in *Gears of War* multiplayer. Knowing the quickest routes between hot spots, how to escape ambush at any time, and where players can get the best line of sight gives you the ability to maximize your kills while avoiding giving your opponents easy ones.

Hot spots are the locations where the most combat occurs. These primarily consist of rings in Domination, map-based weapons, and chokepoints—where multiple routes intersect. Be aware of these locations. They can be ideal for finding targets, but can also be dangerous places to find yourself.

Learn the spawn points of all the map-based weapons and how best to get there. Pulling up the in-game map or using the Tac-Com reveals these locations, making them easy to learn.

Learning your way around the maps not only helps you get to the hot spots first, but it is also beneficial in making a hasty escape. Combine map knowledge with use of the Tac-Com and notifications to be completely aware of what is going on. The notifications in the lower-left corner can let you know when the heavy and special weapons have been taken.

TEAM PLAY

Team play is huge in *Gears of War* multiplayer. A coordinated team nearly always trumps lone fighters. Moving as a team and communicating with each other make you much more effective and aware, which translates to wins. Here are a few tips that can help you and your team get more organized.

WEAPON SELECTION

Some players are more comfortable firing from long distance behind cover while others would rather rush in with a shotgun at the ready. It is good to spread out the starter weapons between the five players, so that all ranges are covered.

Figure out who is best with each and make sure they are equipped with the best weapons. Be sure to take the mode and map that you are playing into account.

Also mix up the grenades that each player carries into the match, as each has its uses in team play. Mask movement or sniper positions with Smoke Grenades, flush out teams from hiding or objectives with Frag and Ink Grenades, mark enemies with Spot Grenades for easy detection, and use Stim-Gas to keep your team healthy during big attacks.

MOVING AS A TEAM

A team is more dangerous when it moves as a group. Opponents are taken down faster and you can rely on your teammates to protect you when attacked. Organize movement across the map and work to flank the enemy's position. Be aware when a heavy weapon is taken by the other team and avoid packing in too close when they possess an area-of-effect weapon such as the Mortar.

GAME MODES

Most of these team strategies are effective in any of the team-based modes, but there are specific tactics that can be used in each. Here we break down each multiplayer mode, including Survival Mode, and give all the information you need to come out on top.

Ribbons are a great way to gain experience and eventually Epic Prizeboxes. We list the ribbons that are specific to each mode, but there are many more available across multiple modes. For the full list, check out the Ribbons chapter in the back of this guide.

DOMINATION

DOMINATION-SPECIFIC RIBBONS

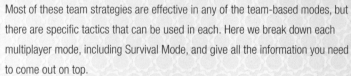

RIBBON	DESCRIPTION
BREAKER BREAKER	MOST CAPTURE POINTS BROKEN.
CAPPER	MOST POINTS CAPTURED IN A MATCH.
DOMINATOR	WON A MATCH WITH ALL THREE POINTS CAPTURED.

Domination is an objective-based mode where three rings located around the map are fought over by two teams in an attempt to control them. Players must step inside a ring to begin the capturing process, which is represented by that team's color filling up a circle. Once it is full that objective is captured for the team.

Getting multiple teammates inside a ring causes the ring to be captured at a quicker rate. As an opponent steps into the ring, all progress is stalled until

only one team resides within the objective. Points are accrued by a team's possession of rings. The first team to reach the required score wins the match.

There are multiple ways that teams can go about playing Domination. With a dominant team, it is possible to circle around the entire map capturing the three rings along the way. Five players in a ring make for a quick capture. The team should be on the defensive at all times. Once the ring is close to being owned, the team should start toward the next objective.

The most effective strategy is concentrating on the two closest rings, knowing that is all you need for a win.

By figuring out where your opponent spawns, you have a good idea from which direction they are more likely to attack. Plus, the relatively short distance required to move between the points makes them easier to defend.

For a lone wolf who is more concerned about leveling up than playing the game, a player can stay on the move as they break and capture rings. Or, one can take cover near a capture point and ambush players who attempt to capture the objectives.

When a ring is just about captured, start moving toward the next ring, as speed is essential in reaching the required score first.

USING GRENADES IN DOMINATION

Tossing a Smoke Grenade into a ring can provide concealment while capturing a circle or even a break attempt. If you see that a ring is being captured, a Frag Grenade, or to a lesser extent an Ink Grenade, can be used to clear it out. Any kind of explosive can be used to possibly get multiple kills.

Stim-Gas Grenades can help a team get that last bit of time necessary to defend a ring during capture. It is visible when a ring is being captured, but Spot Grenades can still be used to reveal players who lie in wait.

FREE-FOR-ALL

FREE-FOR-ALL-SPECIFIC RIBBONS

RIBBON	DESCRIPTION
GOLD	1ST IN A FREE-FOR-ALL MATCH.
SILVER	2ND IN A FREE-FOR-ALL MATCH.
BRONZE	3RD IN A FREE-FOR-ALL MATCH.
BORN LEADER	STAYED IN THE LEAD FOR THE ENTIRE MATCH.

Traditionally, multiplayer in *Gears of War* means some kind of team play. Now you are able to put your skills against the best in a Free-for-All match. Ten players, all out for their own interests, the first to reach the set number of kills wins.

Map knowledge and game awareness are even more valuable when you're on your own—you can no longer rely on teammates to inform you of what is going on. Getting a powerful heavy weapon also becomes more important. Quickly figure out your location when a match begins and head for a nearby weapon.

Typically, long-range combat is tougher to pull off in Free-for-All, so consider taking, or at least picking up, a shotgun. As you move through the map, always consider which weapon to have ready. If you are rounding a corner or entering a tight hallway, carry your short-range weapon.

Do not forget to use your grenades when available. These can be used to disorient your enemy, conceal your movement, flush foes out of a popular hiding spot, and much more. The Spot Grenade comes in handy when heading into an unknown area.

With nine other players on the map, you need to be more cautious. Enemies can be around every turn. Make sure to stay on the move, as you're extremely vulnerable. Do not stay in one location for too long. Listen and watch for any clues to where your foes may be.

As you wait for a respawn after death, check the cameras to find out where your opponents are fighting. Be careful rushing into hot spots; you can easily get overwhelmed.

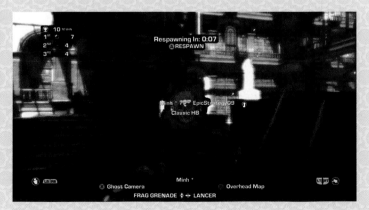

TEAM DEATHMATCH

Team Deathmatch in *Gears of War: Judgment* pits COG versus COG, red team versus blue. The color of your armor is all that distinguishes you from the enemy. Players have unlimited respawns and the first team to reach the set score limit wins.

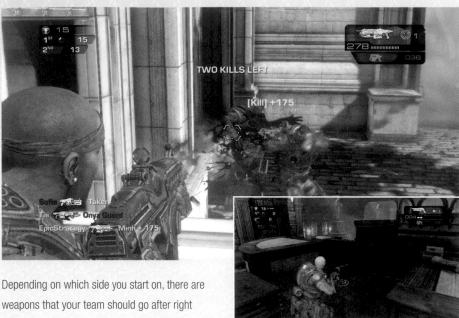

Depending on which side you start on, there are weapons that your team should go after right away. This is where map knowledge comes into play. Figure out where you are on the map and decide whether you're going after one of the map-based weapons or heading to a location where you can take advantage of these hot spots.

It's worth figuring out which weapons each of your teammates are best with. If the match is in the Library and someone excels at sniping, that player should go for the Longshot in the tower or the OneShot behind the clock—depending on which side your team spawns.

TRADE WEAPONS

Remember that you can swap weapons with a teammate by targeting that player and pressing the appropriate button. Therefore, if you're able to get to a weapon quicker than the player that is proficient with that gun, you can grab it and hand it over when you two meet up.

More often than not, an organized team will defeat a team of individuals. Everything we mentioned earlier in the Team Play section holds true in this mode. Communicate with your teammates and try to move as a group.

Be careful moving in on an unknown location while solo or even with a teammate. This is a good way to give the opposing team easy kills. This is especially true if your opponents are moving as one or holding an area as a team.

OVERRUN

OVERRUN-SPECIFIC RIBBONS

RIBBON	DESCRIPTION	CLASS/LOCUST
BEG YOUR PARDON	CHAINSAW A KANTUS WHILE IT'S HEALING.	SOLDIER, MEDIC
BRUTE FORCE	MELEE-KILL A CORPSER WHILE IT'S ATTACKING AN OBJECTIVE.	ANY CLASS
CHAIN OF COMMAND	KILL 5 ENEMIES DEBUFFED BY SCOUT.	ANY CLASS
IRON CURTAIN	PROTECT THE GENERATOR FOR 10 MINUTES.	ANY CLASS
OAKLEY	KICK A TICKER AND SHOOT IT IN THE AIR.	ANY CLASS
SPOTTER	KILL 5 TAGGED ENEMIES IN ONE ROUND OF OVERRUN.	SCOUT
RIGHT PLACE, RIGHT TIME	KILL 5 LOCUST WITH A WELL-PLACED SENTRY.	ENGINEER
HMO	HEAL 20,000 POINTS OF HEALTH FOR YOUR TEAMMATES.	MEDIC
STAY DOWN	MELEE-KILL A WRETCH WHILE IT'S CLIMBING.	ANY CLASS
BATTERING RAM	DEAL 50% OF DAMAGE TO THE GENERATOR IN ONE ROUND.	ANY LOCUST
HOMEWRECKER	DESTROY 5 FORTIFICATIONS IN A ROUND.	ANY LOCUST
NICK OF TIME	DELIVER THE FINAL BLOW TO THE OBJECTIVE WITH 10 SECONDS REMAINING.	ANY LOCUST
ONE BEAST ARMY	DESTROY ALL OBJECTIVES IN AN OVERRUN ROUND.	ANY LOCUST
POINT MONSTER	EARN THE MOST POINTS IN A ROUND AS LOCUST.	ANY LOCUST
SAMPLE PLATTER	PLAY AS 5 DIFFERENT LOCUST IN A ROUND.	ANY FIVE LOCUST
INDIGESTION	KILL AN ENEMY WITH A SWALLOWED GRENADE.	TICKER
INSATIABLE	EAT 10 GRENADES.	TICKER
POP GOES THE WEASEL	BLOW UP 3 ENEMIES AT ONCE.	TICKER
STUNNER	MULTIPLE ENEMIES YOU STUNNED WERE KILLED BY ANOTHER PERSON.	WRETCH
TREE HOUSE PREDATOR	KILL A SCOUT ON A PERCH.	ANY LOCUST
GRENADE FEEDER	FEED 10 TICKERS A GRENADE.	GRENADIER
NICE TRY	WIN A CHAINSAW DUEL AGAINST A MEDIC WHO IS BUFFED BY THEIR OWN STIM.	GRENADIER
ONE MORE THING...	KILL MULTIPLE PLAYERS WITH A FRAG GRENADE WHILE DBNO.	GRENADIER
SCOUTMASTER	HEADSHOT A SCOUT WITH THE BREECHSHOT.	RAGER
TEAM SAVIOR	REVIVE 3 TEAMMATES AT ONCE.	KANTUS
TEAM SHAMAN	HEAL 4 TEAMMATES AT ONCE.	KANTUS
THAT LOVING HEALING	HEAL A KANTUS THAT IS HEALING ANOTHER TEAM MEMBER.	KANTUS
SLAUGHTERHOUSE	KILL A COG WITH REFLECTED BULLETS.	MAULER
SPINNING PLATES	GIB 3 COG WITH A SINGLE SPIN-SHIELD USE.	MAULER
PAVING THE WAY	DESTROY 1 SENTRY WHILE BURROWED.	CORPSER
TUNNEL RAT	DIG A UNDER A FORTIFICATION AND THEN ATTACK AN OBJECTIVE AS A CORPSER.	CORPSER

Two teams take turns playing as the Locust in an attempt to destroy three objectives while the other team defends as the COG. Up to five players can join per side. The Blue side starts as the COG and the red as Locust. After successfully defending the objectives for a given time or after the generator is destroyed, sides are switched. The team to destroy the most objectives wins. In case of a tie, the team with the quickest time wins. If both teams took the same amount of time, it's called a draw.

THE MAPS

The four OverRun/Survival maps are set up in basically the same way with the Locust always attacking from the far west end. They work their way to the east, ending at the generator, which is always near the far side. There are typically two paths entering the objective area, acting as chokepoints. A Troika turret can be found in all of the 2nd and 3rd positions. Only Skyline has a turret at the 1st position. Refer to our Maps chapter for more details about each location.

ABILITIES

Each COG and Locust class has a special ability that can be used by pressing the Left Bumper. Once used, there is a cool down period before it becomes available again. Use these abilities wisely, but do not forget about them and let your allies down.

FORTIFICATIONS

Barriers are present at each objective and range from weakest to strongest: Spikes, Barbed Wire, Blue Electric Fence, and Red Laser. Spikes are destroyed relatively easily with a Ticker, but any weapon can be used to bring them down. COG Engineers are able to keep these repaired with a special repair tool.

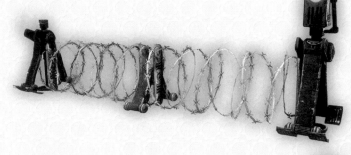

OFFENSE: PLAYING AS THE LOCUST

The offensive team selects from eight Locust before setting out toward their first objective. Only four of these beasts are available at first. Points are accrued as you destroy fortifications, kill the COG soldiers, and other actions. These points can be used to "purchase" a tier-2 Locust.

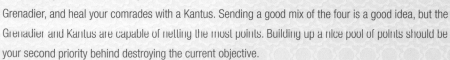

Each of the tier-1 Locust has its uses: chew through fortifications with the Ticker, stun the COG as the pesky Wretch, cause mayhem with the Grenadier, and heal your comrades with a Kantus. Sending a good mix of the four is a good idea, but the Grenadier and Kantus are capable of netting the most points. Building up a nice pool of points should be your second priority behind destroying the current objective.

Take note of what side the COG is spending the most time on and adapt to what they're doing. If they're spending more time on the north side, go south and vice versa. You may need to chew through barriers again, but you'll have an easier time when there are less soldiers around.

THE LOCUST CLASSES

TIER 1		TIER 2	
LOCUST	COST	LOCUST	COST
TICKER	0	RAGER	1500
WRETCH	0	GIANT SERAPEDE	2400
GRENADIER	0	MAULER	3500
KANTUS	0	CORPSER	5000

Since Emergence Day, the Locust have been constant foes of the COG. Seeing Sera as their birthright, the Locust aim to wipe humanity off the planet. Each of the specialized Locust species has a unique loadout and set of skills, just like the COG. At first, you only have access to four Locust types: a Ticker, a Wretch, a Grenadier, and a Kantus.

■ TICKER

EQUIPMENT	NONE
SPECIAL	DASH
DURATION	1 SECOND
COOLDOWN	5 SECONDS
OTHER	B EXPLODE, X EAT GRENADE, RT ATTACK FORTIFICATION

Named for the ticking sound they make while crossing the battlefield, Tickers are mean, nasty little critters that are way more dangerous than they first appear. These fast moving, insect-like creatures can rip apart fortifications with their fore claws as easily as they can a COG Soldier.

The Locust use Tickers as living mobile bombs by strapping Imulsion tanks onto their backs. Their speed and relative small size allow them to access small passages that no one else can use. Another way for them to get across barricades or short walls is for a Grenadier to punt them over.

TICKER CLAWS

Tickers use their front claws to savagely rip apart any barricade in their path. This often wreaks havoc on COG strategy, as they have to contend with destroyed fortifications, leaving them undefended. The first priority for a Ticker should be to tear down enemy fortifications, allowing its Locust allies easy passage through COG defenses. Once destroyed, fortifications cannot be rebuilt, so Tickers should concentrate their attacks on a single fortification to take it down. If more than one Ticker joins the fray, coordinate to focus on one target and quickly eliminate it.

A Ticker's claws are just as dangerous to COG personnel as they are to their fortifications. A Ticker can quickly sneak up with its Dash ability on an otherwise occupied COG soldier. A few vicious strikes of its claws can bring even the strongest COG soldier to his knees.

TICK, TICK, BOOM

While destroying fortifications is important, very few things can cause as much panic as a charging Ticker. Their Dash ability lets them get up close and personal very quickly, often before the COG can react. Once in range of its target, the Ticker uses the Imulsion tank strapped to its back in order to create a massive explosion.

As if the volatile Imulsion weren't enough, Tickers are natural scavengers and eat almost anything in their path. They are particularly fond of tasty, tasty grenades. When a Ticker has a grenade in its belly, it becomes a double threat. Not only does its initial explosion cause significant damage, a few seconds later, a secondary explosion from the grenade can catch unwary COG. This is why the Tick, Tick, Tick of an unseen Ticker is one of the most unnerving sounds a COG soldier can hear on the battlefield.

COG INTEL ON THE TICKER

While it's dangerous to underestimate a Ticker, they are the weakest of the Locust. A few well-placed shots from any weapon quickly ignite the Imulsion tank on its back, destroying the Ticker in the process.

When a Ticker Dashes forward to possibly rend you with its claws or explode on your position, quickly kick the Ticker away, dazing it for a few seconds. During this time, fire a few rounds into its dazed body to finish it off in safety.

◼ WRETCH

EQUIPMENT	NONE
SPECIAL	STUN SCREAM
DURATION	2 SECONDS
COOLDOWN	8 SECONDS
OTHER	A JUMP OVER BARRIER, B MELEE ATTACK, X CLIMB

While Wretches are sometimes seen as little more than cannon fodder, they can be dangerous in their own right. These creatures move with a simian-like gait. They are extremely strong and can leap over barricades with relative ease.

Wretches use their unnatural strength to dish out devastating melee attacks. They have no ranged attacks, so they must get into melee range to inflict any damage. They can quickly cross the distance to a target utilizing Leap to take shortcuts across small walls and other obstacles.

Much like the Ticker, Wretches are very vulnerable to COG fire. They must utilize cover and sneak attacks to have any chance of getting in close to be effective.

HEIGHT MAKES RIGHT

A Wretch's unique physiology makes them well suited to climbing. A Wretch can always see where to climb. Paths are highlighted by claw marks the Wretch can follow.

While climbing can be advantageous in many situations, it really becomes important when facing COG Scouts. Scouts often perch high above the action on

the battlefield, sniping at the Locust. Wretches are the only Locust who can climb up to these roosts to attack the Scout from melee range. Accessing these snipers' roosts

often allows you easy passage to the inside of COG fortifications by avoiding the defenses the COG put in place.

THE WRETCH'S WAIL

A Wretch's high-pitched scream stuns any COG caught in its immediate area in a cone. This scream renders the COG completely defenseless for a few seconds while the Wretch is screaming. While the Wretch can't take advantage of this, because it is too busy screaming, it stops the COG from attacking its allies or the Wretch itself.

If facing a foe alone, the Wretch's Stun Scream does little more than delay the inevitable. But it really shines when working with another Locust. Ideally, the Wretch stuns a COG with its scream, and its allies use the opportunity to attack.

PITCH PERFECT

Before letting loose with a Stun Scream, make sure you are within range. Once you initiate a scream, you are vulnerable for a few seconds. Be near enough to your intended targets for them to get the whole effect.

COG INTEL ON THE WRETCH

When you see a Wretch approaching your battlefield fortifications, you cannot rely on the fortifications to stop the Wretch. It's easiest to take down the Wretch at long range, as it only requires a few shots. Doing this is often easier said than done, given that the Wretch's form of movement is a little chaotic. Take Wretches down before they can reach Climb locations; otherwise, your Scout will be vulnerable. When encountering Wretches, make sure your team is spread out, so the Wretch's Stun Scream cannot affect more than one person. This robs them of their greatest weapon.

■ GRENADIER

EQUIPMENT	GNASHER (PRIMARY), LANCER (SECONDARY)
SPECIAL	THROW FRAG GRENADE
DURATION	N/A
COOLDOWN	12 SECONDS
OTHER	A ENTER COVER, Y SWITCH WEAPONS, RT SHOOT WEAPON

Grenadiers were some of the first Locust out of the hole on E-Day. Their bulky frames and dense body structure allow them to absorb more damage than many of the other Locust. As their name suggests, their specialty lies in lobbing grenades into the midst of their hated COG foes.

Grenadiers are equipped with Gnashers and Lancers. Having both of these weapons makes them dangerous at any range. Grenadiers are extremely deadly at close range. Even when a Grenadier falls in battle, if the cooldown on its grenade is up, it can use it to self-destruct, killing any nearby COG.

FRAG GRENADES

Frag Grenades deal a lot of damage and can be thrown over cover or directly onto priority targets. Grenadiers have an unlimited amount of Frag Grenades, so utilize them whenever possible to maximize the damage potential. If you correctly judge the throwing arc, you can throw grenades over structures to land near the E-hole cover, damaging it without having to fight your way through the COG's fortifications.

Another deadly aspect of the Frag Grenade is its ability to stick to targets. Be careful to stay away from any enemies successfully hit with a Frag Grenade; they can charge you, catching you in the explosion.

FEEDING THE TICKERS

While it's not a job many people prefer to have, using your grenade to feed a Ticker can be a highly effective strategy. If the Ticker stands a better chance of dealing damage, based on the battlefield circumstances, feed it a grenade and let it go.

BLIND-FIRE

Like the COG, the Grenadier can utilize cover to blind-fire at enemies. This is a very effective means of keeping opponents off guard while allies get into better positions. With practice, blind-fire can be used to kill enemy COG in relative safety.

COG INTEL ON THE GRENADIER

While the Grenadiers' ranged fire is just as dangerous as any COG weapon, the real threat lies in their grenades. When facing a Grenadier, be on the lookout for tossed grenades. When a grenade is incoming, quickly try to roll away to avoid getting caught in the blast or, worse yet, stuck with the grenade. If hit with the grenade, accept your fate and don't condemn your allies to share it as well. Get as much distance between you and the rest of the COG and make your peace.

When a Grenadier is down, don't approach it. Even with its last breath it can still set off a last grenade, taking out any gloating COG foolish enough to get too close.

■ KANTUS

EQUIPMENT	CLASSIC HAMMERBURST (PRIMARY)
SPECIAL	HEAL
DURATION	7 SECONDS
COOLDOWN	5 SECONDS
OTHER	A COVER, RT SHOOT WEAPON

The Kantus is a member of the Locust spiritual elite. Their lanky bodies are easily seen on the battlefield. Because of this, Kantus are adept at using cover to protect themselves from enemy fire. They wield the Classic Hammerburst, which fires a burst of projectiles with each pull of the trigger. While this weapon is not dangerous at long range, due to its inaccuracy, it is very deadly in short to medium range.

The Kantus' real strength is in healing allies, even reviving those who fall in combat. Keeping Grenadiers in the fight long past when they should have fallen makes this ability one of the most valuable on the field.

HEALING CHANT

The Kantus is able to harness spiritual powers, allowing it to detect when its allies are injured in combat. When the Kantus performs the healing chant, it heals certain nearby damaged allies over time. While this chant heals all nearby allies except Tickers and Serapedes, it does not heal the Kantus. Make sure to use cover while chanting, as the Kantus is completely vulnerable during this time.

MUTUAL HEALING

While a Kantus can't heal itself while performing the shamanistic chant, it can be healed by another Kantus. By working together, both Kantuses can keep each other alive while giving their allies near limitless health.

DOWN BUT NOT OUT

In addition to keeping allies healed, the Kantus can also revive the Grenadier. If the Grenadier goes down as the chant is in progress, it is revived.

RAGER (1500 POINTS)

EQUIPMENT	BREECHSHOT (PRIMARY)
SPECIAL	RAGE
DURATION	8 SECONDS
COOLDOWN	18 SECONDS
OTHER	RT SHOOT, RT MELEE (WHILE ENRAGED), A CHARGE

As their name implies, Ragers have quite the temper. When they first enter the battle, they attack with their Breechshot, a very powerful, single-shot, long-range rifle. Any COG hit in the head with this rifle is dead in one shot. This is much harder to do than it sounds. The weapon does not possess a scope, so your accuracy must be perfect.

When a player initiates the ability, the Rager immediately drops the Breechshot and transforms into a menacing mass of flesh. At this time, it gains the Charge ability, and can run at super-human speeds towards its intended target.

SNIPING WITH THE BREECHSHOT

As mentioned previously, the Breechshot is an extremely powerful rifle. This weapon is best used at long range against COG soldiers who are hiding behind cover. If there are no Wretches on the battlefield, the Rager should focus on sniping the Scout in his roost. Even if it's impossible to score a headshot on a COG soldier, keep firing rounds into them. The Breechshot is much more powerful than the typical Lancer, making it useful for scoring any kind of hit on the COG.

While bathed in the power of the healing chant during resurrection, the Grenadier is invulnerable to damage for a few seconds. Any Grenadier destroyed by explosives or close-range shotgun blasts is incapable of being revived.

COG INTEL ON THE KANTUS

Kantus should be a priority target for any COG soldiers. As long as they are in the battle, all other Locust are that much harder to defeat. The easiest way to get rid of a Kantus is by using the Scout's Markza to get a clean headshot. This quickly removes the Kantus from the fight, long before any of its abilities can be used to prolong the battle. The Booshka's ability to bounce grenades off of walls to land behind cover is great for taking out Kantus that are hiding.

UNLEASHING RAGE

The real strength of this class is the Rage ability. Anytime the Rager takes damage, activate the Rage ability. This makes it a melee killing machine. Immediately activate the Charge ability to rush into range of any nearby COG. Once you're there, unleash a flurry of melee attacks to quickly destroy any adversary. If by some miracle the Rager survives the duration of its Rage ability, it reverts back into its normal self.

COG INTEL ON THE RAGER

The Rager is best handled at long range while behind cover. This Locust is an expert marksman with the Breechshot and can make quick work of any stationary COG Soldier. The COG Scout should keep an eye out for this sniper and alert everyone on his team. Killing the Rager before it transforms is in every COG Soldiers best interest since it becomes much faster and more deadly once enraged.

Anytime a Rager transforms and comes running after you, alert your teammates so everyone can try to focus fire to quickly down it before it reaches melee combat with any teammates. The best weapons for this are the Gnasher and Booshka.

■ GIANT SERAPEDE (2400 POINTS)

EQUIPMENT	NONE
SPECIAL	REAR UP
DURATION	VARIABLE
COOLDOWN	N/A
OTHER	RT BITE ATTACK, RT SPIT ACID (WHILE REARED UP)

This creature is unlike anything else among the Locust. Its long, segmented body is heavily armored. This, along with its many-legged, swift locomotion, can make it a difficult target for the COG. Because of its many legs, its speed can be surprising, especially when it is damaged. However, most classes are faster than a heavily damaged Serapede.

The Giant Serapede is made up of several segments. Each segment has its own health value, which is easily monitored. This is the only way to accurately judge how much remaining life the Giant Serapede has.

FRIED FOOD

The Giant Serapede's bite is not only extremely effective against barricades, but also COG soldiers. Anytime a COG soldier tries to flank a Giant Serapede to get a shot on the vulnerable tail, it is best to turn and take a bite out of the foe. However, when turning to engage an enemy, make sure not to leave the vulnerable tail area exposed to even more foes.

DESTROYING BARRIERS

Giant Serapedes excel at destroying barriers. Their electrified mandibles make short work of even the strongest fortifications. Giant Serapedes should hide the vulnerable rear of their segmented bodies around corners or behind walls when attacking barricades. This makes the Giant Serapede nearly invulnerable to damage while it's destroying the COG defenses.

REARING UP AND SPITTING

At any time during a fight, the Giant Serapede can rear up on its end segments. This makes the Giant Serapede tower over all other combatants and allows it to see over barricades and walls easily. This is useful because in this mode, the Giant Serapede can launch near endless streams of acidic spit on any COG soldiers hiding behind barricades. The one drawback of this move is that the Giant Serapede must remain immobile and is a much more visible target.

COG INTEL ON THE GIANT SERAPEDE

Though the Giant Serapede is heavily armored, it does have one glaring weak spot—its glowing tail. While it's always advantageous to attack a foe from behind, it is absolutely necessary when taking down the Giant Serapede. These monstrosities are nearly invulnerable from the front.

When a Giant Serapede begins attacking a team member, quickly move behind it while the target flees, leading on the Giant Serapede. Then fire away at its tail segments. Once a segment has taken enough damage, it explodes in a shower of gore, making it possible to move on to the next section. Continue this tactic until you reach the head, putting an end to the Giant Serapede once and for all.

■ MAULER (3500 POINTS)

EQUIPMENT	FLAIL (PRIMARY), BOOMSHIELD (SECONDARY)
SPECIAL	SPIN SHIELD
DURATION	5 SECONDS
COOLDOWN	10 SECONDS
OTHER	A CHARGE, LT RAISE SHIELD, RT FLAIL ATTACK

This hulking behemoth lumbers across the battlefield at a much more sedate pace than other Locusts. A Mauler always carries a large, spiked Boomshield and a deadly Flail. Normally, the Mauler drags its Flail behind as it hunkers down behind its shield. This protects it from almost all projectiles fired at it from its frontal arc. If they need to cross the battlefield, Maulers are capable of short bursts of speed, using their Charge ability. Few sights are more terrifying than a Mauler swinging its Flail as it Charges the COG.

CRUSH

The Mauler's Flail is massive, allowing it to cause enormous damage to barricades and other fortifications. It takes a few moments for the Mauler to marshal all of its strength to smash the Flail down with great force, for maximum damage. The Flail is only useful in close to very short range and has an impact on a relatively small area of effect.

While the Mauler is great for destroying barricades, if it closes with the COG, it is even more dangerous. One hit from a Mauler's Flail reduces even the hardiest COG to ground meat.

SPIN

Because the Mauler is so dangerous, it is often a priority target for the COG. Luckily, the Flail is not the only tool available to the Mauler. The Boomshield is not only useful for protecting the Mauler from enemy COG fire, but it's also a great offensive weapon in its own right. Anytime the Mauler is under heavy fire, yet also needs to quickly cross the distance to its enemy, the Mauler can spin up its shield. Spinning the Boomshield causes all bullets fired at the shield to be reflected and focused back toward the Mauler player's target reticule. These bullets can, and often do, inflict injury to the offending COG.

Activating the Mauler's Spin Shield ability causes it to quickly creep forward, pursuing any nearby COG. If any COG gets caught in the spinning blades of the Boomshield, they are immediately shredded into bite-size chunks. This is an extremely useful tactic to divert attention away from Locust allies while also dealing damage to the COG.

COG INTEL ON THE MAULER

When spotting a Mauler across the battlefield, make it a priority target. It is extremely dangerous at close range and the best tactic is to take it down before it reaches your frontline. The Mauler can absorb a great deal of damage and, thanks to the Boomshield, is nearly invulnerable from frontal attacks while it's active. The only smart time to attack a Mauler head on is when it's charging with Flail swinging and shield down. Get off as many shots as you can at this time. Otherwise, use flanking maneuvers to attack it from its unprotected flanks.

The COG should not engage the Mauler in melee battle, no matter the cost. The Mauler can rip its way through barricades with ease, so it should be stopped, ideally, before it gets the chance. As a champion-class Locust, the Mauler is one of the greatest threats to the COG's defenses, second only to the Corpser.

■ CORPSER (5000 POINTS)

EQUIPMENT	NONE
SPECIAL	BURROW/EMERGE
DURATION	8 SECONDS
COOLDOWN	12 SECONDS
OTHER	RT LEG STOMP

Originally harnessed by the Locust for digging, these huge spider-like creatures are terrors on the battlefield. Not only do they have an enormous health pool, but their tough carapace also offers significant protection from enemy projectiles. Due to these attributes, the Corpser is an excellent siege weapon.

Using their natural abilities, Corpsers are also capable of burrowing into the ground and can swiftly travel beneath the surface, making them incapable of being harmed while traveling this way. One additional benefit of burrowing is that the Corpser can destroy COG Sentry Turrets. The vibrations it causes while traveling blow up any turrets placed over its path.

A Corpser's primary objective is to neutralize any barricades remaining in your team's path to the COG Base. Once this is accomplished, wreak havoc among the COG, taking as many of them down as possible.

DESTROYING BARRICADES WITH LEG STOMP

While a Corpser only has one main attack, that's really all it needs. Its massively powerful Leg Stomp allows it to use its front four legs to slam into a target with great force. This makes short work of COG barricades and other fortifications. If a COG is unfortunate enough to be caught underneath a Corpser's Leg Stomp, they are instantly reduced to COG-flavored jelly.

USING BURROW TO RECOVER HEALTH OR CIRCUMVENT BARRIERS

While the Corpser's ability to travel underground is a useful tool to close in on COG forces, it can also be used to travel underneath many COG fortifications. This is a great tool for quickly reaching an objective when time is running short, giving the COG a nasty surprise if they aren't paying close attention.

Because they are such a dreadnaught on the battlefield, Corpsers often take the brunt of the COG attack. To restore health, a Corpser can burrow underground. Back in its natural environment, the Corpser quickly regains health while out of danger from enemy fire. This ability should be used often to keep this valuable asset in the fight as long as possible.

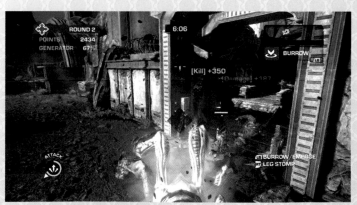

COG INTEL ON THE CORPSER

Looking like something out of a nightmare, Corpsers are terror incarnate on the battlefield. Whenever they appear, make them a priority target. Announce their location to the rest of the team, so everyone can focus fire on this monster. Corpsers are the greatest threat on the battlefield because they can bypass or destroy all COG defenses to quickly reach their objective.

COG should always be on the lookout for the shifting ground which marks a burrowing Corpser and be ready for it when it emerges.

The Corpser has decent protection from frontal attacks due to its armored legs. While it is possible to shoot the Corpser in the head between the legs, it is very difficult because the legs are constantly moving. COGs firing on a Corpser should focus their fire on the underbelly of the Corpser when it rears up to stomp, and on its head and unprotected backside. The Booshka and the Sentry Turrets are the most powerful tools for quickly taking down a Corpser.

DEFENSE: PLAYING AS THE COG

Playing as the defenders, the COG, players can select from four classes: the Engineer, Soldier, Scout, and Medic. Each has its advantages and teams should be a nice mix of the four—depending on how things are going on the defensive front.

The goal is always the same, to protect one of three objectives: one of two E-Holes or the generator. Keep fortifications repaired as long as possible and do not slouch on the support as you fight off the Locust. As the defense, you need to keep the other team from the current objective until the timer hits zero.

If the Locust beasts are moving up one side more than the other, concentrate more firepower on that side. Be sure to keep an eye out though as they may decide to switch. Always have at least one player within sight of the other chokepoint, so there are no surprises.

If you're not getting the needed ammo from Cole, do not be afraid to melee the Locust—especially when attacking an objective. There is a ribbon for doing this to a Corpser.

TROIKA TURRET

Be sure to take full advantage of the Troika Turret, especially as the weaker classes, Engineer and Medic. Scouts running low on ammo may also take advantage of these. Just be sure to use your special abilities when available.

When using the turret, a meter appears in the upper-right corner, where the ammo is displayed. As you fire the turret, the meter goes up, eventually turning red. When it reaches the end, the weapon has overheated and the player must hold the Right Bumper to cool it back down. Try to fire in spurts so you don't waste any time waiting for the gun to recover.

The Troika is destructible just like the fortifications, so it's worth defending for a while—obviously not if the E-Hole or generator is under attack. When playing as an Engineer, check up on the turret's health when you can. If it has taken a beating, use your repair tool to bring it back to full strength.

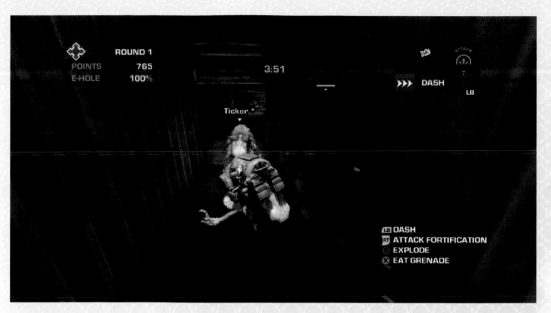

POINTS 765
E-HOLE 100%

ROUND 1

3:51

Ticker

>>> DASH
LB

🅛🅑 DASH
🆁🆃 ATTACK FORTIFICATION
Ⓑ EXPLODE
Ⓧ EAT GRENADE

TICKER ROUTES

Watch out as some maps contain special tunnels just for Tickers. That means they can emerge from a location other than the usual two chokepoints.

THE COG CLASSES

The Coalition of Ordered Governments is always ready to stand on the front line to face the Locust. These soldiers, or Gears, represent the best and baddest the COG has to offer. Each one has a unique loadout and skill set. Choose wisely when you go into battle.

■ THE ENGINEER

EQUIPMENT	GNASHER (PRIMARY), REPAIR TOOL (SECONDARY)
SPECIAL	DEPLOY SENTRY TURRET
DURATION	12 SECONDS
COOLDOWN	18 SECONDS

[Repair] +40

The COG has trained Engineers since before the Pendulum Wars. Their technical knowledge proves invaluable on the battlefield; they have the Repair Tools and the know-how to maintain fortifications. Even the most damaged barricade can easily be fully repaired as long as there is something left for them to work with.

Truly gifted COG Engineers have the expertise to deploy Sentry Turrets anywhere on the battlefield. These turrets have advanced tactical targeting CPUs allowing them to differentiate friend from foe and lock on to any enemy within its significant target range. While extremely powerful, Sentry Turrets consume a lot of energy and can only remain operational for short periods of time before going offline.

All COG Engineers must go through rigorous combat training. Since a COG Engineer is required to be on the frontlines to maintain fortifications, they are trained with an extremely powerful shotgun—the Gnasher. This weapon is ruthless at short range and less effective as the range increases, but its ammo capacity of eight rounds is enough to clear most enemy Locust from the COG Engineer's immediate area.

FIELD REPAIRS

While trying to repair barricades in either OverRun or Survival, be very careful as you must have your Repair Tool equipped and are therefore vulnerable to Locust attack. If a barricade must be repaired, even while enemies are assaulting the nearby area, deploy your Sentry Turret to give you and your team covering fire while you make repairs.

Some fortifications are simply impossible to protect and very little effort should be expended in keeping them up. These barricades typically have low strength and are destroyed rather quickly since they are near the Locust's starting Emergence Holes.

Repairing barricades isn't the only thing your trusty Repair Tool can fix. It can also maintain Troikas! When the COG is pushed back by the Locust, the next areas typically have at least one mounted turret. These Troikas offer extreme firepower and should be kept in peak working order at all times, granting your squad the much needed offense it provides when manned.

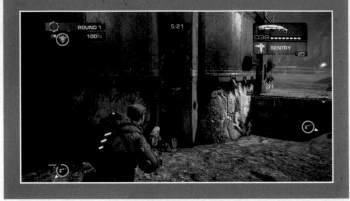

BATTLEFIELD AWARENESS

When defending the E-Hole from Locust assaults always be aware of the remaining strength of nearby fortifications. You can see any damaged barricades' remaining strength, even through walls! When a barricade has a red bar it is near destruction, so repairing it should be a priority. Any barricade your team allows to be destroyed can never be replaced. Protect them as long as you can.

SENTRY ON OVERWATCH

The Sentry Turret is the single most powerful tool the Engineer can use in any OverRun or Survival match. Its extreme firepower can destroy all but the strongest enemies almost immediately. When you deploy the Sentry Turret, it is placed in your current location. Be sure it is in a spot that has excellent line of sight on the area you want to protect.

Deploying the Sentry Turret at the wrong time can mean the difference between holding an area and protecting a fortification and getting overrun by a horde of Locust! Sentry Turrets have a significant cooldown and only remain active for a few seconds, so it is critical that they are deployed only when needed. Be sure to keep your Sentry Turret in well protected or even elevated positions to give it the highest chance of survival and targets to fire upon.

ADVANCED RECON

When reaching later waves of Survival Mode, it's very helpful to run up and place a Sentry Turret within line of sight of a Kryll barrier. This gives your squad some extra time to prepare for the next wave of Locust as your Sentry Turret eradicates all incoming Locust trying to enter through the barrier. If a wave was just completed, do not deploy the Sentry Turret until a few seconds after the countdown has reached zero for the next wave to start.

The Sentry Turret can be best used in two ways. First, it can be used as an advanced scout on one side of the map, letting you know of Locust threats without having a valuable squad member in the location. Second, the Sentry Turret comes into its true strength while helping take down tier 2 Locust enemies like the Mauler or Corpser! These foes take a considerable amount of damage to bring down and the Sentry Turret helps make quick work of them.

LOCUST INTEL ON THE ENGINEER

When encountering a COG Engineer as any Locust class, be on the lookout for his Sentry Turret. Advancing on a position with an active Sentry Turret is suicide. The turret can quickly destroy any foe. If the Sentry Turret is active, you can either wait until it goes offline and powers down or you can destroy it. Preferably, use a Corpser, Mauler, or Giant Serapede, as these classes of Locust are extremely tough. If you don't have access to these classes yet, waiting is the best option.

Getting in close with the COG Engineer is also not recommended since he wields the Gnasher and can destroy all but the toughest Locust in just a couple shots. Grenade tags and long-range weapons are the ideal method of removing the COG Engineer from the battlefield.

■ THE SOLDIER

EQUIPMENT	BOOSHKA (PRIMARY), LANCER (SECONDARY)
SPECIAL	THROW AMMO CRATES
DURATION	6 SECONDS
COOLDOWN	10 SECONDS

COG Soldiers are some of the most elite units trained on Sera. The Pendulum Wars was won in no small part to the training and supplies that these soldiers had at their command. These soldiers are masters of modern-day weapons and put them to efficient and deadly use. Good COG Soldiers know that keeping their squadmates supplied with ammo can mean the difference between life and death. Every COG Soldier has the ability to throw down a crate of ammo that any or all of his teammates can utilize to resupply their depleted weapons.

All COG Soldiers are trained in various weapons, and the most common one is the Lancer. In the hands of trained soldiers, this weapon is extremely deadly in close combat and up to medium range. Attached with a chainsaw, this weapon is designed to easily cut through the tough hides of Locust Drones. Due to its large ammo clip size, COG Soldiers can take out multiple enemies or keep an area suppressed for an extended time before reloading.

New to the COG Soldiers' arsenal is a weapon simply called the Booshka. Now that the Locust have devastated the home nation of Gorasnaya, some of the UIR tech and soldiers are now part of the COG. This weapon was designed and used predominantly in the Pendulum Wars by the UIR. It is excellent at crowd control and destroying large groups of enemies. This grenade launcher has an arcing flight path, and the grenades it launches can be bounced off surfaces to attack unseen Locust for considerable damage.

AMMO RESUPPLY

The Soldier has the amazing utility of providing ammo for his entire team! The ability to deploy an ammo crate is essential in OverRun and Survival. There is no other way to gain ammo for your weapons, short of being killed and choosing your class again. The ammo crate even resupplies the Engineer's blow torch while he is repairing a fortification, which is a very helpful tactic. Another great effect of deploying ammo crates is that standing within its area of effect gains the ammo. Throwing an ammo crate to teammates only requires them to be in range, and they gain the ammo even while in the middle of fighting the Locust hordes!

Playing as the Soldier requires you to be very aware of your teammates' locations and ammo supplies. If your teammates are ever low on ammo, you will see a flashing ammo icon over their head. This means they are dangerously low on ammo and need a resupply as soon as possible. Once an ammo crate is dropped, it does not stay on the battlefield long. Make sure to place it near those who need it! It takes some time before you have the ability to drop another crate of ammo, so be sure you don't throw it into inaccessible areas or use it when it's not needed.

There are strategic times to get everyone's ammo supplies topped off. In Survival, that is between waves. Everyone can quickly gather at the E-Hole and an ammo crate can be dropped for all. This makes the most efficient use of this skill, as it has no limit of how many players can gain ammo by being in its area of effect.

Some of your team may be in hard or impossible-to-reach areas but also need ammo. This is usually the case when the Scout is in need of ammo while in his sniper roost. Ammo crates can be tossed like grenades, so alert your Scout that you are throwing some ammo up to him. He can then keep doing what he does best without wasting the effort and time of climbing down to you.

SUPERIOR FIREPOWER

Soldiers have access to the explosive Booshka, a formidable weapon that can launch grenades at extreme range. The grenades bounce off of the ground and any walls they initially contact. The grenades detonate after coming to a stop after a few seconds. However, the grenade detonates

immediately if it comes into contact with an enemy. When using the Booshka, you should only try to hit enemy targets directly (if you are confident in your shot) since each miss is a waste of a lot of potential damage.

Using the Booshka in conjunction with the Scout's Spot ability is the most effective way of stopping the Locust in any mode. Knowing where they are before they come around corners allows the Soldier to shoot grenades off walls or obstacles to hit the Locust before they can even see any of your COG squaddies. Since the ammo size for this gun is extremely low, make sure to always keep supplied from your ammo crate drops.

The Booshka is absolutely essential for later waves of Survival where the sheer volume of the Locust forces them to be in large roving packs.

A few shots of the Booshka in these circumstances quickly eliminate all but the strongest of Locust classes. Never use the Booshka against Giant Serapedes. Instead, switch to your Lancer to quickly take out their sections from behind, as the Booshka shot can easily miss your target and bounce to another location.

During OverRun and Survival modes there is a high probability that you'll see Locust enemies grouped around fortifications while they try and take them down. In this instance, you should fire the Booshka multiple times directly into the middle of the pack to quickly obliterate all nearby targets.

LOCUST INTEL ON THE SOLDIER

Anytime you encounter a Soldier as the Locust be very aware of any objects landing nearby. They are probably grenades launched from his Booshka! Using the Wretch to quickly stun the Soldier allows the rest of your Locust team to quickly swarm the incapacitated COG. A stunned or killed Soldier cannot supply his teammates with ammo, making all of them weaker. Since the Wretch is fast and fairly small, with the ability to leap over barricades, it is one of your better options for removing the Soldier from the battlefield equation.

Assaulting the Soldier in close combat is very risky; any of your smaller units can easily be chainsawed by the powerful Lancer. Use a Rager, once you have it unlocked, to snipe the Soldier with his Breechshot. It is the safest way of taking down a Soldier until you have access to champion-class Locust like the Corpser or Mauler. With these brutes, you can easily close the distance to any Soldier and quite possibly save your allies by drawing all his fire, keeping the heat off of your weaker teammates.

THE MEDIC

EQUIPMENT	LANCER (PRIMARY), SAWED-OFF SHOTGUN (SECONDARY)
SPECIAL	THROW STIM-GAS GRENADES
DURATION	5 SECONDS
COOLDOWN	4 SECONDS

Being a COG Medic is one of the most honored positions in the COG army. These members of the COG are right in the middle of any significant conflict keeping their squad alive and bringing back soldiers from the brink of death. COG field Medics utilize their extensive knowledge of anatomy to help alleviate all potential life-threatening wounds by effectively using a canister of Stim-Gas.

Stim-Gas is a revolutionary breakthrough in the COG military. Currently, Stim-Gas is produced and placed into canisters that can easily be thrown to any soldier on the battlefield. The canister shatters at their feet and releases healing mists. The chemicals produced from the release of these mists are so powerful they can even bring back soldiers who are killed within a few seconds. COG Medics are able to tell which soldiers are wounded the most through intense mental training. This training allows them to immediately assess which soldiers are in the most need of their supplies. They can then toss Stim-Gas to them while still fighting the Locust hordes themselves.

Being a part of the COG also means intense weapon training on top of all the medical training. COG Medics are typically trained in the use of the Lancer and are also proficient with the Sawed-Off Shotgun. Anyone mistaking the COG Medic for an easy kill is in for a surprise. They are excellent marksmen with the ability to keep themselves alive through amazing amounts of incoming damage (if they drop their Stim-Gas at their feet).

BUFFING HEALTH

The Stim-Gas Grenade is your defining ability as a Medic. Using the Stim-Gas Grenade on allies who are about to engage a Locust assault is the wisest use of your ability. This way, any damage received by the team members who are standing in the healing mists automatically heals. You are effectively increasing their maximum health pool. Don't worry too much about wasting the grenade; your ability has a very quick cooldown, allowing you to use it quite often. This also allows you to continue supporting your team by firing your weapon while your ability is on cooldown.

Don't forget that you can also drop the Stim-Gas Grenades at your feet to buff your own health. Do this if you're in danger or about to face some Locusts with no allies nearby. This gives you a few seconds of increased survivability until your team can get to your position if they are needed. Medics can hold their position against multiple Locust quite easily by protecting themselves this way. But remember to watch your teammates' health. They depend on you to keep them alive!

CHARGED FOR BATTLE

Anytime large groups of Locust are assaulting your position, especially champion-level Locust classes, drop a Stim-Gas Grenade in the middle of your squad's position, making sure to hit as many allies as possible. In Survival, where you fight massive waves of Locust in large groups, it is imperative to keep your team members up through the multitude of attacks they are about to receive.

REVIVING THE FALLEN

Keeping your team alive as long as possible through heals can be tough, especially when fighting endless waves of enemies. Sometimes a squad member is killed but still has a chance of coming back into the fight. If a squadmate is down and they have a red Gears symbol over their body with a red bar slowly draining around it, then they can be brought back to life. You only have a few seconds to send a Stim-Gas Grenade to them, but if you land it near them they immediately revive with full health, ready to fight once more.

STRONG ARM

Learning to control where you throw the Stim-Gas Grenade is essential to being a good Medic. Even if a teammate is across the map, a well-placed grenade can bring your fallen comrade back to life. Make sure to keep mostly clear lines of sight to your squad's fighting position so you can effectively watch as many people as possible.

Even though Stim-Gas Grenades are great for healing and reviving fallen teammates, a Medic's healing power can't prevent all things. Any Locust ability that can gib someone can't be healed through or even revived from. If a COG gets gibbed from any possible attack, there is nothing a Stim-Gas Grenade can do to prevent death. Also, if the COG teammate's body is destroyed in any way, you can't revive them; there is nothing to bring back.

LOCUST INTEL ON THE MEDIC

One of the more annoying enemies you face as a Locust is the Medic. Even though the Medic only has a Lancer and a Sawed-Off, you should not try to face off with her when she is standing in a blue mist. During the time this ability is in effect, it requires massive amount of damage to kill the Medic or abilities that can one-shot. Using a Wretch's Stun Scream is very effective in interrupting her ability to heal. If the Medic deploys her Stim-Gas Grenade on her comrades, she is vulnerable for a short time and this is the best opportunity to attack.

Since the Medic is most likely behind multiple barricades healing her squad, it is best to try and use ranged attacks on her, like grenade throws or suppressive fire from the Grenadier's Lancer. Any champion-class Locust has no trouble facing off with a Medic, as they only have moderate offensive firepower.

THE SCOUT

EQUIPMENT	MARKZA (PRIMARY), SNUB (SECONDARY)
SPECIAL	THROW SPOT GRENADES
DURATION	8 SECONDS
COOLDOWN	3 SECONDS

The UIR has trained some of the greatest snipers Sera has ever seen. These Scouts were the terror of the battlefield during the Pendulum Wars. With their ability to climb to the most advantageous locations and wait for enemy forces for days at a time, they were able to relay information about the Coalition forces fighting them. This provided the UIR perfect opportunities to ambush their enemy.

Even though all current Scouts were members of the UIR, they have sworn allegiance to the Coalition to fight the Locust. Having access to all the weaponry the COG has to offer still hasn't changed the Scout's favored weapon—the Markza. This is the standard marksman rifle that all UIR are trained with. In the right hands, this is an extremely versatile rifle. Scouts excel in medium to long range and have the fire power to lay waste to advancing Locust long before they reach their fortified allies.

The Coalition recently engineered a new grenade called a Spot Grenade. This grenade has the ability to detect all enemy life signatures through any terrain or structures within its sphere of influence. Due to the very nature of Scouts always being in terrain where they have a tactical advantage, it is the standard grenade they are issued in the field. Once thrown to a location by the Scout, all allies can see any enemies traveling near its location (even through walls). This advantage comes with a secondary benefit of giving all squad members bonus damage on any enemy under the effects of the Spot Grenade.

EXTRA EYES

Playing as the Scout is a very important support role. With their ability to deploy Spot Grenades, they are effectively warning their comrades of impending attack from Locust forces. Spot Grenades should be used every time the cooldown is refreshed. Using them at Locust entry points during OverRun and Survival not only allows you to see if any enemies are sneaking past your fortifications, but it also allows your team to see areas they need to rush to defend.

DEBUFFING THE HORDE

Anytime there is a large wave of the Locust be sure to keep your Spot Grenade on them. Your ability coupled with the Soldier firing his Booshka into their ranks can quickly clear out large groups of enemies. This is essential, especially when fighting champion-level Locust classes who have vast amounts of health and take some time to kill.

As you enter any OverRun or Survival map be on the lookout for Special locations that resemble yellow arrows going up walls. In this location, you can climb to an area that only you and the Wretch class can access. These locations almost always provide excellent line of sight on advancing Locust from which you can easily deploy your Spot Grenades to maximum advantage. Be mindful of advancing Wretch forces, as they don't hesitate to climb to your position and engage you.

PRIORITY TARGETS

Using the Scout requires a bit more finesse than the other COG classes. Be judicious about firing your Markza. If you are in your sniper's roost, then it is very hard to get ammo from the Soldier class, as he needs to provide it to the most people he can. For this reason, you should avoid wasting ammo. For example, when a Kantus stops to heal, use the Markza's scope to get in a clean headshot kill.

PROTECTING THE E-HOLE COVER

Sometimes no matter how well you plan there are simply too many enemies to stop from reaching the E-Hole. If any champion-class Locust get close, focus on taking these down first; they have the most health and do the most damage. Sniping the Mauler and Corpser with headshots brings even these brutes down much faster than any of the other COG classes are capable of doing.

While sniping targets from high ground be mindful of the multiple climb points leading to your area. The Wretch usually tries to climb into the Scout's area to engage him or, at the very least, have an easier time of bypassing fortifications. When engaging the Locust in later waves on Survival mode, make sure to take out the mounted Kantus as a priority. This fast-moving unit has the ability to heal allies very quickly and should be given your undivided attention.

LOCUST INTEL ON THE SCOUT

As the Locust encountering Scouts, it is imperative that you utilize cover as much as possible. Any time spent in the open or stopped in any location is a sure way to lose your head. Locust forces should provide covering fire for the Wretch while it gets into position at the climb points. This gives the Wretch a very good chance of surviving and possibly eliminating the Scout threat. After your Wretch climbs into position be sure to use your Stun Scream to help finish off the Scout.

Another great way of taking out the Scout involves having enough points to summon the Rager. With the Rager's Breechshot you can kill the Scout in his perch, especially if he is busy trying to hold off any Wretch advances. One shot to the head with a Breechshot instantly kills any COG. But this weapon does not have a scope, so your aim must be perfect. Keeping Scouts out of the fight essentially helps you keep the rest of your team alive longer since they won't be under the influence of his Spot Grenade debuff.

SURVIVAL

Survival Mode is a co-op mode where five COG characters, controlled by either the computer or by players, defend three objectives while waves of the Locust horde attack. The gameplay is very similar to the defensive round of OverRun, except that 10 waves of Locust attack with breaks in between instead of the continuous onslaught.

The Locust that you face each round are shown in the following table.

TYPES OF LOCUST THAT APPEAR IN EACH WAVE

WAVE	LOCUST
1	TICKER, GRENADIER
2	TICKER, WRETCH, GRENADIER, RAGER
3	TICKER, WRETCH, GRENADIER, KANTUS, RAGER, BOOMER
4	TICKER, WRETCH, GRENADIER, KANTUS, RAGER, MAULER, BOOMER
5	TICKER, WRETCH, GRENADIER, KANTUS, RAGER, CORPSER
6	WRETCH, GRENADIER, KANTUS, MAULER
7	TICKER, WRETCH, GRENADIER, KANTUS, RAGER, MAULER, CORPSER, BLOODMOUNT
8	TICKER, WRETCH, GRENADIER, KANTUS, RAGER, GIANT SERAPEDE, MAULER, BLOODMOUNT
9	WRETCH, GRENADIER, KANTUS, RAGER, MAULER, CORPSER, BOOMER, BLOODMOUNT
10	TICKER, WRETCH, GRENADIER, KANTUS, RAGER, GIANT SERAPEDE, MAULER, CORPSER, BLOODMOUNT

As you can see on the preceding table, the beasts that you face get tough fairly quick. Plus, you will see Locust that you do not face in OverRun. The Boomer wreaks havoc as early as wave 3, launching Boomshots at your party. Kantus riding Bloodmounts appear in later rounds as they heal their allies from atop

their powerful mount. These guys spell double trouble as both need to be dealt with.

Try to keep the fortifications intact for

as long as you can in the early waves. Eventually, the fortifications go down so quick it's not worth dealing with. Concentrate on repairing as an Engineer rather than taking on the Locust who attempt to destroy the fortification. Rely on teammates to fight them off.

Keep the support coming as you progress through the waves. Toss out ammo, Spot Grenades, and Stim-Gas whenever needed and available. Every break between waves should come with an ammo crate so everyone can top off. Unless there are multiple Soldiers, throw it around the current objective to ensure everyone has a fair chance to get some.

DEALING WITH THE LOCUST

Each Locust has the ability to be a pest, but some should be eliminated as soon as possible. Here are some quick tips on how to deal with each beast. Refer to our section on the Locust Classes for more in-depth intel.

TICKER

Tickers are the easiest to eliminate, as one shot blows them up. But if they're able to get past the first line of defense, they can cause some mischief. They have the ability to take out multiple players along with a fortification, so dodge away from one when it rises into a self-detonation.

WRETCH

The Wretch's ability to stun any nearby player makes them priority number one. Fortunately, they are easy to deal with as long as you can get a bead on the quick-moving foes. The fact that they can hop over short walls and fortifications makes them that much more of a pest.

GRENADIER

Grenadiers are the early muscle for the Locust. They carry Frag Grenades as their special ability along with a Gnasher and Lancer. Eliminate these guys with Booshka shots and Markza headshots as soon as they appear, or they can damage the current objective immediately.

KANTUS

Kantus have the power to bring multiple beasts back from near death with their chain heal ability. They tend to hang back, so it's up to the Scout or Soldier to take them down from afar.

RAGER

Ragers are not too bad to deal with until they decide to use their ability and become enraged. Then they are like mini Berserkers, charging at players with increased power. Try not to let them get in close, especially if they have already entered this enraged state. Take them down from a distance or be ready to dodge their charge attack.

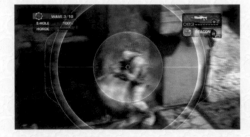

GIANT SERAPEDE

Giant Serapedes are a pain to deal with, as their weak spot is in the tail. Get behind them with a Lancer and they are reduced to just a head in no time.

MAULER

Maulers are tough to take down because they carry a shield. Bullets fired directly at them are bounced back at your allies. Stay away from Maulers, as they have a deadly shield spin and Flail. Get behind them; firing at their rear is the quickest way to down Maulers. Using a Troika Turret while one walks away is best.

CORPSER

Corpsers are armored, so it takes a long time to kill one. Combined with their ability to burrow into the ground, these are one of the toughest Locust to eliminate. As they emerge from the ground they are especially deadly, so stay clear. Getting in close with a shotgun can down one, but be ready for their attack.

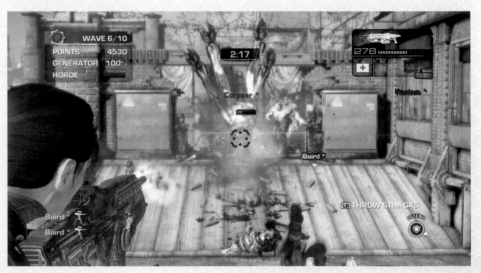

BOOMER

Boomers carry lethal Boomshots, so they are a threat from anywhere on the map. Try to eliminate them with headshots from afar or let a turret take care of them.

BLOODMOUNT

Bloodmounts do not appear until the later waves, carrying Kantus onto the battlefield. They are more of a threat with the healer on top. Take care of the rider first, and then down the beast with consistent gunfire.

FINDING THE RIGHT TEAM

Creating the right team depends greatly on each player's skills and what they are comfortable with. But there are combinations that seem to work better in certain

situations. Each class has its advantages, so try to mix it up.

Every time you die, reconsider what class best suits your current

needs. For example, if the barriers are depleted, try substituting the Engineer with a Soldier. It really comes down to using each class to the best of their abilities and figuring out the best mix of classes that match your playing style.

You can go completely offensive by having three Soldiers with a Scout and Engineer. You may want to substitute the Scout with a Medic when the waves start getting tough. That way, you can keep the Soldiers healthy as they fight the bigger enemies. The Medic must constantly be vigilant as she can get overwhelmed.

A defensive approach may include two or three Engineers. This way, you can keep fortifications up for longer—prolonging the Locust advance. The Soldier will have to be on the ball as he launches his Booshka shots, while a Scout debuffs as many enemies as possible. Keeping all of the Engineers topped off with shotgun ammo can get overwhelming for the Soldier.

If you have a couple good snipers on your team, try out two Scouts. This way, each can watch a chokepoint and keep the Locust debuffed. Be sure your Soldier is on the ball, as they will need ammo almost constantly in later waves. You may even consider another Soldier, but then you have to forego the Medic's heal or the Engineer's repair.

MULTIPLAYER ARSENAL

The weapon selection in *Gears of War: Judgment* includes some incredibly powerful tools. Players choose one starter weapon to carry into battle with their Snub Pistol and grenade. These choices consist of assault rifles, shotguns, and a long-range rifle. The stronger guns lie around the Versus Mode maps, making these spots hotbeds of activity. This chapter provides all the information you need to choose your loadouts and use these tools to their fullest potential.

Each weapon has its own strengths and weaknesses. We explain how to use each one and break down how to get the most out of it. Often, your choice of starter weapon and grenade, along with which map-based weapon to go for, comes down to your preferences. However, it's worth checking out each one to see what they have to offer.

DAMAGE

For a few weapons, damage differs between Versus modes and OverRun. The following table shows how each weapon stacks up.

STARTER WEAPONS

WEAPON	VERSUS DAMAGE	OVERRUN DAMAGE
LANCER	50	50
RETRO LANCER	74	N/A
HAMMERBURST	86	N/A
CLASSIC HAMMERBURST	55	55
GNASHER SHOTGUN	670	670
SAWED-OFF SHOTGUN	670	2500
MARKZA	175	250
SNUB PISTOL	65	65

HEAVY AND SPECIAL WEAPONS

POWER WEAPONS	VERSUS DAMAGE	OVERRUN DAMAGE
BOOMSHOT	900	N/A
BOOSHKA	700	700
BREECHSHOT	280	350
DIGGER	900	N/A
HAMMER OF DAWN	1500	N/A
LONGSHOT	500	N/A
MORTAR	800	N/A
MULCHER	77	N/A
ONESHOT	5000	N/A
SCORCHER	2000	N/A
TORQUE BOW	708	N/A
VULCAN	210	N/A

AMMO COUNT

Each weapon starts with a certain amount of ammo in the gun, but most often you can carry more. Picking up a dropped weapon or an ammo crate gives you ammo up to the max that the weapon can carry. The following table shows these numbers for each weapon along with the size of each magazine. We have included the numbers for OverRun/Survival mode weapons in parentheses as these are often different than in the Versus modes.

STARTER WEAPONS

WEAPON	AMMO	MAX	MAGAZINE	AMMO CRATE/PICK UP
LANCER (OVERRUN)	240 (200)	420 (600)	60 (60)	120 (60)
RETRO LANCER	150	240	30	60
HAMMERBURST	140	200	20	40
CLASSIC HAMMERBURST (OVERRUN)	240 (240)	384 (384)	48 (48)	96 (N/A)
GNASHER SHOTGUN (OVERRUN)	8 (8)	24 (39)	8 (8)	8 (8)
SAWED-OFF SHOTGUN (OVERRUN)	6 (2)	10 (4)	2 (2)	2
MARKZA (OVERRUN)	30 (20)	120 (120)	10 (10)	20 (10)
SNUB PISTOL	24 (72)	84 (132)	12 (12)	48 (12)

HEAVY AND SPECIAL WEAPONS

WEAPON	AMMO	MAX	MAGAZINE	AMMO CRATE/PICK UP
BOOMSHOT	2	7	1	2
BOOSHKA (OVERRUN)	3 (3)	12 (12)	3 (3)	3 (3)
BREECHSHOT	12 (36)	28 (27)	4 (4)	12 (N/A)
DIGGER	2	7	1	2
HAMMER OF DAWN	CHARGE	100%	N/A	100% WITH NEW WEAPON
LONGSHOT	5	24	1	5
MORTAR	2	2	1	2 WITH NEW WEAPON
MULCHER	200	200	88 UNTIL OVERHEAT	100 (UP TO 200)
ONESHOT	8	8	1	8 WITH NEW WEAPON
SCORCHER	102	132	30	102
TORQUE BOW	4	12	1	4
VULCAN	320	320	160	CANNOT ABSORB MORE AMMO

GRENADES

WEAPON	AMMO	MAX	AMMO CRATE/PICK UP
FRAG GRENADE	1	2	1/1
INK GRENADE	1	2	1
SMOKE GRENADE	2	2	1
SPOT GRENADE	2	4	1
STIM-GAS GRENADE	1	2	1
INCENDIARY GRENADE	2	2	2

STARTER WEAPONS

When selecting your loadout, you are only allowed one of the following weapons to go along with the Snub Pistol and grenade. Look out for a dropped weapon or map-based weapon that complements your choice well and replace your Snub Pistol with the stronger gun.

Choosing your starter weapon depends on the range that you expect to fight at and personal preference. Try to take a weapon that excels at close range when fighting on a tight-quarters map such as Streets. A medium- to long-range weapon is ideal if you expect to fight out in the open.

SELECTING A STARTER WEAPON

WEAPON	MAGAZINE SIZE	DAMAGE	RANGE (CLOSE, MEDIUM, LONG)	SPECIAL MELEE ATTACK
LANCER	60	50	MEDIUM	CHAINSAW
RETRO LANCER	30	74	CLOSE-MEDIUM	BAYONET
HAMMERBURST	20	86	MEDIUM-LONG	NO
CLASSIC HAMMERBURST	48	55	CLOSE–MEDIUM	NO
GNASHER SHOTGUN	8	670	CLOSE	NO
SAWED-OFF SHOTGUN	2	670	CLOSE	NO
MARKZA	10	175	MEDIUM-LONG	NO

LANCER

The Lancer is the standard issue rifle for the COG. It has good mid-range accuracy and a huge magazine, which is good because it takes quite a few bullets to take an opponent down. Combine this with a lethal chainsaw melee attack and it's a solid choice for most scenarios.

The Lancer is very effective against the computer, but be ready for dancing opponents online. Players are much more active—jumping back and forth and bouncing off of walls to make it more difficult to take them down. You may empty your entire magazine and end up with a shotgun blast in the face. Be sure to quickly switch to your secondary weapon when under fire and in need of a reload.

The low damage of the Lancer means that you must fire at an opponent for a good amount of time before eliminating the foe. Be careful, as you are an easy target for one-shot weapons such as the Longshot during this time. Be aware of surrounding enemies; a flanking player can easily take you down as you concentrate on your target.

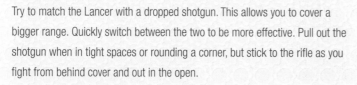

Try to match the Lancer with a dropped shotgun. This allows you to cover a bigger range. Quickly switch between the two to be more effective. Pull out the shotgun when in tight spaces or rounding a corner, but stick to the rifle as you fight from behind cover and out in the open.

CHAINSAW EXECUTION

This weapon is designed to cut through the tough hide of a Locust soldier. To activate the Lancer's chainsaw, hold the B button. This melee attack is designed to eliminate most enemies in a single cut, but beware that it takes a little time to rev up, and taking fire interrupts the rev up but not the revved-up attack.

If your target revs his chainsaw at the same time, a chainsaw duel ensues. Jam on the button to win this battle. This finishing move is extremely satisfying when successful, but try to limit it to unsuspecting opponents. One shotgun blast can end your fun in a hurry.

Walking around with your chainsaw revved is a bad idea. This makes you an easy target. The sound of the running power tool can also tip others off to your intent. Surprise a victim with this execution and quickly move on.

Combining the Lancer's chainsaw attack with a Smoke Grenade can often net you a kill. Stun an enemy with the explosive and walk into the cloud of smoke with your weapon revved to finish your opponent off.

Chainsaw executions take some time to perform, so expect to die soon after making a kill with any enemies close by. Use it as a last resort to at least take one foe down. Otherwise, limit this to single targets or make sure your team has your back.

RETRO LANCER

The Retro Lancer is less accurate than the Chainsaw Lancer prototype, but makes up for it with raw power and a vicious bayonet attachment. Because of its higher damage over the other rifles, it does not require as many shots to take an opponent down.

The Retro Lancer suffers from severe kickback, making it pretty ineffective in long-range battle. Fire the gun in short bursts to accommodate for the gun movement. Concentrate on keeping your aiming reticle down. The high damage of this rifle can take down a user of the other rifles with fewer hits.

Since the Retro Lancer excels at close range, it is good to pair this one with a long-range weapon. The Snub Pistol is decent at this range, but picking up one of the long-range heavy weapons or a dropped Markza gives you more power at that distance.

Use the superior short-range power of the Retro Lancer to fend off those pesky shotgun-toting players. Hipfire against a Gnasher user to take them down before they can send too many shells your way. Beware as the strong kickback throws off your aim in a hurry. Dodge around as you do so to make yourself a more difficult target to hit.

BAYONET CHARGE

The Retro Lancer has a bayonet strapped onto the rifle that makes it a fun weapon to use on unsuspecting foes. To charge an enemy with the bayonet, hold the B button and then use the Left Thumbstick to adjust the angle of your charge. Since a deadly bayonet charge requires a lot of speed, put some distance between you and your target before charging. Your character yells once a sufficient speed has been reached.

Once the charge is initiated, a meter appears under your gun in the top-right corner indicating your remaining stamina. Once the meter turns red, hitting an enemy kills them. The bayonet charge ends when the meter runs out. You need plenty of space to pull off a successful charge, but if your target is too far away, you could end up short.

The charging motion is very similar to roadie running with even less maneuverability. Your character screams as you run, so this lets nearby people know that you are incoming. Charging another player who is also charging your way ends in a double kill. Charging a revved chainsaw ends in your death.

HAMMERBURST

The Hammerburst can be fired quickly by rapidly pressing the Fire button. This does throw off your aim slightly, but it's worth the added damage output.

This rifle produces more damage than the Lancer, but lacks the big magazine size. This is okay, as you can take down an opponent quicker with this gun. Use it to pick off enemies settled in behind cover. Players don't tend to stand still, so you have to get in shots when you can. The muzzle climbs after three shots are fired quickly. If you carefully fire in two-shot bursts, you can avoid the muzzle climb.

It lacks the close-combat damage of the other rifles and lacks a big melee attack, so stick to medium- and long-range distances. Pair it up with a shotgun to cover short distances along with the long range of the rifle.

If you have a team that plays well together and can protect your position, find an elevated floor or platform and spot enemies while you take them down from a distance. The Markza and a number of the heavy weapons are better choices for sniping, but the Hammerburst has a much higher rate of fire than those.

CLASSIC HAMMERBURST
(Pre-Order Bonus)

This classic version of the Hammerburst is only available as a pre-order bonus or when playing OverRun mode as the Kantus. It works well between a short to medium range and has a powerful, six-bullet burst.

The Classic Hammerburst has a decent magazine size and its damage is fairly low. But because it shoots six-bullet bursts, it can quickly deal out the damage—especially at a close range. There is a specific rhythm to trigger pulls that allows the Classic Hammerburst to fire at its maximum speed. If you pull the trigger at the exact moment the weapon finishes firing, a follow-up shot can immediately be fired.

Match the Classic Hammerburst with a long-range rifle so you can cover more range. Keep moving and dodging when you enter a gunfight, as it may take a few bursts to take an opponent down.

GNASHER SHOTGUN

The Gnasher is a deadly weapon at close range and is a popular choice among players online. It is definitely the more well-rounded of the two shotguns. It can also do damage around medium range—especially when aimed.

The preferred fighting space for the Gnasher is short range, but it can be used in a pinch from further away—though the damage done diminishes greatly as the distance goes up. Aim down the gun when you must use this weapon from further away, as this does increase its effectiveness.

Shotgun duels are huge in *Gears* and require experience to get the better of your opponent. Get in some good practice with the Gnasher and you can tear it up with the best of them. Movement is just as important as your Gnasher skills. Skilled movement allows you to dodge incoming fire while still pelting your enemy with buckshot.

Hipfire the Gnasher Shotgun so you can stay on the move. Then aim your

shots when your target attempts to flee or is badly hurt. Aim slightly high when in close, as headshots more often end in death.

SAWED-OFF SHOTGUN

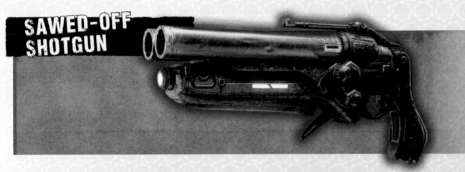

Like the Gnasher, the Sawed-Off Shotgun fires a narrow spread of pellets. Two shortened barrels, each holding a round, make for a devastating weapon at medium to close range. This damage potential is countered by its long reload time and limited ammo.

One squeeze of the trigger fires one of the barrels, but by holding down the Fire button both shots can be fired back to back. The Sawed-Off Shotgun poses a huge risk when you're within range of an opponent wielding one. Be careful advancing against an opponent with this gun.

As a Sawed-Off user, look to grab a rifle with a longer range to complement this shotgun's medium to short range. While firing at longer ranges with your rifle, switch to the Sawed-Off to defend your position as enemies get closer.

This weapon is best saved for medium to close combat. If you can get a good bead on a medium- to close-range foe, this shotgun can kill quickly. Combine a Sawed-Off Shotgun blast with a mantle kick for a lethal combo.

The Sawed-Off's damage at range is higher than the Gnasher, but the distance to gib is just as short and intimate as the Gnasher. For best results, fire with the intention of making both shots land. If both shots aren't true, we recommend quickly resorting to melee attacks against close enemies.

MARKZA

The GZ18 marksman rifle, or Markza, excels at medium-to-long range and has a 1.5x zoom scope along with a 10-round magazine. This incredibly accurate rifle is a new addition to the *Gears of War* games.

Its 1.5x zoom scope makes the Markza the starter weapon choice for snipers. The Markza suffers zero recoil when zoomed in. You will definitely want to find a dropped shotgun so you can defend yourself when someone rushes your position.

Because this weapon excels when aimed and zoomed in, it helps to have an organized team that can protect your position. Look for an elevated level to get a better view of a hot spot. To headshot a healthy player with the Markza, you must land two shots. Be aware of your surroundings. A rogue enemy who slips past your team has an easy kill when you're focused on distant foes.

It is possible to take someone down from close range, but not as quickly as most other weapons. Match the Markza with a shotgun to use when moving around.

SNUB PISTOL

The Snub Pistol is the standard-issue Coalition sidearm with zoom capability and semi-automatic action. To increase the rate of fire, rapidly pull the Right Trigger. Everyone carries a Snub Pistol into a match as their secondary weapon.

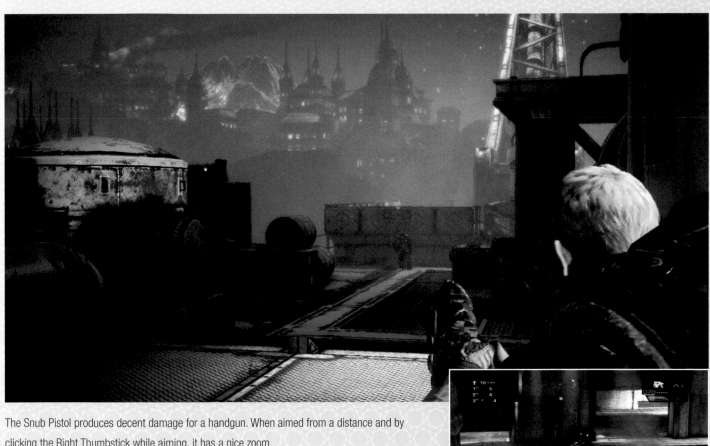

The Snub Pistol produces decent damage for a handgun. When aimed from a distance and by clicking the Right Thumbstick while aiming, it has a nice zoom.

The pistol can be used to complement a shotgun or short-range rifle with decent effect, but there are better options out there. Keep an eye out for dropped or map-based weapons that match better with your primary gun.

GRENADES

Five of the following grenades are selectable for your loadout. Choosing the right one depends on the game mode and where you are fighting—along with the type of weapons you have. Each grenade has its benefits and can complement the right weapon very well. With all grenade types except the Spot, you can martyr yourself (and hopefully your attacker) when you're being chainsawed or retro charged. You can also intimately tag enemies with grenades (except for Stim-Gas) by holding LB and pressing B.

FRAG GRENADES

The Frag Grenade is a standard issue grenade used by both the COG forces and the Locust Horde. It's the most common grenade, and rightfully so, as its blast radius is very large. It causes devastating damage, but it gives the target a little time to get away before going off.

Use the devastating power of the Frag Grenade to take out groups of enemies, or at least flush them out of hiding. Quickly toss grenades at unsuspecting foes by aiming their way and tapping the Left Bumper. All grenades can also be aimed by holding down the Left Bumper. The path of the grenade is shown so you can place it right where you want it.

It's possible to stick a Frag Grenade onto an opponent by hitting the player on the fly. If you get stuck with a Frag Grenade, you'll see an onscreen indicator and hear the classic "clank" sound. If this happens, move toward the closest enemy to try and take them down with you.

INK GRENADES

The Ink Grenade is an infant Nemacyst Inker housed inside a Bolo Grenade casing. It releases a thick black and green poisonous smoke which damages enemies and obscures their vision.

An Ink Grenade causes an area of effect that eats away at enemies' health. It does take a while to completely eliminate a player, so it can easily be escaped. Therefore, it works best when your team can mop up the damaged foes. Ink is very dangerous and can be effectively used as an area-of-denial weapon as well as assisting in kills. Enemies that are hit directly with a thrown Ink Grenade are stained with ink and eventually die regardless if they escape the ink cloud.

Use an Ink Grenade to flush opponents out of hiding while also damaging them as they escape. Switch to your long-range weapon to pick them off as they run away.

SMOKE GRENADES

The Smoke Grenade discharges a thick smoke that completely obscures the vision of anyone inside the cloud. It also makes it impossible for anyone outside the cloud to see what is inside. Use this weapon to disorient enemies or to conceal. This grenade does not damage foes at all.

It is possible to hide a sniper position by throwing a Smoke Grenade down before setting up with your long-range rifle. Then you have a little time to pick off targets before the smoke clears.

Players are unable to spot targets through the smoke, so if you know that an enemy is back there, continue to fire. A Smoke Grenade can also be used to conceal a charging attack, such as a shotgun rusher or bayonet charge. Smoke Grenades cause an upper-body cringe to enemies that stops them firing and forces them to drop heavy weapons and the Boomshield. The detonation of a Smoke Grenade will detonate other grenades. If you see an enemy throwing grenades, you can throw a Smoke to detonate his grenade right in front of his face.

SPOT GRENADES

The Spot Grenade creates a large detection field that displays the position of enemies within it. This highlights any opponent through walls or barriers within the field. This gives your team the location of all enemies in that area.

This allows you to find enemies who may be hiding out. As you run into a particularly busy area, toss this grenade to gain an advantage.

Watch out for the red or blue fields from other players' Spot Grenades and avoid walking through them if possible. Match up the Spot Grenade with a sniper rifle to make finding targets easier.

STIM-GAS GRENADES

The Stim-Gas Grenade is extremely valuable when entering a gunfight in *Gears of War*. It heals the user as he or she stands in the smoke. In OverRun and Survival modes, it has the ability to revive a player soon after being killed.

Match up a Stim-Gas Grenade with a weapon, such as the Lancer, that requires a bit of time to eat through an enemy's health. Drop the grenade and stand in the gas as you take an opponent down.

You should also look out for this from your enemy. If you see a player standing in the blue Stim-Gas smoke, do not even attempt to take the foe on unless you have a high-damage weapon. The only thing that can kill an enemy in Stim-Gas is a headshot or gibbing attack. The color of the Stim-Gas changes depending on the team it is associated with.

INCENDIARY GRENADES

The Incendiary Grenade is the only grenade that you cannot select for your loadout. It is a default map-based weapon for most Versus maps (except Gondola). Toss it at or near an enemy to set the player on fire.

The grenade is extremely lethal with a direct hit, so be careful if you see someone grabbing them. It is well worth an extra effort to get to them first.

Just tossing one of these grenades near an enemy can set the player on fire. It may not be an instant kill, but it can at least get opponents to move out of cover. It does have an area-of-effect, so it can also flush out a whole group.

The Incendiary Grenade is very deadly when blind-fired at short range, so it works as an alternative to a short-range gun. You get two of these grenades when they are picked up, but you must come back to the spawn point to refill the count.

POWER WEAPONS

Power weapons are extremely potent weapons and become a game changer in the hands of a skilled player. These weapons are found around the Versus mode maps at specific spawn locations.

These weapons should be a priority when considering your route from the start, and the spawn points should be visited throughout the match. Some of these weapons are so heavy that your movement is greatly slowed when carrying it around, but others have little effect. Remember that you do not gain ammo for these weapons from an ammo crate, so once it's used up, it's done—unless you pick up another one.

BOOMSHOT

The Boomshot is a powerful weapon that launches an explosive which detonates on impact. It causes an area-of-effect damage, killing anyone in the immediate area. Watch out when firing at close range; it can easily take you out along with your target.

The explosive is launched with a low arc, which causes it to land well short of your target at long distances. Be sure to aim high to compensate for this motion. It may take some practice to get this down, but it's well worth it when you can eliminate groups of enemies with one shot—especially at an objective such as a ring.

BOOSHKA

The Booshka is a grenade launcher with a similar arcing flight path as the Boomshot. These rounds bounce off surfaces though— making it possible to fire around corners. Just like the Boomshot, be aware when firing at a close target as it can take you down too.

Besides finding this weapon on Versus maps, it's also used by the Soldier in OverRun and Survival modes. The arcing path is shown when aiming the Booshka, giving you a good idea where your grenade will bounce when fired.

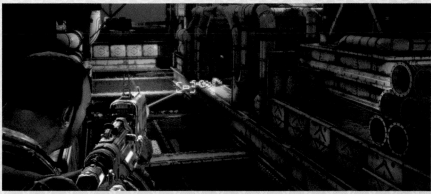

The Booshka does not produce as much damage as the Boomshot, but it's still great for firing into groups such as a ring in Domination. You can also bounce it behind cover to flush enemies out. Direct hits from the Booshka instantly kill.

BREECHSHOT

The Breechshot is a high-powered rifle that is better used at medium ranges. It does not have the scope zoom capabilities as a couple other weapons. Its small magazine size requires frequent reloads, but it can still take down two players before a reload—as long as one is a headshot.

It has the power needed to kill with one well-placed headshot, so it can be deadly in a skilled player's hands. An attached blade makes it lethal in melee attacks too.

Pair this weapon with a shotgun to cover all your bases. Carry the shotgun around as you move through tight spaces and around corners; pull out the Breechshot when you reach the more open spaces.

LONGSHOT

The Longshot Sniper Rifle easily kills with one shot to the head, but its one-round magazine means that you better have some protection around. Hold the Left Trigger to aim and then click the Right Thumbstick to zoom in. There are two zoom magnifications.

This weapon is dangerous in the wrong hands, as it is so deadly with headshots. However, two shots are required anywhere else on a healthy player. And since the Longshot only holds one round at a time, that enemy will probably be long gone before you can get off a second shot.

The Longshot can be effective even if you're not able to get headshots easily— as long as you have teammates in position to finish them off. Communicate to other players where you've injured a foe so they can move in for the kill.

Practicing headshots with this rifle can go a long way toward dominating a match. Just be ready to quickly switch to a close-range weapon if you spot a rushing foe.

MORTAR

The Mortar launches shells into the air. The shells burst and send a deadly explosive onto your enemies, causing an area-of-effect damage. This can be very deadly against a team that is grouped together, such as when capturing a ring in Domination.

To deploy the Mortar, hold the Left Trigger. Then, hold the Right Trigger to set the range, and release to fire the explosive. A meter appears in the middle of the screen that indicates the approximate distance the round will travel before it detonates. The longer you hold the Fire button, the further the round goes. Its distance ranges between 50m to 150m.

When the Mortar is picked up, you do not drop a weapon. Your movement is slowed when carrying it, so be aware of enemies around you or have your team protect your location. Press the B button or Y button to drop the weapon.

This weapon takes a lot of practice to master. It requires either communication from your teammates or an open view to see where the enemies are. Take some time to figure out how far the Mortar fires at each distance mark on the meter.

The Mortar can be blind-fired by pressing the Right Trigger, but be careful when using it at close range or in tight spaces. This weapon can easily take you out in its explosion. Be sure that you have a clear path above, as it will not fire if it's blocked.

MULCHER

The Mulcher doesn't do much damage per round, but its extremely high rate of fire makes it deadly nonetheless. It fires continuously, but it will overheat after some time.

When the Mulcher is picked up, you do not drop a weapon. You are unable to use any other weapon as you carry the Mulcher—switching to another weapon causes you to drop it. In preparation for an enemy, you can slowly pull the Right Trigger to get the barrel spinning. This allows the Mulcher to fire quicker when needed.

The Mulcher slows your movement greatly, but anyone caught in your path as you hipfire does not stand much chance of survival. This weapon is far more stable, and thus more accurate, when you mount the gun on a surface. Move to a low piece of cover and hold the Left Trigger to set the Mulcher on the wall. Watch out, as you are a sitting duck if someone approaches from behind or the sides.

The Mulcher fires continuously as you hold down the Fire button. After about 88 rounds, the gun overheats. When this happens, hold the Right Bumper to cool it down. Fire in short spurts to avoid overheating the gun.

You're pretty much stuck to one area of the map when you decide to grab the Mulcher. If all of the fighting takes place elsewhere, it's not really worth picking up the weapon—movement is just too slow to travel great distances.

ONESHOT

The OneShot is the deadliest long-range weapon in the game if obtained by a skilled player. One accurate discharge of the energy cannon kills on impact—no matter where it comes in contact.

Hold the Left Trigger to aim the gun. Once it locks on a target (indicated by a solid red reticle), press the Right Trigger to vaporize the foe. The OneShot can zoom by clicking the Right Thumbstick. This makes for incredible accuracy.

The OneShot has penetrating capability, so anyone hiding behind your target is also killed. Lining up multiple targets with this weapon and taking them down earns you a ribbon too.

This heavy weapon cannot be fired without aiming first. Plus, a slow charge time means that you must wait for it to lock on. This makes you extremely vulnerable when using it. Wait until you know you are alone or have teammates protect your position.

This weapon uses a red laser when aiming and makes a beeping sound when around hostile targets. These two features of the weapon are telltale signs for a targeted foe to get out of there. If you have teammates in a good position though, this can be used to flush enemies out of hiding.

SPOTTER

Have teammates spot enemies so you can line up shots with the mark. This can make things much easier as you search for targets. Select Spot Grenades for your loadout to mark any enemies in your targeted area yourself.

SCORCHER

The Scorcher is a powerful flamethrower that makes a player extremely dangerous at a short to medium range. A sweep with this weapon can eliminate a group of enemies fairly quickly. Look for this weapon whenever you can; it's a definite game changer.

The Scorcher's flame completely negates a Boomshield. The flame also bleeds over low cover and does impressive damage to enemies ducked behind such cover.

Even though this weapon is so deadly, an opponent with a shotgun can take you down with one shot before you can cause enough fire damage. Constantly scan the area for incoming enemies and ignite them before they can get in close. Use quick movements to avoid their attack.

If you can get a jump on a busy location, such as Domination rings, this weapon is great for clearing out an area. It has the potential to flush enemies out of hiding too.

VULCAN

The Vulcan Cannon has an extremely high rate of fire and has the potential to tear through groups of enemies. A long charge time and limited ammo make this weapon a little tricky to use though.

This heavy weapon is propped onto the shoulder when aiming and causes you to slow down significantly. Watch out as this lack of maneuverability combined with the slow charge makes you an easy target. It's possible for an enemy to quickly move in and take you down with a melee execution before the weapon starts firing.

When using the Vulcan Cannon, you must anticipate where to target and start the weapon early. Against most weapons at a longer range though, you can still mow down an enemy before they can kill you. In preparation for an enemy, you can slowly pull the Right Trigger to get the barrels spinning. This allows the Vulcan to fire quicker when needed. However, the sound of spinning Vulcan barrels is very distinctive and can warn enemies of your presence. This weapon's limited ammo gets used up pretty quickly with its high rate of fire. Fighting next to the weapon's spawn point is your only choice if you want to extend its use.

SPECIAL WEAPONS

Special weapons, just like the power weapons, are found around the Versus mode maps and should be a priority when planning your route. These weapons are pretty unique and all require some finesse to use them successfully.

BOOMSHIELD

The Boomshield can be used as a weapon, but it's more about defense. It can deflect bullets back at opponents, but with reduced movement, and you are vulnerable from behind. The shield can be planted and used as static cover.

Hold the Left Trigger to use the shield as mobile cover. When under fire, adjust your aim to damage your enemies with their own ammo. This is effective against most gunfire, but some weapons have the power to chew through the shield.

Hold the Left Trigger and press the A button to plant the shield in the ground. Now it can be used as stationary cover. To drop the Boomshield, press the Y button to change weapons.

It's possible to plant multiple shields by waiting for another to spawn. Use this added defense around objectives to make them easier to hold. A planted Boomshield will disappear after 10 seconds if it is not picked back up or if a player is not in cover on it. The OneShot will destroy a Boomshield and protect the player behind it.

The Boomshield can be used with most weapons. Scoped weapons, like the Markza and Longshot, cannot be zoomed with a Boomshield. Pick up a launcher weapon, such as a Boomshot, and use it with the shield to be an even bigger threat. If you find a planted shield and wish to knock it down, press the X button from the other side. At this point, it can be picked up and used. A player can also melee with the weapon.

In a team-based mode, find a narrow chokepoint and attract your opponents' attention. Keep them busy as you deflect their shots with the Boomshield while your team attacks their flank.

DIGGER

The Digger Launcher is a Locust weapon. It fires an explosive, bio weapon in a steep arc into the air. The Digger burrows into the ground, ignores cover, and emerges at your target's location. At that point, it detonates in the air—killing anyone nearby.

Hold the Left Trigger to see the Digger Grenade's path and aim with the Right Thumbstick. Press the Right Trigger to send it on its way. The Digger is a great weapon for taking down enemies held up behind cover. A direct hit on an enemy will burrow into its chest for a gruesome kill. The Digger can be fired into the ceiling above the player, and it will emerge from the floor above the player. This is good for surprising enemies on floors above you.

In the open, the Digger is too easy

for an opponent to avoid. Save it for enemies protected by cover. The explosion is big enough that a group of enemies can be taken down at once. The Digger has a very recognizable sound and visual as it digs through the ground, so alert enemies know when one is inbound and can easily get out of the blast radius.

HAMMER OF DAWN

The Hammer of Dawn is very unique. It calls on the power of an Imulsion-powered satellite-based laser system to rain destruction down on your opponents. The beam is guidable while being fired so players can be tracked as they move.

Your target must be outside in order for the satellite to get a bead on the player. Hold down the Right Trigger to release the devastation. The beam can be guided by using the Right Thumbstick to move it. The Hammer of Dawn cannot be blindfired around cover.

It is better to fire the weapon in bursts instead of dragging the beam, as it moves pretty slowly. The weapon does take a couple seconds to lock onto its target, so if the enemy spots the recognizable red laser, it's easily avoided. If you see this telltale sign, roadie run into shelter.

TORQUE BOW

The Torque Bow fires explosive-tipped arrows that are extremely lethal and accurate if used properly. The weapon takes time to use at its full potential, so firing from safe locations or with team support can help greatly in getting kills.

Hold the Left Trigger to ready the bow, and then hold the Right Trigger to aim. Release the Fire button when ready to fire. If the Right Trigger is held long enough, as indicated by a glowing orange reticle, the arrows penetrate and stick into the target before exploding. Hold it too long and it fires automatically.

A fully charged shot results in a straight arrow instead of

dropping off in flight. Once you start to charge the shot, it cannot be cancelled. A fully charged arrow will pass through an enemy's head and continue to fly. The splash damage of the Torque Bow's arrows can still earn kills and damage enemies. It's possible to fire a slightly charged Torque Bow so that the arrow bounces around corners and lands behind cover.

Although the bow can be hipfired, this weapon is a poor choice for short-range combat due to its slow fire time. Match it with a shotgun to complement its long-range capabilities. Getting a good position to fire the bow is key to success.

OVERRUN AND SURVIVAL MAPS

Each of the OverRun/Survival maps is a distinct environment, providing myriad challenges in either mode. We describe each phase of attack as you make your way across the map.

■ ESTATE

Estate is a rambling collection of stone buildings, formerly manicured gardens, and nearly forgotten statuary. The multi-tiered grounds, full of sprawling arches and stonework, lead to the doors of the estate.

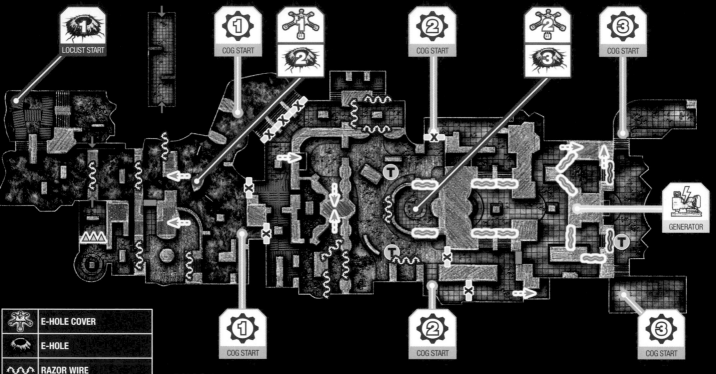

E-HOLE COVER	
E-HOLE	
RAZOR WIRE	
BLUE LASER BARRIER	
RED LASER BARRIER	
SCOUT/WRETCH CLIMBABLE	
SPIKE BARRIER	
WALLED OFF UNTIL NEXT ROUND	
TURRET	

PHASE 1

The path directly under the bridge is the shortest, most direct route to the E-Hole Cover and will likely be the most heavily defended area, at least initially. As the COG, have a Scout occupy the tower overlooking this approach and supply a steady diet of Spot Grenades to identify attackers behind cover and increase the potential damage done to them.

The path over the bridge is a longer route, but may see less resistance. When taking the bridge route, pass the two barriers and bear to the left, past the covered well. From this raised perspective, you can toss grenades at the E-Hole Cover and use Lancer fire to weaken the Cover as a Grenadier. Defenders need to watch this area; there is a Scout spot directly above this location as well.

PHASE 2

Troikas are on the north and south sides of the E-Hole, guarding the nearby entrances to this area. Defenders should man these Troikas and attempt to keep them repaired while attackers should focus on destroying one or both Troikas before making a push for the E-Hole Cover. The central Scout perch gives a 360-degree view of the battlefield and should be manned at all times. Counter with Wretch attacks to kill or occupy the Scout.

PHASE 3

A Troika is to the south of the generator that has an electric fence and laser wire directly in front of it. As the COG, maintain the integrity of this area and force the Locust to the other side. The north side of the map has no Troika but features a Scout perch. Occupy this position and use Spot Grenades to identify attackers coming out of the spawn area. When it comes time to defend the generator, there isn't much available in the way of cover. Stand on the stairwells near the COG spawn area and fire at the backs of foes rushing the generator location.

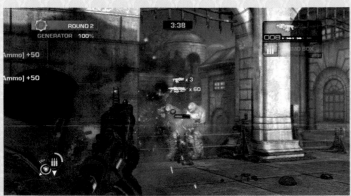

ISLAND

From the Island you can see a desolate ruined cityscape off in the distance, and the Island itself has fared little better. A former working facility, with bombed out buildings, rubble, and a rocky shore, the Island now serves as a battlefield. There are several fully functional bunkers containing useable weapons, making it a deadly, contained landscape.

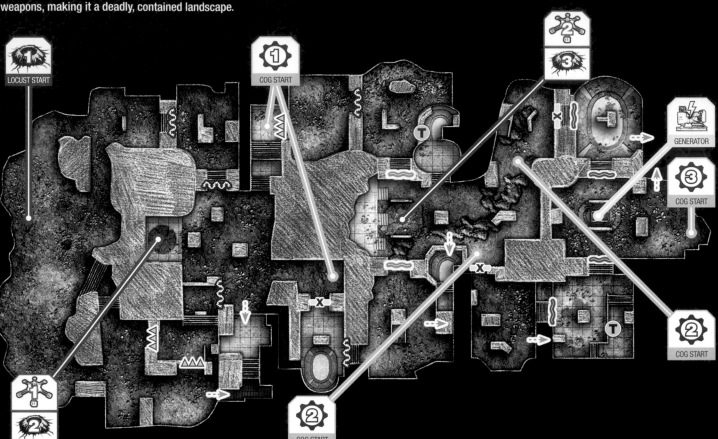

PHASE 1

Occupy the Scout perch to the southeast of the E-Hole Cover during the initial rush. Toss Spot Grenades and provide cover fire for teammates in the vicinity of the barrier south of the E-Hole Cover. The two small staircases to the north of the E-Hole Cover are the other main route for attackers in this small first area. On offense, try using the wall to the south of the E-Hole for cover and toss grenades over the top of it to weaken or destroy the Cover.

PHASE 2

There is a Troika to the north of the E-Hole that can cover the barrier to the northwest. This area is accessible by all classes. It contains a Scout climb spot for quick access. Wretches can also attack this elevated area without going through the more heavily fortified location near the E-Hole Cover. The Scout perch to the south of the E-Hole is a true Scout perch and has views to the southern Locust approach route and most of the area around the E-Hole Cover.

On offense, hop in the back of the pickup truck to the south of the E-Hole as a Grenadier. Use grenades and Lancer fire to destroy the barrier to the north. Weaken or kill enemies in that area before moving in with a heavier class to assault the Cover. Look out for Scout fire from the nearby perch, and send Wretches to kill or distract the Scout(s).

PHASE 3

The Scout perch to the north of the generator is a great spot to defend the barrier to the west, the generator area, and the barrier south of the generator. The Troika to the south of the generator is directly across from the only southern approach and should be used for as long as you can keep it intact. Have the Engineer use Sentry Turrets to slow enemies in this area to maximize the effectiveness of the Troika. When defending an assault on the generator itself, use at least two Engineers to place Sentry Turrets to the east to slow attackers. Then move in close to attack with the Gnasher. Once the Troika to the south and the nearby barriers are destroyed, this route is ready for the heavier troops to move in and attack the generator.

JUNKYARD

The Junkyard is a large industrial facility filled with pipework and cargo containers. The majority of the action takes place in and around the processing center, where there is ample cover, as well as several points of elevation.

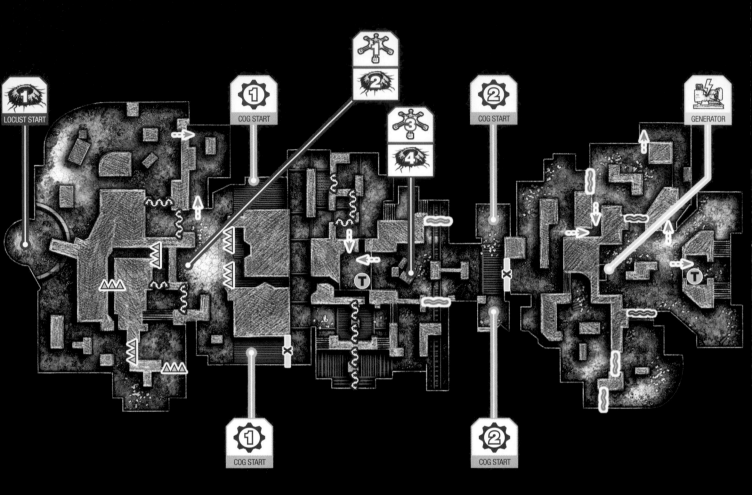

PHASE 1

The Scout perch to the north of the E-Hole has a clear view of the Locust spawn to the west. Use Spot Grenades to identify incoming enemies while the Soldier bombards this area with Booshka rounds. Counter by sending Wretches into the perch. As the COG, watch the central route for enemies taking cover behind the large pipe and firing

upon the Cover on the other side. Take advantage of this route on offense. Once all barriers are gone, the COG can use the short wall to the east of the E-Hole as cover and fire upon incoming Locust.

PHASE 2

The Scout perch west of the E-Hole contains a Troika that is essential for making a last defensive stand of the Cover. There is also a green button in this area that can be pushed. Doing so activates the garbage grinders directly beneath this area. This kills any Tickers that have entered the area via one of the two vents, or it prevents them from entering the area. There is also a green button with the same functionality next to the Scout climb icon on the ground level, west of the E-Hole. The routes to the E-Hole on the north and south side are short, cramped areas that see lots of short-range combat.

PHASE 3

Take advantage of the Ticker tunnel in the center of this area by using Tickers to quickly reach the barriers. Focus on taking out the barriers before moving in to attack the generator with heavier classes. A Scout perch is directly east of the generator with a Troika that has full view of the area around the generator. Utilize this in a last-stand situation. There are also two stairwells in the rear of this position that lead to the Troika. A true, large Scout perch is to the northeast of the generator. This perch has no Troika but decent visibility of the Locust advancing via the northern approach. This isn't the most useful Scout perch. Instead, use the perch near the Locust spawn to spot enemies for your teammates.

■ SKYLINE

As its name suggests, Skyline takes place on the rooftops of a city. This area is littered with ventilation ducts from the buildings, as well as water towers and chimney stacks. There is even an overgrown greenhouse that's fallen into disrepair.

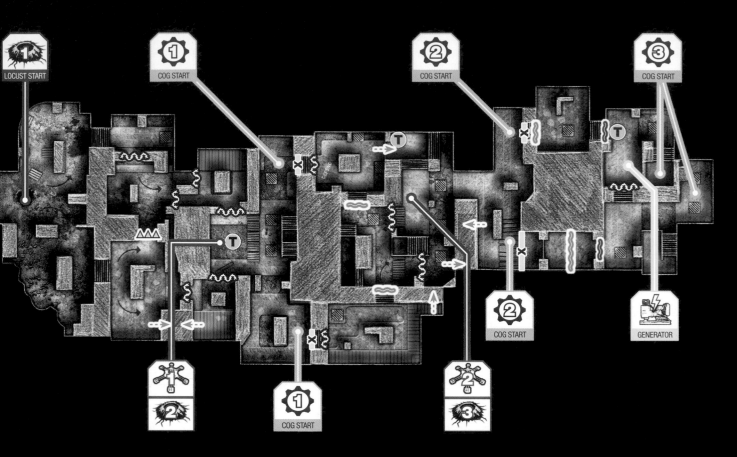

PHASE 1

The Scout perch to the southwest of the E-Hole is an excellent location. You can spot approaching Locust and fire upon enemies attacking the E-Hole, all without dropping down. As the Locust, send Wretches to counter. The Troika next to the E-Hole is useful on defense until all fortifications are gone, after which it will likely get quickly destroyed by Locust attacking the Cover. Fall back to the raised platform to the east and bombard the E-Hole area with Booshka fire. An aggressive Ticker assault via the northern approach can quickly remove all barriers. The Tickers can then move in to attack the E-hole Cover before defenders on the southern end of the map have time to react.

PHASE 2

The Troika on the high platform north of the E-Hole is essential in this round's early stages while fortifications stand. Have an Engineer occupy the lower area to the west, deploying Sentry Turrets to kill or slow enemies while a teammate mans the Troika. The Scout perch southeast of the E-Hole provides a decent perspective on approaching Locust, but it has limited visibility of the E-Hole Cover. Abandon this position when all barriers have fallen.

PHASE 3

The Troika, laser barrier, and electric fence make the northern approach a hazardous one for the Locust. The COG should take full advantage of this defensive position. Attempt to rush past incoming heavies, such as the Mauler and Giant Serapede, to attack their rear. Instead, push the attack on the southern side of the map. This is a large area to traverse with a Scout perch to get past. But once past the final barrier, the generator is right there. Use the Scout perch to the south of the generator to defend its southern approach. There is a stairwell to this platform's rear that other classes can use to reach it.

VERSUS MAPS

Four maps are available in the Versus modes: Gondola, Library, Rig, and Streets. Each of these maps has its own unique features. The following information gives you everything you need to get a head start against your opponents in any of the Versus modes.

GONDOLA

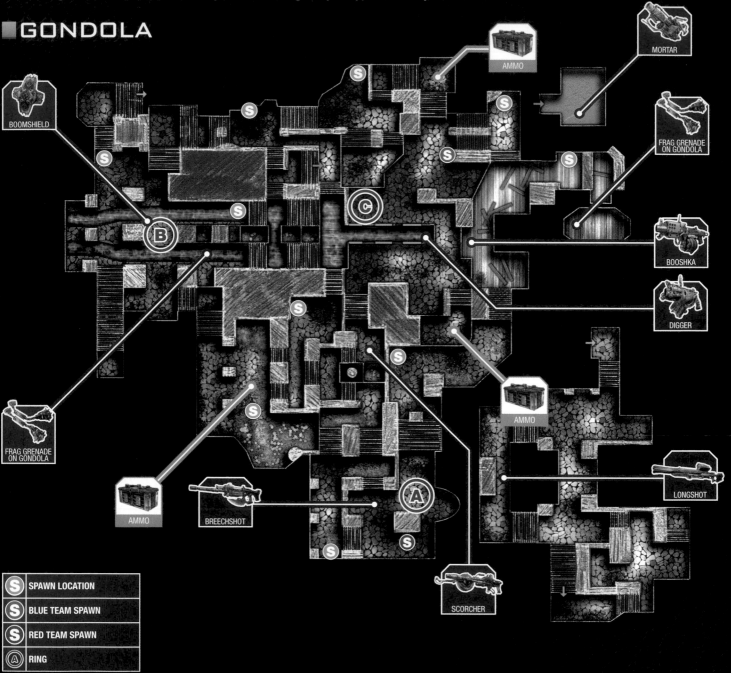

BOOMSHIELD	
MORTAR	
AMMO	
FRAG GRENADE ON GONDOLA	
BOOSHKA	
DIGGER	
FRAG GRENADE ON GONDOLA	
AMMO	
LONGSHOT	
AMMO	
BREECHSHOT	
SCORCHER	

S	SPAWN LOCATION
S	BLUE TEAM SPAWN
S	RED TEAM SPAWN
A	RING

Gondola takes place at Ocean Breeze, a coastal resort town owned by Donaldson & Marlow. A storm looms on the horizon, lending an air of tension to the area.

WATCH YOUR STEP

Remember, in Versus mode you can drop off ledges as a quick way down, but it costs you health.

The main feature of the map is the Gondola, which runs from the docks on the east side up to the resort in the west. Apartments, like the Coastal Villas, and retail businesses, such as Gitte's Hotel, litter this tiered-village, making passageways cramped. The multi-tiered layout often forces you to fight on close stairways and around tight corners.

Because of the constricted quarters, short-range weapons are extremely powerful here. This map offers the Scorcher and Digger Power Weapons, which are excellent tools to get the job done.

DIG CAREFULLY

While the Digger is very deadly, it does not dig through walls or rock. It instead pops out of the ground and detonates right away if it hits an obstacle. Be careful where you aim when using this weapon so it doesn't detonate in your face.

This map has two Frag Grenade locations. Each one rests in a gondola. You can only access the gondolas at the upper levels of the resort or down by the docks. You can chuck grenades from the gondola at enemies passing below you.

FREE-FOR-ALL

Free-for-All is a chaotic melee where everyone guns for each other. Make sure you go after the Power Weapons as quickly as possible. Though not a Power Weapon, either Shotgun has a massive advantage on this map due to its one-shot kill capability at short range.

The action may migrate to the waterfall, but tends to move to the outer corridors and stairways. The Scorcher position tends to be a hot spot on the battlefield due to this weapon's close-range strength.

ROLL AND HOP

Because most battles on Gondola take place in close quarters, you often find yourself in a duel. When this happens, roll and hop to multiple points of cover to avoid incoming fire.

TEAM DEATHMATCH

In Team Deathmatch, moving as a team and watching each other's backs is key. If you like using sniper weapons, grabbing the Longshot and hanging out above the waterfall area is a good plan; you can provide cover to your teammates. If you prefer to fight up close and personal, the short-range Power Weapons let you dominate this area's tight passageways.

The Frag Grenades are always useful. To get the most out of them, toss them into the heavily trafficked area in the map's center, where two streams run between the Boomshield and the Digger.

DOMINATION

To Dominate this map, capture and hold points A and C, which are quickly accessible from each other. Acquire the Scorcher midway between points A and C and stay in between the points to defend both quickly.

If the opposing team has already captured points A and C, don't lose hope! Grab the Mortar on the roof near point C and quickly clear the Domination rings with its massive area-of-effect attack.

LOOK OUT BELOW

When holding point C, keep an eye on the bridge above. Enemies can easily drop grenades or fire from this position in relative safety.

LIBRARY

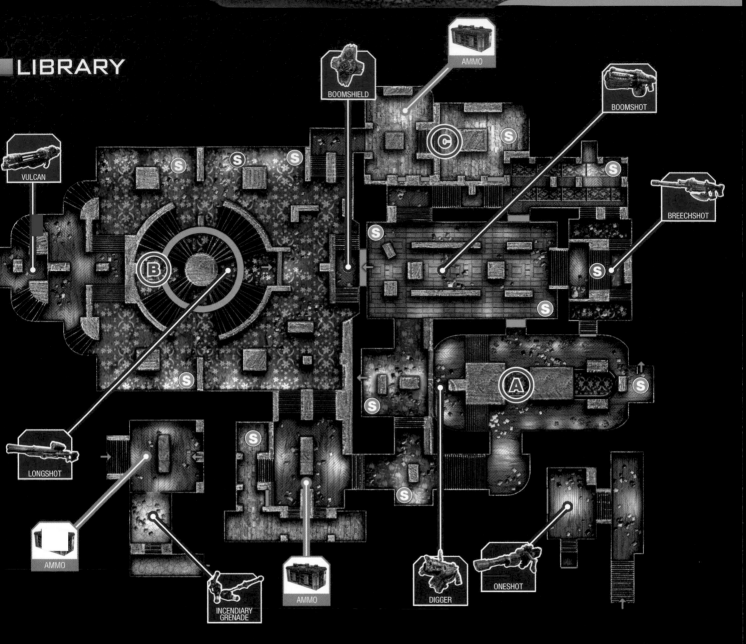

VULCAN

BOOMSHIELD

AMMO

BOOMSHOT

BREECHSHOT

LONGSHOT

AMMO

INCENDIARY GRENADE

AMMO

DIGGER

ONESHOT

This grand old Library survived the Pendulum Wars, only to now become host to your devastating battles. It is mainly an indoor map, filled with multi-floored bookshelves. The aptly named Tower area is an open section with a huge tower at the center. This tower is an excellent location from which to snipe.

On the map's east end, use the secret book in the fountain room to gain access behind the large clock overlooking the main hall and tower. Shoot out the glass and use the OneShot found here on unsuspecting victims below. It's a good idea to have someone stand guard at the south exit while sniping from the clock.

Like any good library, this Library has secrets. In addition to the aforementioned secret book which gives you access to the clock, there is also a secret passage on the lower level running from the tower's southeast to the fountain's west side. Inside the passage is an Incendiary Grenade spawn point.

SNEAK ATTACK

The secret passages can also be used as ambush locations for anyone who accesses the room.

FREE-FOR-ALL

Going for really powerful weapons, such as the Boomshot, Digger, or Vulcan, is a great key to success on Free-for-All. The sniper positions in the clock or on the tower are very vulnerable without a teammate to watch your back, so use them with care, if at all.

Areas like the fountain room and the records room offer great cover, with very little chance of being blindsided by enemy attacks.

TEAM DEATHMATCH

Team Deathmatch allows a communicative team to get some great sniping opportunities. Make sure to have a teammate cover your position if you plan to use the OneShot to snipe from the clock or the Longshot to snipe from the tower. As with any Team Deathmatch, teamwork is crucial.

If you control the sniping positions, you have a much greater opportunity of grabbing the Boomshot from the main hall. With the Boomshot, you can wreak havoc on the opposing team, especially if they are moving in groups.

DOMINATION

Capture and hold B, and then pair it with A. Once captured, Domination Ring B gives you a high vantage point where the Longshot spawns. You can spot and snipe opponents as they attack B or move from C to A. The two circling staircases that lead from B to the Longshot provide cover and cannot be flanked other than by running through the capture circle. This makes them an ideal position to defend. Set up defenders on each staircase to cover both approaches to B, and quickly vault over the wall to fire upon confused enemies on the staircase leading to B.

A is a more ideal position to defend than C. This is due to the nearby Digger spawn, which also serves as a great place to take cover while waiting for defenders. C has little cover and no good weapon spawns nearby. You can easily be attacked from both the east and west while defending C, making it the least desirable of the Library's Domination Rings.

THE VULCAN

Though moving with it is very slow, the Vulcan can allow any defender to successfully hold a Domination Ring on their own for a short time.

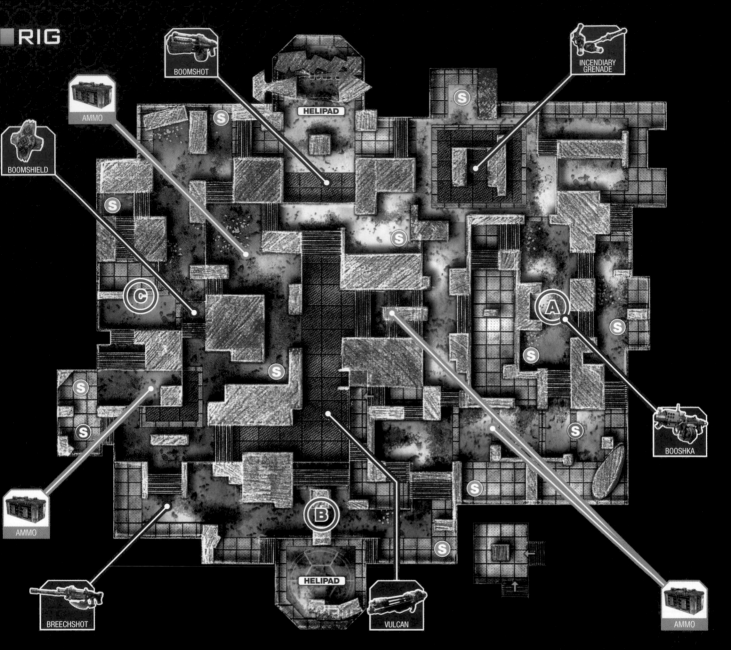

BOOMSHOT

INCENDIARY GRENADE

AMMO

HELIPAD

BOOMSHIELD

C

A

BOOSHKA

AMMO

B

AMMO

HELIPAD

BREECHSHOT

VULCAN

The Gorasnaya Rig is offshore, mining Emulsion. It is littered with cargo containers and offers a great deal of cover. The Rig offers plenty of Power Weapons and a myriad of elevations for you to take advantage of.

The main feature of this map is the King Raven Helicopter. The Rig's northern and southern edges boast Helipads. Mantle into the helicopter and take control of the Troika Turret to lift off. The helicopter flies around to the south Helipad for a short while, then returns to the north, always following a clockwise route.

INCOMING

While manning the Troika, you are susceptible to incoming fire. If the heat gets to be too much, use the entryways as cover and fire back at your attackers with one of your equipped weapons.

FREE-FOR-ALL

In Free-for-All, the helicopter is your best friend. Try to grab the Boomshot before climbing aboard the King Raven. As soon as you board the helicopter, it takes off, leaving your opponents on the ground. While the Troika dishes out a lot of damage, its vulnerability makes using the Boomshot desirable. The Boomshot is superior from a raised vantage point, but be careful to not hit the Troika and blow yourself up!

The Rig's middle is the most dangerous area. Stick to the outer perimeter whenever possible as cover is much more plentiful there. If you aren't fortunate enough to beat everyone else to the chopper, stay on the move. Move between different Power Weapon spawn points while using cover. Avoid the Vulcan Power Weapon; it's a deathtrap in FFA.

TEAM DEATHMATCH

As with Free-for-All, your team should keep on the move. The Rig offers many opportunities for cover and also many opportunities for escape. Avoid going into locations with only one or two means of escape since there are many other areas from which to attack in relative safety. Engineering, and just south of the north Helipad, are great areas to control. You can grab the Boomshot and Booshka Power Weapons, granting your side a significant advantage.

The Vulcan spawn offers an unparalleled view of the map but is also susceptible to fire from all sides. Grab the Vulcan, look for a quick, easy kill or two, and then hop down off of the platform. Otherwise, you quickly become a sitting duck.

DOMINATION

Capture point A is crucial to Domination on Rig. There are four points of entry on A, so guarding it can be tricky. The west entry point is wide open on all but the west side. The south is also wide open, especially from the Vulcan platform.

Even with these challenges, point A is still a strong choice. It contains a Booshka, and the space between A and B makes for an ideal defensive position for both points. They're in close proximity with an ammo crate in between to steadily replenish grenades used in the defense of both points. You can also defend both points from an elevated position, overlooking the capture rings. The Incendiary Grenades in the map's Flare Stack portion north of A can also be used in its defense.

STREETS

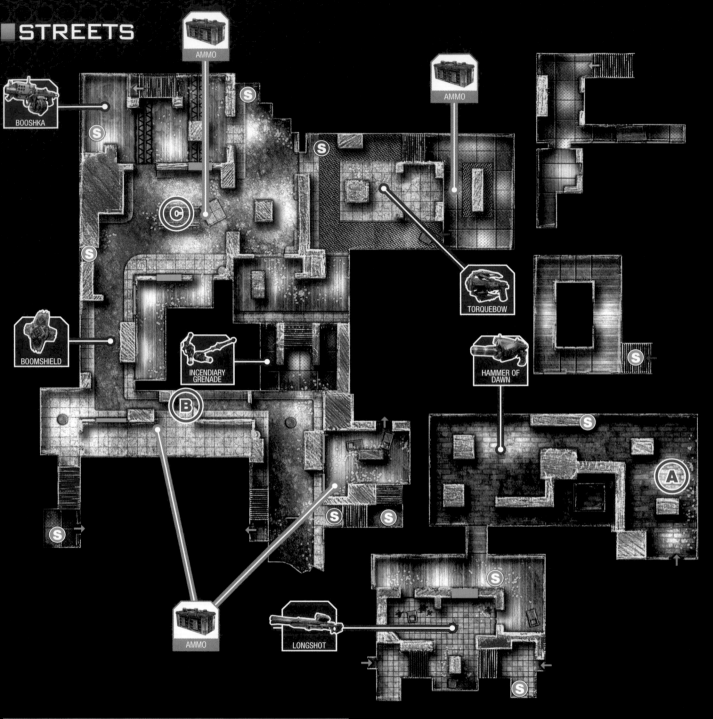

AMMO

AMMO

BOOSHKA

TORQUEBOW

BOOMSHIELD

INCENDIARY GRENADE

HAMMER OF DAWN

AMMO

LONGSHOT

C

B

A

Streets is a compact map, making for quick and intense action.
Consisting of a handful of buildings and stretch of connecting streets,
this map offers both unique opportunities and challenges.

Its strongest feature is the central building containing the Water Tower. From this location you can access any other building except for the Body Shop in the map's northwest corner. Battles are fought on the streets themselves, but also on the rooftops and in buildings.

Controlling the central building with the Water Tower grants you access to the Book Store and the Steel Works. This leaves both ammo crates and the Torque Bow at your disposal. If you blow out the Water Tower's skylight, you can easily drop down to pick up the Incendiary Grenades.

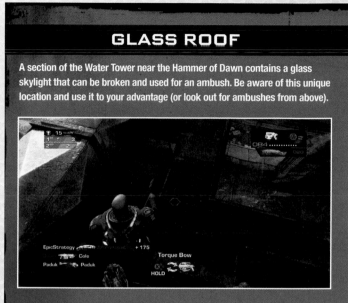

GLASS ROOF

A section of the Water Tower near the Hammer of Dawn contains a glass skylight that can be broken and used for an ambush. Be aware of this unique location and use it to your advantage (or look out for ambushes from above).

FREE-FOR-ALL

Streets offers a fast-paced, close-quarters battle, especially in Free-for-All. Traveling on the streets themselves should be avoided unless you excel at close-range combat. Instead, use the rooftops and the buildings to give yourself adequate cover while fighting off enemies from multiple angles.

In this mode, you have little security trying to use the Hammer of Dawn on the roof. But it can potentially wreak a great deal of havoc as you fire down into groups of opponents squaring off in shotgun duels. The Hammer takes a bit to charge, leaving you vulnerable, particularly to snipers. Anyone claiming the Torque Bow or Longshot should focus on whoever is wielding the Hammer, as it can take down multiple enemies with one shot, before moving to other targets.

DOMINATION

Capture point A is very tempting, but instead, seek to control B and C. Each of these positions has an ammo crate inside it to use while defending the point. The nearby interior section between the two capture points is an ideal position to maintain while waiting for attackers. Go with a shotgun and Frag Grenades to dominate in the short-range engagements near these two capture points.

TEAM DEATHMATCH

The Hammer of Dawn is the most impactful weapon on this map. Positioned on the roof of the central building containing the Water Tower, it is a tempting target for both teams. Grab the Hammer and have a teammate cover you while you skirt the roof's edge looking for enemies to light up in the map's outside portions.

While points B and C are easier to get to, Point A does have a couple of advantages. It gives a team control of the rooftop and the nearby Hammer of Dawn. However, this elevated position takes the most time to get to and is difficult to hold in conjunction with another point. If you find controlling the Hammer of Dawn just too much fun to resist, use it to clear out point C before trying to capture it yourself.

APPENDICES

RIBBONS

Ribbons are awarded every round based on your performance. They are tracked over time, so you can compare Ribbon awards to see how your playstyle stacks up against your friends. Ribbons also get you Epic PrizeBoxes, which in turn unlock skins or give experience.

MULTIPLE MODES

RIBBON	DESCRIPTION	MODES
BOOMBARDIER	KILLED MULTIPLE ENEMIES WITH A SINGLE BOOMSHOT BLAST.	ALL
CHARGE!	RETRO CHARGED 3 OPPONENTS OR ENEMIES IN A ROW.	ALL
FLAMEBROILED	KILLED 3 ENEMIES IN A ROW WITH THE SCORCHER.	ALL
HAIL MARY	BOOMSHOT KILL FROM OVER 100 FEET.	ALL
HAT TRICK	SCORED 3 HEADSHOTS IN A ROW WITHOUT DYING.	ALL
LUMBERJACK	CHAINSAWED 3 OPPONENTS OR ENEMIES IN A ROW.	ALL
MILITARY INTELLIGENCE	3 OPPONENTS SPOTTED ENDING IN A KILL.	ALL
NOTHIN' BUT BITS	KILLED MULTIPLE ENEMIES WITH ONE SAWED-OFF SHOTGUN BLAST.	ALL
ROADBLOCK	STOPPED A RETRO CHARGE WITH THE SAWED-OFF SHOTGUN.	ALL
VENGEANCE IS YOURS	REVENGE KILLED YOUR LAST KILLER.	ALL
WILLIAM TELL OVERTURE	1 TORQUE BOW HEADSHOT, FOLLOWED BY A DIRECT HIT KILL.	ALL
SHISH-KASHOT	KILLED AT LEAST TWO ENEMIES WITH A SINGLE ONESHOT ROUND.	CAMPAIGN, STANDARD MULTIPLAYER
ARTFUL DODGER	FEWEST DEATHS IN A MATCH.	ALL MULTIPLAYER
CARMINE'S STAR	MOST HEADSHOT DEATHS IN A MATCH.	ALL MULTIPLAYER
CLUSTERLUCK	KILLED MULTIPLE OPPONENTS OR ENEMIES WITH ONE GRENADE.	ALL MULTIPLAYER
CONTENDER	MOST MELEE HITS IN A MATCH.	ALL MULTIPLAYER
DEATH BLOSSOM	KILLED 5 CONSECUTIVE OPPONENTS OR ENEMIES WHILE BLINDFIRING.	ALL MULTIPLAYER
DEATH FROM ABOVE	KILLED MULTIPLE OPPONENTS WITH A SINGLE HOD BLAST.	ALL MULTIPLAYER
DEATH FROM BEYOND	KILLED AN OPPONENT OR AN ENEMY AFTER YOU HAVE DIED.	ALL MULTIPLAYER
EVASIVE	LEAST DAMAGE TAKEN IN A MATCH.	ALL MULTIPLAYER
EXECUTIVE ASSISTANT	ASSISTED 10 KILLS IN A ROUND.	ALL MULTIPLAYER
F.I.F.O.	FIRST TO DIE IN A ROUND.	ALL MULTIPLAYER
FIRST BLOOD	EARNED THE FIRST KILL OF THE ROUND.	ALL MULTIPLAYER
GRENADIER	MOST GRENADE KILLS IN A MATCH.	ALL MULTIPLAYER
HEADLESS EVADESMAN	KILLED AN EVADING OPPONENT OR ENEMY WITH A HEADSHOT.	ALL MULTIPLAYER
HEADMASTER	MOST HEADSHOT KILLS IN A MATCH.	ALL MULTIPLAYER
IN THE BLACK	MORE KILLS THAN DEATHS IN A MATCH.	ALL MULTIPLAYER
INVINCIBLE	KILLED 20 OPPONENTS OR ENEMIES WITHOUT DYING.	ALL MULTIPLAYER
MVP	HIGHEST POINT TOTAL FOR THE MATCH.	ALL MULTIPLAYER
NEMESIS	KILLED SAME OPPONENT 5 TIMES.	ALL MULTIPLAYER
NO, WAIT!	KILLED A PLAYER WHILE THEY RELOADED.	ALL MULTIPLAYER
OLE!	GRENADE TAGGED A RETRO CHARGING OPPONENT.	ALL MULTIPLAYER
OPPORTUNITY KNOCKS	KILLED 10 PLAYERS WHILE THEY'RE TAKING DAMAGE FROM ANOTHER PLAYER.	ALL MULTIPLAYER
OSCAR MIKE	KILLED A ROADIE RUNNING OPPONENT OR ENEMY WITH A HEADSHOT.	ALL MULTIPLAYER
PARTICIPANT	EARNED NO OTHER RIBBONS IN A MATCH.	ALL MULTIPLAYER
RAMPAGE	KILLED 10 OPPONENTS OR ENEMIES WITHOUT DYING.	ALL MULTIPLAYER
RETRIBUTION	KILLED YOUR NEMESIS.	ALL MULTIPLAYER
ROUGH DAY	MOST DEATHS IN A MATCH.	ALL MULTIPLAYER
SHUT IT DOWN!	ENDED AN OPPONENT'S KILL STREAK.	ALL MULTIPLAYER

RIBBON	DESCRIPTION	MODES
SMOOTH OPERATOR	HIGHEST K/D RATIO IN A MATCH.	ALL MULTIPLAYER
SPRAY AND PRAY	MOST BLIND-FIRE KILLS IN A MATCH.	ALL MULTIPLAYER
SPREE	KILLED 5 OPPONENTS OR ENEMIES WITHOUT DYING.	ALL MULTIPLAYER
SURESHOT	MOST PISTOL KILLS IN A MATCH.	ALL MULTIPLAYER
TAKIN' YOU WITH ME	KILLED AN OPPONENT OR ENEMY AFTER BEING GRENADE TAGGED.	ALL MULTIPLAYER
TEAM PLAYER	MOST ASSISTS IN A MATCH.	ALL MULTIPLAYER
THE DOUBLE	KILL 2 PLAYERS QUICKLY IN A ROW.	ALL MULTIPLAYER
THE QUAD	KILL 4 PLAYERS QUICKLY IN A ROW.	ALL MULTIPLAYER
THE GRAYSON	KILL 5 PLAYERS QUICKLY IN A ROW.	ALL MULTIPLAYER
THE TRIPLE	KILL 3 PLAYERS QUICKLY IN A ROW.	ALL MULTIPLAYER
THE UNICORN	KILLED 25 OPPONENTS OR ENEMIES WITHOUT DYING.	ALL MULTIPLAYER
UNSTOPPABLE	KILLED 15 OPPONENTS OR ENEMIES WITHOUT DYING.	ALL MULTIPLAYER
YOU'RE IT!	TAGGED GRENADE KILL FROM OVER 50 FEET.	ALL MULTIPLAYER
CLOSE SHAVE	WON A MATCH WITH A MARGIN OF 1.	DOMINATION, FREE-FOR-ALL, TEAM DEATHMATCH
CODEPENDENT	KILLED MULTIPLE OPPONENTS WITH A GRENADE STUCK TO THE PLAYER.	DOMINATION, FREE-FOR-ALL, TEAM DEATHMATCH
EW, STICKY	KILLED 5 PLAYERS WITH A DIRECT STICKY GRENADE HIT.	DOMINATION, FREE-FOR-ALL, TEAM DEATHMATCH
FIRE WALK WITH ME	KILLED 5 PLAYERS WITH FIRE WITHOUT DYING.	DOMINATION, FREE-FOR-ALL, TEAM DEATHMATCH
THE QUAD	KILL 4 PLAYERS QUICKLY IN A ROW.	ALL MULTIPLAYER

DOMINATION

RIBBON	DESCRIPTION
BREAKER BREAKER	MOST CAPTURE POINTS BROKEN.
CAPPER	MOST POINTS CAPTURED IN A MATCH.
DOMINATOR	WON A MATCH WITH ALL THREE POINTS CAPTURED.

FREE-FOR-ALL

RIBBON	DESCRIPTION
GOLD	1ST IN A FREE-FOR-ALL MATCH
SILVER	2ND IN A FREE-FOR-ALL MATCH
BRONZE	3RD IN A FREE-FOR-ALL MATCH
BORN LEADER	STAYED IN THE LEAD FOR THE ENTIRE MATCH.
COUP DE GRACE	FINAL KILL OF THE MATCH.
NEVER SAY DIE	CAME FROM DEFEAT TO WIN A MATCH.

OVERRUN AS COG

RIBBON	DESCRIPTION	CLASS
BEG YOUR PARDON	CHAINSAWED A KANTUS WHILST IT'S HEALING.	MEDIC, SOLDIER
BRUTE FORCE	MELEE-KILLED A CORPSER WHILE IT'S ATTACKING AN OBJECTIVE.	ANY
CHAIN OF COMMAND	KILLED 5 ENEMIES DEBUFFED BY A SCOUT.	ANY
IRON CURTAIN	PROTECTED THE GENERATOR FOR 10 MINUTES.	ANY
OAKLEY	KICKED A TICKER AND SHOT IT IN THE AIR.	ANY
SPOTTER	5 SPOT GRENADE TAGGED ENEMIES KILLED IN A ROUND OF OVERRUN.	ANY
RIGHT PLACE, RIGHT TIME	KILLED 5 LOCUST WITH A WELL-PLACED SENTRY.	ENGINEER
HMO	RESTORED 20,000 POINTS OF HEALTH TO YOUR TEAMMATES.	MEDIC
STAY DOWN	MELEE-KILLED A WRETCH WHILE IT'S CLIMBING.	SCOUT

OVERRUN AS LOCUST

RIBBON	DESCRIPTION	LOCUST
BATTERING RAM	DEALT 50% OF DAMAGE TO THE GENERATOR IN ONE ROUND OF OVERRUN.	ANY
HOMEWRECKER	DESTROYED 5 FORTIFICATIONS IN A ROUND.	ANY
NICK OF TIME	DESTROYED THE OBJECTIVE WITH 10 SECONDS REMAINING.	ANY
ONE BEAST ARMY	DESTROYED ALL OBJECTIVES IN AN OVERRUN ROUND.	ANY
POINT MONSTER	EARNED THE MOST POINTS IN A ROUND AS LOCUST.	ANY
SAMPLE PLATTER	PLAYED AS 5 DIFFERENT LOCUST IN A ROUND.	ANY FIVE
INDIGESTION	KILLED AN ENEMY WITH A SWALLOWED GRENADE.	TICKER
INSATIABLE	ATE 10 GRENADES.	TICKER
POP GOES THE WEASEL	BLEW UP 3 ENEMIES AT ONCE.	TICKER
STUNNER	MULTIPLE ENEMIES YOU STUNNED WERE KILLED.	WRETCH
TREE HOUSE PREDATOR	KILLED A SCOUT ON A PERCH.	WRETCH
GRENADE FEEDER	FED 3 TICKERS A GRENADE.	GRENADIER
NICE TRY	WON A CHAINSAW DUEL AGAINST A BUFFED MEDIC.	GRENADIER
ONE MORE THING[EL]	KILLED MULTIPLE PLAYERS WITH A FRAG GRENADE WHILE DBNO.	GRENADIER
PUNTER	KICKED 5 TICKERS OVER A BARRIER.	GRENADIER
SCOUTMASTER	HEADSHOTTED A SCOUT WITH THE BREECHSHOT.	RAGER
TEAM SAVIOR	REVIVED 3 TEAMMATES AT ONCE.	KANTUS
TEAM SHAMAN	HEALED 4 TEAMMATES AT ONCE.	KANTUS
THAT LOVING HEALING	HEALED A KANTUS WHO IS HEALING ANOTHER TEAM MEMBER.	KANTUS
SLAUGHTERHOUSE	KILLED A COG WITH REFLECTED BULLETS.	MAULER
SPINNING PLATES	GIBBED 3 COG WITH A SINGLE SPIN-SHIELD USE.	MAULER
PAVING THE WAY	DESTROYED A SENTRY WHILE BURROWED.	CORPSER
TUNNEL RAT	DUG UNDER A COG FORTIFICATION AND DAMAGED THE OBJECTIVE.	CORPSER

CAMPAIGN

RIBBON	DESCRIPTION
AND THE KICK IS UP!	KICKED 5 SMALL ENEMIES.
CAN I KICK IT?	MANTLE KICK 5 ENEMIES RESULTING IN KILL.
I'M YOUR HUCKLEBERRY	KILLED 5 ENEMIES IN A ROW WITH ANY TYPE OF PISTOL.
IT'S A TRAP!	KILLED MULTIPLE ENEMIES WITH A SINGLE TRIPWIRE BOW SHOT.
NICE SUIT	KILLED 10 ENEMIES WITH A SILVERBACK.
NONE SHALL PASS	KILLED 10 ENEMIES IN A ROW WITH A TROIKA, CHAINGUN, OR MULCHER.
ONCE MORE UNTO THE BREECH	KILLED 5 ENEMIES IN A ROW WITH THE BREECHSHOT.
PLUG THAT HOLE	CLOSED AN E-HOLE WITH EXPLOSIVES.
PULL!	KILLED A GROUND BURSTING ENEMY IN THE AIR.
RAGE DENIED	KILLED AN ENRAGED RAGER WITH A MELEE ATTACK.

■ MEDALS

Medals are your long-term reward for experience. You can choose a medal to act as your icon for multiplayer matches to show off your proficiency with a specific weapon, or your skill at a certain type of gameplay. Most medals have four levels: Bronze, Silver, Gold, and Onyx. We split up the medals by the game mode that you must play to earn them.

MULTIPLE MODES

MEDAL	HOW TO EARN	CONDITION	TITLE
SERIOUSLY JUDGMENTAL	EARN SERIOUSLY JUDGMENTAL ACHIEVEMENT.	N/A	SERIOUSLY JUDGMENTAL
EMBRY STAR	EARN 30 ONYX MEDALS	20	ALLFATHER
VIP	SIGN UP FOR VIP MEMBERSHIP.	N/A	VIP
SLAYER OF SAMAEL	KILL THE EPIC REAPER IN AN ONLINE MATCH.	N/A	DON'T FEAR THE REAPER
WAR SUPPORTER	PLAY IN 5/10/20/30 GEARS EVENTS.	5	SOCIALITE
		10	MAN ABOUT TOWN
		20	PARTY ANIMAL
		30	HEAD TO REHAB

MULTIPLAYER MODES

MEDAL	HOW TO EARN	CONDITION	TITLE
MVP	EARN 5/25/100/500 MVP RIBBONS.	5	OFFICER AND A GENTLEMAN
		25	ALL-STAR WEEKEND
		100	HUMBLEBRAGGER
		500	HIS ROYAL AIRNESS
FIELD SERVICE	REACH LEVEL 10/20/30/50.	10	GOOD AT GEARS
		20	HONORARY FENIX
		30	SUPER ELITE
		50	GEARS DEITY
VETERAN	PLAY 100/500/2,000/4,000 MATCHES.	100	SHELL-SHOCKED
		500	TWITCHTASTIC
		2000	BEEN THROUGH HELL
		4000	WAR HERO
MATCH WINNER	WIN 50/250/1,000/3,000 MATCHES.	50	MEH
		250	WIN-BAG
		1000	WHO'S A WINNER?
		3000	PROFESSIONAL VICTOR
HEADSHOT	GET 100/500/1,500/4,000 HEADSHOTS.	100	SKEET SKEET
		500	SHARPSHOOTER
		1500	HEADCASE
		4000	PATTY DOMES
EXPLOSIVES	GET 100/500/2,000/6,000 EXPLOSIVE KILLS.	100	POW!
		500	BOOM!!
		2000	KABOOM!!!
		6000	MUSHROOM CLOUD!!!!
MARKZA	GET 250/1,000/3,000/6,000 MARKZA KILLS.	250	MARKSMAN
		1000	TRIGGER MAN
		3000	CONFIRMED KILLER
		6000	SHOOTER MCGAVIN
LANCER	GET 250/1,000/3,000/6,000 LANCER KILLS.	250	CHAINSAW ACCIDENT
		1000	CHAINSAW DEBACLE
		3000	CHAINSAW FIASCO
		6000	CHAINSAW MASSACRE
CLASSIC HAMMERBURST	GET 250/1,000/3,000/6,000 CLASSIC HAMMERBURST KILLS.	250	A GOOD VINTAGE
		1000	CLASSICALLY TRAINED
		3000	DILETTANTE
		6000	STAY CLASSY

MEDAL	HOW TO EARN	CONDITION	TITLE
HAMMERBURST	GET 250/1,000/3,000/6,000 HAMMERBURST KILLS.	250	TO BURST, OR NOT TO BURST
		1000	HAMMERTHIRST
		3000	YOU'RE THE NAIL
		6000	HAMMERBURST HERO
RETRO LANCER	GET 250/1,000/3,000/6,000 RETRO LANCER KILLS.	250	VINTAGE
		1000	OLD-FASHIONED
		3000	ANTIQUE
		6000	RETRO IS OP
GNASHER SHOTGUN	GET 250/1,000/3,000/6,000 GNASHER SHOTGUN KILLS.	250	GUH-NASHER
		1000	WALL-BOUNCER
		3000	GET BODIED
		6000	SHOTGUN NATION
SAWED-OFF SHOTGUN	GET 250/1,000/3,000/6,000 SAWED-OFF SHOTGUN KILLS.	250	BOTH BARRELS
		1000	CLOSED CASKETEER
		3000	LOOKIN' DOWN THE BARREL
		6000	WEARIN' BARRELS
PISTOL	GET 100/500/1,000/3,000 SNUB PISTOL KILLS.	100	PEA-SHOOTER
		500	MAKE MY DAY
		1000	REVOLVER SOLVER
		3000	PISTOL-PACKING MAMA
SPOTTER	SPOT 1,000/3,000/7,000/15,000 OPPONENTS.	1000	SPOTTED YA!
		3000	HEY, HE'S OVER HERE!
		7000	HUMAN LIGHTHOUSE
		15000	THE MOST DANGEROUS GAME
PYRO	KILL 25/100/500/1,000 OPPONENTS WITH FIRE.	25	FIRST DEGREE BURNS
		100	LIKES IT RARE
		500	HELLFIRE
		1000	WATCH IT ALL BURN
MELEE MASTER	KILL 100/500/1,000/3,000 OPPONENTS WITH MELEE.	100	PUNCHED OUT
		500	MORTAL COMBATANT
		1000	SMASH BROTHER
		3000	GOD HANDS
GRENADE MASTER	KILL 200/800/2,000/4,500 OPPONENTS WITH ANY GRENADE.	200	GRENADIER
		800	PIN-PULLER
		2000	GRENADE CHEF
		4500	FRAG KING
SHOCK TROOPER	EARN 100/300/1,000/3,000 "FIRST BLOOD" RIBBONS.	100	QUICK ON THE TRIGGER
		300	MR. ITCHY
		1000	BAD MANNERS
		3000	UP IN YOUR BIDNESS
SPECIAL TEAMS	GET 50/250/1,000/3,000 MAP-BASED WEAPON KILLS.	50	NOWHERE MAN
		250	CAN DO IT ALL
		1000	MULTI-TALENTED
		3000	MASTER OF YOUR DOMAIN
SPECIAL TEAMS	GET 50/250/1,000/3,000 MAP-BASED WEAPON KILLS.	50	NOWHERE MAN
		250	CAN DO IT ALL
		1000	MULTI-TALENTED
		3000	MASTER OF YOUR DOMAIN

OVERRUN MODE

MEDAL	HOW TO EARN	CONDITION	TITLE
THEY'RE COMING	WELCOME TO OVERRUN! COMPLETED ONE OVERRUN MATCH.	N/A	BE GENTLE WITH ME
LOCKDOWN	SUCCESSFULLY DEFEND 5/25/100/200 E-HOLES AND GENERATORS IN OVERRUN.	5	DEFENSE IN DEPTH
		25	BILLY BLOCKADE
		100	LOCUST FAIL
		200	SLAVE TO THE COG
FORT DESTROYER	DESTROY 100/500/1000/2000 FORTIFICATIONS IN OVERRUN.	100	WRECKING BALL
		500	MASTER OF DISASTER
		1000	WELCOME TO SMASHTOWN
		2000	LOOT BRUTE
ANARCHIST	STUN 100/500/1000/2000 OPPONENTS AS A WRETCH.	100	NEEDS A BREATH MINT
		500	HEAD-TURNER
		1000	TRULY WRETCHED
		2000	MASTER ORATOR
SLAYER	KILL 250/1000/3000/6000 OPPONENTS AS COG OR LOCUST.	250	BODY COUNTER
		1000	NOOBICIDE
		3000	CAPTAIN BODYBAG
		6000	SPACE COWBOY
CHAMPION	PLAY AS A 2ND TIER LOCUST 10/100/250/500 TIMES.	10	BENCH WARMER
		100	BAG OF AWESOME
		250	WRECKIN' SHOP
		500	BEASTMASTER
SEARCH AND DESTROY	DESTROY 50/150/300/500 E-HOLES AND GENERATORS IN OVERRUN.	50	TOTALED
		150	IN THE AREA
		300	COGMOWER
		500	BARBARIAN AT THE GATE
FORT FIXER	REPAIR 100/500/1,000/2,000 FORTIFICATIONS IN OVERRUN.	50,000	GREASE MONKEY
		100,000	COME AT ME, BRO
		150,000	FIXINATOR
		200,000	DON'T TASE ME
DEBUFFER	DEBUFF 100/500/2,000/6,000 TIMES.	100	CRYSTAL BALL RUBBER
		500	X-RAY EYES
		2000	ON YOUR KNEES!
		6000	CHUMP KNOCKER
AMMO GIVER	SUPPLY AMMO 100/500/2,000/6,000 TIMES.	100	FRIEND WITH BENEFITS
		500	BACK-SCRATCHER
		2000	QUID PRO QUO
		6000	MAGNIFICENT BASTARD
HEALER	AS A KANTUS. HEAL OR REVIVE 250/750/1,500/3,000 TEAMMATES IN OVERRUN.	250	STREET APOTHECARY
		750	BRING OUT YER DEAD!
		1500	BACON SAVER
		3000	LOVER AND FIGHTER
MEDIC	REVIVE 10/50/200/500 TEAMMATES WITH STIM GAS IN OVERRUN.	10	PARAMEDIC
		50	AMBULANCE CHASER
		200	HE'S DEAD JIM
		500	DR. AWESOME, M.D.

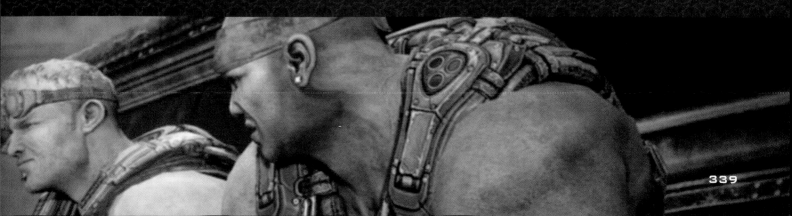

SURVIVAL MODE

MEDAL	HOW TO EARN	CONDITION	TITLE
SURVIVOR	COMPLETE ALL 10 WAVES OF SURVIVAL ON CASUAL/NORMAL/HARDCORE/INSANE DIFFICULTY.	CASUAL	OXYGEN ADDICT
		NORMAL	HARD TO KILL
		HARDCORE	BLACK CHOPPER WATCHER
		INSANE	THERE CAN BE ONLY ONE
DEFENDER	DEFEND THE 1ST E-HOLE UNTIL WAVE 5 3/6/12/25 TIMES.	3	WAVE RIDIN'
		6	BACK OFF, SUCKA!
		12	DEFENSIVE LINEMAN
		25	DEFENDER OF THE HOLE
COALITION	KILL 250/1000/3000/6000 LOCUST IN SURVIVAL.	250	THAT'S A LOTTA BLOOD
		1000	BLOODBATHER
		3000	KILLING MACHINE
		6000	FOG OF WAR
HORDER	COMPLETE 20/100/400/1000 WAVES OF SURVIVAL.	20	MIGHT HAVE A PROBLEM
		100	SEEKING HELP
		400	CERTIFIED HORDER
		1000	KIND OF A BIG DEAL

CAMPAIGN MODE

MEDAL	HOW TO EARN	CONDITION	TITLE
TOUR OF DUTY	COMPLETE CAMPAIGN ON CASUAL, NORMAL, HARDCORE, AND INSANE.	CASUAL	MEDAL OF DUTY
		NORMAL	SEEN SOME ACTION
		HARDCORE	COMBAT VETERAN
		INSANE	GENERAL CHAOS
SURVIVALIST	COMPLETE 10/20/30/40 CHAPTERS WITHOUT DYING.	10	INVISIBLE KID
		20	TOUGH GUY
		30	SURVIVAL ARTIST
		40	INCONCEIVABLE!
DOORMAN	MANIPULATE 200/500/1,000/2,000 OBJECTS IN CAMPAIGN.	200	WHAT'S THIS BUTTON DO?
		500	KNOB-TURNER
		1000	ARE YOU THE KEYMASTER?
		2000	PRESS X TO JASON
TRIPWIRE CROSSBOW	GET 10/50/100/500 IT'S A TRAP! RIBBONS.	10	NOT MY IDEA OF COURAGE
		50	AN ELEGANT WEAPON
		100	THAT'S NO MOON
		500	LET'S BLOW THIS THING
FINISHER	GET 10/50/100/500 EXECUTIONS IN CAMPAIGN.	10	HITMAN
		50	ASSASSIN
		100	DISHONORED
		500	ANGEL OF DEATH
ACTIVE RELOADER	PERFORM 50/100/250/500 PERFECT ACTIVE RELOADS IN CAMPAIGN.	50	GOOD TIMING
		100	DAMAGE, INC.
		250	WOULD YOU LIKE BULLETS WITH THAT?
		500	SECRET SAUCE
HEAVY WEAPONS	GET 50/200/500/1,000 HEAVY WEAPON KILLS IN CAMPAIGN.	50	WEIGHT PROBLEM
		200	GETTING HEAVY
		500	WHOA, THAT'S HEAVY
		1000	FIVE TONS OF OUCH

CHARACTER UNLOCKS

Extra characters are unlocked by signing up for VIP, entering a special code, or by completing certain criteria in-game.

AVAILABLE FROM START

| BAIRD | COLE | SOFIA | PADUK |

UNLOCKED IN GAME

NAME	HOW TO EARN
BAIRD (AFTERMATH)	HAVE ANY ACHIEVEMENT IN *GEARS OF WAR 3*
COLE (AFTERMATH)	SURVIVE THE 10TH WAVE IN SURVIVAL
PADUK (AFTERMATH)	UNLOCKED BY COMPLETING THE AFTERMATH
LOOMIS	BEAT THE MAIN CAMPAIGN (ANY DIFFICULTY)
MINH	EARN 10 STARS ON ANY DIFFICULTY IN THE CAMPAIGN
TAI	EARN 126 STARS ON ANY DIFFICULTY IN THE CAMPAIGN

PRE-ORDER CHARACTERS

These characters are unlocked by a code packaged with your pre-order.

CHARACTER
ALEX BRAND
ANYA
YOUNG DOM
YOUNG MARCUS

VIP EXCLUSIVE

Become a VIP member to unlock the following skins:

CHARACTER
FEMALE ONYX GUARD
ONYX GUARD

MARKETING PROMOTION

CHARACTER	DESCRIPTION	HOW TO EARN
TAI	JUNGLE TAI FROM COMIC BOOK	OBERTO CAMPAIGN, UNLOCKED VIA CODE ON PACKAGES

CHARACTER SKINS

Character Skins are unlocked by a promotional code, signing up for VIP, buying a skin in *Gears of War 3*, making a purchase from Xbox Live Marketplace, and when opening a PrizeBox. These skins are strictly cosmetic—offering players more customization options and possibly making you stand out more on the battlefield.

CAMPAIGN
Earn 80 Stars.

PROMOTIONAL
Look for codes on Brisk and Lipton tea.

SKELETAL (GLOW)

BRISK

VIP EXCLUSIVE
Become a VIP member to unlock the following skins:

ARCTIC ARMOR

BIG GAME

DARK CARNIVAL

PLAID (ANIMATED)

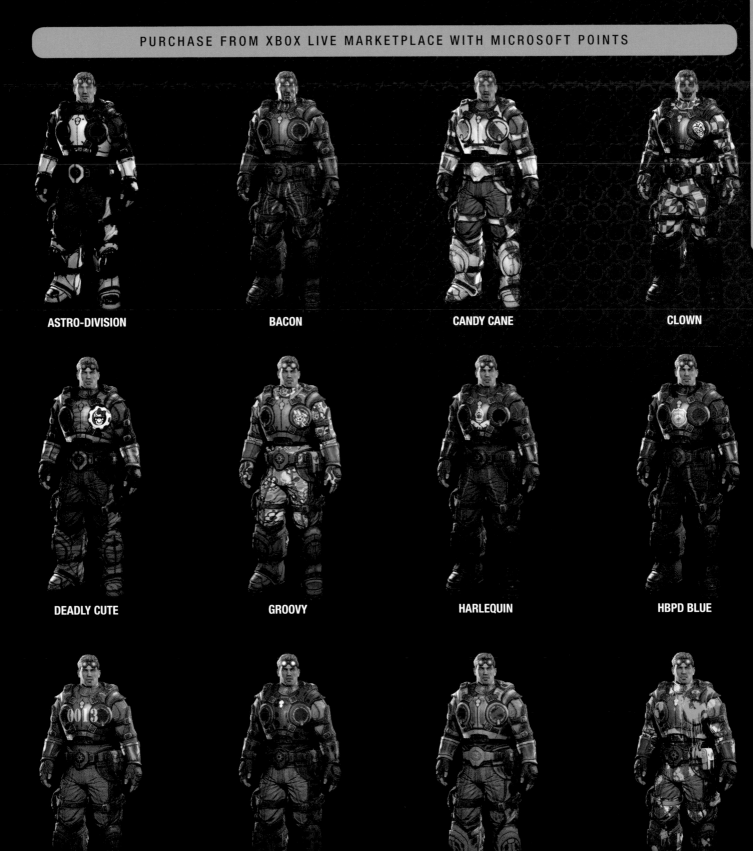

PURCHASE FROM XBOX LIVE MARKETPLACE WITH MICROSOFT POINTS

ASTRO-DIVISION

BACON

CANDY CANE

CLOWN

DEADLY CUTE

GROOVY

HARLEQUIN

HBPD BLUE

INMATE

LADYBUG

NEON

PAINTBALL

PROGRAM   SKELETAL   SUPER HERO   TIGER STRIPES

ZOMBIE   BURNING (ANIMATED)   CASCADE (ANIMATED)   CRACKED (ANIMATED)

DIGITAL (ANIMATED)   DOUBLE RAINBOW (ANIMATED)

UNLOCKED FROM PRIZEBOXES
The following Character Skins can be found inside PrizeBoxes.

CHROME
PRIZE BOX: NORMAL

COPPER
PRIZE BOX: NORMAL

CEL SHADED
PRIZE BOX: EPIC

MUMMY
PRIZE BOX: EPIC

BEE
PRIZE BOX: RARE

GOLD
PRIZE BOX: RARE

WEAPON SKINS

Weapon Skins are unlocked by a promotional code, signing up for VIP, buying a skin in *Gears of War 3,* making a purchase from Xbox Live Marketplace, and when opening a PrizeBox. Some skins are even animated—great for attracting more attention.

GAMEPLAY

	SKIN	WEAPON	HOW TO UNLOCK
	REAPER SLAYER	ALL	KILL AN EPIC REAPER

MARKETING PROMOTIONS

	SKIN	WEAPON	HOW TO UNLOCK
	BIG GAME	ALL	BRADYGAMES GUIDE, UNLOCKED BY CODE INCLUDED IN THIS BOOK
	BRISK	ALL	LOOK FOR CODES ON BRISK AND LIPTON TEA
	LAMBENT	ALL	GAMESTOP POWERUP PROMOTION, UNLOCKED BY CODE FROM GAMESTOP
	PAINTBALL	ALL	MS EXPERT ZONE, UNLOCKED BY CODE FROM EXPERT ZONE
	TEAM METAL (BLUE)	ALL	LIVE GOLD CARDS, UNLOCKED BY CODE ON CARD
	TEAM METAL (RED)	ALL	LIVE GOLD CARDS, UNLOCKED BY CODE ON CARD
	TEAM PULSE (ANIMATED)	ALL	SOCIAL MEDIA PROMOTION, UNLOCKED BY CODE
	WEB	ALL	BEST BUY REWARD ZONE PROMOTION, UNLOCKED BY CODE FROM BEST BUY

VIP EXCLUSIVE
Become a VIP member to unlock the following skins.

	SKIN	WEAPON
	ARES BRONZE	ALL
	FLAMES OF JUDGMENT (ANIMATED)	ALL
	HAZARDOUS	ALL
	HOT ROD	ALL
	ZEBRA	ALL

PURCHASE FROM XBOX LIVE MARKETPLACE WITH MICROSOFT POINTS

	SKIN	WEAPON		SKIN	WEAPON
	8 BALL	ALL		MELON FARMER	ALL
	AURORA (ANIMATED)	ALL		MOD CULTURE	ALL
	CANDY	ALL		PINK RABBIT	ALL

UNLOCKED FROM PRIZEBOXES

All of the following skins are unlocked separately after opening a PrizeBox, as opposed to the previous skins that are unlocked for all guns at once. Find these inside PrizeBoxes.

SKIN	WEAPON	TYPE OF PRIZEBOX
BURN SPRAY	LANCER	NORMAL PRIZEBOX
	RETRO LANCER	NORMAL PRIZEBOX
	HAMMERBURST & CLASSIC HB	NORMAL PRIZEBOX
	MARKZA	NORMAL PRIZEBOX
	GNASHER	NORMAL PRIZEBOX
	SAWED-OFF SHOTGUN	NORMAL PRIZEBOX
	BOOSHKA	NORMAL PRIZEBOX
CHROME	LANCER	NORMAL PRIZEBOX
	RETRO LANCER	NORMAL PRIZEBOX
	HAMMERBURST & CLASSIC HB	NORMAL PRIZEBOX
	MARKZA	NORMAL PRIZEBOX
	GNASHER	NORMAL PRIZEBOX
	SAWED-OFF SHOTGUN	NORMAL PRIZEBOX
	BOOSHKA	NORMAL PRIZEBOX
GOLD	LANCER	RARE PRIZEBOX
	RETRO LANCER	RARE PRIZEBOX
	HAMMERBURST & CLASSIC HB	RARE PRIZEBOX
	MARKZA	RARE PRIZEBOX
	GNASHER	RARE PRIZEBOX
	SAWED-OFF SHOTGUN	RARE PRIZEBOX
	BOOSHKA	RARE PRIZEBOX
RIB CAGE	LANCER	RARE PRIZEBOX
	RETRO LANCER	RARE PRIZEBOX
	HAMMERBURST & CLASSIC HB	RARE PRIZEBOX
	MARKZA	RARE PRIZEBOX
	GNASHER	RARE PRIZEBOX
	SAWED-OFF SHOTGUN	RARE PRIZEBOX
	BOOSHKA	RARE PRIZEBOX
ONYX (ANIMATED)	LANCER	EPIC PRIZEBOX
	RETRO LANCER	EPIC PRIZEBOX
	HAMMERBURST & CLASSIC HB	EPIC PRIZEBOX
	MARKZA	EPIC PRIZEBOX
	GNASHER	EPIC PRIZEBOX
	SAWED-OFF SHOTGUN	EPIC PRIZEBOX
	BOOSHKA	EPIC PRIZEBOX
XBOX (ANIMATED)	LANCER	EPIC PRIZEBOX
	RETRO LANCER	EPIC PRIZEBOX
	HAMMERBURST & CLASSIC HB	EPIC PRIZEBOX
	MARKZA	EPIC PRIZEBOX
	GNASHER	EPIC PRIZEBOX
	SAWED-OFF SHOTGUN	EPIC PRIZEBOX
	BOOSHKA	EPIC PRIZEBOX

ACHIEVEMENTS

Gears of War: Judgment contains a total of 50 Achievements worth 1000 Gamer Points. None of the fifty Achievements are "secret" and the requirements are all clearly explained. Some will be very difficult to unlock, particularly Lion Heart and Superstar, but they can all be unlocked with enough time, practice, and skill. Good luck, soldier.

CAMPAIGN ACHIEVEMENTS

The bulk of the Achievements are unlocked through the Judgment Campaign. Depending on your prior *Gears of War* experience, consider playing through each section once on Normal or Hardcore difficulty without accepting the Declassified option. Then immediately replay the section with the Declassified option while it's fresh in your memory. Most sections can be completed in under five minutes, making them the perfect size for repeat attempts at harder difficulties. The Judgment Campaign is structured very differently from the campaigns in previous games in the series; it's not enough to survive to the end of the section, but you're graded on your performance with Stars. Follow the strategies outlined in the walkthrough for help in earning three Stars on every section

CAMPAIGN PROGRESSION

	ACHIEVEMENT	REQUIREMENT	GAMER POINTS
	THEY CALLED HIM KARN	COMPLETE CHAPTER 1.	10
	OPEN ARMS	COMPLETE CHAPTER 2.	10
	THE REAL THING	COMPLETE CHAPTER 3.	10
	TAKE BACK THIS CITY	COMPLETE CHAPTER 4.	10
	I TOLD YOU	COMPLETE CHAPTER 5.	10
	THIS ONE'S NOT OVER	COMPLETE CHAPTER 6.	10
	FRIENDS	COMPLETE AFTERMATH.	10

CAMPAIGN COMPLETION

	ACHIEVEMENT	REQUIREMENT	GAMER POINTS
	DETERMINED	COMPLETE ALL CAMPAIGN CHAPTERS ON AT LEAST CASUAL DIFFICULTY.	0
	STEEL NERVES	COMPLETE ALL CAMPAIGN CHAPTERS ON AT LEAST NORMAL DIFFICULTY.	0
	IRON FIST	COMPLETE ALL CAMPAIGN CHAPTERS ON AT LEAST HARDCORE DIFFICULTY.	25
	LION HEART	COMPLETE ALL CAMPAIGN CHAPTERS ON INSANE DIFFICULTY.	50
	PARTY PEOPLE	PLAY ANY SECTION IN 4 PLAYER CO-OP.	0
	BLOOD BROTHERS	COMPLETE ALL CAMPAIGN CHAPTERS IN CO-OP.	50

DECLASSIFIED MISSIONS

	ACHIEVEMENT	REQUIREMENT	GAMER POINTS
	CHALLENGE ACCEPTED	COMPLETE YOUR FIRST DECLASSIFIED MISSION.	5
	NEVER GIVE UP	COMPLETE AT LEAST 20 DECLASSIFIED MISSIONS.	10
	QUALITY SOLDIERING	COMPLETE ALL DECLASSIFIED MISSIONS.	50
	SERIOUSLY JUDGMENTAL	COMPLETE ALL DECLASSIFIED MISSIONS ON INSANE DIFFICULTY	75

COG TAG RECOVERY

	ACHIEVEMENT	REQUIREMENT	GAMER POINTS
	NEVER FORGOTTEN	RECOVER 10 COG TAGS DURING THE CAMPAIGN.	0
	VETERAN REMEMBRANCE	RECOVER 25 COG TAGS DURING THE CAMPAIGN.	0
	RESPECT FOR THE FALLEN	RECOVER ALL 48 COG TAGS DURING THE CAMPAIGN.	20

STARS

	ACHIEVEMENT	REQUIREMENT	GAMER POINTS
	A PEEK INTO THE FUTURE	WATCH AFTERMATH TEASER.	0
	THE AFTERMATH	UNLOCK AFTERMATH.	20
	RISING STAR	ATTAIN 50 STARS ON AT LEAST CASUAL DIFFICULTY.	0
	SHOOTING STAR	ATTAIN 75 STARS ON AT LEAST NORMAL DIFFICULTY.	20
	STAR STRUCK	ATTAIN 100 STARS ON AT LEAST HARDCORE DIFFICULTY.	50
	SUPERSTAR	ATTAIN ALL STARS ON INSANE DIFFICULTY.	50

STATS & AWARDS

Nearly every action you take in *Gears of War: Judgment* has a corresponding ribbon or medal, whether playing campaign or multiplayer modes. Your play also earns your player profile experience points (XP), which determine your player level. Earning ribbons and medals earns you bonus XP! The more you play, the more XP, ribbons, and medals you'll earn and, in turn, the faster you'll unlock these Achievements. The other appendices in this section detail the requirements and bonus XP awarded for every ribbon and medal.

RIBBONS AND MEDALS

	ACHIEVEMENT	REQUIREMENT	GAMER POINTS
	RIBBON MASTER	EARN 3 UNIQUE RIBBONS IN ANY SECTION (CAMPAIGN).	10
	PROUD WEARER	EQUIP YOUR FIRST MEDAL.	5
	READY FOR WAR	EARN AT LEAST ONE ONYX MEDAL.	20
	SYBARITE	EARN THE ONYX "WAR SUPPORTER" MEDAL.	50

PLAYER PROGRESSION

	ACHIEVEMENT	REQUIREMENT	GAMER POINTS
	LEVEL 5	REACH LEVEL 5.	5
	LEVEL 10	REACH LEVEL 10.	10
	LEVEL 20	REACH LEVEL 20.	10
	LEVEL 30	REACH LEVEL 30.	15
	LEVEL 40	REACH LEVEL 40.	25
	LEVEL 50	REACH LEVEL 50.	25
	LET'S DO THIS	ACHIEVE LEVEL 50 AND CHOOSE TO RE-UP FOR ANOTHER TOUR OF DUTY.	50
	FEARLESS	ACHIEVE LEVEL 50 A SECOND TIME AND CHOOSE TO RE-UP FOR ANOTHER TOUR.	50
	UNSTOPPABLE	ACHIEVE LEVEL 50 A THIRD TIME AND CHOOSE TO RE-UP FOR ANOTHER TOUR.	50

MULTIPLAYER

These 11 Achievements reward you for seeing all that the multiplayer component of *Gears of War: Judgment* has to offer. These Achievements encourage you to play with every COG and Locust class, attain victory on every map, and find success in all gameplay modes. Whether you're a multiplayer expert or a bullet-sponge, you're bound to unlock each of these Achievements over time.

	ACHIEVEMENT	REQUIREMENT	GAMER POINTS
	DEATH TO LOCUST	KILL WITH ALL CLASSES OF COG.	10
	DEATH TO COG	KILL WITH ALL CLASSES OF LOCUST.	10
	SURVIVOR	COMPLETE WAVE 10 ON ALL MAPS IN SURVIVAL MODE.	10
	GLOBE TROTTER	WIN A MATCH ON EVERY MAP IN ALL VERSUS MODES.	10
	JACK OF ALL TRADES	WIN 10 MATCHES OF OVERRUN.	10
	TEAM LEADER	WIN 10 MATCHES OF TEAM DEATHMATCH.	10
	ALL ROUNDER	WIN ONE MATCH IN FREE-FOR-ALL, TEAM DEATHMATCH, AND DOMINATION.	10
	ROAMING FREE	WIN ONE MATCH ON EVERY MAP IN FREE-FOR-ALL.	10
	TEAM ON TOUR	WIN ONE MATCH ON EVERY MAP IN TEAM DEATHMATCH.	10
	OVERRAN	WIN ONE MATCH ON EVERY MAP IN OVERRUN.	10
	DOMINATOR	WIN ONE MATCH ON EVERY MAP IN DOMINATION.	10

Get Social with BradyGames!

- **Become a Fan on Facebook**

- **Follow @Brady_Games on Twitter**

- **Watch strategy videos on our YouTube channel**

Insider Information on Facebook!

Gain access to insider information just by "Liking" BradyGames on Facebook!

Giveaways
Enter giveaways on some of our biggest titles!

Exclusive Content
Get sneak peeks and sample sections from upcoming titles!

Quizzes
Take quizzes to test your knowledge on newly released video games!

Polls
Voice your opinion in polls ranging from video games to pop culture!

MadCatz SFXT Fightstick

Sneak Peeks

Which Diablo III Class are you?

If the Avengers fought, who would win?

GEARS OF WAR®
JUDGMENT
COLLECTOR'S EDITION
DIGITAL EDITION AVAILABLE!

This digital version contains all the content from the printed version, including:

> **CAMPAIGN WALKTHROUGH:** Get complete coverage of the entire walkthrough.

> **MULTIPLAYER COVERAGE:** Learn to master every game mode, including the new OverRun class-based experience.

> **MISSION DECLASSIFIED SYSTEM:** Discover how each mission changes and the best ways to adapt. Tactics for getting a three-star ranking included!

> **DETAILED MAPS:** Illustrated maps for every single-player and multiplayer map contain mission objectives, Declassify locations and more!

ONLY $9.99!

DIGITAL EDITION AVAILABLE IN THE iBOOKSTORE AND GOOGLE PLAY

COG TAG VIDEO WALKTHROUGHS!
FIND ALL 48 COG TAGS!

> Created by the author while on-site at Epic Games, each video walkthrough provides a quick run-through of every chapter revealing the location of all 48 COG Tags. No spoilers here—the videos only highlight the collectibles and leave the storyline intact!

VIDEOS AVAILABLE ON
XBOX LIVE MARKETPLACE

BRADYGAMES®
www.bradygames.com

EPIC GAMES
www.epicgames.com

GEARS OF WAR.
JUDGMENT

Written by Doug Walsh, Michael Owen, Kenny Sims, and Jim Morey

Maps illustrated by Rich Hunsinger

DK/BradyGames, a division of Penguin Group (USA) Inc.

800 East 96th Street, 3rd Floor

Indianapolis, IN 46240

ISBN 13 EAN: 978-0-7440-1465-5

Printing Code: The rightmost double-digit number is the year of the book's printing; the rightmost single-digit number is the number of the book's printing. For example, 13-1 shows that the first printing of the book occurred in 2013.

16 15 14 13   4 3 2 1

Printed in the USA.

CREDITS

TITLE MANAGER
Tim Fitzpatrick

MANUSCRIPT EDITOR
Matt Buchanan

BOOK DESIGNER
Tim Amrhein

PRODUCTION DESIGNERS
Julie Clark
Tracy Wehmeyer

BRADYGAMES STAFF

GLOBAL STRATEGY GUIDE PUBLISHER
Mike Degler

EDITOR-IN-CHIEF
H. Leigh Davis

LICENSING MANAGER
Christian Sumner

MARKETING MANAGER
Katie Hemlock

DIGITAL PUBLISHING MANAGER
Tim Cox

OPERATIONS MANAGER
Stacey Beheler

ACKNOWLEDGMENTS

BradyGames extends sincere gratitude to everyone at Epic Games for their generous hospitality, unrivaled support, and true partnership on every project. *Gears of War: Judgment* was no exception to this, and working with you was once again a real pleasure. Very special thanks to Chris Mielke, Chris Perna, Prince Arrington, and Dominic Acquarulo—without your dedication and indispensable assistance, these guides would not be possible—thank you! The following folks at Epic helped make sure this guide's accuracy, thoroughness, and quality measured up, and for that we cannot thank them enough: Andrew Bains, Alex Conner, Jacob Lawyer, John Liberto, Christine Neville, Brian Roberts, Wes Swain, Donald White, and Rich Wilt.

DOUG WALSH: My involvement with *Gears of War* has been a source of great pride and enjoyment over the past seven years, and I was thrilled to learn the franchise would continue on after the events at Azura. Not only did it mean that we fans would get to return to Sera for another battle with the Locust, but that I would be once again heading back to Epic's studios. On-site at Epic, my coauthors and I get to enjoy an environment, hospitality, and level of assistance that is without equal. Simply put, these strategy guides would not be possible without the support of Chris Mielke and Dominic Acquarulo. Thank you both! Spending weeks away from home is never easy, but everyone I come into contact with at Epic helps make it a little easier and for that I'm grateful. I want to also once again thank Mike Degler, Leigh Davis, and my editor, Tim Fitzpatrick, for your continued support and for being such great people to work with. Lastly, to my wife Kristin: I know the time apart is always tough, but I've got four little words that make it easier to bear: twelve months to go!

MICHAEL OWEN: I would like to thank the following people, as this guide would not have been possible without them: To Dominic Acquarulo and Chris Mielke at Epic Games for giving us access to everything we needed. I wouldn't be writing this if Leigh Davis hadn't given me this opportunity, so thank you, and to Tim Fitzpatrick for his incredible work in bringing this guide together.

A big thanks must go out to Jim Morey for all of his *Gears of War* expertise and to my co-author Kenny Sims, as getting this done on time was only possible with his huge help. Thanks to Doug Walsh for his great work on the single-player side and Rich Hunsinger for creating the beautiful maps. Last but not least, I thank my wife for putting up with my absence and making sure things still got done around the house while I was busy.

RICH HUNSINGER: I'd like to thank the BradyGames staff for their support on this project, as well as the highly talented authors that helped make this guide a reality: Michael, Kenny, Doug, and Jim. Good work, boys! Special thanks goes to Epic's own Chris Mielke and Dominic Acquarulo, who provided all of the assets I could possibly ask for—thanks Dom, you rock, and I couldn't have gotten home for the holidays without your help! Congrats to Ash on your promotion, buddy! I also couldn't have gotten all of these maps completed without the incredible support of my beautiful wife Kate, who takes care of everything while I'm on site and buried. Thanks, baby girl!

JIM MOREY: Thanks to my fellow authors Michael Owen, Kenny Sims, and Rich Hunsinger, and a special acknowledgment to my friend Doug Walsh for first introducing me to BradyGames to work on a new game called *Gears of War* back in 2006! Thanks once again to the good people at Epic Games for the warm hospitality. And finally, all the love in the world to my wife Jessica and son James. Let's DO THIS!